# THE COUNSELOR-IN-TRAINING

Century Psychology Series

Kenneth MacCorquodale
Gardner Lindzey
Kenneth E. Clark

*Editors*

# The Counselor-In-Training

**Susan K. Gilmore**

*University of Oregon*

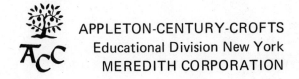

APPLETON-CENTURY-CROFTS
Educational Division New York
MEREDITH CORPORATION

to
Leona Tyler

# Contents

# Preface

When I first began supervising counselors in training, I was flattered by the number of students who wanted to observe or co-counsel with me so they could improve their interviewing skills. However, the ineffectiveness of charisma as a teaching tool soon began to outweigh any personal gratification in hearing students say, "That was just beautiful; I don't know how you do it!" Describing explicitly "how you do it" and developing a teaching procedure which would result in students learning how to counsel more effectively, without their having to depend upon lengthy and intimate contact with a highly skilled, seasoned counselor became very important to me.

That was seven years ago. Now over twenty groups of from six to eight persons, under the direction of about ten different pairs of leaders, have completed the 11-session practicum described in Section Four. Feedback from the participants about the practicum is a regular part of the training experience. In addition two major studies, the results of which will be published soon, have systematically evaluated the effectiveness of the practicum, using both self-report questionnaires and objectively rated behavioral measures of counseling skill. Thus far, I am quite encouraged and optimistic because the 11-session practicum, together with the materials concerning the content, purpose, and process of counseling presented in Sections One, Two and Three, apparently do teach people "how to do it." The gratification now comes from hearing students marvel at their own increasing skill level.

The practicum participants have included beginning masters' students in counseling, advanced doctoral students in counseling psychology, staff members of a neuropsychiatric hospital (psychiatrist, nurses, nursing assistants and rehabilitation counselor), students in a community college vocational-technical program, teachers, and ministers. Many participants have reported that not only has their effectiveness with clients and patients improved, but also they have experienced positive changes in their ability to communicate more effectively with their colleagues and their families. There is a feedback form at the end of Session 11 inviting you to send written comments about your experience with the practicum and the materials. I would like to emphasize that I would value very highly receiving both positive and negative comments and suggestions for improving the materials. I would then compile and publish the comments and suggestions.

I have tried to be clear about the limitations of this book, throughout. There is much more to becoming a competent counselor than is provided here. Specifically, this book does not provide counseling setting information (i.e., information about schools, hospitals, churches, clinics, etc.) and it does not provide sufficient information about particular counseling procedures (e.g., standardized testing, systematic desensitization, role playing, rational decision-making techniques, etc.) which would allow the reader to master these techniques. What is possible, using the materials in this book, is that an individual can significantly improve his ability to:

(1)    communicate his sincere understanding and acceptance of other persons,

(2)    facilitate the forward movement of verbal interactions so that other persons are more able to make choices or changes or to reduce some of the confusion in their lives,

(3)    give and receive constructive verbal and written feedback concerning the strengths and weaknesses of his own and others' counseling skills.

Whereas doing these three things well, is not all there is to learning to provide effective counseling assistance, I believe they are all necessary in order to become a competent counselor and, therefore, should concern every counselor-in-training.

There are several individuals to whom I would like to express my gratitude.

Gordon and Kate Gilmore, my parents, and Duane Gilmore, my brother, whose values and life styles were the primary source of philosophical assumptions about work, human relationships, and aloneness which permeate my thinking and writing and being, are three of the finest people I know.

Dr. Patrick W. Fraleigh, my husband, who is not only a competent counseling psychologist and thus a very helpful critic, but is also an uncommonly fine man who has lovingly and patiently provided unlimited support and encouragement throughout the writing process, consistently helps make it possible to be all that I am becoming.

Dr. Sandra P. Chernoff, a very dear friend and an exceptionally skillful psychologist, who has worked closely with me in developing, testing out, and modifying the practicum procedures from the beginning, has in addition taught me more about the courage to be human, regardless of how painful or difficult or absurd life is, than all the existentialists I have read.

Margaret Ewell Nichols and Dr. Roberta Shockley Ray are members of the same *karass* I belong to (according to Kurt Vonnegut, Jr. [1963] ". . . Bokononists believe that humanity is organized into teams, teams that do

God's will without ever discovering what they are doing. Such a team is called a *karass* by Bokonon ... p. 14."). We have been members of the same *karass* for over 10 years, during which time life certainly has been busy, busy, busy; so it helps to know there are two such people on your team.

Mary K. Collins, who typed the manuscript from my pencilled scribblings and never lost her sense of humor or her good will, helped make the preparation of this book much more pleasant.

Dean Leona E. Tyler, my teacher, to whom this book is dedicated, has had more to do with the way I think about counseling and the way I counsel than any other person. Because I am pleased with the way I think about and do counseling, I am indeed grateful to her — which is the same effect she has had on hundreds of students and clients in the course of her career. I joyfully join a chorus of men and women who have publicly sung her praises. She is the most consistently constructive human being I have ever encountered.

S.K.G.

# LIST OF FIGURES

# Section One

THE
CONTENT
OF
COUNSELING

# I  OVERVIEW – THREE DEVELOPMENTAL LIFE TASKS

There probably is not a single aspect of human experience which is irrelevant to counseling. If you try to identify a topic that would never arise in the course of counseling, you no sooner think of it than you can also imagine a person and situation wherein it might be very important. If you take the position that some topics are much more important than others or that some problems are far more appropriate than others, you run the serious risk of imposing your own hierarchy of values and concerns on the individuals who seek your assistance. However, if you do not have some system for sorting and evaluating the topics and concerns which comprise the content of counseling, then you are in the untenable position of not knowing whether what gets discussed in counseling is any more or less helpful than something else which might be discussed. What every counselor needs is a substantive framework which will allow him to answer two questions: (1) In what way is what we are talking about important to discuss? and (2) Are there other things which also should be discussed? Such a framework for organizing and evaluating counseling content must, however, be sufficiently flexible to allow the counselee to determine its unique configuration.

An analogy which comes to mind is the use of wire mesh, "chicken wire," in building a parade float or a temporary stationary display. Because of its malleability, the chicken wire can be shaped to provide a basic framework for nearly any representation. Brightly colored flowers of various shapes and sizes or various colors and textures of paper are then anchored to the framework, giving it beauty and meaning. Parade floats are only temporary structures, of course, but so are counseling relationships. Counselors do not need Mt. Rushmore materials to carve out configurations of their clients which will endure all time and clime. But counselors do need a flexible framework which is sufficiently substantive to anchor and support the bits and pieces that give a person's life beauty and meaning and sufficiently malleable to accommodate to the unique shapes and themes of people's individually patterned lives. The purpose of Section One is to present and discuss a three-category classification system for organizing the content of counseling. The system is designed to be both substantive and flexible.

Most people who are attracted to counseling as a profession abhor stuffing human beings into categories; sorting, classifying, labeling, and cataloguing clients seems to contradict a basic belief in the uniqueness of each person and, perhaps worse, it seems to violate a basic value concerning the dignity and worth of each individual. It is not uncommon to hear counselors say: "You can't classify human behavior in any meaningful way, because every human is so different!" or "Counselors who establish rigid categories and insist that other people fit into them treat people as if they were just a bunch of sheep or rats or monkeys!"

In this first section, a system for organizing the content of counseling will be presented and discussed. The position taken in this book is that every counselor already has some internal scheme for processing and interpreting the content of his interactions with clients, which he has developed during the course of living his own life. The question is not "Should I use a classification scheme for making sense of my interactions?" but rather "What classification scheme *do* I typically use and is it adequate?" It may be that the classification scheme you presently use, whether or not you could explicitly state it, works quite well most of the time. The point is that until you examine it, you do not really know if or when it is working well. Examining your own interpretative schemata, that is, being systematic about the way you think about the content of a counseling interaction, need not result in your being coldly analytical, impersonally objective, authoritarian, or rigid. However, if you are *not* systematic in your thinking, planning, and self-evaluation, you and your clients are at the mercy of your good faith and good fortune to see you through. For someone who is accorded the rights and responsibilities of a professional role, that is simply not good enough. What is required is that in your efforts to make sense of counseling interactions, you bring to bear all that is humanly possible for guiding your understanding. Such a requirement presupposes that you have examined and developed ways of thinking about human behavior which allow you to process and interpret the specific content of a particular counseling interaction in a manner that yields a clear and complete understanding of the individual with whom you are interacting.

Whether you adopt the classification scheme presented below or develop one of your own, the scheme which you use to organize the content of counseling should be simple enough so that you can remember it easily and utilize it conveniently. On the other hand, the scheme you use should be sufficiently comprehensive so that you do not ignore or distort important facets of the content of your interactions with clients. As was stated earlier, your content classification system should help you, while you are actually engaged in counseling, answer two questions easily and quickly: (1) "In what way is this important to discuss?" and (2) "What else is important to discuss?"

In Section Two we will examine the purposes of counseling in greater detail; at this point the general purpose of counseling will be defined as helping people of all ages and in a variety of settings cope constructively with the business of being human. The three dimensions of human existence with which counselors can be of particular assistance are: WORK, RELATIONSHIP, and ALONENESS. Each human being, at every developmental stage in his life, must somehow come to grips with these three dimensions of existence. At different developmental stages, the three dimensions – Work, Relationship, and Aloneness – present different developmental tasks and make different demands upon the individual. The general purpose of counseling, helping individuals cope constructively with human existence, is more specifically defined according to the developmental life task areas upon which the counselor and client focus their attention.

Figure 1 contains examples of human concerns in the three life task areas for different developmental stages. The examples are only illustrative and are not meant to be an exhaustive summary or a priority ranking of developmental tasks and demands which are important in counseling.

Every person, at each developmental stage, is faced with the question, "What are you *doing* with the limited time, energy, and resources available to you?" The pattern of responses the individual makes to that question constitutes his Work. Every person, at each developmental stage, is faced with the question, "How are you *moving* in relation to the movement of other persons?" The pattern of movements away from, toward, and alongside persons comprises the individual's Relationships. Every person, at each developmental stage, is faced with the question, "Who are you?" The individual's responsiveness to and responsibility for *being* a separate and unique person are disclosed in the constellation of choices he makes in the face of his Aloneness. At any point in a person's life, the extent to which he views himself and is viewed by others as constructively coping with life, depends heavily on what and how he is doing, moving, and being.

The content of counseling can be sorted into these three developmental life task areas:

| *Work* | *Relationship* | *Aloneness* |
|--------|----------------|-------------|
| Doing | Moving | Being |

The utility of any content classification system for counselors can be evaluated in terms of how much it helps the counselor organize, make sense of, and guide the counseling interaction. The system should facilitate the counselor's identifying in what way the content of the client's statements is important to him, as well as identifying what important content has not been mentioned by the client. In other words, you organize and interpret a client's statements according to their implications for one or more of the three life task areas and you identify missing or ambiguous information by reviewing what you understand about the client in each of the three life task areas.

We will first explore each of the areas separately and then examine their

FIGURE 1.  Examples of Life Tasks of Concern to Counselors.

DEVELOPMENTAL STAGES

| | Infancy and Childhood | Adolescence | Early Adulthood | Middle Age | Old Age |
|---|---|---|---|---|---|
| **WORK** | Explore and manipulate the world around | Help at home | First job and/or continued education | Possible job change | Retirement |
| | | Cope with school work | | Re-enter school | Alternatives to remunerated activity |
| | Acquire language and concepts | Vocational exploration | Continued vocational planning | Redefine vocational aspirations Prepare for retirement | Cope with real and arbitrary limits |
| **RELATIONSHIP** | Approach others | Reciprocity or "taking role of the others" | Marriage and family | Break-up of family with loss of children | "Generation gap" |
| | Allow others to approach | Share outside family group | Friendship | | Share the wisdom of experience |
| | Differentiate family, friends, strangers | Sexual identity | Coworkers | Change roles in marriage | |
| | | Cooperation and competition | Community relations | Importance of friends and coworkers | Cope with loneliness |
| **ALONENESS** | Allow "mothering one" out of sight | Uniqueness and accountability of self | Ability to maintain oneself and help care for others | Loss of parents | Face one's own death |
| | Stand and walk alone | Relationship to higher order of meaning (Religion, Humanity, etc.) | Tolerate being misunderstood | Meaning of physical suffering and death | Loss of spouse |
| | Separate sense of "me-ness" | | Carve out personal philosophy of life | Continued integration of philosophy of life | Loss of friends |
| | Self-initiated play | | | | |

interrelatedness. Section One will close with an example of how the three category system can be used to organize the content of an ongoing counseling interaction as well as guide the direction of that interaction.

## II WORK

Walter S. Neff has contributed what is probably the single most comprehensive, well organized, and readable analysis of work in a book entitled *Work and Human Behavior*, 1968. After considering over fifty definitions and meanings for the noun and verb forms of "work" given in Webster's International Dictionary and after examining definitions of "work" utilized by anthropologists, sociologists, psychologists, economists, historians, and other social scientists, Neff concludes that

> Work is a distinctively *human* activity, although other animals carry through a great number of work-like activities. The direct links between instinct and action appear as it were, to be "broken" in man. While animals other than man are generally limited to living in the world as they find it, man is capable of *altering* the features of his environment so that life will be (as he sees it) more secure, more satisfying, or more pleasurable. So far as we can discover, the essentials of what is meant by work are to be found in this "planful alteration of certain features of man's environment" (p. 253).

> Work is neither a blessing nor a curse, but simply one of the major conditions of man's existence. Through work, a naked half-ape, equipped with neither fang nor claw, has been able to establish his sway over stronger and better armed animals, virtually extinguishing the latter in the process. Through work, we have domesticated useful animals, tamed the land, learned to control many of the indifferent and inimical forces of nature. Through work also, we have developed the most efficient means of subjugating and killing our fellow men, which, of course, is the darker side of the process. The entire aggregate of human culture, for better and for worse, is a product of work; without work, it is difficult to say how we would have become human at all (p. 259).

Against this backdrop of the structure and function of work in the history of the human species, we will focus on the meaning of work in the life of a developing individual.

An individual by his very nature is always doing something. Regardless of how random or quiescent or self-defeating a person's behavior may at times appear to be, it can be understood in terms of the purposes it serves. This is another way of saying that all human behavior is purposive and/or is goal-directed. The range of things humans of various ages can do is indeed extensive; the potentialities for one individual would be staggering, if you had to list them. However, the number of things one individual will actually do in the time and space he occupies throughout his life is considerably limited. A person's work, as the term is used here, refers to the limited pattern of activity in which he engages for purposes of "altering the features of his environment so that life will be (as he sees it) more secure, more satisfying, or more pleasurable."

## Development of Work Patterns

It is difficult to specify precisely the point when a young developing human being can be said to begin responding to Life's question, "What are you going to do?" in a reflective and planful manner. After a youngster has acquired sufficient language to respond verbally, it is, of course, easier to construe the pattern of his choices concerning how he spends his time and energy, as the result of conscious thoughts and intentions and plans he possesses. Nevertheless, if you observe the intensity and persistence with which a toddler stacks blocks, fits a smaller box inside a bigger one, points to and names familiar objects and persons, attempts to deposit his feces in a prescribed receptacle, struggles to become increasingly mobile, etc., it is not difficult to view such activities as belonging to the category we have defined as Work. Even for the prelanguage child, it is possible to classify much of his behavior as patterned activity designed to planfully alter certain features of his environment. In a very real way, these activities constitute the child's work and they have profound, lasting effects on his developing humanness.

At later stages of his development much of the individual's activity is concerned with what we more typically think of as work, i.e., chores at home, attending school, volunteer services, and employment. The definition of "worker" and the demands of work change as a person moves through the developmental stages; but the significance of work as a basic dimension of being human is unchanged. Whether the individual is remunerated directly or indirectly and whether the individual is expanding his work behavior or curtailing his work activities does not alter the importance of work in his life. In order to participate fully in his own humanness, an individual must be able to work; that is, he must be able to planfully alter his environment so that his life will be, from his own point of view, more secure, more satisfying, and more pleasurable. If, at any developmental stage, an individual views himself as incapable of having a significant impact on his environment because of deficits within himself or outside barriers that make the environment unalterable, he will begin to suffer as a human being. In your role as counselor, you will be called upon to assist persons with the dimension of their existence we have identified as Work: (1) when they pass from one developmental stage to another and the definitions and demands of work change; (2) when they experience deficits within themselves which prevent them from having a significant impact on their environments; and (3) when they encounter unyielding environments which block their efforts to live a secure, satisfying, and pleasurable life.

Many counselors work in institutions which have as their major reason for existing to assist individuals of various ages in becoming more fully functioning workers: schools and colleges, employment services, vocational rehabilitation services, and federal and state economic opportunity programs. Also a large number of counselors staff programs designed to assist persons develop as workers within institutions whose primary commitment may be to detention, incarceration, treatment of mental illness, promotion of business and industry, or the training of persons with special educational problems, e.g., deaf, blind, retarded, crippled, etc. The counseling profession, since its beginning, has been closely identified with the Work dimension of human existence. Counselors have provided and continue to provide assistance to persons struggling to answer the question, "What are you going to do?" It is somewhat of a puzzle to this writer why many counselors in training are frequently disparaging of counseling activities devoted to assisting persons cope constructively with the life task area called Work. In view of the significance of work for the humanness of the species as a whole, for the development of the individual, and for the identity of the profession, it would seem reasonable that counselors-in-training might regard Work as the most important content area of counseling.

## III   RELATIONSHIP

One frequently encounters the romantic notion that the individual can be master of himself and his fate, divested of all hampering ties, a free-soaring bird. Such notions create grave confusion. Complete individual autonomy is unthinkable. The dictum of Theocritus, "Man will ever stand in need of man," is borne out by all of modern psychology and anthropology. Man's social character is fixed in his biological nature. For at least the first half dozen years of his life, the human infant is utterly dependent on his elders. By the time those years have passed, he possesses deeply rooted social habits. And beyond that, all that makes us most human — communication, self-awareness, sympathy, conscience — is dependent on interaction with other beings of our own kind (Gardner, 1965, p. 91).

The second category in the content classification system stated above is Relationship and to this category belong the myriad of interpersonal relationships upon which a person's very survival and developing humanness depend. Few things are more obvious than that human beings are social creatures — that relationships with other people are absolutely necessary for an individual in the process of becoming and being a mature, fully functioning person who can cope constructively with exigencies of existence. The structure, function, and quality of human relationships are so complex that it is difficult to develop this second category in a way which does justice to the richness and subtlety of relationships, but which does not become so complicated and unwieldy that it is useless to the practicing counselor. What we need is a relatively simple category which will help identify and review the basic dimensions of relationships and which is sufficiently portable that it can be carried from one counseling interaction to another. With this in mind, the following discussion is presented.

Every client's relationships can be viewed in terms of the movements between himself and others and the purposes those movements serve and/or are intended to serve. A relationship between one person and another is never static; a person is always in the process of moving toward, away from, or alongside the other people in his world. The general purposes of survival and humanization which are served by the movements between persons are, more specifically: (1) physical and emotional care; (2) support and encouragement; (3) instruction and guidance; (4) cooperation for achieving mutual goals; and (5) continuity and stability.

At each developmental stage, Life poses the question, "How are you moving in relation to other human beings?" Regardless of your client's age, that question can be answered in terms of his ability and willingness to move toward, away from, and alongside others for purposes of giving/receiving physical and emotional care, support and encouragement, instruction and guidance, and for purposes of cooperating and providing continuity and stability to one another.

## Physical and Emotional Care

When you began the course of your life and again as you complete the course of your life, the importance of other persons giving you physical and emotional care is most obvious. During the middle span of your life, your giving physical and emotional care to others is most obvious. There really is never a time when you or any other human being does not need to be actively engaged in giving/receiving physical and emotional care. Even during those years when you are most capable of caring for yourself — when you are sufficiently experienced, healthy, strong, and independent to be "on your own" — it is terribly important to be "connected" with other humans. It is very unfortunate if a person ceases to be tied to other humans — if he loses his personal moorings. What may appear to be the ultimate in freedom turns into a nightmare of senseless drifting amidst a sea of humanity.

Many modern lyricists have written about the giving/receiving of physical and psychological care necessary in relationships; however Paul Simon has in the simple verses of "Bridge Over Troubled Water"* captured the essence of our discussion here.

> When you're weary, feeling small,
> When tears are in your eyes, I will dry them all;
> I'm on your side. When times get rough
> And friends just can't be found,
> Like a bridge over troubled water
> I will lay me down.
> When you're down and out,
> When you're on the street,
> When evening falls so hard
> I will comfort you.
> I'll take your part.
> When darkness comes
> And pain is all around,
> Like a bridge over troubled water
> I will lay me down.
> Like a bridge over troubled water
> I will lay me down. . . .

At the beginning each of us is small and at the end each of us is weary; but in between there are many times when we feel both small and weary. It is terribly important that each of us is able and willing to take one another's part — to be a bridge and to accept another's comfort across troubled water.

An inquiry which you may find useful with clients of all ages is, "Who takes care of you?" and "Whom do you take care of?" There are a number of ways to ask about this dimension of movement between a client and the significant people in his life: "Who keeps track of you — who knows if your big toe hurts, or if your head aches, or if you are constipated?" "Who could get in touch with you any time of the day or night — who knows your comings and goings enough to track you down?" "Who counts on you to be there to help them — who really relies on your assistance?" "Whom do you know all about — whether they are glad, sad, nauseated, worried, ashamed, pleased, etc?" Regardless of your theoretical orientation, this kind of information is critical to a complete understanding of your client. Whether you think in terms of the sources of social reinforcement in your client's life or his sources of existential meaning, you will need to know about the giving/receiving of physical and psychological care in your client's relationships.

If we were to reduce human relationships to nothing but taking over for

* © Paul Simon. Used with permission of the Publisher.

one another during childhood and old age, illness and personal crisis, we would
run the risk of glorifying dependency. Individuals of all ages who are coping
constructively with life are able to accept a dependent role and they are able to
be depended upon. However, they are also able to move out on their
own — away from significant others in their lives and to encourage and support
others' efforts to move away from them. It is this blend of dependence/
independence, or moving toward/moving away from which characterizes the
fully functioning person.

## Support and Encouragement

Each person, at each developmental stage, needs to have relationships which will
encourage and support his efforts to become more independent — to move out
on his own, to take risks, to explore, to grow and develop and change. Such
relationships can exist with parents, teachers, friends at school, colleagues at
work, with a marriage partner, friends in the community, relatives, and with a
counselor/therapist. Unfortunately, many times the individuals who occupy
these roles are not eager to see a person become more independent. Instead of
encouraging and supporting such growth and change, they often, unwittingly
and unconsciously, attempt to block such movement by withdrawing support
and encouragement. An important aspect of understanding a client's relationships is knowing whether he sees the important people in his life as facilitating or
hindering his development as an individual. Are the important people "calling
forth independence from him" or does he have to "wrench it from the hands of
those who control him?"

   We are quick to associate problems of balancing dependence and
independence, moving toward and moving away from, with the relationships
between teenagers and parents. However, the same issue is at stake between
husbands and wives, teachers and school administrators, ministers and congrega-
tions, intimate friends, between counselors and clients, etc. Whether or not an
individual is willing to try something new and unfamiliar, to commit himself to
something uncertain and ambiguous, to risk failing and possibly looking foolish is
heavily dependent upon there being some relationship from which he gains
encouragement and support to move out on his own.

   Some inquiries which you may find useful with clients of all ages are,
"Who is pleased with your efforts to be you?" "Who would be more pleased if
you tried something *you* really wanted to do, even though you failed miserably,
than if you hadn't tried at all?" "Can you think of a time when someone
else knew you felt that way about something *they* wanted to do?" Relationships
which are devoid of a minimum of mutual support and encouragement are
typically experienced as binding, burdensome, controlling, ingrown, possessive,
and personally destructive. Relationships which are characterized by a high
degree of mutual support and encouragement to move away from, as well as to

move toward, are typically experienced as freeing, flexible, expanding, creative, and personally constructive. Any choice or change in his life which a client may be contemplating will be directly influenced by the degree of support and encouragement present in his relationship with you and with others.

## Instruction and Guidance

The third basic function of interpersonal relationships is the giving and receiving of instruction and guidance. If we think of an individual's power in terms of his ability to make things happen the way he intends them to happen, then it is clear that knowledge, experience, and skill are significant sources of power. Particularly in a complex technological society, the knowledgeable, experienced, and skilled individuals are more likely to be personally powerful. Of course, "making things happen the way you intend them to happen" is not only a matter of personal power, but is also dependent upon the environment, which can either hinder or facilitate your actions. Increasing attention is being paid to the fact that environments which are highly structured, densely populated, and organized through large bureaucratic systems hinder the actions of individuals and leave them feeling impotent and insignificant. Nearly all the clients you will encounter in the course of your professional life exist in environments (schools, churches, communities, families, businesses, etc.) which hinder and thwart their efforts to act. Nevertheless, there are vast differences in the degree of personal power experienced and exercised by individuals who exist in equally hindering environments. Given equally difficult situations, the difference between an individual who feels powerless and unimportant and one who feels he can make things happen the way he intends them to happen is largely a matter of his knowledge, experience, and skill.

It is reasonable to assume that all human beings by nature are eager to learn. Scientific evidence and personal experience point to the fact that man is basically designed to acquire knowledge, experience, and skills which will allow him to master and control himself and the world about him. However, to acquire sufficient knowledge, experience, and skill, the developing individual must be willing to receive instruction and guidance from others. Each of us has had a unique personal history of learning from others, including our parents, teachers, friends, and employers. For some it has been overall, an exciting, mutually rewarding, independence-producing experience of gaining increasing power and self-esteem. For some it has been largely a boring, dissatisfying, debilitating experience resulting in increasing frustration and self-doubt. For others it has been an uneven mixture of satisfaction and frustration.

By the time a person is old enough to be sent to you as a client or to voluntarily seek to become your client, he also has a unique personal history of learning from others. Because early survival and maturation are so heavily dependent upon older humans instructing and guiding younger humans, the experienced teaching the inexperienced, the skilled training the unskilled, etc., we tend to think of learning from others as an exclusively vertical process. The movement in such exchanges between persons is experienced as from above to below, from superior to inferior, from bigger to smaller, from "one up" to "one down." In all probability, your clients will construe the counseling relationship as another vertical process. As a result of their individual histories of learning from others, they will enter the relationship with very different expectations of how you will move in relation to them and how they should move in relation to you. Therefore, there are two very important reasons for you to gain an understanding of how your client relates to other persons when it comes to giving and receiving instruction and guidance: (1) the sources of power to make happen what he intends to have happen are knowledge, experience, and skill, which most frequently are acquired directly from or under the supervision of other persons, and (2) the way he construes the counseling relationship and his expectations concerning it are heavily influenced by his personal history of learning from others. As you listen to your client and think about this content area we have called the client's Relationships, it is helpful to ask yourself, "Do I have a picture of what the client is like when he is giving and receiving instruction and guidance?" "What kinds of circumstances and what kinds of people does he find it easy to learn from and to teach?" So much of being the kind of person who feels he can make things happen the way he intends them to happen depends upon learning from and teaching others, "Does he have ready access to that process of acquiring personal power and significance?"

Before we turn to the fourth and fifth purposes served by human relationships, namely "cooperation to achieve mutual goals," and "providing continuity and stability," there is a special case of humans instructing and guiding one another which deserves mention. We have discussed how the young, developing person's survival and maturation depend upon learning from others. We have noted the relationship between skilled and experienced humans instructing and guiding the unskilled and the inexperienced so that they might grow in personal power and importance. We have seen that most instruction and guidance is experienced as a vertical process, from above to below. It is no surprise, therefore, that many people, from young adulthood to old age, fail to participate in one of the most meaningful and satisfying instructional experiences available to them – teaching someone else about themselves. Husbands and wives enter marriage assuming that their spouse should somehow know all about them. Friends set up a tyranny of intuition which is based on the assumption that the more you care about me, the less I will have to teach you about me. Love is viewed as a state of knowing all about another person without having to be told. Probably the fact that so few individuals have experienced the joys of a mutual, reciprocal, horizontal, rather than vertical learning process, accounts for their awkwardness and cautiousness when it comes to teaching someone else about themselves and learning about that other person directly from him or her. For example, married couples spend years disappointing one another sexually, without ever attempting to teach one another what each considers the most meaningful and satisfying aspects of making love. Friends tolerate one another's inability to say the right thing or offer sympathy and support because it never occurs to them to teach one another directly and explicitly how to be most helpful. Young people who are dating one another persist in relating in painful ways because each one, in turn, assumes that "girls really like to be treated that way" or "guys like girls who act like that," and neither one tempts to teach the other how he or she prefers to be treated. Teachers continue to register displeasure with their colleagues' comments but assume there is nothing they could do to inform one another about how to listen or make suggestions.

Many of the ways in which people cause one another disappointment and grief are a result of not knowing what else to do. Often times what a client interprets as a lack of genuine caring, or even viciousness on the part of a significant person in his life is more a result of the client's not having taught that person how to care for him in ways that are acceptable and effective. It is not uncommon for a client to believe that because he has let it be known that what another person is doing is not pleasing, the other person will then automatically know what would be pleasing. Many feelings of "You don't really care," and "You're not even trying" could be avoided if individuals actively engaged in a process of instructing and guiding one another about themselves. Thus, in your efforts to understand a client's relationships, particularly a client of junior high age or older, it is important to listen for indications that he is able to move toward others for purposes of teaching others about himself.

## Cooperation

In our consideration of the remaining two purposes which human relationships serve, cooperation and continuity, we will be more concerned with the movement of persons alongside one another. In your efforts to assist clients cope constructively with the second life task area, that is, Relationships, it is helpful if you have a way to think about one of the more complicated processes humans engage in, namely, cooperating to achieve mutual goals. We will begin looking at cooperative behavior with some rather elementary and obvious statements, such as "You can't run a three-legged race by yourself," and "Rarely does anyone attempt the Hallelujah Chorus alone." On the other hand, "Even a small group of sculptors can't give a one-man show," and "What someone else says during a soliloquy doesn't count for much." However, "It is usually easier to move a piano if there are at least two piano movers," and "Driving from Providence to Santa Cruz usually goes a lot faster if you take turns at the wheel." The point is that, by definition, there are some things which simply cannot be accomplished by one person acting alone; there are some things which, by definition, must be accomplished by one person acting alone; and there are some things which usually are more efficiently and effectively accomplished by two or more people. We will concentrate our discussion on the nature of movement between and among persons engaged in activities which either must be accomplished cooperatively or usually are accomplished more efficiently and effectively when they are done cooperatively.

One way to view cooperative movement among persons is in terms of time and space. For example, cooperation sometimes involves acting in the same place at the same time, for example, both parents attend a parent conference concerning their eleven-year-old son. But cooperation can also involve acting in a different place at a different time, for instance, "I will need to have the car by 4:30 so I can pick up your parents and the cake before the bakery closes." Looking at cooperation this way, there are two other combinations of time and space, acting in the same place at a different time and acting in a different place at the same time. These combinations of the spatio-temporal dimensions of cooperation are illustrated in Figure 2. An example of acting in the same place at a different time would be a married couple both attending community college, taking turns attending classes, and babysitting. Examples of cooperating by acting in a different place at the same time involve simultaneous, parallel tasks, such as mother getting the children ready for a picnic while father packs the car. The other examples are drawn from musical performances which depend on cooperative vocalization and athletic performances which depend on cooperative movements.

The individual who is capable of and willing to cooperate with others in all four ways is, of course, more versatile and flexible and, thus, can cope

FIGURE 2.    Examples of the Spatio—temporal Dimensions of
Cooperation

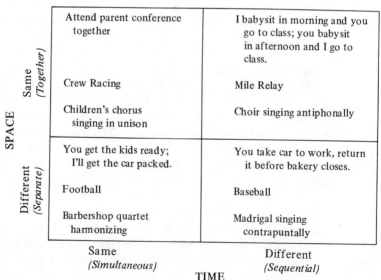

constructively with a wider range of situations which demand cooperation. Unfortunately there are people who only know one way to cooperate; for example, they view every cooperative venture as a three-legged race — "We must do exactly the same thing at the same time or we aren't really cooperating." Also, there are people who think of cooperation strictly in terms of doing their own part very well, but fail to recognize the tremendous importance of transitions from one sequence to the next. For example, many a relay team loses, not because the four runners are too slow, but because they are unable to pass the baton quickly and smoothly.

There are limitless numbers of situations and tasks which require that people be willing and able to cooperate with one another. There is considerable variety in the way cooperation can occur. The chances are very good that as a counselor you will be faced with having to assist individuals with both their willingness and ability to engage others cooperatively. Regardless of your counseling setting — whether you interact with teachers and students, parents and teachers, husbands and wives, parents and children, supervisors and employees, patients and treatment staffs, etc. — you will need to be able to understand the extent to which your clients can move alongside others in a cooperative effort to achieve mutual goals.

## Continuity and Stability

The final purpose served by interpersonal relationships which we will consider is the provision of continuity and stability. This dimension of relationship also involves people being willing and able to move alongside one another. Our earliest experiences with others, namely, the "mothering one or ones," set the scene for the lifelong expectation that it is connectedness with other human beings which makes life at least minimally stable and orderly. Even when the "mothering one" is absent a great deal, quite inconsistent, or neglectful in meeting a child's needs, she is still his major source of stability. A child can easily weather moving around from one neighborhood to another, from one town, state or country to another, if the people with whom he is moving remain constant. In a later section (see Section Three — Acceptance, pp. 147-178) we will discuss the Optimal Range of Change within which humans function best. At one extreme is Chaos — a completely random world devoid of stability or continuity; at the other extreme is Constancy — a completely predictable world wherein nothing ever changes. Humans do not function well at either extreme; that is, humans need to live in a world characterized not only by stability and continuity, but also by novelty and change. For the infant and young child, stability and continuity are almost totally dependent upon the "mothering one or ones." Gradually, the child begins to derive some sense of stability from familiar objects, e.g., a blanket, a stuffed animal, a cup and spoon, the sound of a music box, etc. A growing awareness of routines concerning sleeping, eating, bathing, the regular comings and goings of other people (siblings, parents, grandparents, baby sitter provides continuity in the developing youngster's life.

It is difficult to say exactly when a little human being begins to realize that there is another kind of stability and continuity in which people participate, namely, choosing to be with one another. "I'll save you a seat on the bus." "You can be my best friend forever, okay?" "Mrs. Rogers' husband got transferred and she isn't going to be our teacher anymore." "No, I certainly don't think 'we both ought to go out with other people for a while' and I don't think you do either!" "But the fact you were there and understood what was happening means more to me than anything you or anybody actually did." In the beginning people are there just because that is the way things are; but before long there comes the realization that people can choose whether or not to be there — that *I* can choose whether or not to be there. Moving alongside another person takes on meaning beyond cooperating to achieve mutual goals. Choosing to sit beside the same person each morning on the bus has almost nothing to do with both of you getting to school. It has everything to do with belonging to someone else, having a place beside them, and being able to count on them.

In a sense, this aspect of relationship is like counting on your own fingers and toes; although they are at the farthest edges of you, they are connected to you and readily accessible. In the same way that you cannot count on the fingers of a tightly clenched fist, counting on another person cannot result from a stranglehold grasp of that person. Unlike fingers and toes, other people can disconnect themselves from you and cease moving alongside. The stability and continuity which people provide for one another must be, with the exception of the earliest stage of development, freely chosen or else it is not stability, but enslavement; it is not continuity, but bondage.

As a counselor, you may interact most frequently with young people who are just beginning to struggle with the paradox of freedom and commitment in relationship; or you may interact most frequently with people who are bound up with years of entangled, knotted relationships. Regardless of your counseling setting or the age of your client, it is important to gain a sense of the client's willingness and ability to move alongside another person for purposes of giving and receiving stability and continuity. Many of the decisions a client faces, the changes he may want to have happen, or the confusion he may experience (any one of which could be the reason he sought your assistance) depend upon the degree and quality of stability and continuity provided by his relationships with other persons. The following questions and statements illustrate the significance of this dimension of Relationship in the content of counseling interactions:

> "But your wife doesn't seem to understand that waiting on you hand and foot makes it harder and that her just standing quietly by while you claw your way back to being a whole man again, is what would help the most."

"Even though it's not very clear, what are some of the reasons why you question whether going steady with Sally would be best for both of you?"

"So your mother-in-law thinks that the reason Stephen is having difficulties reading, is because after the divorce you went to work and are not home when he gets home from school?"

"Knowing that Don will have to travel one week out of every month for a year, the question is what can you do not to become suspicous, distrustful, and estranged from one another, right?"

"Unless I am talking directly to Carolyn or hearing her read or paying attention to her in some way, she acts angry or hurt. If I pay attention to the other children, she takes it as a personal rejection of her."

Stability and continuity in relationship, and the feeling of belonging which accompanies them, are the result of individuals consistently choosing to move alongside one another, even when there is nothing in particular to do together. Such a process of connectedness and relatedness is not easily learned and cannot, by its nature, be completely captured. In the words of *The Prophet*, by Kahlil Gibran*

> But let there be spaces in your togetherness,
> And let the winds of the heavens dance
> between you.
> Love one another, but make not a bond
> of love:
> Let it rather be a moving sea between
> the shores of your souls.
> Fill each other's cup but drink not from
> one cup.
> Give one another of your bread but eat
> not from the same loaf.
> Sing and dance together and be joyous,
> but let each one of you be alone,
> Even as the strings of a lute are alone
> though they quiver with the same music.
> Give your hearts, but not into each
> other's keeping
> For only the hand of Life can contain
> your hearts.

* From *The Prophet* by Kahlil Gibran. Copyright 1923 by Kahlil Gibran; renewal copyright 1951 by Administrators C.T.A. of Kahlil Gibran Estate and Mary G. Gibran. Reprinted by permission of Alfred A. Knopf, Inc.

> And stand together yet not too near
> together:
> For the pillars of the temple stand apart,
> And the oak tree and the cypress grow
> not in each other's shadow. (pp. 15–16).

We will now turn to the third and final category in the content classification scheme for counselors: ALONENESS.


## IV   ALONENESS


A person who is constructively coping with his Aloneness is rarely lonely; but he is also rarely unaware of his separateness. He experiences himself as being very much a part of humanity; but he also experiences himself as set apart from every other human being. He participates in the unity of mankind, but he also remains a unique, one-of-a-kind man. To cope constructively with Aloneness is to confront your own separateness, your set-apartness, your uniqueness, and affirm your own Being. At different developmental stages, your personal affirmation of Being will tend to focus on different aspects of human existence. In the following discussion of Aloneness we will examine these existential realities in the same order that they become foci for the developing individual: Uncertainty, Choices, Uniqueness, and Death.


### Uncertainty

Although we cannot specify the day or week in which an infant begins to differentiate between himself and the rest of the world, the process appears to be related to his experiencing some things as "always there" — fingers, toes, nose, etc. Then there are things that are almost always there — my blanket, my mother, my stuffed duck, my blue plastic cup, etc. With the developing sense of "me" being a cluster of body parts, feelings, movements, smells, noises, and objects, including other people, that somehow fit together, there also develops an awareness of the uncertainty of existence. The world is not always what it appears to be: beads that disappear under blankets are gone forever; stairs are not where they were; lids that did fit on bottles do not anymore; Mother, who was there, is not there now; a little hand that is carefully guiding a mashed banana/strained apricot mixture to a waiting open mouth stops off at an ear. Inevitably, with the differentiation of "me" and "mine" comes uncertainty; the world is not always what it appears to be; things do not always happen when and how you expect they will; you cannot always do what you were *sure* you could do (WORK) and move (RELATE); existence is increasingly characterized by greater uncertainty.

There is no escape from the contingent, unpredictable nature of existence. Even the individual who attempts to eradicate the ultimate uncertainty — Death — by choosing the moment of his suicide, has no absolute guarantee that he will be successful. Many of us know of, or have worked, with individuals who have made what appeared to be foolproof suicidal attempts and failed. The probability may be very high that a bullet or a leap from a bridge or a massive dose of barbiturates will fix the final moment, but it is, nonetheless, a matter of probability and not a certainty. Whereas it is not particularly productive to spend time conjuring up hypothetical examples of the foolproof suicide with a probability of success that approaches 1.00, it is useful to focus on the extent to which uncertainty pervades human existence. Such focus urges us to raise the question, "What does it take to cope constructively with the uncertainty that surrounds?" "What keeps the individual from being ungulfed?"

As we have already discussed, the individual's Work and his Relationships are significant sources of strength and buoyancy and purpose. But Work and Relationships are also shot through with uncertainty. Our efforts to do get interrupted, thwarted, and sometimes obliterated; our movements in relation to others get delayed, deflected, and sometimes completely blocked. Again and again we are thrown back on ourselves with the imperative *to be* in the face of nothing to do and nowhere to move. In those hours, the courage to confront a contingent world and affirm one's Being must come from within each of us. No other person, no job, no institution can shoulder that responsibility. There is no affirmation of Being by proxy.

You may identify with the theistic stream of existentialism and declare that affirmation of one's own Being comes through a blind leap of faith and commitment to God; the ultimate in confronting uncertainty is to commit yourself to God in the face of there being no completely compelling reason to do so. You may identify with the atheistic stream of existentialism and declare that affirmation of one's own Being comes through living at the edge of the precipice and steadfastly refusing to leap blindly into nothingness; the ultimate in confronting uncertainty is to be in active revolt against the seductive security of faith in God. These two streams of existentialist thought are in direct opposition to one another concerning what constitutes the courageous response to the uncertainty of existence; but they are in complete accord concerning *who* must respond. Each individual, alone, must come to terms with the uncertainty of Being.

In counseling with an individual, it is neither necessary nor possible for the counselor to decide what is *the* courageous response for his client. What is possible and may be necessary for the counselor is to assist his client become aware that in one way or another his client does respond to the uncertainty of existence and that there is more than one way to respond. Specifically, he can pretend that everything is exactly as he would like it to be; or he can refuse to think about it altogether or he can confront contingency head-on and declare, "I am and I stand here."

Each year thousands of children must somehow come to terms with the uncertainty that results from their parents' divorcing. It is all too easy to view the child of divorced parents as victimized by the selfishness of immature adults, when, in many cases, much greater stability and consistency are the actual results of separation or divorce. The truly victimized child is one who is never asked to wait, to endure disappointment, to face failure, to suffer his own pain, or be exposed to the suffering of others. While we are not advocating suffering for its own sake, nor is there the slightest suggestion that a youngster should be dealt with harshly or cruelly for the sake of building character, there is reason to believe that those persons who can cope constructively with uncertainty throughout life are individuals who were not shielded from disappointment and suffering in their early years. Parents and teachers and the counselors with whom they consult, who attempt to create a phoney world of certainty by denying such realities as: "Sometimes I make mistakes, I'm not always right" "Sometimes I'm cranky and grouchy and I don't want to talk with you or anybody else" "Sometimes I'm frightened and unsure about what to do" "Sometimes I hurt in ways that neither you nor anybody else can do anything about" "Sometimes I feel as if life isn't worth it" perform a hideous disservice to the developing youngster. The probability that a youngster will be able to stand alone and affirm his own Being in the face of uncertainty is enhanced, not guaranteed but enhanced, by having had some access to similar self-affirming processes within the significant others in his world.

## Choice

Many of us have had profound personal experiences of affirming our own Being which we would characterize as "oceanic" or "peak" experiences. It is no accident that such terms are used to describe self-affirmation in that, quite literally, a journey to the ocean or to the top of a mountain can alter one's perspective so thoroughly that contemplating and confronting the relationship between oneself and the vast, uncertain world is inescapable. Even though we have to face aspects of ourselves that are shameful, useless, and frightening, the total experience is one of cleansing and renewal. We descend the mountain or return from the ocean with both a sense of urgency and resolution which have been expressed in the familiar lines:

> . . . the strength to change that which can be changed
> the serenity to accept that which cannot be changed
> and the wisdom to know one from the other.

Many of us have also had the discouraging experience of our serenity being quickly shattered and our urgency being rapidly dissipated by the noise and routine of the daily life to which we return. Whereas we recognize the importance of breaking away from daily routine and of seeking new perspectives, it is not possible for most of us to live on the mountain top or to seclude ourselves at the ocean. Therefore, if we are to live lives characterized by both strength and serenity, vitality and tranquility, lustiness and harmony, then we must somehow discover resources within ourselves, rather than relying on frequent setting changes, to regain and maintain perspective.

It is possible for anyone in any situation to live a meaningful life if he is willing to recognize and commit himself to the basic principle: The way I make my choices makes all the difference. Individuals who are coping constructively with the uncertainty of human existence are individuals who actively choose what they will do, how they will move, and who they will be. Life does not *happen* to the person who is confronting and coping with his Aloneness; he makes his life happen and makes himself — affirms his Being — in the act of choosing. This principle applies in situations which are as dehumanizing, painful, and hideous as that described by Victor Frankl in *Man's Search for Meaning* (1963).

> We who lived in concentration camps can remember the men who walked through the huts conforting others, giving away their last piece of bread. They may have been few in number, but they offer sufficient proof that everything can be taken from a man but one thing: the last of the human freedoms — to choose one's attitude in any given set of circumstances, to choose one's own way.
>
> And there were always choices to make. Every day, every hour, offered the opportunity to make a decision, a decision which determined whether you would or would not submit to those powers which threatened to rob you of your very self, your inner freedom; which determined whether or not you would become the plaything of circumstances, renouncing freedom and dignity to become molded into the form of the typical inmate.
>
> . . . in the final analysis it becomes clear that the sort of person the prisoner became was the result of an inner decision, and not the result of camp influences alone. Fundamentally, therefore, any man can, even under such circumstances, decide what shall become of him — mentally and spiritually. He may retain his human dignity even in a concentration camp (pp. 104—105).

The probability is very remote that any of you who are reading this book will be required to endure unspeakable torment, such as was inflicted in Nazi concentration camps. Nevertheless, each of you faces the same basic question concerning how you, individually and alone, will respond to the fact that being human means you must choose your human Being.

The practicing counselor will encounter numerous instances when a client construes his life as devoid of meaningful choices. The most common deterrent to making self-affirming choices which are necessary in coping constructively with Aloneness is an attitude and posture taken by the client that, "Oh well, it doesn't really matter; I don't care anyway." The element in an individual client's life that blocks him most thoroughly from making meaningful choices is his own indifference. Physical suffering, prejudice, injustice, severe personal loss, financial disaster, and the threat of death rob the individual of many meaningful choices. But only his indifference blots out choice altogether. This is not to say that all things matter equally or that some things do not really matter. But no one can make out a list of "things that don't really matter" for another person, each of us must choose what does and does not matter to him.

In most cases when a client says, in one form or another, "It doesn't really matter, anyway," that is not a complete description of how he feels about himself or his situation. It is not so much that he is lying, but rather that he has learned to say, "I don't care," when he feels one of several things he is unable or unwilling to say more directly. "It doesn't matter" and "I don't care" are frequently substitutes for one of the following:

I'm not worthy of having a preference; I don't deserve to make a choice.

I'm afraid of having preferences or making a choice because it may displease someone else, or it might turn out wrong. I might make a mistake.

I'm in conflict about what I really want and I'd rather stop caring than resolve the conflict.

I've been hurt in the past when I cared about something and I'm not willing to risk suffering again.

If I act like I care or that something matters, then other people will know where I'm vulnerable and they could hurt me.

If I care enough to make a choice, then I'm responsible for the outcome and my life is so painful I shouldn't have to be responsible.

While it may be true that the individual who adopts the crouched and/or broken posture reflected in the above statements, may momentarily avoid conflict, fear, vulnerability, and disappointment, the price he pays is his dignity, his freedom, his integrity — his very Being. In Frankl's words, he becomes "the plaything of circumstances."

To a counselor who is trying to understand an individual client or consult with the parents, teachers, or employers of a client, the way in which the client is coping with his Aloneness is terribly important. This means the counselor must understand the client's capacity to make choices; his capacity to decide what matters and what does not matter to him; his willingness to recognize and commit himself to the basic principle: "The way I make my choices makes all the difference." Until a client can be encouraged, persuaded, or convinced that his making choices really does matter, there is no point in discussing what the alternatives are, what it would take to make various possibilities actualities, or what the costs and payoffs might be. Although it has more to do with the process of counseling than the content of counseling, it should probably be noted that one of the more effective ways to encourage a client to care about his own choices is, within the context of your own genuine caring for him, inviting him to risk acting as if he cared enough to actively choose.

## Uniqueness

The third focal point in our discussion of the nature of Aloneness is the existential reality that each individual must come to terms with the fact that he is unique. If an individual is in the process of affirming his own Being through actively choosing his own way, then he, more than anyone or anything, is the designer of his life's pattern; he is the composer/conductor of his life themes. However, even if an individual ignores or refuses his opportunities to choose and winds up dancing to someone else's tune or patterning himself according to someone else's design, that particular person's life is nevertheless unique.

On the face of it, being unique sounds great; after all, who wants to be just like everybody else! But uniqueness does not stop with "not being like everybody else"; unique means being unlike *anybody* else. Although you share many things in common with other persons, no one, absolutely no one, is exactly like you. No one has or ever will experience life exactly as you do. No one can understand totally what life is like for you. There is an impenetrable barrier, an untraversable distance, an unbridgeable gulf between you and every other person. Being unique means being separate and alone.

It is possible to observe the developing youngster become aware of his own uniqueness. At first there are only fleeting thoughts: Does anybody else have my name? Are there any other Marty Grahams in the world building a sand castle on a beach just like this one? Really, nobody ever made a picture just like this one before? As the awareness of uniqueness – and the separation and aloneness which go with that awareness – begin to crescendo in adolescence, a frantic flurry of conformity consumes most young people. Great effort is expended on looking like, talking like, walking like, sneering like, smelling like, everybody else in my school, on my block, or in my gang. But, in time it becomes very clear – no matter what I do, how I look or dress, or talk – nobody really understands me. At this point the individual is in a position to confront his Aloneness directly and to not shrink from the unalterable reality that he, like every other human being, is fundamentally unique and separate. No longer need he be driven to wear *the* right clothes, say *the* right words, find *the* right person, or do *the* right thing to erase his separation. Henceforth, he becomes free to wear, say, relate, and do what he chooses as right for him. He becomes free to participate joyfully in the process of increasing understanding between himself and others, once he has relinquished the unreal ideal that somewhere there is a magical someone who will understand him totally. He becomes free to delight in the wonder of words, awkwardly chosen and haltingly spoken perhaps, but increasingly effective in conveying his meaning to another, once he has abandoned the search for a magic language that everybody always understands completely.

Many people never recover from their adolescent horror of being unique, separate, and alone. Instead of actively affirming authorship of their own lives, they become incidental characters in the autobiographies of others. While it is imperative for an individual to be willing and able to play a support role in relation to significant other persons, it is immoral for an individual to reduce himself to nothing but a member of the supporting cast in someone else's life drama. Undoubtedly the question will be raised, "But what if a person doesn't want to be unique, separate, and alone; what if he (or, more likely, she) is happier just being like others?" The question makes no sense, in that it implies a choice which is not available to human beings. You cannot choose to not be unique. The question makes as much sense as asking, "But what if a person doesn't want to die; what if he or she would be happier living forever?" Uniqueness, and therefore separateness and aloneness, are immutable conditions of human existence. Those conditions can be an invitation for the individual to engage in a lifelong process of seeking directions and destinations of his own choosing or those same conditions can be a burdensome and depressing reality which the individual spends his life trying to deny or ignore.

In either case, the individual may present himself to a counselor for assistance. For the individual who has already confronted the fact that he is unique and thus alone, his purposes in seeking counseling may be to identify possible directions his life could take or to discuss the manner in which he will make the continuous series of choices that together determine his unique life course. For the individual who has not yet come to terms with the fact that he is unique and singularly responsible for the direction his life takes, counseling may provide the first situation in which he has felt sufficiently safe and personally worthy of addressing the questions: "What do *I* want my life to be?" "Where do *I* want to head?" "What shape do *I* want my life to take?" In order for a counselor to be of assistance to individuals who are attempting to cope with human Aloneness, that counselor must listen carefully for the content which discloses the client's struggle with uncertainty, choices, and uniqueness. The major battlefield upon which confrontation with uniqueness is conducted, is the awareness that nobody, including a skilled counselor, is ever going to understand me completely. The enemy to be vanquished is the false hope that there is anything I can do, say, or be that will eradicate my uniqueness and alleviate me of the responsibility for choosing myself — my Being. The paradox of skillful counseling in the content area Aloneness is, that from a relationship characterized by incomplete although extensive understanding, limited but far-reaching acceptance, imperfect albeit effective communication, a client can gain the courage to create himself by himself.


## Death

Our final focus on the human existential realities which define the individual's Aloneness is, appropriately, death. If, as a counselor, you are frequently called upon to counsel with terminally ill clients and their families and friends or with bereaved clients, you will need to study the meaning of death in human experience beyond what we will be able to discuss here. However, the fact that life is terminal is a basic, inescapable reality for each of the limited number of clients with whom you will work in the course of your own life. It is not so much that the moment of death is uncertain or that the experience is one which cannot be completely shared, that makes the individual's own death a central focus of his Aloneness, because very few, if any, human experiences are either exactly predictable or completely communicable. The significance of death, as it relates to counseling, is that *time* is absolutely limited for each of us. This, of course, is so obviously the case that it often goes by unnoticed. On the one hand, we live in a society that is obsessed with doing more and more in less and less time. We seem to be driven toward discovering and inventing ways to make living more instantaneous; "instamatic" has replaced "automatic" as the most attractive aspect of an object, a process, or a person. On the other hand, we seem to be equally driven to avoid and to ignore asking ourselves "Why?" "What for?" "How come?" It is very easy to slip into a faulty line of thinking that begins: Time is valuable, therefore time-saving devices and ways of doing things are also valuable. The difficulty is that time, unlike money and S & H Green Stamps, cannot be saved. You can take less time to do something, but you cannot stop spending it — until it is all gone.

There are a variety of experiences that can sharply focus attention on the cold impersonal fact that one's time is running out. Some of them are obvious, such as observing the passing of the Old Year in Times Square, New York City; reading a poster that says, "Today is the first day of the rest of your life"; attending a funeral; meeting the 6'2" son of a friend you have not seen since you were classmates; or trying to answer a child's question about what it is like to be "older." Some experiences are more subtle, and perhaps more shocking, such as hearing your heart beat and realizing that some day it will be silent forever, planting a tree which will never be big enough to shade your day, or reading your name in the University Library card catalog followed by the year of your birth and a dash and a blank space — to be filled in later. While we would probably agree that it is not constructive to be highly preoccupied with the unrelenting passage of time and the inevitability of death, it is also not constructive to be totally oblivious to diminishing time and the increasing proximity of death.

Suppose that you have recently visited your physician for a routine annual examination, and it is his conclusion that you are suffering from inoperable, terminal cancer and have about one year to live. Eliminating the possibility that either his diagnosis or prognosis are in error, would you want to know that you have but one year of life left? In other words, it is not a matter that he thinks you may have cancer and there is nothing that can be done to treat it, you *in fact* have terminal cancer and *in fact* have but one year to live. Would you want to know that? People differ greatly in their response to this possibility. Some say, "No, I would not want to know, if there isn't anything that could be done about it, because I'd be so worried and depressed that I couldn't enjoy the last year." Some people say, "Yes, I would want to know, because even if there wasn't anything I could do about it, there'd be a lot of things I'd do differently that year." Other people say, "Yes, I would want to know, but it probably wouldn't change my life very much, because I'd try not to think about it and just go on living naturally." There are some few people who also say, "Yes, I would want to know, but it probably wouldn't change my life very much"; however, their reason is much different, "because I try to live each day now as if it is part of the last year I'll be here."

Being informed that you have only one year to live, almost forces you to ask yourself: "What for?" "How come?" "Why?" would I choose to do one thing rather than another. The individual who would not want to know he had merely a year to live is in essence saying: "I do not want to grapple with questions about my basic purpose in living!" The individual who would want to know, but also knows it would not change his life because he simply would stop thinking about it, is in essence saying: "I don't think it's normal or natural to struggle with questions about the purpose of my life!" The individual who would want to know because he would do many things differently is in essence saying: "I don't think about the purpose of my life often enough, and knowing I had just a year to live would force me to come to grips with my life!" The rare individual who would want to know he had one remaining year to live, but who also knows that his life would not be drastically altered by such information is in essence saying: "I have faced the question of my purpose in living and daily I struggle to hammer out the answer!"

Human beings' sense of time and the units of time that are real to them vary a great deal. Most people can imagine what it might be like to have a year or less to live; that is, they can imagine that it would probably not be something they would lose track of or forget very easily. However, if the time limit were extended to three or five or ten years, the fact that human existence is terminal beins to lose its impact on many people. Some individuals have to be experiencing death as an immediate threat in order to focus on questions about the purpose and meaning of their lives. It is not your responsibility as a counselor to hit people over the head with the fact that they are going to die.

However, the questions and concerns that arise in counseling with an individual do not make sense unless they are viewed in terms of that individual's basic purpose in living. For example, when a young man struggles with a decision about military service and the draft, a personally satisfying choice is unlikely to result from considering only the legal and political aspects of the decision. What may at best have to be a compromise choice among competing, contradictory values hardly stands a chance of being a decision the young man feels right about, unless he has considered the increased probability of being killed, what risking death means to him, what his purposes in serving in the Armed Forces would be, and what his purposes in refusing to serve in the Armed Forces would be. Another example of a situation which occurs increasingly frequently in counseling involves the decision to change career fields after age forty-five. The longer the period of formal training and experience in any one career field, the more difficult it is to radically alter a career pattern. For a physician, or logger, or architect, or fisherman who has devoted twenty years or more to one line of work to consider another career possibility most certainly means he or she must address the question: "What is most important in the time that remains?" Again, there is no decision or problem that a client faces which can be fully understood by the counselor or the client himself unless it is viewed in the context of the client's basic purpose in living. A person's basic life purpose is not necessarily something he can describe or define in precise and eloquent language; but he discloses his basic purpose in the way he chooses to spend his limited time.

There are many counselors who would definitely rather not think about death, especially their own. They would be likely to point out that a person ought to focus on living, not on dying; after all, you can do something about living and there is not anything you can do about dying. The difficulty with such a view is that living and dying are not two separate processes or phases of existence. Each of us is quite literally in the process of dying; for some of us it will take longer than for others of us. Each of us is also quite literally in the process of living. But it is simply not the case that some of us are in the process of living and others in the process of dying. The existential process each one of us is engaged in is simultaneously a living/dying process. Affirming one's own Being, achieving the full stature of humanness, constructively coping with Aloneness necessarily include an awareness and acceptance of the fact that human existence is simultaneously a living/dying process. If a counselor narrows his focus to "living" and ignores dying, he is less likely to ask himself, or anyone else, questions concerning the purpose for being one way as opposed to another. He is likely to become preoccupied with questions concerning the mechanics of living, that is, "How can a person live a more ––– life?" (The blank is filled in with terms such as meaningful, satisfying, full, happy, contented, mature, self-actualizing, creative, relevant, useful, complete, etc.). But being human involves more than answering "how to do it" questions. Being human means answering the question, "Why do it at all?" An individual is more likely to find answers to his questions about how to live life, if he has begun to deal with the basic question of "Why am I living?" That basic question comes into focus as the individual realizes that he is not always going to be living; that, in fact, he is presently dying on his feet. If you, as a counselor, are going to be of assistance to a person struggling with questions about how to live life, then your focus on human existence needs to include dying as well as living. You need to be able to assist the person ask and answer the basic question of "Why am I living?"

If a counselor narrows his focus to "dying," however, and ignores living, he is less likely to ask himself, or anyone else, questions concerning how to translate purposes for living into concrete actions. He is likely to become preoccupied with abstract thoughts of Being and non-Being. It is not enough, in your role as counselor, to assist a person develop an essay entitled "My Purpose for Being" which has little or nothing to do with how he actually chooses to invest his time. In addition to the basic question of "Why am I living?" you need to be able to assist the person ask and answer the question "How do I realize my purpose for living through choosing how I spend my time?"

Before summarizing the discussion of Aloneness, it probably should be re-emphasized that we are looking at the *content* of counseling and not the *process*. Hopefully, no one would conclude from the above discussion on death that it is the counselor's job to point a verbal finger at the client and demand to know: (1) "What is your basic purpose in life?" (2) "How are you realizing that purpose?" and (3) "In light of the fact that you are going to die some day, are you giving these things sufficient attention?"

The intended effect of the discussion of Aloneness is that you would enter the counseling process with a preparedness to hear and understand some specific things about the individual human being seated across from you. In addition to his concerns with what he is doing about Work and how he is moving in Relationship with people, he, by the very fact that he exists, must somehow come to terms with his existence. For each human being that means, in a world that is not always what it appears to be, full of other human beings, none of whom will ever understand me totally, I cannot escape making the unique pattern of choices that, looking backwards in time from the point of death will be my essence. None of the other creatures works in the sense that man works; none of the other creatures relates in the sense that man relates. And no other creature carves out his Being in the sense that a man chooses to be who he is. Humans work together and they relate with one another, but the individual, alone, chooses to be who he is. Understanding the Aloneness that characterizes each person's existence frees you, as a counselor, from being overly cautious in your efforts to help a client cope constructively with living and dying because, even if you were intentionally trying to do so, you cannot choose another person's Being for him. Understanding Aloneness also frees you from being overly zealous in your efforts to help because, regardless of how thoroughly you understand a person and his situation, he and only he is in a position to design and define who he is.

## V   SUMMARY AND APPLICATIONS

In the beginning of this section concerning the content of counseling, the position was taken that each counselor needs to have some way of organizing the vast amount of personal information a client typically discloses in even the first interview. You need to be able to answer the question, "In what ways are these particular episodes, persons, feelings, thoughts, problems, questions, etc., which the client is describing, important to him?" Also, you need to have some way of organizing the content which the client relates in order to answer a second question: "What else, which the client has not yet mentioned, might also be important to him?" It is your responsibility as a counselor to receive the bulky and amorphous life packages which some clients present and then to sort through and organize the contents, jumbled though they may be, in such a way that both you and the individual client are better able to understand and appreciate the substance of his life. With other clients your responsibility may involve receiving a life package that initially appears to be just a barren brown box, easily tossed aside because of its lack of substance. Then, you must engage the client in a process of identifying the content he left out of the package, probably because he finds it hard to believe you are really interested in "all that stuff." A counselor needs a content classification system for organizing and managing "all the stuff" a client says about himself; he also needs such a system to facilitate finding and gathering important "stuff" that the client, for one reason or another, does not share spontaneously.

We have discussed the three categories of a content classification system based on three life tasks which are an integral part of each stage of human development, Work, Relationship, and Aloneness. At any given point in an individual's developmental history, he will be deeply immersed in all three life task areas; that is, he will be doing, moving, and being, simultaneously. Even if a client is highly organized and quite articulate, he, of course, is not going to present three neat little bundles tagged "Work, Relationship, and Aloneness. " Instead, he will probably describe various life experiences that in most instances reflect all three life task areas. There is no point in trying to classify a particular experience as belonging to one category *rather than* another. For example, it is pointless to concern yourself with whether a client's description of quitting his job after an argument with his boss about the company's dishonest business practices tells you more about his Work, his Relationships, or his Aloneness. Most things a client says, tell you something about him in each content area, so the question you need to ask yourself is: "If I were to describe this person in terms of his Work, his Relationships, and his Aloneness, could I give a full and accurate account?"

While we can recognize the three life task areas as separable dimensions of human experience, clearly they are not separate, distinct, and unrelated compartments of a person's life. In fact, it is the interrelatedness of the content areas that is usually most important. In Section Two, The Purpose of Counseling, we will be discussing choice, change, and confusion reduction as the three major purposes of counseling. Rarely is it the case that a client is confused or needs to make choices or changes in one content area without that affecting the other two content areas. Thus, it bears repeating that the important question is: "Are you organizing the content your client communicates in such a way that both of you are better able to see how he is coming to terms with the basic, interrelated, developmental tasks concerning Work, Relationship, and Aloneness, which are the defining characteristics of humanness?"

### The Case of Warren Lopez

To illustrate further how you might utilize the three-category classification system to organize the content of a counseling interaction, two brief, hypothetical case studies will be presented.

Harold Stromme has been boys' counselor in a suburban junior high school near Seattle, Washington for three years. During this time he has developed a reputation among the teachers for being very approachable and helpful in consulting with them about their interactions with students. Late in the Spring, Mr. Collins, the art teacher, talked with Mr. Stromme about some difficulties he was having with an eighth-grade student named Warren Lopez. Mr. Stromme had only met Warren once, but remembered him as being a good-looking, dark-complexioned boy of Mexican-American descent, somewhat small in stature, but well-developed and self-confident in his carriage. Mr. Collins described Warren as having considerable artistic ability, particulary in sculpting and pottery-making, and as being one of the most promising art students Collins had ever taught.

For several summers, a large resort on the coast of Washington had sponsored a series of art shows, including two weeks when the work of very young Pacific Northwest artists was featured. Mr. Collins had informed Warren of this and strongly encouraged him to submit several of his best pieces, plus the wood carving he was then completing, for possible inclusion in the show. However, since the time he first mentioned the show, Mr. Collins has watched Warren become increasingly disinterested and unproductive in his art class. Warren no longer works in the art room after school or during his free period; he has missed two regular classes because of "not feeling well." His English teacher commented the other day to Mr. Collins that Warren and another student appeared to be having a pretty heated argument in the hall before class. Mr. Collins thinks that the more enthusiastic he has been about Warren's entering the art show, the more distant and resistant Warren has become. Any efforts to discuss it have been met with silence and blank looks from Warren.

Mr. Stromme agreed to talk with Warren, if he were willing to do so. Warren reluctantly complied with Mr. Collins' request that he go see Mr. Stromme for purposes of discussing the obvious change in his performance in the art class. Mr. Stromme began their discussion by clearly, but briefly, describing all he knew of the situation and stating he believed that Warren might find it useful if they were to discuss it. Warren looked skeptical, but went on to say he was "just under a lot of pressure."

*Mr. Stromme:* "Lota' stuff coming at you all at once?"

*Warren:* "Yeh, well both my father and Mr. Collins are sorta' . . . oh, I don't know."

*Mr. Stromme:* "Could you tell me a little about your father?"

*Warren:* "Well, he's in charge of all the produce for the Safeway Stores in greater Seattle."

*Mr, Stromme:* "He manages the buying and distributing?"

*Warren:* "Yeh, well sort of — see, we moved here from Texas about seven years ago, and my father came to Wenatchee to pick fruit, then we moved to Seattle and he got a job at Safeway. Since then he's worked his way up 'til he's in charge of all the produce stuff for eight different Safeway Stores."

Because of the straightforward manner in which Mr. Stromme approached their meeting and the genuine interest he displayed in what Warren had to say, Mr. Stromme quickly established sufficient rapport with Warren, that in the course of their forty-minute interview Warren was willing to share the following information:

Seven years ago, Mr. and Mrs. Lopez moved to Washington with their three daughters, ages eleven, twelve, and thirteen, and their seven-year-old son, Warren, to follow the fruit crops with other Mexican-American families. The following year, when Warren was in the second grade, Mrs. Lopez delivered twin boys. Since then, the family has moved to Seattle; the three girls each completed high school or received a General Equivalency Diploma, and then left home to marry. Warren's father, age thirty-eight, was very successful in his first full-time job with Safeway Stores and has been steadily advanced to his present managerial position. This past year, after the twins entered first grade, Mrs. Lopez, age thirty-six, went to work in a florist shop where she designs and makes flower arrangements. The family has been very closely knit and even though the girls are married and live from 10 to 30 miles away, the larger family gathers for dinner each Sunday after Mass.

About three weeks ago, Warren's father asked him to assist with inventory after school and on the weekends. When Warren told his father

that he needed to stay after school to work on his art project, Mr. Lopez
let him know just how thoroughly he disapproved of a young man
spending all of his time playing with clay and wood! Warren's mother had
always encouraged him to pursue his interest in art, but she felt she could
not say much this time because Warren's father was so opposed to it. Mr.
Lopez wanted Warren to learn to work hard, to go to college and to get a
degree in accounting or law or medicine. Warren told Mr. Stromme that he
could understand how his father felt, because they had always been so
poor, and he *really* did not want to disappoint him. Warren was not sure
that Mr. Collins could understand how his father felt and besides, he was
not sure it would be right to talk to anyone outside the family.

So, for the first time in his life, Warren found himself in a position
of not being able to talk to anyone and not being able to please the people
he valued most. As a result, he had stopped talking to anyone and, for
the most part, he had stopped doing anything he did not absolutely have
to do.

The purpose of this example is not to solve Warren's problem with the
"right" answer. Undoubtedly you can think of several ways Mr. Stromme might
assist Warren in resolving the conflicts. However, if you apply the three-category
classification system to Warren and his situation, you can see that the third
category, Aloneness, stands out as the major arena of confussion and conflict. As
far as Work is concerned, it is clear that Warren has not yet decided what kind of
work he will pursue and that it is too early to make a final decision anyway.
It is true that Warren's conflicts are showing up in his work. but merely
deciding whether to finish his project and submit it to the art show, or to work
for his father after school will not resolve the basic question of who should
design Warren's life. His conflicts are also affecting his relationships with both
his mother and father, with Mr. Collins, and with some of his peers. But again,
the basic conflict would not be resolved by trying to improve Warren's
relationship with any of these people. One month ago, Warren enjoyed excellent
relationships with all persons concerned! The only thing that addresses the basic
issue and thus puts Warren in a position to begin resolving his conflicts, is the
question, "How do you see yourself making your choices about how to spend
your time and energies?"

When Warren begins to grapple with the larger question of how he should
plan his life, who should influence his plans and to what extent, the specific
questions about entering the art show, working in inventory, talking with his
parents, etc. can be answered more easily. If Warren had some idea of how much
he felt his father's wishes should influence his choices, then Mr. Stromme might
assist Warren find ways to discuss that with his father and with Mr. Collins.
However, before such a strategy would be appropriate, Mr. Stromme needs to
assist Warren in asking himself questions in the Aloneness category concerning

uncertainty, uniqueness, not being understood, separateness, the inevitability of making choices, and the significance of time.

With the information given above, Mr. Stromme knows the least about Warren in content area three, Aloneness. That is reason enough for Mr. Stromme to focus their attention on it because they do not yet have a very complete picture of Warren as an individual, separate and alone. However in this case, exploring the area of Aloneness will do more than fill in the missing information; it will also provide a beginning basis for facing conflicts and concerns in the other two content areas as well.

Receiving and sifting through the information being provided by a client, reviewing the three content areas of that particular client's life, and then seeking additional information or clarification in one or more of the life task areas can be accomplished during the session itself. You have merely to take a moment and think it through, asking yourself the question, "If I were to describe this person (e.g., Warren Lopez) in terms of his Work, Relationships, and Aloneness, could I give a full and accurate account?" In the case of Warren Lopez, Mr. Stromme will need to understand more about Warren's struggles with Aloneness in order to answer "yes" to that question.

### The Case of Sigrid Hartman

The other hypothetical case which we will consider in order to illustrate the utility of the three-category content classification system, came to the attention of Sandy Campbell, an elementary school counselor in Decatur, Illinois. Miss Campbell had established regular biweekly consultation sessions with the first, second, and third grade teachers; these six teachers, a special educational consultant, and Miss Campbell met as a group to share problems and solutions they experienced in working with children and parents. During their second meeting in September, Mrs. Miles, one of the first grade teachers, wanted to discuss a conference she had had with Mrs. Sigrid Hartman, the mother of two girls, ages six and seven. The youngest girl, Gretchen, has from the beginning of school started each morning on the verge of tears; she was a week late entering school because Mrs. Hartman could not get Gretchen to quit crying while the two girls were supposedly dressing for school. Elsa, the older girl, now a second grader, was described by her first grade teacher as extremely shy and unsure of herself, although her academic progress was average or above. Both girls appear to be terribly frightened of other children and very reluctant to join in any group activity.

Mrs. Hartman, who is very concerned about the situation, spent over an hour talking with Mrs. Miles and at the conclusion asked if it might be helpful to talk with the school counselor as well. As a result of her conference with Mrs. Hartman, Mrs. Miles was able to share the following information with the consultation group.

Sigrid Hartman was born in Germany in 1943; she was the youngest of three children. When she was two, Sigrid's parents and her brother and sister were all killed at home during a bombing raid. Sigrid grew up in a Protestant orphanage where she lived from 1945 until 1962, when she was nineteen. During her second year of training as a dental technician, Sigrid moved to an apartment, but she usually returned to the orphanage on the weekends to assist with the program. When she was twenty-one and had been working in a laboratory for over a year, she met and married Ernst Hartman, a G.I. stationed in Germany. In 1965 they moved to the United States and settled in Ernst's home town in Pennsylvania. Ernst was never able to secure steady employment and after moving from place to place for four years, with Sigrid working as a waitress or a domestic servant, she decided to divorce him. So with their two small daughters, she moved to Decatur, where she knew a couple who had lived in Germany. Sigrid found a job as a maid in an older motel; she and the girls were provided a three-room apartment as part of her wages. Although she had made an effort to find work as a dental technician, Sigrid was unable to gain reciprocity for her German certification and so she took the first job she could find.

In contrast to her own childhood, surrounded by other children in the orphanage, Sigrid's daughters rarely interact with other children outside of school. Because her job is most demanding on the weekends, Sigrid has never become acquainted in or joined any of Decatur's church groups. Her friends from Germany live at some distance and they rarely visit one another more than once every couple months. In view of their meager income, Mrs. Hartman and the girls are very creative and resourceful in occupying what little free time she has by making good use of a nearby park and playground, the city library, free concerts, and her own accordion which she brought with her from Germany. The time they spend together is the best part of the day for each of them.

If we apply the three-category classification system to Mrs. Hartman and to Elsa and Gretchen, we can quickly identify the life task areas in which change needs to occur. It is clear that the two girls are not coping constructively in their relationships with people, other than their mother. If we focus on Mrs. Hartman, it is clear that while she is working and doing as well as she can at this point, she could certainly use some skillful career counseling.

The consultation group with whom Mrs. Miles discussed the Hartmans agreed that Miss Campbell was in the best position to meet with Mrs. Hartman and talk about alternatives to her present work situation. Also, they concluded that, as a group, they could help the two teachers who have the Hartman girls in class plan and implement ways of assisting the girls learn to become more comfortable and skillful in their interpersonal relationships at school.

There may be some temptation to ask, "Who needs a three-category content classification system to help the Hartmans; good common sense would do the job!" In the first place, good sense is not all that common and, in the second place, there are many choice points where a partial view of the client's life results in a counselor forging ahead — all the way to a dead-end. For example, in the case of Sigrid Hartman and her daughters, it would have been relatively easy for a counselor to pounce on the trauma of Mrs. Hartman's early childhood and speculate that somehow she is communicating her unresolved fears to her daughters. Or it is conceivable that a counselor might conclude that the children of any recently divorced parents would be very hurt and angry and would express their hostilities by having difficulties at school. One of the best checks against a counselor offering premature interpretations and partially accurate explanations, is a willingness to take whatever time is required and to make whatever effort is necessary to understand the client in all three developmental task areas. If you are able to describe your client in terms of his Work — what he is doing, his Relationships — how he is moving, and his Aloneness — who he is, you are in the best position to formulate the purpose of counseling with him and to engage in a process that will realize that purpose.

# Section Two

## THE
## PURPOSE
## OF
## COUNSELING

# I  OVERVIEW — THREE COUNSELING CONTRACTS

There are several different phrases which could be used to represent the topic of Section Two; we could discuss "the goals of counseling," "the objectives of counseling," the "intended outcomes of counseling," or "the directions and destinations of counseling." Although they suggest slightly different shades of meaning, none of these phrases seems particularly better than the others and they all can be designated by the rather simple phrase, "the purposes of counseling." Clearly, something ought to happen as a result of counseling. Whether you call that "something" an outcome, a goal, or a destination does not matter nearly as much as your being able to think and talk about the purposes of your counseling in such a way that you and your clients hold a similar view of what it is you are trying to accomplish together.

## Importance of a common purpose

You are much more likely to plan effectively and to complete your plans together, if you and your client have a common purpose that is clear to both of you. For example, if an unmarried pregnant high school student seeks counseling for the purpose of deciding what she should do about her situation, you are more likely to be of help to her, if you define the purpose of counseling as assisting her make the series of choices which faces her, than if you define your purpose as changing her self-concept and degree of self-esteem so she views herself as a worthwhile person. The latter purpose may in fact be an outcome of counseling with her, but it is not the primary focus or the central purpose of your meeting together.

Or, to cite another example, suppose a young man in the middle of his freshman year in college seeks counseling because he "just doesn't know where he's going or who he is or what to think about himself." He is more likely to be able to use your help if you define the purpose of your meeting together as assisting him clarify and reduce the confusion in his life, than if you define the purpose as getting him to choose a major and change his study habits. It may well be that as the two of you work for clarification and a reduction in his confusion, he will then see his way clear to declare a particular major and/or see the necessity for acquiring additional study skills. However, you are more likely to reach that point if initially you have truly accepted his definition of the purpose of your meeting together as being "to sort stuff out so he isn't confused." It certainly could be the case that this is not the best time for him to choose a major or change the way he studies and that reducing his confusion about himself is all that is required now. In both of these examples and in general, counseling will proceed more smoothly and more effectively if you and your client are headed in the same direction, seek the same outcome, are traveling toward the same destination, are pursuing the same goal, have the same objectives or, more simply, if you share the same purpose.

In Section One we defined the general purpose of counseling to be *helping people of all ages and in a variety of settings cope constructively with the business of being human.* With that general purpose in mind we were able to focus attention on three developmental task areas, Work, Relationship, and Aloneness, which are major dimensions of the business of being human and which together provide the content of counseling. We are now in a position to demand a more specific definition of the purpose of counseling by asking, "What does it mean to help people cope constructively with their Work, Relationships, and Aloneness?" If the answer to that question is to be useful to the practicing counselor, it will require a definition of the purpose of counseling that accomplishes two things simultaneously. In the first place, a useful definition of the specific purpose of counseling needs to be cast in terms that both the counselor and client can readily understand and apply to their experience of meeting together. If the client thinks he is there "because he needs to get some things decided" and the counselor thinks the client is there "to more fully participate in his own becoming" they will probably have more difficulty communicating with one another and achieving their purposes, than if they both viewed the purpose of their meeting together as assisting the client with some of his choices. If a counselor persists in defining the purpose of counseling in terms that, from the client's point of view, seem to have no bearing on why he thought he sought counseling, communication between them will be seriously jeopardized and the client will probably terminate counseling prematurely.

The second requirement in order for a definition of the purpose of counseling to be useful to the practicing counselor, is that it be cast in terms which will enable both the counselor and the client to judge whether or not, or the extent to which, they are accomplishing their purpose in meeting together. Although it may sound simpleminded, a question you ought to be able to answer regarding any particular client is "How will you know when you have finished —what would things look like at the end of successful counseling with this person?" Whether your counseling with any particular client takes one session or one hundred and one sessions, you need to understand and describe the purpose of your sessions in such a way that you and your client are able to evaluate if, when, and to what degree your explicitly stated, mutually agreed upon purpose is being achieved.

Although it is sometimes more confortable and usually much easier to think about the purpose of counseling in broad general terms, such as "coping constructively" or "becoming a more responsible citizen" or "being a better father" or "living a more complete life" or "finding oneself" or "losing oneself," etc., these statements of purpose do not offer much help in evaluating the effectiveness of counseling. Assuming that it is important to both the counselor and the client to assess the value and effectiveness of their efforts together, then it is necessary to define the purpose of their counseling with sufficient clarity and precision that they both know what it is they are trying to accomplish and they would both recognize it, if and when it happens. If a counselor persists in defining the purpose of counseling in vague, general, abstruse terms, he probably is also unable or unwilling to plan the process of counseling systematically or carefully and he is probably unable or unwilling to evaluate the results of his counseling efforts.

## Tyler's Counseling Objectives

To answer the question, "What does it mean to help people cope constructively with their Work, Relationships, and Aloneness?" we need a definition of the purpose of counseling which both counselors and clients would regard as accurately describing their common intentions and expectations for meeting together and which would allow them to evaluate the extent to which they are accomplishing their mutually agreed upon intentions and expectations. In the third edition of *The Work of the Counselor,* Leona Tyler (1969) has provided such a definition of the purpose of counseling. As part of a larger classification system, which includes categories for the content and process of counseling as well, Tyler identifies three major classes of counseling objectives: Choice, Change, and Confusion Reduction. (Tyler also refers to the Confusion Reduction category as "Doubtful" because it includes those clients for whom it is initially unclear whether the purpose of counseling is Choice or Change.) Throughout the remainder of this book we will use Tyler's three categories to define and discuss the purposes of counseling in more specific terms. The definition we are adopting is that the purpose of counseling is to assist people of all ages and in a variety of settings make choices, make changes, and reduce personal confusion concerning their work, relationships and aloneness. In an effort to translate this definition of the purpose of counseling into the language of practice, Figure 3 includes examples of counseling purposes for each counseling content area.

Two-dimensional diagrams, such as Figure 3, make interesting additions to a textbook, especially when they possess the lovely symmetry of Figure 3. However, breaking the monotony of rows and colums of printed words is hardly

**FIGURE 3. Examples of Specific Counseling Purposes.**

PURPOSE OF COUNSELING

| CONTENT OF COUNSELING | Choice | Change | Confusion Reduction |
|---|---|---|---|
| Work | Go on to college<br>Declare major<br>Return to school<br>Change jobs | Acquire new study habits and skills<br>Reduce overly critical supervisory style<br>Increase ability to use leisure time | Explore career possibilities<br>Realistic appraisal of abilities<br>Assess chances for advancement |
| Relationship | Go steady at age 13<br>File for divorce<br>Interracial marriage<br>Place parent in nursing home | Improve ability to converse in social situations<br>Acquire ability to fight with spouse constructively<br>Eliminate frequent references to personal disability<br>Reduce fear of crowds | Gain more accurate view of how regarded by others<br>Appreciate differences in need for privacy between self and others |
| Aloneness | Break with parents<br>Use drugs<br>Declare conscientious objector status<br>Have abortion at age 40 | Confront and accept personal failure<br>Acquire ability to travel unaccompanied<br>Increase capacity to please or reward oneself<br>Face terminal illness courageously | Reorient after death of spouse<br>Confront contradictory values encountered at college<br>Gain perspective on personal responsibility for alcoholic husband |

sufficient justification for devising a 3 x 3 classification of counseling purposes. Unless these categories make a difference in the way you are able to think about, plan for, implement, and evaluate your counseling they really are not worth remembering. On the basis of what numerous graduate students have reported in advanced practicum supervision sessions, it seems that one of the best ways to use the Choice, Change, Confusion Reduction categories is to view them as potential contracts that could be negotiated between you and your client.

## Counseling — A Contractual Relationship

A contract between two or more persons is an explicitly stated agreement to do something. After a contract has been negotiated, it is reasonable for the persons who participated in its formulation to expect that each person will do his part to make happen the something that was agreed upon. In the case of a counseling contract, at times the counselor and the client may have very similar parts to play in fulfilling their contract with one another; at other points they may do very different things in order to complete the contract. For example, a young man who has been blinded in an industrial accident seeks the assistance of a rehabilitation counselor for purposes of finding a job or entering a training program. When the counselor and client are working together to clarify and fully understand what factors are most important (e.g., personal values, family commitments, previous experiences, special aptitudes, etc.) for the client to consider in his plans and decisions, the roles they play appear quite similar. Of course, it is expected that the counselor will be especially skillful in facilitating the kind of communication between them which will result in a clear and complete picture of the client and his situation. In contrast, when the counselor is reporting on and interpreting the client's scores on a battery of tests, the part each of them takes is obviously quite different. But in both instances, whether the counselor is communicating *with* his client or presenting information *to* his client, it is useful to view their interaction as a contractual relationship.

In this example, the rehabilitation counselor and the young blind man would together formulate a contract in the Choice category. That is, they would agree that, using whatever processes are most suitable, their purpose in meeting together is to assist the young man survey career possibilities, select several possibilities to be explored in greater depth, rule out the least likely and least attractive of these possibilities and then choose which possibility to plan and pursue. To describe their relationship as "contractual" is simply to say that they have agreed to do something together; they both know what the something is; each one expects to do his part and expects that the other person will do his part in making the something happen. Together they formulate the contract which describes their purposes in meeting and they will continue working together to fulfill their contract.

Whether the purpose of counseling in any given case is Choice, Change, or Confusion Reduction or some combination of these, the counseling relationship can be viewed as contractual. The advantages of viewing the purpose of counseling in terms of a contract which is negotiated between the counselor and the client are:

1.  The purpose of counseling becomes the mutual concern of the counselor and the client; both the counselor and the client become responsible for formulating a statement of their purpose in meeting.

Stating their mutually agreed upon purpose as a contract to be fulfilled fosters an attitude of joint responsibility for the counseling process selected to fulfill the contract.

2.  The purpose of counseling becomes explicit; both the client and the counselor have a clear understanding of why they are meeting and what they can expect of one another. Explicitly stating their mutually agreed upon purpose as a contract to be fulfilled allows and encourages both the counselor and the client to evaluate their progress toward fulfilling the contract.

As was suggested earlier, Tyler's (1969) three categories of counseling purposes, Choice, Change, and Confusion Reduction, utilize terms which both counselors and clients readily regard as accurately describing their common purposes. People seek counseling because they need or want to make some choices; they seek counseling because they need or want to change; and they seek counseling because they need or want to become less confused. Clients literally think and talk about their purposes in seeking counseling in these terms. One way to increase the probability that the purpose of your counseling with a particular person is mutually agreed upon is to jointly formulate an explicit counseling contract in terms of Choice, Change, or Confusion Reduction.

These three categories of counseling purposes utilize terms which are also amenable to evaluation. Clients *can* tell whether or not they have made a particular choice or a series of choices with which they were struggling; clients *are* able to evaluate their progress toward making specific changes which have been identified as necessary or desirable; and clients *are* able to assess to what extent confusion about themselves and their worlds has been reduced. One way to increase the probability that the outcome of your counseling with a particular person will be mutually evaluated is also accomplished by jointly formulating an explicit counseling contract in terms of Choice, Change, or Confusion Reduction.

We will next consider in greater detail the formulation of a counseling contract in each of the three counseling purpose categories, Choice, Change, and Confusion Reduction. It is impossible to discuss the negotiating of a counseling contract to accomplish a certain purpose without reference to the processes available to fulfill the contract. However, it should be recognized that neither this section nor any other section in this book provides a description of all the available techniques for realizing the purposes of counseling. The materials presented in Section Three and the exercises and assignments in Section Four are concerned with teaching the counselor-in-training what and how to communicate in order to move the counseling process from the initial stages of understanding the client and his situation to the formulation of a counseling contract. Skillful interviewing is a necessity in the negotiation of any counseling contract, but additional information and techniques must be mastered in order for a counselor to fulfill specific counseling contracts involving Choice, Change, or Confusion Reduction. The following discussions of the three counseling contracts will close with suggested resources that can be used to acquire the information and techniques which are not presented in this book, but which are required in order to achieve certain purposes of counseling.

## II  CHOICE

In Section One we discussed Choice as one of the existential realities of being a separate, unique individual. Not making choices is not something a human being can choose to do. In the extreme case, a human can adopt a very passive, indifferent, undirected posture in relation to the way he spends his time and energy; but even then he cannot escape the fact that he is choosing such a posture and that it could be different if he chose to make it be different. This is not to say, of course, that all things are possible for humans or that there are no limits on what an individual can choose. Each of us always makes choices among limited possibilities and, in many cases, such as extreme poverty, profound physical disability, stigmatization, and prejudice, the limits on choice are irrational, unnecessary, or unjust. Nevertheless, the individual cannot escape choosing his response to the limited possibilities which confront him concerning how he will spend his time and energy. Making choices is a defining characteristic of humanness.

The general purpose of counseling was defined in Section One as assisting people to cope constructively with their humanness. Earlier in Section Two that general purpose was defined more specifically and included assisting people make choices concerning their Work, Relationships, and Aloneness. Actively engaging in rational decision-making is one of the hallmarks of a psychologically mature individual. If a person is old enough to be viewed as a client, it is appropriate to regard his making rational decisions as an important and valuable process for him to engage in actively. When a person faces typical choices characteristic of his particular developmental stage or when he confronts choice-points precipitated by changes in his personal life situation (see Figure 3 for examples), one of the most rational and sensible responses he can make is to seek counsel with someone who is both willing and able to assist with the decision-making process. Rather than giving evidence of immaturity, character-logical weakness, or psychological dysfunction, requesting the assistance of a competent counselor who sees his task not as one of making choices for the individual, but as facilitating the individual's making his own choices, is evidence of maturity, strength and psychological competence. Unfortunately the general public tends to use a "disease model" interpretation of anyone's seeking counseling for any reason; that is, a client is viewed as emotionally ill and the purpose of counseling is to cure him of his sickness. Whereas there is very little you can do to make sweeping changes in the way the general public views counseling, counselors, and clienthood, unless you have access to the mass media, you can make certain that you personally do not harbor such a view of counseling and that you do not subtly communicate that you expect clients to be a very sick and troubled lot. At any developmental stage, seeking counseling assistance for purposes of making choices ought to be viewed as a normal, natural, appropriate, and sensible decision.

## Helping the Client To Define His Purpose

The easiest way to find out why a person has sought your assistance is to ask him. However, if you begin the counseling interaction by asking your client, "What is your purpose in seeking counseling?" he will probably become somewhat defensive. When the question of purpose is posed in that manner, it implies that the client must somehow justify to you why he is there. This is not a very effective way to begin what is supposed to become a cooperative, trusting relationship. You should simply assume: (1) the client has a legitimate purpose in requesting counseling assistance and (2) his general purpose can be understood more specifically in terms of making choices, making changes, and/or reducing confusion in his life. Your task is to inquire about his reasons for seeking counseling in such a way that he does not become defensive, but instead joins with you in an effort to define his purpose specifically in one or more of the three purpose categories, i.e., Choice, Change, or Confusion Reduction.

There are several key questions that you can ask a client, the answers to which will allow you to ascertain in which of the three purpose categories the counseling contract or contracts will be formulated. This list of key questions ought not to be viewed as a set of diagnostic indicators (analogous to temperature, blood pressure, pulse, etc.) which are evaluated before the counseling process begins. Asking one or more of the following key questions is part of the counseling process — formulating a contract is part of the counseling process. Everything which we will discuss in Section Three, concerning how a competent counselor can proceed most effectively, applies to the formulation of a counseling contract. In fact, skillfully communicating understanding, acceptance, and sincerity (which is the subject of Section Three) is probably more important during the initial stages of counseling and during the contract negotiation stage than at any other time. Assuming that you will introduce key questions in a manner consistent with the descriptions of effective counseling process given in Section Three and that you do not regard the suggested questions as a script for the Interrogator's role in a mythical play entitled, "The Counseling Inquisition," we will proceed to the questions and two possible client responses which would result in your tentatively concluding that Choice was to be the major purpose of counseling.

*Counselor:*    Perhaps we could begin with the question of what brings you to the Counseling Center?

> *Client #1:*    'Cause I have to decide on a major and I've never really thought about anything but Business Administration — but I don't know if that's really what I want.

> *Client #2:*    I just don't know what I'm going to do; my husband has been out of work for four months and he's started drinking a lot. I thought if I didn't nag him he'd go find a job but he hasn't really tried and this has happened before and I've just about had it.

If you already know the client, that is, if you were a high school counselor and the individual before you is a teacher-colleague, you would probably ask the above question in a manner that would appear flip or arrogant to a client you had just met in a Counseling Center for the first time. To the teacher you might simply say:

*Counselor:*    Well, what's on your good mind, Allen?

> *Client #3:*    What's on my good mind is that I know of three kids in my senior English class who are starting to mess with really heavy drugs and I don't know what to do about it — if anything.

> *Client #4:*    Not much is on my good mind and that's the problem — sometimes I think I ought to go back to school and get my administrator's credentials or at least finish my master's degree in English or something 'cause I just seem to be going along without much direction right now.

If you have some advance information about the client either because he has completed a written intake form, such as a counseling goal check list, or he has been referred, that information needs to be acknowledged in some manner.

*Counselor:*    I have read the form the secretary gave you and it was very helpful, but I think it would also be useful if you could just summarize how you decided to seek counseling at this time.

> *Client #5:*    Yeh, I checked a lot of things on that form and some of them don't really matter as much, but mostly I feel I need to set some goals or something 'cause it seems like I just keep going around in circles.

> *Client #6:*    Why I decided to come in now is because I have a friend who said it really helped her — she didn't know if she could get admitted to college at her age, and she's older than I am, and she said there are tests that you can take that tell you what you might be good at or like to do.

*Counselor:*    When Reverend Gilbert asked if I could meet with you, he indicated that there were several things you might like to discuss but he preferred that you tell me about them. So maybe you could begin by describing some of the things you hope may happen in our discussion.

*Client #7:* What I wanted to talk about has to do with Reverend Gilbert and the church. It seems like I just keep getting more and more involved in the church and I think my husband and children are suffering — I need to sort things out and set some priorities and stick to them. I just can't keep doing everything I'm trying to do now.

*Client #8:* I've been going to Reverend Gilbert's church all my life and my family are really active in stuff and see I've been dating an exchange student from Africa and my family's really upset — so they go, "You're just doing this to hurt us" and my mother cries and my father won't even speak to Golinza so I'd just like to talk to somebody who isn't in the middle of it and who understands — 'cause I have to decide what I'm going to do this summer; Golinza has to go back in August and they want me to work at church camp all summer so I won't see him.

In some instances a client may have been referred under considerable pressure and that also can be acknowledged in your question.

*Counselor:* I recognize that coming here is much more your wife's idea than yours, but suppose you were a little more convinced that counseling might help, what would you say could happen or should happen?

*Client #9:* My mother has lived with us for the past two years — she has a separate room and bathroom and sort of a sitting room-porch — and it has worked out just fine until the last month when she had another slight stroke. Well, my wife agrees that she isn't that much of a problem to take care of, but Mary thinks we ought to talk about what happens if Mother gets really sick and I just don't think you can plan things that way — we'll just have to wait and see. But Mary thought if we both talked to you about it that it might help and I'm willing to talk about it — maybe a person can make plans like that or at least talk about different possibilities.

*Client #10:* My wife thinks I'm not happy in my job or that I could be a lot happier — and I don't have any real plans or goals for the future and sometimes that really does get to me — I suppose it would be good to talk about that.

*Counselor:* As I understand the situation, Debbie, your father insisted that you talk with me because he does not want you to quit school or get married and he thought maybe you would reconsider if we talked about it. Now I've told him that I'm not about to try to talk you in or out of anything but I would be happy to discuss it with you, if you see any point in that. Can you say what value, if any, you see in our talking together?

*Client #11:*   The reason I said I'd talk to you is because I know Dad is really worried and I don't want to hurt him. Last year he married this woman — my mother died when I was eight — and before Sylvia moved in we had a housekeeper; well, I don't like Sylvia and I don't know why he married her, but that's not why I want to get married. Tom and I have been going steady for two years and we feel we are ready to get married, but I know how Dad feels about it. So I really am willing to talk to someone 'cause I don't want to make a big mistake and then have to live with it forever.

*Client #12:*   I've told Dad a hundred times that I'm not going to drop out of school forever and I'm not even sure that getting married is the best thing, but I don't know what else to do — and, yah, I'm willing to talk about it but I don't think I should have to give up the baby if I don't want to.

If assistance in making choices is the major purpose for a person's seeking counseling, then one of the above questions (or a variation of one of them) will result in his making some reference to decisions, plans or choices he needs to make or he will refer to goals, priorities, or direction he needs to establish. Upon hearing the client make such a reference to decisions, plans, choices, or goals, etc., a counselor knows that most likely the nature of the contract between himself and the client will be one of facilitating rational decision-making. A detailed description of that process is beyond the scope of this book, but in general it will involve the counselor assisting with the gathering of relevant information from a variety of sources, helping sort out and summarize the information so that the relative value and importance of various bits of information stand out clearly, and working with the client to anticipate and evaluate the results of one choice over another or the outcome of one plan as opposed to another.

## Negotiating a Counseling Contract

What we have referred to as contract formulation and negotiation bears no resemblance to the activities of the United Auto Workers or to the Teamsters' Union. A counselor may very well never use the word "contract" in his interactions with a client. Whenever a counselor is working with a client to make explicit what the client's major purpose is in seeking counseling, what can be done to realize the client's purpose, and what they both are actually going to do to realize the client's purpose, he is negotiating a contract, whether or not he calls it that. The contract negotiation process may proceed quite rapidly and expectations of what is to take place between you and your client may be clear to both of you in ten minutes time. By the end of an hour interview, however, you ought to be able to provide a summary statement that describes at least a tentative contract between you and your client. Twelve such summary statements will be given below for purposes of illustrating typical contracts in the area of Choice. The twelve statements come from the hypothetical examples given above and they assume that considerable information and understanding has passed between the counselor and clients since the clients made the responses given above. In each case, it is expected that the statement could be made within two hours of the beginning of counseling, however.

## Examples of Choice Contracts

Client #1

*Counselor:*    Our time is about up today; let me just summarize what I understand we've agreed to do. You are going to make arrangements with the secretary to take the two tests we discussed and also set up an appointment with the Head Adviser in the School of Business to talk about career possibilities with a bachelor's degree in business. The test results won't be ready for about ten days, but that will give us an opportunity to talk more about how you would deal with your father's disappointment if you decided not to go into his business with him. And there may be other things that come up, after you've had a chance to think about our discussion today, too. I will find out what and where information is available about marine biology before next week. Does that pretty much cover it from your point of view?

Client #2

*Counselor:*    Let's see, we've agreed to meet next week at this same time and just to be sure we're both headed in the same direction, let me say how I see things and then you can correct or add anything that looks different to you. The first decision you have to make is whether to try to get Mark to get help with his drinking problem again or to just let him go — figuring that you've tried that three times already and he always quits before the treatment is complete. When you think about the children and trying to keep the family together then it seems like you should do *anything* to get him to go for help; when you think about the fights and the money then you just want *out.* You're going to think about this more this week. In the meantime you will go out to the Community College and find out if you could get back into an LPN training program and what financial assistance might be available, if you do decide to go back to school. What you'd like us to do is go over the different factors on which you will base a decision about your marriage and talk about which ones are the most important and which ones are the least important to you. If you do decide to talk with Mark and he wants to come in, then I would try to arrange to see him before our next session. But unless I hear from Mark, I will assume that my focus is on you and the decisions you face.

Let me just say that I think the decision to come in today was a very good one and probably took some courage on your part. Is there anything else we should look at before we close today?

Client #3

*Counselor:* My understanding is that you are going to approach the students and ask to talk with them about the whole drug scene and the choices they're making. I won't enter the picture except to consult with you — since you have pretty good relationships with them already and they'd be more likely to believe that you're not going to blow the whistle. I will leave a copy of that list of common drug names and the brief descriptions of their various effects in your mail box. I'll also get a copy of the law and some suggestions about how a teacher can operate within the law and still be of some help to a minor child. But otherwise I'll wait for you to get in touch with me, if you'd like to talk about it further. Okay?

Client #4

*Counselor:* As we've talked about it, Al, it seems like one of the questions you have is whether I'd be willing or interested in really looking at the whole situation and talking about the pros and cons of administrator's credentials vs. the master's degree in English or the larger question of whether to stay in education for the rest of your life. The answer is yes, I would, and I think it would probably be helpful if we did. Let's set up a time when we have an hour or more and take a look at what you see as possibilities, what has to be considered first, and so forth. I'll locate the guidelines for state certification for administrators; you bring your transcripts and that evaluation of your remaining work for the master's degree. We will probably want to get together more than once, because I think the conflicts between you and Jeannie over what you should do will take a little while to sort through.

Client #5

*Counselor:* From what we've talked about today, it seems that the most pressing concern is deciding whether to remain here living with your parents, to move into an apartment but keep your job, or to move to another town and find another job. But that decision depends on just what it is you'd like to do with your life and where that's most likely to take place. In order for us to get some handles on this, I'd like you to get three sheets of paper, divide them in half and label one side "Advantages" and the other "Disadvantages." For each alternative (remain at home, move to an apartment, and move to another city), jot down as many things as you can think of that are positive and negative about each one. When we meet next week, I'll read through them with you and probably some major themes will begin to stand out. If we can identify what's most important about where you live, and with whom, where you work, and doing what, then we can begin talking about plans to make those things happen.

Client #6

> *Counselor:*  I'm very glad you came in; your friend gave you good advice. I don't want to sound like "all women returning to school after being out for a number of years are just alike" — because nothing could be farther from the truth. But there are a number of things that you would probably be surprised to find out are common experiences — such as feeling like a stupid fool when you walk into a classroom full of eager, bright young people who all look like straight "A" students — or some of the problems at home that result from your being gone for longer periods or having to study, and so forth. So in addition to arranging to take the interest and aptitude tests, you are going to get in touch with one or more of those women on the list who have agreed to let me refer other women who are thinking about going back to school. Then next week we will meet again and talk about your family's reactions to your thoughts about coming back; I will have the schedule of classes for next term available by then, so we can also look at that. If the test results are ready we can also look at them. Now are we moving too fast, or is this where you hoped we'd be by the end of our session today?

Client #7

> *Counselor:*  Since we seem to be at a sorta' natural stopping place and our time is about up, let me describe what I understand to be the purpose of our meeting together and then let's see if that fits with your understanding. You'd like to talk with someone who is somewhat neutral about, or at least uninvolved in your particular church, who can think things through with you and help you come to some understanding of why you are so heavily involved with the church. With that kind of understanding, you would then be in a better position to plan ways to limit your activities but, at the same time, do those things in the church which are essential for you to see yourself as a responsible, committed Christian. It's as if you need to look at yourself and the whole situation and then make some choices which will restore balance within yourself, within the family and between you and the church. I don't see my role in this as, for example, uncovering some deep-seated guilt complex that's compelling you to be overly involved — although guilt certainly may play a part and we would want to understand that — but rather I see myself as encouraging you to assess the whole situation, to be realistic about time and energy, to make your choices and stick to them. You will then know if that makes the kind of difference you are hoping for. I'm not sure how long it will take — it isn't going to happen overnight, but it does not seem necessary to drag on for months either. So if this makes sense to you, we will continue assessing the situation next week when we meet and expect to begin planning where limits might be imposed.

Client #8

> *Counselor:* As I've listened to you talk about this whole thing — the importance of your family to you, the fact that this is probably the last year you will be living at home before going off to college, the fact that you really would like to work at church camp, and that you do not see your relationship with Golinza as having long-term potential — it is sounding to me as if you've pretty much made your decision about this summer. However, what is still very unsettled and unsettling is the question of what do you do when your values and the choices you believe are right for you are in real conflict with your parents' values and the choices they think you should make. It seems to me that focusing on that question and finding ways to handle those conflicts may be the most important thing we do together — does it make sense to you to see our working together in this way?

Client #9

> *Counselor:* What we have discussed today is very helpful. When your wife first came in two weeks ago, she was very concerned about a number of things — your mother's failing health, the children becoming increasingly independent and invested in their own high school activities, her concerns about finding a part-time job or returning to school — and I think she was feeling pretty isolated and weighted down by the possibility of having to make all the decisions by herself. Your willingness to join the effort to look at changes within the family structure and to plan with her about how to cope with those changes will probably reduce her anxiety considerably. As the focus of your marriage shifts away from child-rearing and you have an opportunity to focus more on one another, it makes sense to me that you both would benefit from talking over the choices open to you and examining your process of making those choices. So I'm suggesting that the three of us meet together for two or three sessions in which we would do just that — look at the choices concerning the children, your mother, the time the two of you have together, and so forth — and look at the ways you both would like to see those choices and plans be made. Does that sound reasonable to you?

Client #10

> *Counselor:* Just to be sure my thinking is moving in the same direction that yours is, I'd like to review some of what we have covered today and then look at what we expect to do next week. After spending seven years working your way through school, supporting a wife and three children, then locating the insurance job and making enough money so your wife could quit her job and go back to school, it's a little rough to hear from her that she really isn't satisfied with what you've accomplished. Nevertheless, you recognize that there are many times when *you* aren't

really satisfied either, As I explained earlier, you have access to the services
of the University Counseling Center both as a graduate who needs career
counseling and as the spouse of a current student, namely, your wife. It
would be a shame not to take advantage of that and I'm glad you've
decided to. What this means is that you and I will gather enough
information about you from tests and from your descriptions of the kinds
of things you really enjoy, feel competent doing, can see yourself getting
really involved in, and so forth, and put that together with information
about career possibilities for someone with a general social science degree.
We should then be able to identify several possibilities that are worth
exploring in greater depth. I think the concern that both you and your
wife express that the more excited she gets about finishing her degree and
teaching, the more important it is for you to be working at something that
really makes a difference to you — that you care about — is a realistic
concern. So — you are going to make arrangements to take the tests and
I'm going to do my homework on the range of job possibilities with a B.A.
in the social sciences. And next week when we meet, you will have
reviewed every job you've ever held, starting with the paper route, and
made some notes to yourself concerning what you liked and didn't like
about each of them. Is there anything else for next week that I didn't
cover?

Client #11

*Counselor:*    Well, I couldn't agree with you more, Debbie, that two
people who are expecting to spend the rest of their days with their lives
intertwined in marriage ought to give that decision some very careful
thought — individually and together. So I'm glad that both you and Tom
want the three of us to meet together to discuss it. I realize that I am
somewhat biased towards encouraging people to hold off marrying 'til
their education is completed, but I can honestly say that I see the purpose
of our meeting will be to look at the advantages and disadvantages for you
two people to marry now — and I believe there are *both* advantages and
disadvantages. At this point I'm not sure which there are more of — but
I'm very sure that the three of us looking at them squarely is an advantage.

Client #12

*Counselor:*    Before we end our discussion today, Debbie, I'd like us to
have as clear a picture as we can of what we can expect of one another.
During the next four and a half months, until the baby comes, you are
obviously going to be facing a lot of decisions and will have to interact
with a lot of people about what you are going to do — as you know this
district still has the archaic policy of refusing to let you attend regular
classes, but at least they regard it as appropriate for me to work closely
with you, if you want it that way — and I hope you do. I see myself as a
source of information, a place where you can talk about your thoughts,

feelings, and the choices you face — and someone who cares a great deal about what happens to you. I don't have any rigid ideas about how things should be as far as getting married or not getting married, keeping the baby or not keeping the baby, dropping out of school or continuing on home instruction, and so forth. I've seen each of those alternatives work out well and I've seen them not work out. What I am absolutely convinced about — yah, even rigid about — is that you look at all sides of the choices and make those decisions that make the most sense to you, rather than letting the next four and a half months just happen to you. If we stay in pretty close contact I think the chances are greater that you will make plans and decisions that you later will be satified were the best choices. So that's why I want to see you at least every other day — if even for fifteen minutes until things are more settled and I want you to feel free to call me at home if you define the situation as one in which it would be helpful to talk. For instance, if you are feeling very depressed and isolated or if you feel you need some information that I might help you find or if you simply need to talk, I would expect that you would get in touch with me right away. You can expect that I will arrange my schedule so that we indeed do have a chance to talk quickly and frequently, as circumstances dictate. Does this describe how you see the two of us working together?

Whether or not you will be called upon to formulate Choice contracts comparable to those given above is heavily dependent upon the setting in which you work. However, one of the characteristics of counseling is the amazing diversity of situations and concerns that people bring to a counselor in any one setting. What that diversity demands of you is skill in locating relevant information about a tremendous range of topics and a working knowledge of how to facilitate rational decision-making and planning. As indicated earlier, presenting techniques for locating relevant information and for facilitating rational decision-making is beyond the scope of this book. However, the following references should be helpful in acquiring those techniques.

## Readings

1.  Becker, G. M. and McClintock, C. G., 1967. Value: Behavioral Decision Theory. *Annual Review of Psychology,* 18, 239—286.
2.  Goldman, L., 1961. *Using Tests in Counseling.* New York: Appleton-Century-Crofts.
3.  Roth, R. M., Hershenson, D. B., and Hilliard, T. (Eds.), 1970. *The Psychology of Vocational Development.* Boston: Allyn & Bacon.
4.  Tyler, L. E., 1969. *The Work of the Counselor.* 3d Edition. New York: Appleton-Century-Crofts.

## III  CHANGE

The second category of counseling purposes within which counselors and clients negotiate contracts, Tyler (1969) calls *Change*. It is true that all successful counseling involves change in the sense that things are different at the close of successful counseling from what they were at the beginning. If a client has made some choices or plans or established some goals or determined the direction he is headed, certainly we could say change has occurred. However, Change as it is being used to identify this second category of purposes has a much narrower meaning, and it does not include anything and everything that might be different from the beginning to the end of counseling. An easy way to understand Change as a counseling purpose is in terms of a client wanting to do, think, or feel some specific thing more often or less often or in some situations, but not others. The contract that is negotiated between the counselor and his client is designed to change specific actions, thoughts, or feelings so that they occur more frequently or less frequently or under one set of conditions, but not under other conditions.

### Difference Between Choice and Change

We will consider several examples. A high school student may think of himself as very shy and lacking in confidence; he may feel very anxious and be unable to speak clearly and fluently whenever he is called upon to talk in speech class. If he requests assistance from the school counselor, it would be for purposes of changing his actions, feelings, and thoughts concerning giving a speech. His choice to do something about his situation has already been made; change in his behavior is his purpose for seeking counseling.

If an elementary teacher requests the assistance of the school counselor to help control a hyperactive youngster who will not remain seated for more than two minutes' duration, change in the youngster's behavior is the purpose of counseling. The teacher's decision has already been made; that is, the youngster should learn to sit in his seat for longer than two minutes at a time. We are not at this point concerned about the ethics of the teacher's decision — whether it is good or bad to try to teach a hyperactive child to sit in a chair. We are only concerned with the fact that assistance is being requested to change behavior.

Taking another typical case, a counselor in a rehabilitation agency was asked to assist a truck driver who, after a serious back injury, became very depressed and resigned himself to total unemployment. In order for the ex-truck driver to consider returning to gainful employment of any kind, he may first need to learn how to care for himself, drive a specially equipped car, regain sufficient stamina to work an eight-hour day, and stop viewing himself as a hopeless invalid. Change in certain behaviors, thoughts, and feelings must occur before any realistic planning and decision-making can be undertaken.

Finally, a request for help which is frequently directed to ministers and priests involves general inability of husbands and wives to communicate with one another. In those instances when a couple has decided not to dissolve their marriage until they have made a genuine effort to learn to communicate satisfactorily, the purpose of seeking counseling is to change. The contract negotiated between the couple and the clergyman should be designed to help them learn to do some things more frequently — for instance, listen carefully, and some things less frequently — for instance, bring up old grievances, and some things in one situation but not another — for instance, avoid critizing one another publicly. The feature which is common to these several examples is that the purpose of counseling is to bring about change in behavior — change in the way the clients think, feel, or act.

The reason that it is important to distinguish between Choice and Change is that the contracts which are negotiated and the processes which follow are different for these two counseling purposes. In the previous subsection, Choice, numerous examples were given of contracts designed to facilitate rational planning and decision-making. In the present subsection, Change, examples will be given of how to negotiate a contract designed to facilitate the modification of specific behaviors. If a counselor does not know how to engage his clients in different processes depending on the purposes the clients have in seeking counseling, then there would hardly be any advantage in differentiating Choice from Change. However, if a counselor is aware that different procedures are available and are differentially successful in bringing about Choice and Change, then obviously it is worth whatever time and effort is required to clearly understand whether his client's purpose is primarily Choice or Change and then to negotiate with his client a contract which will realize that purpose.

This book is limited to a presentation of techniques for beginning the counseling process and moving it forward through the process of negotiating a contract for Choice, Change, or Confusion Reduction. As was true of the subsection on Choice, suggested resources on techniques for bringing about Change will be given at the end of this subsection. It is assumed that you recognize that in order to become proficient in the application of these Change techniques, you will need to receive carefully supervised practicum training in utilizing behavior modification procedures.

## The Counselor as "Behavior-Modifier"

Before we proceed to further examples of key questions and the client responses which indicate that Change is the purpose of counseling, we will briefly consider the counselor's understanding of and attitudes toward people who seek counseling for purposes of changing their behavior. We have progressed considerably from the early 1500s to the present In that we no longer view persons whose behavior needs to change as "demon-possessed." It was indeed humane when we stopped labeling individuals "especially sinful" and began labeling them "mentally ill." It will be even more humane when we stop labeling people "mentally ill" and begin describing and explaining their behavior in terms of the advantageous and disadvantageous ways they have learned to conduct their lives. (See Saslow [1966], Kanfer & Saslow [1969], Szasz [1961].) If you view the clients who seek your assistance as "demon-possessed" and your function as "casting out demons," it would probably be better if you did not keep score because any systematic evaluation of your work is likely to be rather discouraging. If you view the clients who seek your assistance as "mentally ill" and your function as "healing mental disease," your position is not much improved in that systematic evaluation of your work would probably disclose a relatively unimpressive "cure rate." However, if you view the clients who seek your assistance as "persons who need to learn to modify their behavior" and your role as "teaching them to behave in new and different ways," you will probably find it personally rewarding to systematically evaluate your work for the simple reason that effective procedures for teaching people how to behave differently have been and continue to be developed. Although the role of caster-out of demons and/or healer may be more powerful and prestigious than the role of teacher, there is something to be said for efficacy. At present, the counselors and/or psychotherapists who are clearly most effective in changing behavior are those who work with their clients to create situations in which the clients learn new ways of acting, thinking, and feeling. Recently, such counselors are being referred to as "behavior modifiers"; their primary function is teaching.

Leonard P. Ullmann (1969) has expressed a viewpoint very similar to the position taken in this book concerning counseling and/or psychotherapy which is intended to bring about Change.

> The model that in my opinion most closely fits the work of the behavioral therapist is that of teacher. The teacher helps people change in ways that will have presumably favorable consequences. The object is the engendering of skills. This is more than conformity; a good teacher aims not only for solution to a set of problems, that is, rote memory, but also for an approach to future problems; that is, creativity.
>
> The therapist is faced with another human. Every therapist endeavors to help. Every therapist shares certain role characteristics such as training, social recognition, and the like. The behavioral therapist has in his repertoire a number of strategies and maneuvers. *These are in addition to and do not replace interviewing skills.* [Italics added] ...
>
> For the client, the behavioral or educational model means that he is treated as a normal human being, who, under certain limited and specifiable conditions, acts in a manner that does not serve him well and

therefore is changeworthy. He is not a "phobic" or a "schizophrenic" or a "sexual deviate." He is a worthwhile person who serves himself and his community well the vast majority of the time, but who, in certain restricted situations, emits behaviors that he himself or others find upsetting and wish to change. The first point, then, is that there is a basic respect for people implied in the very model. The second point is that the client has the same obligations as any student: to work with his teacher. The teacher has the responsibility of effective lesson design, reinforcement of good performance, and pacing of stimuli to fit the student's needs and growth.

All of these procedures have in common a direct, tutorial approach by the therapist rather than an indirect approach in which some hypothesized internal personality construct is altered prior to changed overt behavior. Behavior therapy or behavioral counseling is not the use of any single technique but rather a way of thinking about the helping relationship that in operation leads to the use of a selection of techniques based on psychological principles. Finally, new techniques are being constantly introduced and older procedures are constantly being modified. Again, behavioral therapy is not the use of specific techniques, but the application of general principles or effective independent variables in experiments from learning and social psychology laboratories.

... That behavioral procedures are not that simple does not mean that procedures cannot be specified; it does mean that there is a technology that must be learned and that a set of good intentions and new words are not enough (pp. 68–69).

It is beyond the scope of this book to summarize the general principles of human learning and social psychology upon which behavioral counseling technology is based. In an effort to make the examples of Change contracts realistic and authentic, references will be made to behavioral counseling techniques which are not herein described or explained in detail. It is up to the reader to locate descriptions and explanations of such techniques in the suggested references; and, it should be reiterated, it is up to the counselor-in-training to secure adequately supervised training in the use of behavioral counseling techniques if he expects to become a proficient behavioral counselor.

## Identifying Change as the Purpose of Counseling

The format for presenting examples of key questions and client responses which lead to the conclusion that Change is the purpose of counseling will be the same as the format used for Choice. Six counselor questions will be presented; the responses of two hypothetical clients will follow each counselor question. The first three key questions are very similar to three of those presented in the

Choice subsection; these questions can be used very early in any initial interview. The client's response is what takes the interview in the direction of negotiating a Change contract, in contrast to a Choice contract. The last three key questions would be more likely to occur after the interview is underway and you have a hunch that Change is probably the primary purpose for counseling. As you read the counselor questions and the client responses, put yourself in the place of the counselor and try to anticipate the type of contract that might be negotiated with each client. After all twelve client response examples have been given, an example of a Change contract for each client will be presented.

*Counselor:*     Perhaps we could just begin with the question of what brings you here?

> *Client #1:*     Well, you probably know I was just elected District MYF treasurer and I have to go to the Council meetings and sometimes maybe I'll have to lead meetings or speak and stuff — and I have to give reports at the District meetings. Well, I can keep the books okay and my Mom can help me, if I need it — but I don't think I can talk in front of all those people — and if I ever have to lead devotions or something, I'd probably just faint or get sick or something. Dad said he thought I should talk to you . . .

> *Client #2:*     I guess you know Jack and me better than anyone — and since we've both been coming to church regularly and Jack's gotten really interested in the basketball league, things have been a lot better, but we still fight so much and maybe its just me — but it seems like we should be able to get along better or not hurt each other so much — I just thought maybe you could tell me something I could read or do or something.

The second key question, designed to reveal the client's general purpose for seeking counseling, tends to focus attention on the events that led up to making an appointment.

*Counselor:*     I have read the Personnel Form you completed and that was helpful in my understanding your purpose in seeking counseling, but I think it would also be helpful if you could say how it was that you decided to come in for counseling at this time.

> *Client #3:*     Early last week Mr. Arnold, from the front office, came over to Supply, where I'm assistant manager, and told me that my name had been mentioned for the new opening in Promotion and that if I was interested in being considered to ask that my file be activated. Well, I'm very interested and have wanted to get into Promotion from the beginning — plus the fact that it would be a good advancement, both in salary and position. So I activated my file, but there's just one thing about

it — I know the position involves some travel and I'm scared to death of flying. I told my manager about it and he said you might be able to help.

*Client #4:*    Well, I've been with this company for eight years and they know I'm the best driver they've got, but the last two performance ratings — you know in the "Comments" place — said I was sometimes hard to get along with — "belligerent" I think he said. Well, I was so mad the first time I could've punched him in the nose, but my wife kinda' calmed me down and then, anyway, the supervisors changed — and I really like this guy who's in charge now. Well, when he said the same thing that the other guy said and Art, he's one of the other drivers that I know pretty well, he said he could see what they meant — I got to thinking maybe it really is me. So Art said he'd talked to you once about a problem and was glad he did — so I decided to make an appointment.

When you already know that another person has strongly encouraged a client to seek counseling, such as a teacher recommending to a student that he or she talk to you, it is useful to focus a question about the purpose of counseling directly on the *client's* purposes in seeking counseling.

*Counselor:*    I know that Mr. Nichols asked you if he could talk with me about the difficulty you've been having and that that was okay with you. We didn't have a chance to talk very long, but even if we had, I would be most concerned about what *you* would like to see happen as a result of you and me talking together.

*Client #5:*    Mr. Nichols is really worried, I know, 'cause he thinks I'm going to get in a lota' trouble, but I'm really kinda' worried too, 'cause I don't like what I've been doing either. I'd just like to have friends and go out and have a good time and just have things be okay—but ever since I got in ninth grade I just keep having problems . . . I guess I'm scared if I don't pet and stuff or go all the way that the boys just won't have anything to do with me — I don't know, 'cause I keep saying I'm not going to do that any more and then it just happens all over again. But Mr. Nichols said if I was really serious about changing, then you could probably help me and I thought it over and I really do want to be different.

*Client #6:*    What I want is to be able to study — I just can't make myself do my assignments or study for tests or nothing — it's all I can do to sit there through those stupid classes — but if I don't get C's or better this time then I can't play on the varsity basketball team and this is my last year in high school, and I have a good chance to start at center. So Mr. Nichols said you'd help me get going or find out how to study or whatever — just so I don't get any D's or F's this time — I mean on the next two report cards, until the conference games are over and 'til after state tournament — if we get that far.

After the interview has begun, if you have some indication that Change is the client's primary purpose for seeking counseling, you can use one of the following three questions to clarify further the nature of the changes which the client hopes will happen.

*Counselor:*     One of the ways we might think more specifically about our purpose in meeting together is to raise the question, "If we were 100 percent successful, exactly how would that look or what would that be like?"

> *Client #7:*     Well, I would be able to accept Sherrie and treat her like any other of my sister's children. If she has a seizure while I'm there or if someone begins talking about it, I should be able to take that in stride — or maybe even help out, if there's anything to do. Right now I just feel so guilty because I know it's hard enough on my sister just having an epileptic child — but my being so revolted and frightened just makes it worse, I'm sure. So if we were 100 percent successful, I would think and feel about Sherrie just like I do the other children — her being epileptic wouldn't matter at all — I'd treat them all the same.

> *Client #8:*     I suppose if we were 100 percent successful my daughter would turn out to be a normal young lady — but I *have* to remember that she's not "normal," I mean she's not like other little girls — I never thought being extra smart could cause so much trouble, but ever since they told her in the third grade she was very "gifted" and "special" I can't get her to do anything — she won't read or work on her projects — she has a butterfly and bug collection — and she won't clean her room or practice the piano anymore. If I ask her why she just says she doesn't want to be "special" and that "boys hate smart girls." So I guess to be 100 percent successful, I want her to stop some of the silliness, but mostly she should start doing some of the things that she used to really enjoy — I just want to help her adjust, I guess.

In addition to looking forward in time to what a 100 percent successful outcome of counseling would be, the client's purposes for Change can also be understood in terms of his past.

*Counselor:*     Sometimes it is possible to get a clearer picture of just what you'd like to have be different by asking the question, "How do you think things got this way — you have probably given it quite a bit of thought before today, how do you understand it?"

> *Client #9:*     I don't know, it just seems like I'm a lot more unsure of myself, especially around girls. When I was in junior high — or even before — we lived on a farm and nobody went out on dates or stuff — I mean mostly you just did things with your family or at church. Then in junior high some of the guys with older brothers went to parties I guess, but 'course my family doesn't believe in dancing or movies — but when

Dad went to work in town and we moved I didn't have my rabbits or the horses to take care of — and everyone in this school goes steady or at least they go out a lot — I just think I never learned to talk to girls — so even the girls at church I don't talk to and there're a couple of them that I'd really like to get to know.

*Client #10:* I really think a lot of women have this same problem, I know several women teachers who would have made very good principals, but because they were afraid of having authority over men, they chose not to go into administration. But I would really like to have an opportunity to influence education — both the kids and the teachers — and I think I can do that in this new job — but I know I have to get over being afraid of giving orders or even making a strong recommendation to both males and females. I don't think I'm so unusual; when my husband was alive we always made decisions together, but he generally took the lead or at least publicly he dominated. I was very comfortable with that and so was he, but I didn't have much chance to know what it was like to be in a position of obvious authority. So I think I got this way just because that's the way things are — but I'd like it to be different — except I don't want to become a domineering old lady who just hands out orders. There must be some happy medium.

There are, of course, many questions that could be considered "key" questions in that they unlock the area of central concern to the client, and they open up the client's primary purpose for counseling. The final example, is a question designed to identify significant other persons who may have an investment in a client's changing or modifying his behavior.

*Counselor:* It is becoming clearer to me what you think ought to change, and I'm wondering if there are other people who also share your concern; or to ask it another way, "Is it just up to you and me to decide what changes should happen for you?"

*Client #11:* There are others who are concerned, like my children, but yes, it's up to me to work it out with you — how I can get over this. I'm sure my children, especially my son, find it very upsetting to see me cry or have to leave the room every time their father's name is mentioned . . . or when certain music is on or on special days . . . and, of course, they have had to put up with me this way for ten months now . . . but they are very understanding and except for encouraging me when I said I was going to see you, they've never mentioned it. I haven't seen many of our friends, just because I don't want to even be around them anymore . . . he was everything to me and I try to make myself get out . . . but I know I'm such a burden to people because I am so depressed . . . it's up to me, allright, but there are others who would be affected if I could just get over it . . .

*Client #12:*    I haven't thought about it much and yet it seems like I
don't think of anything else. My mother and father *really* want me to lose
weight and they've tried everything — sent me to doctors and clinics,
bought special equipment, tried to talk to me about it themselves. When I
really think about it, I realize just how much pressure from my parents
there is for me losing weight. But this time it's my idea to come here and
my parents are going to stay out of it. I'd really like to lose weight for
them, but mostly I realize that I'm not ever going to get a job if I don't
lose at least sixty pounds. I'm tired of being a fat slob that everybody
thinks is lazy.

These twelve hypothetical clients have introduced a wide array of concerns
from the three content areas: Work, Relationship, and Aloneness. The
counselors with whom they are talking would no doubt be found in a variety of
settings, such as schools, employment services, rehabilitation agencies, churches,
private industries, college counseling centers, and mental health clinics. Although
they are diverse people in very different settings, all twelve clients have a
common purpose in seeking counseling: they all want to change their behavior.
They expect counseling to help them modify the way they think or feel or act.
Assuming that considerable information and understanding will be communicated between a counselor and a client during the initial interview, the counselor
ought to be able to move from the client's beginning statements regarding
change to at least a tentative Contract for Change by the end of the first session.
In order to gather enough relevant information so that the counselor and client
can plan an efficient, effective program to bring about the desired changes, they
may need to continue describing and defining the intended counseling outcome
(i.e., the purpose) of counseling for several sessions. Nevertheless, by the end of
interview one, the counselors working with the twelve clients presented above
ought to be able to summarize a tentative contract concerning each client's
expectation of change.

It was suggested that, as you read the twelve client responses, you should
speculate on the type of contract which could be negotiated with each client. An
example of a Change Contract for each of the twelve cases will be given below.
In each case there are undoubtedly several equally justified ways to approach
changing the person's behavior and/or his situation. Your idea of what the
contract should be like may be different from the example given, but it also may
be as good or better a way to proceed. In many cases we do not have adequate
research evidence to conclude that one procedure is superior to all others. The
advantage, however, of thinking about the counseling relationship in contractual
terms and the purpose of counseling in specific outcome terms is that questions
about the general effectiveness of a particular procedure and the specific success
of that procedure with a particular client are more likely to be addressed and
answered. Therefore, whether or not you *agree* with the contracts which were
negotiated is less important than the fact that you are in a position to think

about and discuss which is the most effective way to proceed with counseling in each of the twelve cases presented above.

## Examples of Change Contracts

Client #1

*Counselor:* I would like to review our contract, before we end our discussion today, so we are both clear on what's going to happen. I know it seems completely impossible to think that you will ever be able to speak to a whole church full of people, but it *can* be done and probably less painfully than you might think. What we have to do is be very sure we plan together small enough steps toward our goal that you can manage each one and feel okay about it before we go on to the next one. Now we agreed that to start, you will assist with taking up the collection next Sunday, right? I will inform Mr. Tryon, who's in charge of ushers this month, that you will be assisting. And you'll do that for one or more weeks, depending on when you and I feel you're ready to take the next step, which is you come up to the platform from one of the front pews where you'll be seated and read the announcements which pertain to youth activities for that week. You and I will have gone over those announcements before Sunday morning when you have to read them; you can practice in the empty sanctuary and at least once when only I am there to hear them. We will do that for a couple of weeks 'til we agree you are ready for step three — reading the Scriptures. We will again practice here in my office at least once and in the sanctuary at least once before Sunday morning and you can practice other times on your own. This time you will sit with me on the platform throughout the service.

Now I don't know *exactly* how long it will take 'til you are comfortable reading something to a church full of people — but I am confident that if we plan it together, role play each phase ahead of time, take small enough steps and talk about the progress we are making each week, it shouldn't take very long — you don't have to go into a year of psychoanalysis to get over what is a very common fear. And, yes, I'm very busy, but it certainly is worth it to me to be able to participate in your gaining self-confidence and becoming more comfortable in assisting people to worship together — it's not a sacrifice at all, it's a very reasonable and pleasurable way for me to invest some of my time. So I'll get in touch with Mr. Tryon today — you will be calling him in a day or so — and we will meet next week at this same time — okay?

Client #2

*Counselor:* I realize your hopes are very high that you and Jack can improve your marriage and I don't think that is unrealistic. There is every reason to expect that Jack will be willing to discuss the possibility of your joining the Marriage Study Group. As I said, I have a great deal of confidence in the couple who is leading the group; they are both trained in marriage counseling and have experience working with groups. You ask Jack to call me and I'll talk with him about it; then the next step would be for the two of you to meet with the group leaders and discuss your joining the Study Group. If you want to buy two of the books I know they're using — *The Intimate Enemy,* by George Bach and Peter Wyden and the *Mirages of Marriage* by Lederer and Jackson — I think that's fine. Although, I think you need to be careful not to run away with things. If you rush out and buy the books and then start reading little passages to Jack, pointing out how miserable he is or you are, and so on, I think he will be less likely to want to join the group. This is something you want to do together, as much as is possible — in fact, unless both partners are at least minimally agreed that they want to work on changing their marriage, they are not eligible for the group. You are probably more enthusiastic than Jack is at this time, and that's all right; you both don't have to be ecstatic about it to be eligible — but I think you will need to instruct yourself not to oversell it or try to push Jack into it.

I will speak to the group leaders and tell them I may be referring you folks and I will wait to hear from Jack. If things don't work out as you'd like them to, you will get in touch with me again, right?

## Client #3

*Counselor:*    From our discussion, it appears to me that your fear of flying, which as I've explained is technically termed a "phobia" is quite specific; that is, you are not afraid of other forms of transportation or of heights, in general — and I think you are correct in thinking that you learned to be afraid of flying because of the tragedy with your brother. It's also true that understanding your feelings about your brother's accident by reliving that whole period of time, probably would not reduce your present fear of planes. The procedure which is most likely to result in your being able to fly with minimal anxiety is called "systematic desensitization" and I'm going to give you a mimeographed description of that procedure and, generally, how it works. There is a reference at the bottom of the page there, if you want to read more of the research about the procedure. As indicated in the description there are two things for you to do to get started. One is to begin building a "hierarchy," that is, a series of about eight scenes which become increasingly anxiety-provoking — you might, for instance, begin with a scene involving taking someone else to the airport and then build other scenes that go all the way to your boarding a plane, and taking off for a transcontinental flight. I will help you build your hierarchy beginning next session, after you've had a chance to work on it first. The second thing is to take this tape recording of instructions for relaxing and play it through once each day. You'll need to locate a quiet place in the house where you can go through it undisturbed. This is all explained on the sheets there, but let me just say that we will begin the actual process of desensitizing you to flying, after you have learned to relax thoroughly when instructed to do so and after we have built your particular hierarchy. I can't say exactly how long it will take us to do these things, but we will work together on both of them, so we can begin desensitization as soon as possible. Okay, you have the tape and the description and we are set up for one week from today. If there are any questions or problems, you can of course reach me here, even before our next appointment . . . otherwise, I'll see you in a week.

Client #4

*Counselor:*   We have agreed that it is the explosive, angry outbursts that need to be controlled or eliminated and that they are most likely to occur immediately after someone has criticized you for one reason or another. I think it is important to note that it is not frustration alone that leads to the angry outbursts — as you described it there are numerous occasions, like when you are working on a piece of equipment or when the children are bugging you, and so forth, that you become irritated and angry, but don't go into a towering rage over it. At this point it does seem to be associated primarily with being criticized or challenged in some way. What we need to do is teach you another response to take the place of the outbursts. It also appears that once you are out of the situation in which the criticism was directed toward you, once you get some distance on it, you very quickly calm down and can "think straight" again. So it looks as if what we need is a way for you to leave the situation long enough to collect your thoughts — a sort of delaying tactic or "time out" that you impose on yourself.

What I want you to do between now and next week is to make a list of as many situations as you can think of that have or could result in your becoming enraged. What we will do with the list then is begin recreating some of those situations and sort of act out different ways you could delay the angry outburst. You may have heard about or even done something like this before — it's called "role playing." The interesting thing is that even though it's not actually real and you and I are just playing roles, it has an impact on your behavior out there. Sometimes I will have you play your own role and I will be the "criticizer"; sometimes I will have you be the "criticizer" and I will play your role. But together we will figure out ways for you to manage your temper better and we will work together to put those into practice here. Do you have any questions about what you are to do for our next session?

Client #5

*Counselor:*   I think we have a clearer understanding of what both you and Mr. Nichols are concerned about — it isn't simply that you might get pregnant or that your sexual activity is bad and "nice" girls don't do that — but more it's that you're developing a style of relating to boys in which you're just an object and not a person — intimacy doesn't occur within a relationship based on genuine caring and mutual respect, but rather it's a matter of grabbing whatever physical pleasure the moment may hold — and "so what" about you as a person, or him as a person — and that's not a very satisfying way to relate. I'm not minimizing the importance of unwanted pregnancy and that's why I've given you that printed information on preventing pregnancy — but I'm as concerned about your present inability to set any limits on sexual intimacy — to insist that intimacy, and I mean more than just the act of intercourse, that intimacy be an expression of mutual caring and respect.

This year we have been able to establish a really good working relationship with the local YWCA and YMCA staffs and with the blessing and understanding of the school board, the local medical association and the ministerial association, we have begun several discussion groups for ninth grade students. These are mixed groups, both boys and girls, and they are led by a psychologist and a social worker who are specially trained to work with young people in groups. My understanding is that they talk about relationships — what it takes to have a really satisfying and constructive relationship — both between males and females and between friends of the same sex. There is a chance also to learn how to communicate better — and, what would be especially useful to you, there is a chance to learn ways to set limits without rejecting the other person or destroying the relationship. Now I know this sounds kinda' scarey, but everyone else is in the same boat and the people who are leading the groups are used to helping you get over being scared. So what I want you to do is meet with a group at least one session — there is an opening in the one that meets on Saturday morning — then during the week you and I will meet together again to see if you think the group will be helpful and if you want to continue with them.

Now, as I explained, the details of our conversation are strictly confidential and I will not be discussing them with anyone, without first clearing that with you — at this point I see no need for me to discuss this with anyone. I know you very much don't want to talk with your parents about it, but we will need a written permission, signed by one of your parents, in order for you to participate in the group. What I would suggest is that you talk with one or both of your parents and tell them that you and I have talked today because you've been sorta' concerned and confused about dating, and so forth, and that I suggested that you join the Saturday morning group. This is a brief, one-page description of the group — its purpose and the procedures that are followed — which I will give you to show to your parents. If they have additional questions or they would like to talk with me for any reason, they can reach me here at school any day of the week and I'd be very happy to talk with one or both of them. As soon as you bring back that permission form — it's with the description there — I will notify the group leaders that you will be joining the group and they will be expecting you. So, I will hear from you within the next couple days, okay?

## Client #6

*Counselor:*    Okay, so we've agreed you start going to classes regularly and stop complaining about how stupid and irrelevant they are and I will never try to get you to admit that really they are interesting and that they really are good for you. All we are interested in is a system for getting you to do C work or better. From your standardized test scores it's clear that you can read and comprehend what you're reading fairly well — which is fortunate — otherwise we would have to teach you how to read, first. Writing seems to be more of a problem, although you did say that last year when you were free to write on anything in your health class, you wrote a good paper on sexual deviance — so it looks as if you can write if you're interested in the topic.

Well, the first step is for me to get ahold of the guy I told you about, Don, who thinks he wants to be a teacher and see if he is still willing to do some tutoring. Assuming that he is, then the three of us and the basketball coach will meet together and set up a program of rewards and penalties for you. For example, you have an essay due in English class in three weeks; okay, you and Don will work out a daily schedule of the time you should spend and the daily progress you should make on writing that essay. Some days it might be that we'd agree you don't need to do anything on it, but, say on the weekend, it might be agreed that you should spend whatever time it takes to develop an acceptable outline for the essay. On the days you complete everything that was agreed upon for you to do, then you can attend basketball practice the full time. If you fail to meet the contract that was negotiated for studying, then you either don't get to attend practice at all or for only half of it, depending on what you did accomplish. It's pretty clear the coach won't be able to work with a team whose center is there half the time or every other day; so it's in your best interest to see that you meet the daily studying contracts. Don will clear you for practice each day.

You have considerable control over a system like this because you get to have a big say in what is expected or contracted for the next day. Each morning Don will meet you before school, talk to you and look at what you've done and then clear you for full or half practice or bar you from practice for that day. Don will contact the coach about the outcome of your meeting each morning. I will work very closely with Don to assist with any problems that might arise and to generally supervise the system. In addition you can make appointments with Don or myself or your

teachers to get help with any particular part of your studies. The first
thing we need from you is a list of all your classes and the assignments for
each class, plus your daily schedule, both in school and out. You will need
to keep a running record of the contracts you and Don work out and the
outcome of each morning meeting. I will explain that more, when we all
meet together, which will be as soon as I can arrange it — I'll send you a
note in your first period class. So, are we in agreement about the first
step?

Client #7

*Counselor:*     I think I have a clear picture of the way things are now in
that you don't want to go to your sister's home, you become anxious if
she comes over, if Sherrie is with her, and you find yourself unable to stay
in the room, when someone begins talking about Sherrie being epileptic — and I think I have a clear picture of how you would like to change
your behavior. If we dug around in your past we could probably unearth
some traumatic experience which involved someone having a seizure or
fainting and you feeling panic-stricken and powerless to cope with the
situation. However, even if we were quite successful in uncovering an
earlier experience which has made Sherrie's epilepsy horrifying and
disgusting to you — there's just one problem with that — such psychic
excavation often produces great insights into a person's feelings, but it
usually does not result in any appreciable change in his behavior. So if it's
change in your behavior, both feelings and actions, that we are trying to
accomplish — then we will have to do more than simply understand how
you got this way.

There are two approaches to this that I want us to pursue at this
time. In the first place I want you to become better informed about
"epilepsy" — or "seizure disorder" — as it is more accurately termed.
There is a national association that provides literature which is accurate
and understandable to the layman; the librarian at the city library would
be happy to assist you locate such information, I'm quite sure. If you have
any trouble I will help you locate it myself. But I want it to become less of
a mystery to you. The second thing I want us to do is what has been called
a "guided fantasy." We will together construct a series of about eight
different scenes involving Sherrie's epilepsy, that begins with, for example,
your imagining that you are watching a movie of Sherrie blowing out the
candles on her third birthday cake during which time there is absolutely
no evidence of a seizure. Sherrie would not be present in the fantasy of
watching the movie. Then we would progress in scenes where there is
greater risk that she might have a seizure in your presence. Finally, we will
construct a scene where she actually does have a seizure in your presence.
In the calm and comfort of this office, I will instruct you to relax as much
as you can and then we will proceed through each scene. I will instruct

you to vividly imagine each scene, which will undoubtedly be somewhat anxiety-provoking to you. Although I don't enjoy inflicting pain or discomfort on people, in this case the momentary discomfort you experience here is offset by the value to you of becoming free of this particular fear or phobia. It is often surprising to people that going through a guided fantasy, such as I've described, each week for several weeks, could make that much difference. But it does. Each week it becomes less and less frightening and unpleasant and each week it becomes easier to approach the real-life situation. I do not know just how long it might take, nor am I saying that such a procedure is 100 percent successful in every case. However, nearly all of the individuals with whom I have used such a procedure have begun to experience changes in their attitudes and feelings within the first two sessions and in many cases have been free of a particular phobia within six weeks. Whatever your experience is, we will continue to work on the phobia until it is gone. For next session, then, I want you to begin outlining the eight scenes; just write out eight brief descriptions on separate three by five cards. See if you can construct the entire set; if you have difficulty I will help you with it during our next session. Also, you should by then have had a chance to have gone to the library, located some information and begun reading about epilepsy. Are there any questions about expectations for our meeting next week?

## Client #8

*Counselor:*    I find myself in a position of wanting to assist you do two things that seem contradictory — on the one hand I would like to see you become more relaxed and matter-of-fact about having a "special" or "gifted" child — almost as if it makes no difference — you would relate to her as you would relate to any of your children, without special regard to I.Q. On the other hand, I would like to see you become aware of and sensitive to experiences which are characteristic of very bright youngsters which do not present themselves as frequently to less intelligent youngsters . . . such as the fact that very bright youngsters are sometimes threatening to teachers who feel they can't provide enough interesting learning experiences for such children. To accomplish these seemingly contradictory purposes, I am proposing two courses of action.

I want you to read a number of articles and studies and biographical descriptions concerning very intelligent or "gifted" children. I will need to do a little research and gather together some material I have myself and some references which we may need to send for through the library. I will have that ready for you next week. As you read the materials we can then discuss how it applies to your own situation. The other approach I want us to take is to identify current, troublesome interchanges between you and Beth and then you and I will do some role playing of alternative ways to handle those situations. It seems that you need to communicate to Beth

that her being very intelligent and feeling quite different from other
youngsters does not constitute an excuse for being irresponsible — like no
matter how bright she is, it's reasonable to expect that she will clean her
room, do her schoolwork, and so forth. And, perhaps even more
importantly, we need to develop your skills in giving her permission to be
very bright — that is, your ability to communicate that it's okay to be
different; it's okay to be Beth. So during this week, while I'm gathering
some materials for you to read, I want you to jot down enough of a
description of these troublesome interchanges between the two of you,
that you and I can do some role-playing next week. Does this make sense
to you — is it clear what I am proposing?

Client #9

> *Counselor:*   Let me summarize what I think we have agreed to do and
> you check me to see if that's how you see it, too. In the first place, moving
> from the country to town was like skipping about three grades, as far as
> social relationships — especially boy-girl relationships — are concerned. So
> there's a lot of information and experience that everybody but you seems
> to have. As far as information is concerned, I am going to help you locate
> material to read which I know is accurate, easy-to-read, and sensible. We
> will also discuss what you read and work on finding the answers to any
> questions or confusion which the readings don't take care of. As far as
> experience is concerned, you and I will talk about, plan, and then role-play
> ways you can begin having rewarding experiences with girls, especially.
> Between sessions you will carry out whatever we've agreed upon and
> practiced — such as a five-minute conversation with at least two different
> girls either at school or at church.
>
>       In the second place, because of your parents' and your religious
> beliefs about what are acceptable ways for boys and girls to relate to one
> another, there are a number of activities which are open to others, but are
> ruled out for you — such as movies, dances, parties where kids are smoking
> or drinking, and so forth. So our plans for ways you can begin having
> rewarding experiences need to fit within your religious beliefs and values
> or else we would wind up with you in terrible conflict or feeling very
> guilty. Although I do not share your beliefs about what is acceptable and
> what is sinful, I don't have any problem working within your framework
> or code of what's right and wrong. There isn't any reason why you'd have
> to be able to take a girl to a movie in order to learn how to be confident
> about and really enjoy dating. But I'm assuming that we are not trying to
> prove that going to the movies or not going to the movies (or dances, and
> so forth) is right or wrong. We are simply assuming that for you movies
> and some other activities would be wrong and therefore, we won't
> consider them — other than to talk about feelings of being left out or
> something like that, which you might experience. What we are focused on

is how to get you from where you are now — scared to death to talk to girls — to the point where you can talk to girls, have fun with a group of both boys and girls, go out on a date with a girl and not feel either frightened or guilty.

Then the third thing is that we've agreed that it would be a mistake to try and hide your concerns from your parents and even though they may be skeptical, they probably will be willing to talk with me or with your pastor about me — so you are going to talk with them — and we've gone over how you could best do that. And early this week, I will call your pastor'and talk with him about the purpose of our counseling, and ask him about reading material your church recommends. I realize it's possible for everybody to get all upset about this and be mad at you for even coming to see a school counselor in the first place, but if we are absolutely honest, patient and open with your parents and your pastor, my prediction is that they will be very encouraging and supportive. If they're not, we'll figure out what to do when we come to it. Now, is that how you see our agreement?

Client #10

*Counselor:*    You know, I'm afraid that even just a year ago I would have listened carefully, as I've done today, and tried to understand just what it is you'd like to change about yourself and then like a typical male I'd have probably done one of two things — encouraged you *not* to enter the hurly-burly of public school administration or told you to go ahead, but to just relax and be yourself and stop worrying. However, I have recently begun to appreciate some of the subtle, even unconscious, ways I have been guilty of male chauvinistic thinking and feeling — and so, I have a much better grasp of the sorts of conflicts and subtle barriers you will face as a professional woman in a position of authority.

Fortunately, within the last several years, with the development of behavioral approaches in counseling and psychotherapy, there are specific techniques and procedures available to us that will result in the sort of personal changes you are seeking. I'm referring to the use of role-playing and behavior rehearsal and assertiveness training in particular. If you wish, I can give you references which describe the procedures and also report the results of using behavioral approaches in situations similar to your own.

The first step is for us to get a very clear, accurate, and detailed description of what you presently do when a situation seems to call for you to assert yourself or be aggressive in any way. For that reason, I want you to begin keeping a daily log (which you should write in at least once a day) of situations which you view as requiring assertiveness from you. Jot down enough information so that next week we can re-create any one of the episodes: what were the circumstances, who said what, what did you do, what were the results of what you did, and generally how you felt about the whole episode. In addition to our observations and impressions of you during the role-play of the situations, we will tape record the role-play and, after listening to it, discuss further what and how you communicated or failed to communicate. Our efforts will be directed toward developing responses which communicate the blend of firmness/ gentleness and assertiveness/flexibility which you wish to achieve. So we will meet next week then, and you will bring your log, right?

Client #11

*Counselor:*   From what we've discussed, it is apparent that your husband's sudden death left you with tremendous responsibilities and very little knowledge of how to cope with them all by yourself. It is very understandable that you would feel nearly overwhelmed, lost, and alone. But as you have said, your grief and despair have persisted much longer than you feel is normal or tolerable. There are two approaches that it seems to me we should take in order to lift your depression and restore you to a relatively normal existence. You need to "work through" — that is, understand and accept — the tremendous range of feelings which are attached to your husband's death. For example, it may surprise you to know that it is very common for a bereaved husband or wife to feel considerable anger and frustration at being left with all kinds of responsibilities and yet also feel that it is completely inappropriate to be hurt and angry— not only is it unacceptable, but it also seems futile because there's no place to direct the anger. Depression can be thought of as "frozen rage" — a sort of psychological state in which you feel everything and nothing all at once. As long as you stay depressed, the seemingly futile and inappropriate anger does not have to be acknowledged or expressed. I am not saying that all of depression can be explained in this way, but it is a very good hypothesis or guess to check out — that your depression, in part at least, serves the purpose of keeping you from having to feel and express anger. Here in the counseling situation, which is contained and set apart from the rest of your life, it will be possible to seriously consider and examine the feelings of anger which may very well be part of what you are experiencing inside, but are failing to find acceptable outward expression for.

In addition to acknowledging, understanding, and accepting the range of feelings, which are often contradictory to one another, we need to plan ways for you to comfortably reestablish meaningful and rewarding interpersonal relationships. At this point the role "widow" is nothing but ugly and painful to you — but whether or not you remarry, it is possible to build satisfying, rewarding relationships with others (and not just other widows) that are not dependent upon your having or not having a mate.

To accomplish both of these we will use our sessions as a laboratory to try out different ways to cope with your feelings — through discussion and role-play. And we will also use some of our time as a planning session to work out "homework" assignments to be accomplished between sessions. Then we will go over the results of your "homework" — such as taking a friend to lunch — during our next session. In order to know exactly where we are beginning and to be able to check our progress, I want you to keep a daily log of your activities for one week. That isn't a very pleasant task, but it's necessary in order for us to evaluate our progress and plan the steps you need to take. Just get yourself an eight and a half by eleven notebook of some kind and take one page for each day; divide the page into Morning, Afternoon, and Evening. Each day, record at least once what went on during those three periods of time. Write down what you were doing, with whom, and for how long; also, note down whether you see yourself as having been more depressed, less depressed, or experiencing about the same degree of depression that you were experiencing when you came here today. You can indicate this with just the letters M, L, and S if you like — or work out another system to code your relative degree of depression. In the back of your notebook I want you to start a list of everything you can think of that is a personally gratifying activity or experience for you — such as, taking a hot bath, reading a good book, dancing, talking seriously with a teenager, wearing perfume, going to church, playing bridge, and so on, whatever you can think of that pleases you.

Is it clear now what I want in this notebook; and is the direction we are headed clear and understandable to you?

Client #12

*Counselor:* We have spent some time talking about your past efforts to lose weight and your present motivation to lose. I want now to be very clear and even blunt about what I see as involved in your losing seventy pounds. In the first place dieting, perhaps more than any other behavior change effort, requires a considerable willingness to suffer over a long period of time. If we are *very* successful and you are able to lose steadily without major setbacks, we can expect about a one and a half to two pound loss per week, on the average. Now that means between thirty-five to forty-seven weeks, most of which will be sheer hell. Not only will you be in a nearly constant state of deprivation from what you have learned to regard as a normal eating level, but you are also going to have to exercise much more than you ever have in the past. In addition to that, you will have to begin keeping a record of absolutely everything that goes in your mouth and a record of exercises; most people find the record keeping irritating in the beginning, but they get used to it by the twelfth week. There will be an elaborate set of rules about what you can eat and when, which you get to help work out. You will find me to be interested in you, sympathetic, and a source of ideas for how to control yourself and learn to govern your eating with rational choices — as long as you give clear evidence that you are committed and trying by keeping the contracts we negotiate each week. I will help you figure out what is reasonable to expect of yourself each week, but the responsibility for judging whether or not you will be able to keep our contracts is primarily yours. If you fail to keep a contract — such as no snack after dinner, unless it's meat, fish, or poultry — you have the option to get in touch with me immediately and renegotiate the contract on the basis that we both misjudged. But there's an undefined and limited number of times you can get away with that. If you persist in breaking contracts, which during our weekly session you agreed were reasonable, you are through.

In order to supervise a weight loss program, particularly in the beginning stages, it is necessary for me to change my typical style of relating to clients. Usually, I am a very warm, perceptive person — I am not particularly judgmental. I'm very accepting and interested in whatever is important to a client. That's genuinely how I feel, with rare exceptions. However, I have found that that is not a helpful way to relate to most obese clients. Particularly in the beginning you will find me to be interested in nothing but your weight and your efforts to diet. If you have broken contracts I will be angry. If you have kept contracts but not lost weight, I will be puzzled and interested in solving the problem in terms of reduction in calories or increase in exercise or both. If you have kept contracts and lost weight, I will be pleased. As time goes on and it is clear that you are successfully managing your weight-loss program, you can earn the right to talk with me about other things. Until that time, I do not care how lonely, depressed, anxious, self-conscious, ashamed, guilty, ugly, and so forth, you feel; I will probably just ignore comments which would lead us to discuss such topics. I am not interested in how you learned to overeat or what are the deep-seated, self-destructive reasons for your overeating; I'm only interested in your present efforts to stop overeating.

Nothing you could do would affect your life more than losing weight and learning to rationally choose what you eat. I do not have any trouble staying invested in and excited about your losing weight — as long as you are honest and keep trying. If I find you have been dishonest or that you are not really trying — and though you might fool me for a week or two, I'd detect it pretty quickly — you are all through. Now I know this sounds harsh and it may be unnecessarily harsh for you — but it is exactly how things are. Working with me can be very pleasant and I know a lot about ways to keep the suffering from getting you down — but I will turn off like a light switch if you don't abide by the rules — rules, let me remind you, that you have an opportunity and a responsibility to help determine.

There are some things which are not negotiable: (1) you must get a notebook and write down everything you eat after you eat it; (2) you must weigh every morning and record it in your book; (3) you must work out an exercise program with which I will help you, if you need help; (4) you must work out a system for reducing your caloric intake — whether you count calories or not is up to you, most obese people know more about calories and how much it takes for them to lose than the average physician; (5) you must consult regularly with a physician to check your general physical health; (6) you may not use any medication for purposes of suppressing your appetite.

Between now and one week from today when we meet again, I will expect that you will have purchased a notebook, recorded everything you've eaten, worked out an exercise program and put it into practice each day, weighed and recorded your weight every morning, seen a physician with whom I will consult, thrown away any appetite suppressors, and thought about how you're going to eat less. This week you are free to eat anything you want; but you must do all of the other tasks. Next week you will start your dieting program — you *can* start sooner, but next week we will begin, if you haven't already.

Are you prepared to participate in as rigid a system as I've outlined and commit yourself to it 100 percent?

There are a number of counseling settings in which any and all of the twelve hypothetical clients described above might seek help to change their behavior, i.e., thoughts, feelings, and/or actions. Family physicians, ministers, and priests, counselors, and therapists in private practice and in public mental health clinics can easily encounter such a wide diversity of clients in a week's time. Settings which provide counseling services to a specific population, e.g., schools and colleges, will probably be asked to assist with a somewhat narrower range of client requests for change. Settings with a more narrowly defined reason for existing, e.g., the employment service, some rehabilitation agencies, etc., will probably be asked to assist with an even narrower range of client requests for change than the array of requests represented by these twelve hypothetical clients. Nevertheless, it is not difficult to imagine that a counselor or psychotherapist in any setting would be called upon to work with or provide an effective referral for any one of the twelve clients. Regardless of the setting in which you function as a counselor, you will very likely not be able to escape being asked to help directly or help by providing an intelligent referral for individuals who need and want the diversity of changes which were sought by the twelve clients just discussed.

We are a long way from knowing exactly what techniques to apply to help bring the desired changes for every client who seeks counseling and/or psychotherapy. However, we are no longer in a position where one approach works about as well as another and thus a counselor/therapist is free to choose whatever procedures he happened to learn or that suit his personal style best. Your comfort with a procedure is no longer an adequate or an ethically justifiable basis for planning how you will assist a client change. The evidence is strong and clear that behavioral approaches to counseling and psychotherapy result in far greater success when Change is the purpose of counseling/psychotherapy. Whenever you are faced with a client who wants and needs to change his behavior, either you need to know to whom you can refer him for behavioral counseling/psychotherapy or you need to have acquired sufficient skills and competencies in behavioral theory and techniques in a recognized training institution, so that you can assist him directly. Talking with him and hoping that when he gets a few insights things will straighten out is no longer a viable alternative for anyone but a well-meaning but untrained layman who is given neither professional status nor money for being a good friend.

The following references describe behavioral approaches to counseling and psychotherapy when Change is the client's purpose for seeking assistance. They can be used as resources for counselors who have already received basic training in the theory and techniques of behavioral counseling or as sources of information about behavior change procedures, which will assist you in making intelligent referrals to adequately trained counselors and psychotherapists.

## Readings

1.  Bandura, A., 1969. *Principles of Behavior Modification.* New York: Holt, Rinehart and Winston.
2.  Franks, C. M. (Ed.), 1969. *Behavior Therapy.* New York: McGraw-Hill.
3.  Krumboltz, J. D. and Thoresen, C. E. (Eds.), 1969. *Behavioral Counseling.* New York: Holt, Rinehart and Winston.
4.  Whitely, J. M. (Ed.), 1969. Behavioral Counseling. *The Counseling Psychologist,* 1, 1–108.
5   Kanfer, F. H. and Phillips, J. S., 1970. *Learning Foundations of Behavior Therapy.* New York: Wiley.

## IV    CONFUSION REDUCTION

The third and final category of counseling purposes within which counselors and clients negotiate contracts is called *Confusion Reduction,* based on Tyler's (1969) classification system. Confusion Reduction, as it will be used here to designate a whole category of specific counseling purposes, is more far-reaching and complex than simple "clarification" which is the first step toward negotiating any counseling contract. That is, Confusion Reduction is more than the initial phase of all counseling interactions. It is true that in the beginning of a counseling interaction, which eventually becomes defined as a Choice situation or as a Change situation, there may be considerable confusion which must be clarified and eliminated. The communication process between counselor and client is designed to bring about such clarification and eliminate any confusion so that Choice or Change can be accomplished. However, there are several kinds of distressing life circumstances in which neither Choice nor Change, as we have defined them earlier, are called for — and yet the client experiences a profound and pervasive sense of confusion.

## Loss of Structure — Cause for Confusion

Confusion Reduction, as a separate category of counseling purposes, is most closely tied to inadequacy of the structure with which an individual is attempting to perceive and understand daily life. For example, an assumption which most of us make about how to get along in life is that "If I know what other people expect of me, I will be less likely to make a lot of mistakes or unwittingly disappoint people." There are countless mechanisms we utilize to figure out what other people expect of us, such as: what they actually say they expect, what they do not actually say, but what seems to be implied by the way they respond nonverbally (frowns, blank looks, smiles, etc.) and spoken or unspoken rules about how people in general behave here ("Everybody in this department calls everyone else by his first name" or "People don't strike up a conversation with anyone just because they happen to be on the same elevator or subway").

Each of us has a complicated set of assumptions, built up from his own life experiences, which concern what it takes to get along at work, with other people and in relation to oneself. For most people, many, and maybe even most, of those assumptions would be difficult to state clearly and simply. Nevertheless, that set of assumptions about life in general, together with the mechanisms each of us has developed to perceive and understand specific daily events, are what bring order, consistency, and predictability into each of our lives. The set of assumptions plus the perceptual mechanisms provide the structure by means of which we function in our daily lives. If for some reason, the set of assumptions and/or the perceptual mechanisms we have developed do not seem to work any more or have somehow vanished, we experience a tremendous amount of confusion, which usually interferes seriously with our daily functioning.

When an individual feels very confused and reports that he just cannot seem to function as he would like to, it may mean that he is facing some choices which, once made, will result in his being able to function again. It may mean that he needs to make some changes which, once accomplished, will result in his being able to function again. However, it also could mean that the person has suffered the loss of part or all of his basic structure for living and only a process of building a new structure or rebuilding the old structure will reduce his confusion sufficient to restore his functioning. When such an individual seeks counseling assistance, his purpose is to become less confused so he can function again. The restructuring process which will accomplish such Confusion Reduction must necessarily deal with the person's basic assumptions about life in general, especially his basic assumptions about Work, Relationships, and his Aloneness, and it must necessarily deal with the person's perceptual mechanisms whereby he represents the events of daily living to himself.

You, as a counselor, need to be able to ascertain whether the confusion a client is expressing is associated with choices or changes, which are yet to be made, or his confusion is associated with inadequacy of basic personal structure; the process of counseling ought to be different in each case. If confusion is merely an outgrowth of unmade choices, then negotiating a contract to engage the client in a process of rational decision-making is what is required of the conselor. If confusion is an outgrowth of unrealized changes, then negotiating a contract to engage the client in a process of modifying his behavior is what is required of the counselor. But if confusion is an outgrowth of inadequacy of structure in the client's life, then what is required of the conselor is negotiating a contract which will engage the client in a process of building a new structure or rebuilding an old structure. Confusion Reduction, the third and final category of counseling purposes, applies to those clients who seek counseling because the structure (i.e., the set of basic assumptions and the perceptual mechanisms) with which they make sense out of life is no longer adequate; they feel confused and unable to function as they would like to.

## Identifying Confusion

Two types of human experience which frequently include loss of structure and therefore lead to profound confusion will be briefly outlined. If a counselor is aware of the kinds of circumstances that often result in structure loss and confusion, he is more likely to discern when a particular client's primary purpose in seeking counseling is Confusion Reduction. He will more quickly negotiate a Confusion Reduction Contract which will engage the client in an effective restructuring process. The following outline is intended to provide clues for detecting Confusion Reduction as the primary counseling purpose. Not everyone who experiences one or more of the following things will require Confusion Reduction counseling. Also, a person who could definitely benefit from Confusion Reduction counseling would not necessarily have experienced any of the following. However, it bears repeating that the counselor who has some awareness of the kinds of circumstances which frequently result in structure loss and confusion is better equipped to discern the need for Confusion Reduction counseling.

I. Loss of Structure Through Major Life Change.

   A. Sudden Onset $\longrightarrow$ Structure Obliterated.

     1. Self: physical disability, e.g., loss of arm or leg, facial scars, heart attack.

        drug induced psychological changes, e.g., recurrent hallucinations, addiction.

        personal failure, e.g., expelled from school, bankruptcy, sexual impotence, frigidity.

        new or unfamiliar role demands, e.g., older sister to brand new baby brother, retirement, return to school after many years, share room for first time.

     2. Significant Others:

        no longer accessible; e.g., death, divorce, moved away, serious illness.

        radical change in values or style, e.g., religious conversion, financial status increase.

        disapproval and/or vindictiveness, e.g., hostile attack, sharp withdrawal or rejection, dishonesty – lying, cheating, conning.

     3. Setting:

        move to a new neighborhood, community, or state.

        job change, e.g., desk work after being a field man.

        changes in institutions, e.g., old, downtown church razed.

   B. Gradual Onset $\longrightarrow$ Structure Eroded.

     1. Self: aging and/or chronic disease.

        retarded youngster facing increasing school demands.

        skills becoming obsolete with increased automation.

        inability to form close personal relationships.

     2. Significant Others:

        diminishing contact with previously close friend or family member.

        more accelerated job advancement of friend.

        growing independence of one's children.

        aging of parents.

        gradual reduction in previously commonly held values among family and/or friends.

     3. Setting:

        policies governing job role and activities gradually redefined and revised.

        church doctrine revised and reinterpreted.

        small town becoming a city.

        increasing crime and violence in previously safe neighborhood.

II. Loss of Structure Through Personal Examination and Evaluation of
Previously Distant Events.

   A. Refocusing of Time Perspective, e.g., long-range career planning,
contemplating one's own death, increased knowledge of history.

   B. Expansion of Personal World, e.g., increased knowledge of or
contact with other cultures, religions, political-social systems.

   C. Increased Knowledge of Self, e.g., insight into egocentric or
self-aggrandizing motives, awareness of one's own sexuality, shift in
appraisal of personal strengths and weaknesses.

When a person experiences major changes in his life or begins examining
new ideas which were previously very foreign to him, he typically passes through
a period of ambiguity and uncertainty — a period of confusion — before he is
able to sort things out and make whatever choices or changes seem necessary
and/or possible. However, for some people, the period of confusion never ends.
They often begin doubting many of their basic assumptions about life and
distrusting their own perceptions of reality. In some cases the individual's
assumptions and perceptions are quite appropriate and accurate; in some cases
the individual's assumptions and perceptions are fallacious and distorted.
Regardless of the accuracy and trustworthiness of his assumptions and
perceptions, from your point of view, if the individual lacks confidence in them
and is thus very confused, your task as a counselor is to assist him build a new,
more adequate structure in his life or rebuild the old structure, which would be
adequate if he had confidence in it. Except in cases of marked disorganization
and dysfunction, you and the client together make the judgments concerning the
desirability and/or necessity of building a new structure.

## Identifying Confusion Reduction as the Purpose of Counseling

In order to illustrate the range of client concerns which fall in the Confusion
Reduction category, we will continue with the same format of presenting several
hypothetical cases. Because Confusion Reduction is usually a more difficult
counseling purpose to identify and define than either Choice or Change, we will
devote more attention to combinations of key questions which are helpful in
recognizing Confusion Reduction as the primary purpose of counseling. The fact
that eight, rather than twelve, hypothetical cases are presented will allow us to
focus on the counselor's questions more extensively. The diversity of client
concerns which fall in the Confusion Reduction category is probably greater and
more complex than the range of concerns in either the Choice or Change
categories. Thus, the smaller number of hypothetical cases presented should not
be interpreted as indicating that Confusion Reduction is a less important
counseling purpose. After the eight hypothetical cases have been presented, a
Confusion Reduction Contract, appropriate for each case, will be suggested.

*Counselor:*   Perhaps it would be best to begin with the question of what brings you here.

   *Client #1:*   Yah — like, man, I'm not making it anywhere.

*Counselor:*   I want you to think back to when it wasn't like this and talk to me about what it *was* like then — let's take a year ago at this time, where were you, what were you doing, who was on the scene. . .

   *Client #1:*   Like you mean last fall? — well, I was right here, but it was really beautiful, I was just starting with this group — I play the electric organ — and we were really starting to groove on each other — we had several one-nighters. I was like so naive — I mean like I learned to play the organ in church and what I knew about life was like zero — well, J. G., the lead guitar, and this chick I was seeing got busted in December — on the 24th, at a party — and I was in church . . . I was in church — well, it's been a downer ever since.

Some clients, for whom Confusion Reduction is the primary counseling purpose, do not sound particularly confused, even though they may have experienced a considerable loss of structure. Nevertheless, their questioning of basic assumptions and/or distrust of their own perceptions can be just as real and their need for Confusion Reduction counseling be just as pressing.

*Counselor:*   Why don't we begin with the question of what brings you here.

   *Client #2:*   Well, I probably shouldn't even be talking to you 'cause I know there are kids who are really in bad shape — but I, I don't know, I just feel like things aren't right somehow.

*Counselor:*   You're not sure you really ought to be here — maybe somebody else needs the time worse than you do — but still it feels like things should be different some way.

   *Client #2:*   Yah, but I don't know how they should be any different or how they *could* be any better, really. See, I come from a very good family — I mean they're all big successes — both my parents have doctorates; my father is a chemist at Albany-Fordyce and my mother teaches sociology at the U; I have an older brother who is a junior at Stanford in premed.

*Counselor:*   Everyone in your family has run up quite an impressive success record.

   *Client #2:*   Yah, and including me — 'cause I get very good grades — I'm active in a lot of stuff, including being Vice President of the Student Council. I date some — although mostly I go with a group of kids who have a lot of the same interests I do. I'm really very happy . . .

*Counselor:*   The picture I'm getting is that you've pretty much got everything going for you and, for the most part, you are quite happy — and yet there is a kinda' growing feeling that something doesn't fit or is missing or . . .

> *Client #2:*    Right, like it's all too easy or too good or something.

*Counselor:*    Like it can't last, maybe?

> *Client #2:*    Well, no . . . more like maybe it *will* last forever, I mean just go on and on like a lovely novel with pretty people and a happy ending — but life isn't like that — or it doesn't seem like it should be.

When Confusion Reduction is the client's primary purpose, it is often very difficult to translate his concerns into a neat "statement of a problem." As in the case of Client #2, if you ask "Well, what's her problem?" it is difficult to say, precisely, what her problem is. Some counselors become almost cynical at this point. "Her only problem is that she doesn't have any problems and thinks she should!" A much more constructive viewpoint depends upon your recognizing that many clients seek counseling with personal concerns which cannot be easily formulated as "a problem." When a client's purpose is not necessarily to solve a problem, you can actually block communication and delay formulating a contract by insisting upon adopting a problem-solving approach to the client's concerns. Problem-solving is more likely to be inappropriate in cases where Confusion Reduction is the primary counseling purpose than when either Choice or Change is the purpose. If you regard assisting a client to examine his own basic assumptions about life, to evaluate his own ability to fully and accurately perceive daily experiences, and to understand the unique structure and direction of his own life as a legitimate counseling purpose, that is, if you regard Confusion Reduction as a legitimate counseling purpose, then you must be able to inquire about the specific purpose of meeting together in terms other than "What's the problem to be solved?"

*Counselor:*    Maybe we could begin with your telling me how you decided to see a counselor at this time?

> *Client #3:*    I decided to see a counselor at this time because it appeared to be the most reasonable of the alternatives that I was considering. You see, my problem, if I can so label it, is that I happen to be fifteen years old and while I am quite prepared, intellectually, to cope with my course work at the University, I am markedly unprepared, interpersonally, to cope with many of the social demands which characterize campus life. I, of course, anticipated that such would be the case and I made the decision, in consultation with my parents and prep school instructors, to pursue my studies here at the University in spite of the personal conflicts it would likely precipitate. My field is mathematics, although I have a strong interest in music, as well.

*Counselor:*    So you made the choice to be here, knowing that socially it would be difficult at times, and you're pretty much satisfied with that decision — yet the feelings of being "out of place" or "out of step" are quite real and sometimes painful.

> *Client #3:*   Yes, they are — sometimes surprisingly so. I live with a family who are close friends of friends of my parents and the whole arrangement seems to be working out quite satisfactorily. I enjoy considerable independence, but I nevertheless feel included and have a sense of "belonging." I don't want to give you the impression that I'm terribly lonely or isolated, because I certainly am not. However, it does seem to me that it would be beneficial if I had a place where I could go, routinely, to discuss the conflicts and problems which I have encountered and, undoubtedly, will continue to encounter.

*Counselor:*   Someone who can act as a sounding board — perhaps as a collaborator or consultant — but mostly someone who knows you, has some feeling for what you're like — what's important to you, where you're headed, what you're struggling with — and someone you can count on having ready access to . . .

> *Client #3:*   Sorta' sounds like a substitute for my parents, doesn't it? . . . Well, I guess that's all right — not unreasonable.

*Counselor:*   It makes sense to arrange to have someone in that role, whether or not it resembles a parental role?

> *Client #3:* ,   Yah, just because I'm on a college campus and very mature in some ways, I realize that I am still fifteen years old and I don't want to start trying to be twenty and it seems as if I could subtly start thinking that way — and expect myself to be something I'm not.

Sometimes the question, "How did you decide to seek counseling at this time?" produces a description of the events leading up to the first appointment, but it may still be very unclear what the client wants to have happen as a result of counseling, that is, what his purpose is. You will then need to inquire again and probably in a different way in order to clarify the client's purpose in seeking counseling. This is more likely to be true when Confusion Reduction is the primary purpose of counseling.

*Counselor:*   Why don't we begin with your telling me how you decided to see a counselor at this time?

> *Client #4:*   Yes, well, my youngest daughter is a sophomore here now — we live in Clarkston — I am an attorney and have practiced law there for, well, it will be twenty-five years in April — anyway, Jennifer, that's the daughter I want to talk about, Jennifer's mother is an alcoholic and has had to be hospitalized much of the past three years and I think that has been very hard on Jennifer. She has two older sisters, but they were already in college before their mother got so bad that she had to be hospitalized, but I think Jennifer was still young enough that it really

shook her whole world. She seemed to be all right her first year in college — although I guess she didn't have many friends — but toward the end of this past summer, she comes home during the summer, she became involved with this young couple, who live together and they have a child, but they're not married, I don't think — anyway, she started spending every hour of the day and night she possibly could — or so it seemed anyway — with this couple. Now I don't have anything against hippies, but it just seems to me that this isn't the best kind of psychological environment for a young girl who has always lived in a small town and is in many ways very immature — but I don't want to tell her she can't associate with them — 'course I don't think it would do any good anyway — she comes home nearly every weekend and spends the entire time at their house and I don't want to say she can't come home — but — well, so I don't know what to do about the situation or even if I should be worried about it — kids are different nowadays — but, well, I thought you might have some suggestions.

*Counselor:*  So on the one hand, you can understand why Jennifer may be reaching out to this couple, who have apparently sort of taken her in — because of the difficulties with her mother — but on the other hand, it doesn't seem healthy or in her best interest — but then again, you're not sure just how to evaluate the situation — how to tell if it is serious or maybe you're just overreacting.

*Client #4:*  I thought that I understood Jennifer very well and we've always been able to talk — more than with the other girls, even — but this has me really stumped — maybe I'm just trying to hang on to her — she's the baby, of course, and her mother is so — well, she just isn't the same person anymore.

*Counselor:*  One way we may get a little clearer picture of your major concerns is for you to talk about what you think might happen or are afraid might happen, if you did nothing — if for instance, I said, "Just ignore it, you don't really have anything to be concerned about."

*Client #4:*  Well, I'm not sure I *could* just ignore it — although that might be the best thing — I don't know — I guess I'm afraid that she may be feeling rejected or lonely and that she will just be at the mercy of whomever is nice to her and then, of course, she could just get involved in all kinds of trouble — drugs or she could get pregnant or I don't know — and I know I can't lead her life for her — but . . .

*Counselor:*  . . . but, somehow there must be a way to sort this out and make some sense out of it.

In addition to the question, "What might happen if you did nothing or if our counseling were completely unsuccessful?" we will consider two other key questions which help the Confusion Reduction client focus on his purpose in seeking counseling: (1) "If an acquaintance of yours asked you why you were going to see a counselor, what would you say?" and (2) "How would we know when we were through counseling; how would we be able to tell we had done what we started out to do?" These two questions or variations of them will be introduced in the remaining four hypothetical examples of Confusion Reduction cases.

*Counselor:* Perhaps we could begin with the question of what brings you to the Counseling Center?

> *Client #5:* Okay, well I'm just a freshman and I'm going to major in journalism, I'm pretty sure. Well, I've lived in a large city all my life — New York and Chicago, mostly. My family just moved to Palm Beach when I came to Illinois. I live on campus in a dorm, which is okay, except that I'm really having trouble with the guy I'm rooming with — we didn't know one another, we were just assigned to the same room. Ralph is okay — well, in fact, there's a lot about him that I really like, but man, we just live in different worlds.

*Counselor:* Ralph is the roommate you didn't know before you were assigned to live in the same room?

> *Client #5:* Yah, he's from a small town in Indiana and has lived on a farm all his life — he's okay, I mean he's not just a dumb farm kid, but we just don't have anything in common — like he goes to bed at eleven o'clock and he listens to this country music all the time and if you mention anything about women he just gives you this blank stare or kinda' silly smile. Well, at first I thought this just can't be, I mean like no way . . . but he sorta' grows on you and there really is a lot to him.

*Counselor:* So even though he is very different from yourself and it's like living with someone from another planet, you have come to sorta' like him . . .

> *Client #5:* . . . What really bothers me is that I've never known anybody who thinks like he does or sees life like he does and he's not the only one — there's a whole bunch of guys in the dorm like that.

*Counselor:* It's hard to communicate with Ralph and with the others.

> *Client #5:* Well, I don't know — no, I don't think it's lack of communication — 'cause we can talk a lot — it's more that we're just so different — it's our backgrounds, I guess — and I don't know why it even bothers me . . .

*Counselor:* Let's see if we can get a better handle on what's bothersome about this by asking, "What if some good friend of yours from New York, whom you'd known quite a while, somehow found out you had gone to see a counselor and he asked you 'What in the world are you going to see a counselor for?' Other than, 'It's none of your damn business!' what might you say to the friend?"

*Client #5:*   Well, let's see — if I thought he was really interested, I'd probably just tell him that the people are really different here — I mean especially the kids from small towns and off farms and that I thought I really understood people pretty well — see I might major in psychology, instead of journalism — but since I came here — I guess there's a lot I don't know — I mean, 'cause the people here are just really different.

*Counselor:*   Over time you've developed some pretty effective ways of getting with people — understanding what they think, how they feel, why they do the things they do — but somehow that's not working so well since coming here — people don't respond like you think they're going to, especially some of the guys in the dorm?

*Client #5:*   Yah, right, and so I'm wondering what's with me — maybe I could find some people more like me and that would be fine, except I'd really like to understand what's going on with all these other guys.

You will probably encounter more clients who seek Confusion Reduction counseling if you work with high school and college students. However, older adults experience loss of structure and the nearly overwhelming confusion which attends structure loss quite frequently also.

*Counselor:*   I see from the intake form you completed that you were referred by your minister. Maybe you could begin by telling me what you both hoped might happen for you here at the clinic.

*Client #6:*   I talked to Reverend Gray a couple of times since my wife died — he took care of the funeral and talked to the kids — she had a miscarriage and they couldn't get the bleeding stopped . . . we were out on a camping trip, so she'd lost a lot of blood before we even got to the hospital and she has the wrong kind of blood so they couldn't find enough before she was gone — 'cause it was just an hour after we got to the emergency room.

*Counselor:*   One minute you're just a happy family out enjoying a camping trip together and then within only a few short hours everything is just wiped out . . .

*Client #6:*   . . . yah, I — ah — I was pretty much wiped out — but the kids — the kids were really great — Reverend Gray helped a lot and my sister came down from Baltimore — well, in fact, she and my wife's brother and sister just left.

*Counselor:*   And it was Reverend Gray who suggested you come here . . .

*Client #6:*   Yah, he thought it might be a good idea to get someone more outside to help kinda' think it through . . . sometimes the family can't see things 'cause they're so close to it and they kinda' get in the way — without meaning to.

*Counselor:*  Like there are a lot of decisions and plans which have to be made and people — just trying to be helpful — tend to take over and want to make them for you?

*Client #6:*  Well, I really appreciated all they did — and my wife's aunt is going to stay with us for a while and take care of the house and the kids. I'm a house painter and this is our busiest time, of course. Everything is getting back to normal — the kids are in school, except for Danny — he's just four — so most of the plans are worked out for now — but I keep feeling like there's something I'm not doing right or what if I do the wrong thing — like with the kids or something — like I can't keep track of everything — but things *seem* to be okay, I don't know . . .

*Counselor:*  Sorta' like it's on the edge of going out of control any minute?

*Client #6:*  Yeh, but I know that isn't true — or at least I don't think that's true, but then I just don't know —

*Counselor:*  This may seem like an abrupt shift of gears, but it may help us understand your feelings a little better, just imagine with me for a minute that you and I have worked together for awhile and things seem to be a lot better, what would that look like — how would we know that we'd accomplished what we set out to do?

*Client #6:*  Well, I don't really know, but I guess — I guess I'd know things were okay — that the kids are okay mostly — that I was doing the right thing by 'em, I mean, I think Shirley's sister and my sister both think that the kids need a mother — which they do — but I think they should stay together and with me, and that's the way it's going to be — but sometimes I'm not sure that I'm right — and I thought if I talked it over with a counselor or a doctor or someone who knows, that I could find out either more about how to take care of them — you know — right, I mean, or you'd advise me that maybe I shouldn't try to keep 'em together . . . but I'd know where I stand —

*Counselor:*  So by our talking about the whole situation — but mostly about you and the kids — you'd have a better idea of whether you ought to be thinking about other arrangements or plans for them or whether things are best with the family together and what you really ought to do is concentrate on how to be both father and mother to them . . . ?

*Client #6:*  Yah, I'd know how I ought to think about it or whether there's anything to think about, other than just raising 'em right.

As you can see, defining the specific purpose of counseling when Confusion Reduction is the general category of counseling purposes requires a balance of asking questions and paraphrasing (See Section Three — Communication). While it is imperative that you understand your client's purpose, in order to negotiate a contract for accomplishing his purpose, you must also take care not to question and probe in such a manner that your client feels on-the-spot to justify his presence in your office. The rather delicate balance between probing and paraphrasing is especially important to maintain with a Confusion Reduction client. Because it is often more difficult for a Confusion Reduction client to be specific about his purpose in seeking counseling, because he is less certain about his assumptions and less confident about his perceptions, he is more likely to conclude that he probably should not have come for counseling. The harder you press the question "What are you doing here?" the more rattled and defensive he will become. Your questions and paraphrases should be designed to give him permission to share his confusion with you, at the same time that they help clarify the nature of the confusion and what he would like to do about it.

*Counselor:*    I guess it's been about six months since we last talked — about scholarships and loans, as I recall — what brings you in today, Marilyn?

> *Client #7:*    Well, I remembered what you said about things not working out sometimes, even when they look like they're all set and that I should come back if that happened. Well, I got my scholarship to State and my folks were going to help out with the rest — well, actually, they still want to, but I'm not sure they should. See my little brother, Kevin, has leukemia, I mean they're pretty sure that's what it is, but they don't know how long . . . you know, or what will happen.

*Counselor:*    . . . That's terrible, Marilyn, I'm really sorry — I almost don't know what to say — I guess because there really isn't anything that's "right" to say. You must be experiencing some very difficult feelings.

> *Client #7:*    Well, at first I just wouldn't even believe it, I mean, not Kevin — 'cause I'd read about it some in Health and I still can't believe that he really might . . . die — I mean it doesn't even sound real when I say it . . .

*Counselor:*    Something within you just won't accept that he's so sick he could die.

> *Client #7:*    But I *know* he's sick and I just don't want to make it worse for my parents — they're the ones who should need to see a counselor, but I just don't know what to do.

*Counselor:*    Like it's screaming inside of you, "Do something — do something!" but there's nothing anybody can do?

> *Client #7:*    The doctors are doing all they can and my parents are doing everything that they can and it just seems like I need to keep myself together, so I'm not more burden to them — and I thought talking to you might help.

*Counselor:*    . . . that maybe if we talk about it here you could get a grip on yourself and be able to help more?

*Client #7:*   Yah, I guess ... I'm not sure how I can help, I do stuff around the house more, but Mom and Dad say to just go on with life as normally as we can — that I should go ahead and go out and have fun — but that just doesn't seem right to me ... I don't know — I'm just not sure about anything anymore.

*Counselor:*   Let me ask, Marilyn, does anyone know you were going to talk with me today?

*Client #7:*   I told Jeff, he's the boy I've been dating, and we've been really close friends for quite a while — I've been talking to him a lot.

*Counselor:*   Well, Jeff probably knows you fairly well, it sounds like, and he would probably have some idea of what might be the most helpful thing that could happen from your talking with me about yourself and Kevin and your parents — what do you think Jeff thinks about it?

*Client #7:*   He thinks it's really a good idea, if fact, he really encouraged me to come because he doesn't feel like he should influence me about going out 'cause he thinks I need to think about it and decide on my own — not just about that, but to talk about how it affects everything and sorta' get my thinking straightened out — and my parents can't really do that for me either — but Jeff thinks, and I agree, that somebody outside the situation could help me see it better.

The final hypothetical Confusion Reduction case, Client #8, follows immediately.

*Counselor:*   Marty, I know that both your parents and your teacher, Mr. Chambers, told you that I would be talking with you today, but I'm not sure they made it real clear what we would talk about — can you just tell me why you think we are meeting together?

*Client #8:*   Yah, because they put me in the Special class and I don't wanna' stay there — I wanna' go back to the regular fifth grade — *they* think I'm retarded, but I'm not — my mother says that I've always been slow — but I'm not retarded. Can you be dumb and not retarded?

*Counselor:*   It sounds like there's a difference between "dumb" and "retarded" — "Dumb" is like slow, but it's okay — and "retarded" is like something's wrong with you, you're not okay — is that what makes the difference for you, Marty?

*Client #8:*   Well, I think — that the M.R.'s in the Special class — the teachers call them M.R.'s but not to their face, and they mean the really dumb ones — "the weirdos." There's nothing wrong with my brain, I just don't use it. My mother says I don't listen, but sometimes I just forget.

*Counselor:*   Deep down, Mother doesn't want you to be in the Special class either?

*Client #8:*   Well no, she thinks I don't need it, but my Dad gets mad and says she's pushing me too hard and I wouldn't even care, except my friend Donald lives on the south side, you know, and now I have to go on a different bus — 'cause we get out earlier — and I don't know anybody in the M.R. class.

*Counselor:*   Marty, it seems like maybe your mother and father see things a little differently, as far as you and school are concerned — could you say what some of those differences are — like Mom thinks I should "blank" but Dad thinks I should do "blank" — can you fill in the blanks?

*Client #8:*   Yah — like Mom thinks I should come home after school and study . . .

*Counselor:*   . . . and Dad thinks —

*Client #8:*   Dad thinks — well, he knows that I like to go over to the high school and watch them practice — see he knows one of the coaches and sometimes Mr. Carter gives me a ride home.

*Counselor:*   Let's take another example like that, as far as school is concerned, Mother thinks you should . . . what?

*Client #8:*   pay attention to what the teacher says —

*Counselor:*   . . . and Dad thinks?

*Client #8:*   He just thinks that — well, he just thinks — I don't know . . . why do we have to do this?

*Counselor:*   That's a good question, Marty, I'm trying to figure out the same thing — why *should* we talk to one another, what about and why and how would we know when we should stop talking, other than that we're tired of talking?

*Client #8:*   Well, my Mother wants you to talk to them so I don't have to stay in the Special class and Mr. Chambers wants you to talk to me so I'll shut up and stay in my seat, I guess —

*Counselor:*   Well, what about you, Marty, what do you want us to talk about?

*Client #8:*   I don't care — well, I sorta' care but I just wish they'd make up their minds. Maybe if I talk to you and then you talk to them, then I won't have to go back to the Special M.R. class — except, I really like the fish tank in there, but I can't sit still 'cause I don't know anybody or what I'm supposed to do — maybe you should talk to my mother.

*Counselor:*   Seems like the most important thing, Marty, is to get it settled so that everybody's got the same story on how things should be — so one place to start is for you and me to talk for just a little while longer, today, about how *you* think things should be.

It is true that clients who seek counseling because they have experienced structure loss and are confused will invariably, show signs, verbally and nonverbally, of distress. However, the distressing feelings which are present in

Confusion Reduction clients range from mild apprehension to overwhelming panic and from "feeling somewhat down" to "being buried in the depths of depression." It is important to understand and accept the anxious and/or depressed feelings which usually accompany the need for Confusion Reduction, but the mere presence of anxiety and/or depression should not lead you to conclude that Confusion Reduction is the client's purpose. It is the combination of life change (sudden or gradual) resulting in loss of structure (questioning of basic assumptions and perceptual mechanisms) together with some degree of distress (anxiety or depression) which leads to the conclusion that Confusion Reduction is the client's primary purpose.

It is not possible, within the limits of this section on counseling purposes, to survey or discuss all the counseling processes and techniques which have been developed to assist a client with Confusion Reduction. In general, this involves mastering counseling skills which help a client build new structure into his life or remodel an older structure which is not longer adequate or safe to continue using. The communication techniques, discussed and illustrated in Section Three, are especially important in working with a Confusion Reduction client. Consider your initial efforts to identify the client's general counseling purpose, your continued efforts to define his purpose more specifically, and your further efforts to formulate and negotiate a contract with him to accomplish Confusion Reduction, and it is obvious that communication skills are at a premium with the Confusion Reduction client.

We will assume that the counselors with whom the eight hypothetical clients have been interacting are skillful communicators and that they have a thorough understanding of the significance of structure and structure loss to a human being. By the end of the first interview, each of the eight counselors ought to be able to offer a statement summarizing his understanding of the client's purpose in seeking counseling and his understanding of the initial contract they have negotiated to accomplish the client's purpose. An example of such a contractual summary statement for each of the eight Confusion Reduction clients is given below.

## Examples of Confusion Reduction Contracts

Client #1

> *Counselor:* Our time is about up for today and you may feel like we've just rapped about a lot of stuff and "so what?" but I'd like to just take a minute and share some thoughts with you. I know you came today because you told your Mom that you would, but I also sense some feelings within *you* that, while life is at best a hassle, maybe it doesn't have to be a total bummer — maybe it doesn't have to be just a random series of disconnected distractions. I happen to think that everyone has to find his own thing and nobody can do it for him — but I also think that "finding

your own thing" doesn't mean you can't talk with anybody else in the process. Maybe I'm naive too — but I'm really convinced that things don't have to be so fouled up for you and that our talking about it can make a difference. There's a whole range of possibilities for how you're going to get your game together, especially as far as how you spend your time and what you're going to do about other people. I'd like to see us look at some of those possibilities together.

Okay, so much for the hard sell. I'm very concerned about the fact that you can't concentrate — there's a lot of stuff roaring around in you and some of it doesn't fit together so well — your music, the whole church scene with your folks, your own religious experiences, the drug scene, your experiences with sex — all the stuff we've just sorta' touched on but couldn't possibly talk about in depth in one meeting — I'm not surprised you can't concentrate. While I don't think there are easy answers or even complete answers, I am convinced that it's worth it to be engaged in a process of trying to carve out your own answers and that it makes sense to talk with someone like myself as part of that process. So I'd like us to continue meeting on a weekly basis; does that make sense to you?

> *Client #1:*   Yah, it makes as much sense as anything does, and I really would like to get it straightened out so I could at least think about it or stop thinking about it, if I want to. Are you going to talk to my doctor, too, like you said you might?

*Counselor:*   Yes, I understood that to be okay from your point of view and, as I said, it may be helpful to both of us, if I talk with him and get his impressions of any physical factors involved.

> *Client #1:*   Do you think I'm crazy?

*Counselor:*   No, I don't think you're crazy — you mean like do I think you should be locked up?

> *Client #1:*   Yah — like shipped off to the funny farm . . .

*Counselor:*   No. We talked about suicide as a way out and you said you were sure you weren't in danger of attempting suicide and gave your reasons why not or what would stop you — I accept that, take it seriously — I believe you that suicide is not an alternative you would choose. I'm sure it feels pretty crazy inside of you a lot of the time and that's one of the things I expect will change with our talking. You may always be aware of a kind of madness in life — like Zorba the Greek — but it doesn't have to be this constantly being invaded or overwhelmed by it.

There's one thing I want you to do this week, which you may not find especially pleasant, but I want you to do it anyway — I want you to get a notebook of unlined paper, like a sketch pad, and some different colored pens and each day this week I want you to write or draw something about that day — it could be something that's happened —

whatever seems important. Next week when we meet, we'll look at it and talk about it — now obviously I'm not interested in evaluating how well you write or draw — that's not the point. The point is that I want us to be able to focus on and communicate with one another about some of your day-to-day experiences — and this is one way I've found that it's possible to do that. Does that make sense — or is it clear what I want you to do?

Client #2

*Counselor:* Before we end our session today, I'd like to summarize and share some of the thoughts and feelings I've had as we've talked and then I want to make a couple of suggestions for how we might proceed. Are you familiar with Salinger's *Franny and Zooey*?

> *Client #2:* No — I've read *Catcher in the Rye* and some of the *Nine Short Stories*, but I really like Salinger —

*Counselor:* Well, it's a little risky for me to refer to a character in a book — in that it may sound as if I'm saying, "Well, my dear, you're just like Franny in *Franny and Zooey*, so why don't you go read all about yourself and things will probably become much clearer to you!" And that's not my intention! But there are some things that Salinger deals with there that I think are very much related to the kind of struggle I see you engaged in. Just briefly, Franny returns home from college for a visit and interacts mostly with her brother, Zooey, but with her mother, also. She is a very bright, perceptive young woman who has become thoroughly and bitterly disillusioned with the sham and hypocrisy and compromise that characterize everything and everybody, including herself — pompous professors who perform, rather than teach; college men and women, who are capable of much more, but settle for superficial, exploitative relationships; and her own inability to carry out a pure act of altruism or love — all examples of the phoniness of people's lives, including Franny's own life. Relating this to you and why I thought of it — it seems that you have become painfully aware of the fact that you cannot escape the egocentricity of your own motivation — that no matter what you do, however lofty or noble or altruistic it may appear to others or to yourself, there is the growing awareness that it has personal payoff to you — even if you deny yourself something and supposedly sacrifice for someone else, you derive the benefit of feeling good, helpful and pleased with yourself for being self-sacrificing. Does this ring any bells or am I way off track?

> *Client #2:* No, I know what you mean, all the social service and volunteer work that I do and just being the one who gets to help all the time — it's like it puts other people down or something — but I really don't feel better than other people — but maybe I really do — oh, I don't know — how can it be wrong to want to help other people? And yet it doesn't seem fair.

*Counselor:* It's a hard question — personally, I don't think there's a simple answer, but I'm convinced that it's possible to struggle with the question, as you are, and work out an answer you can live with. The way I see myself being of use to you is in helping clarify the question and in being a source of information about ways others have dealt with the question — such as Salinger in *Franny and Zooey*. It's also been dealt with by Ayn Rand and Reinhold Niebuhr and numerous other writers. What I'm proposing is that we focus on the whole area of your desire to help others — the feelings of wanting to be helpful, the effects on you and on others when you help and when you don't, and so on. There are several ways to approach the issue, such as: reading about it, both fiction and nonfiction; talking with others — from different walks of life and perhaps with different values than your own; and monitoring and reviewing your own daily experiences of giving and receiving help; our relationship here can be another source of understanding if we choose to focus on the process between us.

> *Client #2:* I'm not really sure what all is involved, but I'd like to know, I mean, I'd like to talk about because it effects so much of everything.

*Counselor:* Well, if it makes sense to you, why don't we begin with *Franny and Zooey*. I'd like you to read it this week and next time we meet we can talk about it and about connections you've made between it and your own experience. There's a section right at the end about shining your shoes for the Fat Lady that's probably especially important for us to understand in terms of your daily experience — but let's just see how it goes for you. It may even turn out that this is not a productive way to approach the issue and if that were true, we'd just come at it a different way — but I think this has promise — so one week from today, right?

## Client #3

*Counselor:* It seems as though we've arrived at a sensible arrangement — we will meet together every two weeks for this semester, and then we will decide about a future meeting schedule. If you feel it would be helpful to discuss something between sessions, then you will call and make an appointment, in addition to our regular biweekly sessions.

> *Client #3:* Right — and I appreciate your willingness to do this.

*Counselor:* Well, I frankly am looking forward to meeting with you and I'm glad we have established regular meetings rather than having it be on a "call in, if you want to" basis only — because, I think you mentioned it first, you might have a tendency to view making an appointment as a sign of weakness or immaturity, if things weren't going too well — whereas *now* you can see it as sensible and, actually, an indication of strength to make such arrangements.

> *Client #3:* I think most people are that way — regard it as appropriate to seek assistance when they need it least and find it difficult to accept when they need it most.

*Counselor:* There's one additional thing I'd like to share with you — I think our interaction today has been very candid and direct and that seems to me to be a very important style for us to maintain. I think I told you that initially I was somewhat off-balance with your high level of verbal skill and your intellectual ability — I don't see fifteen-year-old math majors every day. There may be occasions when you could become impatient with my slowness to track what you are communicating or with what may seem to you like general obtuseness on my part. Well, two things occur to me — one is that I will have to guard against becoming intimidated or defensive, if that happens — if I am having to struggle, and two, you are going to have to interact with a lot of people who will feel intellectually inferior to you and incapable of relating with you. We have an opportunity to look at that and talk about it in a way which can make relating to people, like myself, mutually rewarding — to you and to them. But this will require a degree of honesty and directness, such as we have enjoyed today.

> *Client #3:* I have certainly enjoyed talking with you today and I especially appreciate your not trying to find some big problems that you're just sure all so-called geniuses must suffer. And you're right about my perfectionistic tendencies; I probably would have trouble admitting it would be helpful to see you — so I too am glad we have established a regular meeting schedule — in fact, I feel somewhat more organized — as if I have my bearings a bit better — just from having talked with you today.

*Counselor:* Good, well I'll see you in two weeks and, perhaps, before.

## Client #4

*Counselor:* I hope as we have talked that it has been clear to you that in no way do I think it's foolish for you to be so concerned about Jennifer — many's the time I've wished parents were more concerned about the continuing development of their teenagers. I think I can appreciate both the feeling of wanting to protect her from making what might be a tragic mistake and at the same time feeling you must let go and allow her to make her own choices and lead her own life. It is very difficult to sort it out in a way that makes sense and takes everything into account. I'm going to make a proposal on the basis of what you've said about Jennifer and particularly what you've said about your relationship with her.

It seems to me that Jennifer has shown good judgment and been quite reliable in the past — even though she has been somewhat protected from having to make a great many serious decisions. Also, it seems to me that the two of you have developed a solid, honest and open relationship — particularly in contrast to her relationship with her mother.

*Client #4:*     Yes, I think both of those things are true.

*Counselor:*     Well, there are three things I would advise you to do. The first one is that I think you should make an appointment with Jennifer — by that I mean tell her that you would like to talk with her about some concerns you have about her investment in the couple — her friends. Rather than try to have it come up casually or just spontaneously, tell her directly that you'd like to talk about it with her and ask her to indicate which of several times you name, when you would be available, would be most convenient for her — or ask her to suggest another time if none of those works. Allow yourselves plenty of time — an hour or more — and be sure you are somewhere where you won't be interrupted. And then simply tell her as clearly and honestly as you can what you are concerned about. Let her know, as you have let me know, the depth of your concern and that you have many mixed and conflicting feelings about it.

*Client #4:*     You mean just tell her exactly what I think and feel?

*Counselor:*     That's right — if you represent yourself accurately you won't appear either close-minded or thoroughly disapproving, because from my interaction with you, I find you to be undecided and uncertain about what you think of the situation, and that's a reality she should be expected to deal with — the fact that you are unsure and let her know that, will probably call forth the most mature and responsible response from her that's possible. And she is certainly old enough to be asked to respond to your concerns and uncertainties. The outcome of such a talk or perhaps several such talks, will likely be that both of you will see things somewhat differently and probably be able to understand one another's viewpoint better.

The second thing is that you make no effort to prevent her from seeing the couple. During your talk you should tell her that you are not going to try to discourage her or block her from seeing them — that at this point, you simply want to understand it. However, tell her that because of your concern and not knowing which way to turn that you did have a conference with me — give her my name and invite her to come in and talk with me, if she would like to or if she finds herself in some difficulty and wants to talk to someone on campus quickly. I will alert the receptionist to make an appointment for her immediately, if she calls in.

Then the third thing is that one month from now, or sooner if you feel it's necessary, I would like us to get together again and assess, together, if things seem to be getting sorted out. It may be that Jennifer would want to be included in that session, but that should be her decision.

Does that seem workable from your point of view?

*Client #4:*    Yes, it does — I'm a little apprehensive about talking with her, but as you've pointed out, we have been able to talk in the past and I'll be letting her know about my apprehensions anyway. It's reassuring to know that there's a person down here she can go to if she needs or wants to — and I would like to meet with you again ... I guess I can call and make an appointment, just as I did this time.

## Client #5

*Counselor:*    Let's just review what we've agreed makes sense for you to do before we end our session today. As I understand your major concern or what's at the center of things for you, it's not so much that you're lonely or don't have anybody to talk to — 'cause, actually there are lots of people to talk to — it's more a matter that the people here are so very different from any you've encountered before and you're left not knowing how to respond to them or how to understand them ... now, it would be possible just to write them off and search out people who are more like yourself and figure mid-Westerners are just weird — why bother?

*Client #5:*    Yah, but I don't really want to do that.

*Counselor:*    With your interest in journalism and writing and psychology — that seems like a really close-minded or narrow way to deal with the situation ... and we talked about writers, like Steinbeck, who seem to have a sense of life that takes in the whole country — they're not tied to just one corner of the U.S. — like in *Travels with Charley.* So your thought is that you could do something like Steinbeck did traveling across the country — feeling the texture of life, seeing the colors and patterns, tasting and smelling the very fabric of living — but you would concentrate your travels on this part of the country and the people who seem so different.

*Client #5:*    Yah, I don't have a camper, but that's okay — maybe even better for me — 'cause I'll probably learn more just being in bus stations and hitchhiking around on the weekends. And then Ralph has asked me to go home with him over Thanksgiving and so I'll probably get some insights being around his family and friends, too.

*Counselor:*    So then as you do this, you're going to write down your experiences — in journalistic style — and ask Mr. Little and Mrs. Lloyd in the Journalism department to critique them for you — and maybe consider submitting something for publication, right?

*Client #5:*    Well, they probably won't be good enough to publish but I think Mr. Little and Mrs. Lloyd would be willing to talk with me about them and maybe I'll get a better idea if I have some potential or if I even like writing.

*Counselor:*   And then the part about your wanting to expand your own world of experience and yourself, as a human being, to be able to understand and accept and respond to more of life — we will have a chance to talk about, here, and focus on the ways you are being shaped and changed — the way things are getting sorted out differently for you.

> *Client #5:*   Yah, I think I need someone to — like you say — kinda' help me sort it out as I go.

*Counselor:*   Well, that makes all kinds of sense to me and I'd just like to say that I really respect the way you're going about this — it would be so easy to simply close off and figure it isn't worth the effort — and I really look forward to sharing the process you're going through with you — and I agree, I think I can be helpful in your sorting it out and making sense out of what now seems very foreign and strange.

So you're going out to Brownsville and Thornton this weekend and then next week, at this time, we'll talk about it and whatever else may have come up in the meantime, okay?

> *Client #5:*   Yah, I'm sure glad you don't think I'm really weird for being concerned about it, 'cause I was sorta' wondering — and I'll make an appointment with the secretary for next week, right now.

### Client #6

*Counselor:*   I think I have a fairly good picture of your situation and some sense of the confusion that you are feeling. Since your wife's death, things have begun to get settled down — you aunt's being with you helps out quite a bit at home with the kids, but it's unclear just how long she'll be with you — and the other family members have helped out a lot, but you have some concern that they not take over too much, especially on what happens with your children. Reverend Gray suggested that maybe someone like myself could advise you about the children — whether they are getting along all right without a mother or whether you should be thinking of placing them in a foster home or whether it's even necessary to be thinking about it.

> *Client #6:*   It's just hard for me to know about these things and like I told you, I know Shirley would want the kids to stay together and that's what I want to, unless it would be best for them some other way.

*Counselor:*   We've talked quite a bit about what life is like for you and the kids on a day-to-day basis — the time you're with them, the kinds of things you do together, the rules that operate around your home, and so on — and I find no reason to tell you that you really ought to think about finding a foster home for them — in fact, I think that's in the opposite direction of what makes sense to me.

*Client #6:*    Well, that's a relief, because I really don't want to give them up — but I'd be willing to if it was best.

*Counselor:*    What I do think you ought to do, however, is begin to find some ways that you and the kids together can sort things out and have confidence in the decisions that you make together. And there isn't any reason why the kids can't be a part of that process in fact, it would be in their best interest, as far as their own growth and development is concerned, if they did share the responsibility for deciding on how life should be for all of you.

*Client #6:*    And I think they could do it, too, especially the two oldest ones.

*Counselor:*    I'm sure you know that there are just mountains of books and articles written on how to raise children; some of them are very good and many of them are worthless. I don't know how much chance you get to read or how willing you are to read something I'd suggest, but there's a paperback book called *Between Parent and Child* by a man by the name of Haim Ginott — it's spelled H-A-I-M — that's his first name, and G-I-N-O-T-T is his last name — here — I'll jot it down — well, I think it would be worth your time and effort to read his book. It's very down-to-earth and sensible and I think it would give you some ideas on the best way to relate with the children.

*Client #6:*    Well, I don't read a lot, but I will get it and read it, if you think it will help.

*Counselor:*    Now, of course, a person can't learn everything out of a book and I don't think that book or any other one is going to answer everything, but I think it may help you build some confidence in yourself as a parent. The other thing I want to suggest is that you find out about a group in the city who operates an Adlerian Family Counseling Clinic — the psychologist's name who coordinates the program is on this card. There are all kinds of people associated with this program — physicians, ministers, psychologists, and they work very closely with the public schools. The program is based on the ideas of Alfred Adler and takes its name from his work — anyway, they have regular family counseling sessions and parent study groups where you can go talk over your own problems and, maybe even more importantly for you, learn from observing and interacting with other parents who are talking about problems with their youngsters.

I know you are busy and that this sort of activity is quite foreign to you anyway, but I'd like you to find out about it and go, at least once, to see for yourself if you think there may be something in it for you. They often hold evening and weekend meetings just so the program won't conflict with work and with school — 'cause kids and teachers are involved, too.

> *Client #6:*   Well, I'm not much good at talking, particularly in a group, but like I said, I'll try anything once if I think it would help me understand better or feel like I know what I'm doing — so, yah, I'll find out about it.

*Counselor:*   What I think would be best for us, would be to meet again in about three weeks or a month and check out with one another how things seem to be going.

> *Client #6:*   Yah, well I'd like to do that, okay.

*Counselor:*   Does a month seem too long?

> *Client #6:*   Well, it seems like quite a while — maybe three weeks — although I guess I could call you if something came up.

*Counselor:*   Absolutely — and I would expect that you would do that — yes, by all means, you can call if something changes radically or an emergency comes up or if you continue to feel as confused as you have.

> *Client #6:*   Well, I think I have a better handle on things now — and I really am relieved about not sending the kids away . . . and I will get that book and I'll find out about this family counseling thing.

*Counselor:*   Well, why don't we set up an appointment for three weeks from now with the understanding that, if you feel it is necessary or would be helpful, you can call and make an appointment before that time, okay?

### Client #7

*Counselor:*   Before we stop talking today, Marilyn, I'd like us to take a few minutes more and look at the value and importance to you of talking about Kevin and your parents and how you're feeling about yourself and the whole situation. You expressed some misgivings about whether you ought to need to talk about it.

> *Client #7:*   It just seems like I'm being such a baby and I know it's so much harder on my folks — but I guess it really does help, because I feel better able to cope with it some already.

*Counselor:*   When something like this happens to a family, there's just no way anyone can say exactly what they should do or how they should respond to it — but it does seem to me that what you are doing — of trying to face the situation directly and deciding almost day by day and week by week how to cope with it — is the most responsible and constructive thing you can do. It's sort of a combination of carrying on with life, as normally as possible, and at the same time recognizing that things aren't normal, that *nothing* is quite the same.

> *Client #7:*   I know it doesn't do any good to run away from it and, yet, I don't think it's good to think about it all the time either.

*Counselor:*   That's where I think counseling can probably be the most help to you, Marilyn . . . it can be a place where you can go to think about it, talk about it, and give yourself permission to let down and experience the feelings of confusion and despair that you really can't allow yourself out there, day to day . . . and I'm encouraging you to make use of me and of this setting in that way — I see it as appropriate and something I am very ready and willing to do.

> *Client #7:*   Well, I really appreciate it — 'cause I know it helps to talk, but my parents can't always be expected to be ready to listen to me, when they are hurting so much themselves and I don't want to put them in that position — I mean, I think we should talk and all, but I don't want them to all the time have to help me — and the same with Jeff.

*Counselor:*   Does it make sense to you that we would set up a regular time for you to come in — even for a half hour or fifteen minutes each week — just to see how it's going?

> *Client #7:*   Yah, it would probably be a good idea, 'cause I'd probably go through the same thing each time, otherwise — sorta' talk myself out of coming in.

*Counselor:*   Of course, because it is not clear how rapidly it may progress or what the chances are, even though we know they are very remote, that Kevin might recover . . . you may very well want to talk longer than thirty minutes or sooner than a week, depending on how things develop — but we'll adjust our meetings to whatever does happen.

> *Client #7:*   Well, I don't know if you know how much I appreciate the time you've taken, 'cause I'm really grateful.

*Counselor:*   I think I do, Marilyn, and I appreciate your saying so; I hope it's clear to you, also, that it's important to me and personally rewarding to be of help to you — it's not something that requires sacrifice, nor am I burdened down with it — or with you — it's something that I choose to do and I want to do it. I'm glad I'm able to. So I'll see you next week at this same time, unless I hear from you sooner, okay?

## Client #8

*Counselor:*   Well, this has been helpful to me, Marty, to get a better picture of the whole situation and particularly what you would like to see happen. Let me just go over quickly what we've talked about and then we'll see if we can do something to get things straightened out. Okay? First, there's you — and you don't especially want to stay in the Special class — mostly because you don't know anyone in there and you have trouble sitting still and it messes up the bus you'd like to go home on, right?

*Client #8:*    Well, I just don't like to be pushed around so much.

*Counselor:*    Okay, then there's your mother and she doesn't think you should be in the Special class at all — 'cause it sounds like the school is saying there's something wrong with you — and she thinks mostly you don't try hard enough, right?

*Client #8:*    Yah, she thinks I'm lazy — but sometimes I really do have trouble understanding what the teacher wants.

*Counselor:*    Then there's your father and he doesn't particularly care whether you're in the Special class or not — just so you can be sure and go to high school and he, like you, would like to see it get settled, right?

*Client #8:*    Yah, that's right.

*Counselor:*    Finally, there's Mr. Chambers, the Special class teacher and he wants something done with you, because you cause so much disturbance in his class — but he doesn't necessarily think you should stay in there, right?

*Client #8:*    Yah, I think he's just fed up with me.

*Counselor:*    Okay, I think I have the story straight from your point of view. This whole thing has gotten pretty confused — but I think you and I are in the best position to get it unconfused. In the first place, I want you and myself and Mr. Chambers to go over your standardized tests — the ones you took in class and the ones you took alone with him — not today, but within a couple of days. And I want all three of us to look at the results of those tests and some of your school work from last year and I want all three of us, including you, to understand why you were transferred to Mr. Chambers' class in the first place. Then I want the three of us to look at what's happened since you were transferred and ask ourselves why it isn't working out and what should we do about it.

*Client #8:*    What about my mother?

*Counselor:*    Well, we will go through the whole thing again with her here — so she has a chance to say what she thinks, too. Now, Mr. Chambers makes the final decision about where you will be assigned — but I know that he will listen very carefully to what you say, what I say, and what your mother says, before he makes the decision.

*Client #8:*    Oh, I thought you had to decide . . .

*Counselor:*    No, Mr. Chambers does, but I feel I have a part in helping make the decision — mostly what I'm doing is trying to get it sorted out so a good decision, that hopefully, everybody's pleased with, can get made. So the next step is to get you and me and Mr. Chambers together within a couple of days, okay?

*Client #8:*   Yah, that's fine — am I supposed to go back to the Special class 'til then?

*Counselor:*   Yah, I think that's best for now, 'til we get it sorted out and know how it's going to be. In the meantime, and I don't think this is going to drag on much longer with you not knowing — but in the meantime, it probably would help the whole process, if you could kinda' cool it in Mr. Chambers' class — like try not to keep things in a constant turmoil —

*Client #8:*   Yah, okay — but I don't like being pushed around — but, yah, I'll shut up more.

## Summary

Regardless of the setting in which you counsel, you will encounter individuals, like the eight clients just described, who for one reason or another have experienced a significant loss of structure in their lives and as a result are quite confused. As we have seen, the onset of such confusion may be sudden because of a rapid, radical change in the person's world or the onset of confusion may be a gradual process which accompanies transitions from one developmental stage to another. Individuals who are questioning their basic assumptions about life and/or have lost confidence in their typical ways of perceiving and adjusting to daily living are likely to present themselves for counseling in any one of the variety of counseling settings available in a small town or a city. They may appear to be very disturbed or depressed; they may appear to be only mildly distressed. They may seem nearly overwhelmed with problems; they may seem to be nearly problem-free. While it is true that some clients who are facing difficult Choices or who need to make Changes in their lives will also experience considerable confusion, there are clients who are not facing any particular Choice or Change, and yet they are confused. These latter individuals have been identified as Confusion Reduction clients.

The position taken in this book is that an important and legitimate purpose for an individual's seeking counseling assistance is to reduce the confusion in his life — to sort things out, to find new ways to look at life, to reorganize or restructure the way he sees himself, other people, and the direction and meaning of his existence. In order to be able to respond to a client seeking Confusion Reduction counseling, you must recognize the legitimacy of his purpose, understand the importance of a personal structure for the individual and understand the significance of structure loss in a person's life. A complete description of the counseling skills required to assist the individual remodel old or build new structure in his life is beyond the scope of this book. However, the following references should be helpful in acquiring the requisite understanding and skill.

## Readings

1.   Erikson, E. H., 1959. Identity and the Life Cycle. *Psychological Issues*, Monograph 1. New York: International Universities.
2.   Kelly, G. A., 1963. *A Theory of Personality*. New York: Norton.
3.   Maher, B. (Ed.), 1969. *Clinical Psychology and Personality: The Selected Papers of George Kelly*. New York: Wiley.
4.   Rogers, C. R., 1951. *Client Centered Therapy*. Boston: Houghton-Mifflin.
5.   Tyler, L. E., 1969. *The Work of The Counselor*. 3d Edition. New York: Appleton-Century-Crofts.

## A Final Word on Counseling Contracts

We have examined thirty-two different counseling contracts in the three categories of counseling purposes: Choice, Change, and Confusion Reduction. Some of the contracts make use of the same or similar techniques, such as role playing, but they all have been individually tailored to the specific needs of the individuals with whom they were formulated and negotiated. You could probably generate another thirty-two contract examples and although they would undoubtedly resemble some of those presented here, they would also be unique to the particular persons with whom they were negotiated. In order to formulate and negotiate a counseling contract that is individually tailored to accomplish the particular purpose of a specific client, you will need to remember four things:

1.   *Don't hurry.* You cannot possibly understand everything you need to know about a client and his situation in a few minutes. Although you should be able to gain a clear enough picture of his purpose in seeking counseling by the end of the first interview, in order to plan with him for the next session, it may be several sessions before the purpose is sufficiently clear to apply a particular procedure.
2.   *Don't mess around.* At the same time that you must allow both yourself and the client sufficient time to understand his purpose fully, there is no place in counseling for aimless wandering and poking into this corner and that bit of history of the client's life. Counseling ought to be purposive activity and it is primarily your responsibility to structure it that way.
3.   *You can't know everything, already.* Techniques and procedures are being developed and introduced into the professional literature every year, which, if you knew about them, would probably make quite a difference in the contracts you negotiate that year. There is nothing wrong with needing to consult the literature or a specialist in a particular area, before you negotiate a counseling contract. Clients do

not regard that as inadequacy on your part. There is plenty wrong with remaining ignorant of available procedures for realizing a client's purpose.

4. *Rid yourself of silly ideas about how people should live.* If you have a very narrow view of the way people ought to conduct themselves, you are likely to ignore or refuse to consider some of the Choices or Changes or Structures which could be instrumental in a client's realizing his purpose. This does not mean that you should have *no* idea of how people ought to live; it simply means that you should know what those ideas are and that they should be subjected to your own rational analysis and to your colleagues' evaluation.

In some ways this Final Word may sound negativistic; however, it does seem to be true that people remember well those things that are ruled out or forbidden. Of course, even if you manage to never violate any of these four prohibitions, your competence as a counselor depends upon what you do more than what you do not do. So while it is important not to hurry, not to mess around, not to ignore new procedures, and not to have silly ideas about people, it is more important to understand, accept and communicate your genuine caring to a client. Section Three, which follows immediately, is concerned with these positive aspects of the counseling process.

# Section Three

## THE PROCESS OF COUNSELING

# I OVERVIEW – CHARACTERISTICS OF THE COMPETENT COUNSELOR

In 1957 Carl Rogers published what could now be called a critical article in the literature that concerns the process of counseling and psychotherapy. Rogers' clear and concise statement of what he considered to be the "necessary and sufficient conditions of therapeutic personality change" specified three therapist attributes: *congruence, unconditional positive regard*, and *empathic understanding*. Rogers' discussion focused on the characteristics of the therapist as a person and definitely deemphasized the significance of any particular things the therapist might say or do. Based on his professional experience as a practitioner-researcher-teacher, Rogers stated that the process of therapy (or counseling) is highly dependent upon the kind of person the therapist is. In fact, Rogers takes the position that the personal qualities which the therapist communicates to the client are vastly more important than any particular procedures or techniques the therapist has mastered.

For constructive personality change to occur, it is necessary that these conditions exist and continue over a period of time:

1. Two persons are in psychological contact.
2. The first, whom we shall term the client, is in a state of incongruence, being vulnerable or anxious.
3. The second person, whom we shall term the therapist, is congruent or integrated in the relationship.
4. The therapist experiences unconditional positive regard for the client.
5. The therapist experiences an empathic understanding of the client's internal frame of reference and endeavors to communicate this experience to the client.
6. The communication to the client of the therapist's empathic understanding and unconditional positive regard is to a minimal degree achieved.

No other conditions are necessary. If these six conditions exist, and continue over a period of time, this is sufficient. The process of constructive personality change will follow (p. 96).

If there is any startling feature in the formulation which has been given as to the necessary conditions for therapy, it probably lies in the elements which are omitted.

For example, it is not stated that these conditions apply to one type of client, and that other conditions are necessary to bring about psychotherapeutic change with other types of clients.

It is not stated that psychotherapy is a special kind of relationship, different in kind from all others which occur in everyday life. It will be evident instead that for brief moments at least many good friendships fulfill the six conditions.

It is not stated that special intellectual professional knowledge — psychological, psychiatric, medical, or religious — is required of the therapist. . . . Intellectual training and the acquiring of information has, I believe, many valuable results, but becoming a therapist is not one of these results.

It is not stated that it is necessary for psychotherapy that the therapist have an accurate psychological diagnosis of the client. . . . I am forced to the conclusion that such diagnostic knowledge is not essential to psychotherapy. It may even be that its defense as a necessary prelude to psychotherapy is simply a protective alternative to the admission that it is, for the most part, a colossal waste of time (pp. 100–102).

Ten years later, in a book entitled *Toward Effective Counseling and Psychotherapy*, Truax and Carkhuff summarized and discussed the sizeable amount of research that was stimulated by Rogers' 1957 formulations. During that ten-year period, Truax and Carkhuff, who are responsible for the largest portion of research in this area, reformulated Rogers' original "necessary and sufficient conditions" and have suggested three "central therapeutic ingredients" — *accurate empathy, nonpossessive warmth* and *authenticity* or *genuineness*. Although Truax and Carkhuff (1967) attribute the major impetus for their own research to Carl Rogers, they offer a helpful review of the writings of other psychotherapists and counselors in which they were able to identify constructs sufficiently similar to empathy, warmth and genuineness that the reader is able to see a convergence of theoretical positions.

Despite the bewildering array of divergent theories and the difficulty in translating concepts from the language of one theory to that of another, several common threads weave their way through almost every major theory of psychotherapy and counseling, including the psychoanalytic, the client-centered, the behavioristic, and many of the more eclectic and derivative theories. In one way or another, all have emphasized the importance of the therapist's ability to be integrated, mature, genuine, authentic, or congruent in his relationship to the patient. They have all stressed also, the importance of the therapist's ability to provide a non-threatening, trusting, safe, or secure atmosphere by his acceptance, nonpossessive warmth, unconditional positive regard, or love. Finally, virtually all theories of psychotherapy emphasize that for the therapist to be helpful, he must be accurately empathic, be "with" the client, be understanding, or grasp the patient's meaning.

These three sets of characteristics can, for lack of better words, be termed *accurate empathy, nonpossessive warmth* and *genuineness* (p. 25).

Leona Tyler, whose writings have had a tremendous impact on the practice of counseling, might well have been cited by Truax and Carkhuff as another practitioner whose conception of the counseling process closely parallels Rogers' view of therapy. The second edition of Tyler's *The Work of the Counselor* (1961) places particular emphasis on two therapist characteristics (empathy and warmth) which Tyler calls *understanding* and *acceptance.* In the recent third edition of *The Work of the Counselor* (1969), Tyler makes explicit the parallels between her own conception of the essential qualities of the counseling encounter and the Rogers-Truax-Carkhuff formulations.

At the very heart of the counseling process is a *meeting* of counselor and client. Whether they meet for fifteen of fifty minutes, whether they talk about symptoms, explore feelings, or discuss facts and schedules, whether the client confronts the counselor alone or as a member of a group — whatever influence counseling has is related most closely to the nature of the relationship that grows out of this encounter.

The reason it has been difficult to analyze what good counselors *do* in this situation, so that others can be trained to do likewise, is that the essential components are attitudes rather than skills. By his actions, words, gestures, and facial expressions, the counselor must communicate *acceptance, understanding* and *sincerity* (p. 33).

Figure 4 summarizes the characteristics of the competent counselor as presented by Rogers in 1957, Truax and Carkhuff in 1967 and Tyler in 1969.

In addition to the three essential qualities of the competent counselor, Tyler names and discusses a single basic skill which is common to all types of counseling in all of the various counseling settings — *Communication.* Here again the agreement among theorists/practitioners is nearly unanimous — communication skills are either obviously assumed to be or directly discussed as being vital to effective counseling or psychotherapy. The terms used to describe communication skills have ranged widely, for example, "listening with the third ear," "accurate data-processing and retrieval," or "really getting with the person and telling it like it is." However, in the interest of consistency and clarity, Tyler's terminology is used throughout this book. Understanding + Acceptance + Sincerity x Communication   Skills = Effective   Counseling   Encounter.

FIGURE 4.     Characteristics of the Competent Counselor

| ROGERS (1957) | TRUAX AND CARKHUFF (1967) | TYLER (1969) |
|---|---|---|
| Necessary and Sufficient Conditions of Therapeutic Personality Change. | Central Therapeutic Ingredients | Essential Qualities of the Effective Counselor |
| Empathic Understanding | Accurate Empathy | Understanding |
| Unconditional Positive Regard | Nonpossessive Warmth | Acceptance |
| Congruence | Genuineness or Authenticity | Sincerity |

Understanding, together with acceptance, together with sincerity, all amplified by skillful communication, lead to an effective counseling encounter.

The remainder of this Third Section has one purpose: to provide different ways of viewing the four components which together give rise to effective counseling or therapeutic encounter. These different views could be thought of as analogous to contemporary television coverage of a ball game or a parade or a political event. There are the *close-ups* where the camera zooms in on some fine detail of the central event; there are the *aerial shots* where the central event is viewed within its larger context; there are the *medium-range shots* where the central event action can be easily followed; and there are the *split-screen shots* where two or more things which are normally not juxtaposed can be tracked simultaneously. We will attempt to capture these different perspectives as we view the essential components of the effective counseling encounter.


## II  UNDERSTANDING


According to Tyler (1969), "To understand is simply to grasp clearly and completely the meaning the client is trying to convey" (p. 36). If it is possible to describe understanding in such clear and simple language, then why does it seem that really understanding another person is such a complicated and difficult process? The same paradox stated another way points to the fact that people go around understanding one another every day and, in addition, people have done that for ages, long before anyone ever thought about counseling or psychotherapy — so why all the fuss about the importance and the difficulty of training counselors to be understanding? Using the "television coverage" analogy, we will attempt to resolve this paradox by first taking an aerial view of understanding in the context of human relationships in general. Next we will move into a middle-range view of understanding in the counseling relationship, and then move to a close-up view of *what* to understand about the client and *how* to understand it. In the close-up views of what and how to understand, we will juxtapose descriptions of understanding and hypothetical client-counselor interactions designed to illustrate a high degree of understanding.

From the instant an infant arrives, and probably before, he is actively involved in trying to grasp the meaning of himself and things around him. Most of his time and energy is dedicated to bringing order to the chaos outside himself and the incessant changes within himself. As his ability to control what he sees, touches, and tastes increases, the world becomes more predictable and thus more meaningful. Turning his eyes toward a sound source predictably results in seeing something new or something familiar; reaching out and grasping in a particular direction predictably results in holding his own foot. With the acquisition of locomotor skills and language, the individual's ability to predict and assign meaning to himself and his world seems almost limitless. The process of understanding is basically the same for the toddler who is trying to grasp the full meaning of a bright red rubber ball as it is for the scientist who is trying to grasp the full meaning of a bright shiny moon.

## Understanding — Dynamic Interaction

A particularly important arena of understanding for both the toddler and the scientist is that involving other people. A unique feature of people, that both the toddler and the scientist must appreciate, is that unlike rubber balls or moons, people "understand back." Grasping the full meaning of, and/or being able to predict people is, obviously, a very difficult task because of how complex people are. But what is already a difficult task is further complicated by the fact that if you get "close enough" to understand a particular individual, you are also close enough for him to begin understanding you. This dynamic interaction between the one who is trying to understand and the one being understood is inevitable and inescapable whenever one individual attempts to understand another.

There are many ways, of course, to cope with this situation. One solution for people in general, and for each of us some of the time, is to remain sufficiently removed from one another that the complicating interaction is at a minimum. When we do that, of course, we also reduce the degree of understanding that it is possible to achieve. In a world where there is literally less and less physical space per person, and mass media are increasingly pervasive, it appears that remaining removed from one another is being ruled out as a way to cope with the difficulties encountered in understanding one another. Another solution has been to settle for a rough approximation of what someone else means, or a rough guess as to what he will do, and not be too concerned about the times you are wrong. Again, in a world in which more and more time is spent involved with other people — a world in which the nature of work has less to do with things, and more to do with people-oriented goods and services — being wrong about what a person means, or what he is going to do is more serious. On an even larger scale, with change occurring at an accelerating rate and the tremendous potential for vast destruction, there is a sense of urgency about not making mistakes concerning what others mean, or what they will do — our very survival may depend on achieving a thorough understanding. The last type of solution we will consider, which people in general have developed to cope with the difficulty in understanding one another, is very much like the way understanding is achieved in counseling. That is, every effort is made to get close enough to understand one another in depth at the same time that effort is made to understand the dynamic interactive process of trying to grasp one another's meaning.

Good parent-child relationships, satisfying marital relationships and solid friendships are all characterized by a sustained effort to move toward the other person and also to understand both the process and the outcome of moving toward one another. A basic mechanism of such understanding has been described by G. H. Mead (see Morris [1934] and Strauss [1964] ) as "taking the role of the other." By putting yourself in the other person's shoes and looking out from his vantage point, it is easier to grasp what he means and predict what he will likely do. The invitation to take the role of another comes early with such requests as, "Think how that makes Mommy feel when you do that!" Later, it more probably will sound like, "How would you like to be me and have to deal with you?" or "Reverse the situation, is that the way you want me to treat you?" This way of coping with the difficulty and complexity of human interaction, namely, "taking the role of the other," is usually called "empathizing," and as already stated, is most like the way understanding is accomplished in good parent-child, marital, or friendship interactions, as well as in a counseling relationship — which we will focus on now as we shift from this rather sweeping aerial view of understanding in human relations to a more middle-range view of understanding in the counseling relationship.

In summary, we have examined the paradox of why understanding — grasping another's meaning — is so important and so difficult in counseling. The process of humans understanding one another seems commonplace and something one begins learning early. However, much of the so-called understanding between persons results from a combination of simplifying matters by staying out of one another's way, and settling for only rough estimates of one another's meaning. In contrast, those persons who are engaged in an attempt to understand one another clearly and completely, find it to be both difficult and demanding.

At the same time that the above remarks are intended to underscore the arduousness of trying to understand another person, they are also intended to have an encouraging effect on the counselor in training. Even though counseling is a demanding activity, you have spent a lifetime being prepared for it. All of your efforts to understand other people, and particularly your understanding of those relationships which have been both close and meaningful, are applicable to understanding as a counselor. There are many ways in which the role of counselor is like that of a good mother or father, husband or wife, friend or teacher. But there are also characteristics of the counselor's role which distinguish it from all the others: (1) limited reciprocity and mutuality; (2) limited time, place and involvement; (3) initial commitment to termination.

## Limited Reciprocity and Mutuality

In an age when there is considerable emphasis upon questioning, redefining, and removing restrictions, it may seem anachronistic to talk about the therapeutic use of limits. But greater freedom to choose and greater freedom to change does not alter the fact that when one chooses or changes, some things are ruled out as others are selected, and some things are eliminated as others are elected. By limiting reciprocity and mutuality in the counseling relationship, the chances that the counselor will be thoroughly understood by the client are very slight. However, the choice to limit a relationship in this way opens up the possibility for both the client and the counselor to understand the client in great depth. The time and energies of both counselor and client are invested in understanding the client; the counselor in particular is actively involved in processing messages from the client in order to more clearly and completely capture the client's meaning. The process of representing the client, that is, placing the client before both of them, allows the client to correct the distorted portions of the counselor's representation, and by successive approximations, a clearer more complete picture of the client emerges. Whereas it is not desirable for the counselor to be a total enigma to the client, neither is it necessary that all facets of the counselor's existence be clearly and completely understood. Even when there is considerable commonality in the counselor's and client's experience of some parts of their lives, it is frequently quite irrelevant and inappropriate for the counselor to share that with his client. In short, the counseling relationship is characterized by two people focusing on only one of them, rather than on each other.

## Limited Time, Place, and Involvement

A second way in which the counseling relationship is intentionally limited involves the choice of topics to be discussed and when, where, and how extensively they will be discussed. It is patently obvious that the counselor will seriously limit his understanding of the client if he is the sole and arbitrary judge of what should be talked about, when, and for how long. On the other hand, neither is the counselor free to wander about aimlessly hoping something of significance will turn up. Because of a desire to be "spontaneous" and to avoid being authoritarian, counselors are often loath to deal with the limits of time, place, and topic. Unfortunately, their counseling interactions are like dictionary definitions of spontaneous: "impulsive, instinctive, automatic, and mechanical, engaging neither the mind nor the emotions." A productive counseling interaction — one that promotes understanding — falls somewhere between a business meeting with a fixed agenda, and an uncharted encounter between two friends engaged in mutual psychic exploration. Subsequently we will be taking a close-up look at the "what to" and "how to" of understanding. It suffices to say at this point that the counselor's willingness to work within certain constraints on time, place, and topic facilitates the forward movement of counseling.

## Initial Commitment to Termination

The final limitation which we will consider now is contained in the fact that from the outset, a counseling relationship is intended to be transitory. The initial commitment to eventual termination places a very valuable constraint on the counseling process, namely, counseling should contribute to the client's being better able to go on alone. This is not to say that the client should be freed from all need of counseling in the future. There will very likely be future situations in which the client could benefit greatly from a counselor's assistance with personal choices and/or changes. What it does say is that the counseling process should foster greater self-understanding and independence within the client. If only the counselor gains a clearer and more complete understanding of the client, while the client himself learns to passively endure his own personal confusion, then the risk is high that the client will also acquire a debilitating dependency on the counselor's understanding. The best safeguard against such an outcome is a process in which both client and counselor actively participate and work together to understand the client. To facilitate this cooperative effort, the counselor avoids any esoteric, magical mumbo-jumbo or parading of his intuitive prowess. Rather the counselor uses his special skills in listening and talking as a model for the client; this usually results in the client becoming more skillful in listening and talking to himself and to others. Because the counseling interaction is terminal and usually relatively brief, understanding on the part of the counselor should promote greater client self-understanding which the client can readily translate into other dimensions of his life.

We are going to adjust our "video camera range" again and zoom in on *what* it is that the counselor and client need to understand and *how* the counselor in particular makes that happen. The unit of our analysis is no longer as broad as "people in general"; we are now focusing in on a particular person in transaction with his unique world. What both the counselor and client need to grasp clearly and completely is the meaning of *this* client interacting with his own special situation. Regardless of the later course of counseling or psychotherapy — whether it is primarily Choice or Change or Confusion Reduction that needs to occur — the initial task is always the same: to gain an understanding of the client in transaction with his world.

## Three-phase Model of the Understanding Process

At any point in time, understanding what another person is doing, thinking, and feeling is an amazingly complicated perceptual-cognitive task. Using a three-stage model, the understanding process can be represented as follows:

FIGURE 5.    The Process of Understanding

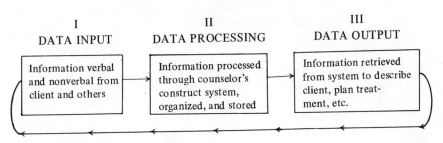

| I<br>DATA INPUT | II<br>DATA PROCESSING | III<br>DATA OUTPUT |
|---|---|---|
| Information verbal and nonverbal from client and others | Information processed through counselor's construct system, organized, and stored | Information retrieved from system to describe client, plan treatment, etc. |

Obviously this is a crude and simplistic model of a highly refined and complex process. Nevertheless, the model can serve us well in the sense that if we share the same framework and some of the same terms, the chances are much better that we will be able to understand and keep track of one another. This is especially true when what we are trying to understand and track is very complicated; there are so many places to get off track and misunderstand. I trust that the parallel between you trying to understand my writing about the understanding process and either of us trying to understand a client talking about himself is clear. In both instances, it is helpful if we share the same framework and some of the same terms. It is for this reason that the data processing system (Phase II) to be outlined below is comprised largely of nontechnical terminology. The value of using nontechnical terms or common sense language for understanding another person is discussed and defended by Fritz Heider in his pivotal work on interpersonal perception entitled *The Psychology of Interpersonal Relations* (1958).

Before proceeding to the data-processing system (Phase II), two other points need to be made. The first concerns the wisdom of having a well-defined or clearly specified system at all; the second concerns the dynamic vs. static quality of the system as indicated by the continuous loop in Figure 5. There are practitioners who would discourage the beginning counselor/therapist from using any predetermined data-processing system. Instead, the novice would be encouraged to learn to empty his head of preconceptions and biases and simply listen carefully to what the client says verbally and nonverbally about himself. The counselor is to become a *tabula rasa* upon which the client writes and sketches an image of himself. A question arises, however, concerning how rasa anybody's tabula can become.

Unfortunately, there is no reason to believe that it is even possible for an adult human to divest himself of all predetermined ways of receiving information, regardless of how desirable it might be. The fact that the counselor possesses a language and a personal history of experiences stored in the terms of that language and that the client is also using that language is inescapable. Rather than attempting to rid himself completely of preconceived notions, which is, no doubt, impossible, the counselor's efforts should be directed toward acquainting himself as thoroughly as he can with what his preconceptions actually are. With that kind of self-knowledge, the counselor is in a position to plan what kinds of preconceptions he would like to possess. For example, two terms which are associated with a tremendous range of experiences are "sex" and "religion." Rather than trying to divest yourself of all preconceived ways of receiving a client's messages about sex and/or religion, what makes more sense is first to discover your present preconceptions about sex and religion and then, if necessary, plan ways to modify those preconceptions in ways that facilitate understanding clients' messages. We will discuss how counselors can accomplish planned modification of their own preconceptions in the section dealing with Acceptance which follows.

Those practitioners who object to talking about data-processing systems are usually concerned about a very important aspect of understanding another person, namely, appreciating the uniqueness of each individual. There is no disagreement between the position taken in this book and the position of those who believe that the counselor must understand each client as a separate and unique person rather than as a collection of diagnostic categories. Any disagreement is over what constitutes the best means for accomplishing this end. Instead of attempting the impossible, namely, suspending all personal data-processing systems, the position taken here is that the counselor should develop a data-processing system which guarantees that each client's unique and individualized pattern or mode of existence will emerge clearly as the counselor and client interact.

This then brings us to the second point which concerns the dynamic quality of the data-processing system. It is imperative that the counselor be willing to forgo the personal expectations that he will understand the client either immediately or totally; instead, the counselor must be willing to begin a series of successive approximations through which the client's meaning becomes increasingly clear and more complete. But the increasing clarity of such a series depends on the counselor's willingness to encourage the client to correct or modify the counselor's representations (Phase III), so that distortion is reduced.

This is indicated in Figure 5. by the "conveyor belt" continuous loop; client input affects counselor output which, in turn, affects further client input so that the next counselor output can more accurately represent what the client is trying to convey. Keeping in mind that what we are trying to develop is a highly individualized representation which captures the client's uniqueness, and that we develop such a representation through a series of successive approximations from which the client helps remove the distortion, let us now turn to the system.

## Person-Situation Transactions — The T-Formation

As was discussed in Section One, there are three major life task areas, Work, Relationship, and Aloneness, with which every individual must cope throughout his entire life. At different developmental stages, each area is dealt with differently; during some periods one area is more central to the person's existence than are the other two. For some people the three areas blend together into a complimentary combination of activity and meaning; for other people there is constant conflict among the activities in one area and the demands of the other areas. As was discussed in Section Two, people seek counseling or are "encouraged" to seek counseling when at least one of three conditions exists: (1) they are facing a choice or choices in one or more of the three life task areas; (2) they desire personal change or changes in one or more of the three life task areas; (3) they have become very confused (either suddenly or gradually) about how to organize and make sense out of life in one or more of the three life task areas. Before a counselor or therapist, regardless of his theoretical persuasion, can agree to assist a client with either making decisions or modifying his behavior or reducing the confusion in his life, the counselor or therapist must be able to represent to himself, to the client, and to his professional colleagues, an accurate picture of this particular client in transaction with his world.

Figure 6 which has been dubbed the "T-formation" is one way to think about person-situation transactions.

As a client begins to disclose himself and his situation (Phase I) the counselor receives and processes this information (Phase II) and then represents the client-in-transaction for correction or confirmation by the client (Phase III). Using Figure 6 as a guide, during Phase II, the counselor sorts incoming information into data that primarily belong to the Person, and data that primarily belong to the Person's Situation. This is a crude, initial sorting into "inside information," that is, within the person, and "outside information," that is, outside the person's skin. Once something has been sorted into Person or Situation (inside or outside) information, it can be further sorted into one of several relatively stable or enduring categories under the two major headings. On the Person side those subcategories are: Values, Interests, Abilities, and Expectations. On the Situation side, the subcategories are: Family and Other Personal Commitments, Opportunities, and Social/Cultural Rules. Since the

FIGURE 6.    The Person-Situation T-formation.

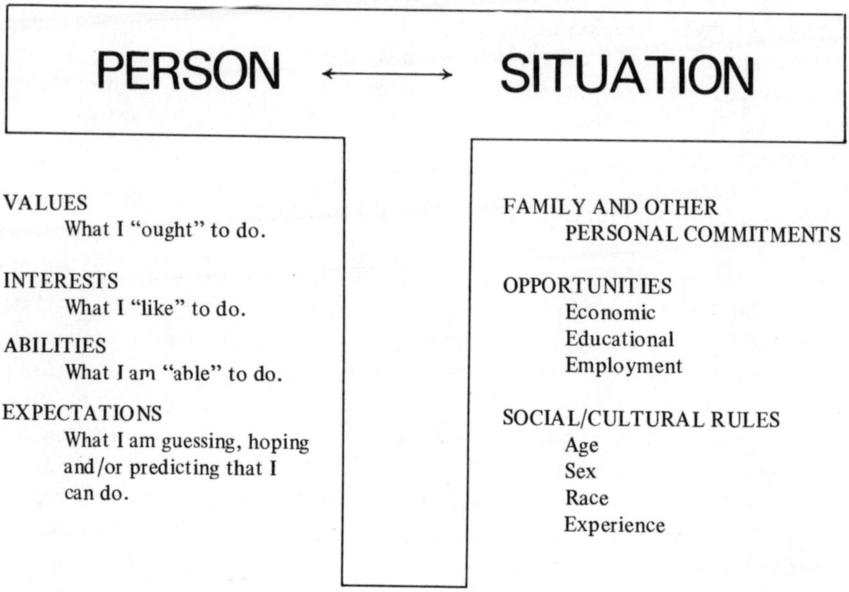

```
 _____
|                                                      |
|    PERSON  ←————————→  SITUATION                      |
|_____|_____|
                              |
VALUES                        |    FAMILY AND OTHER
    What I "ought" to do.      |         PERSONAL COMMITMENTS
                              |
INTERESTS                     |    OPPORTUNITIES
    What I "like" to do.       |         Economic
                              |         Educational
ABILITIES                     |         Employment
    What I am "able" to do.    |
                              |    SOCIAL/CULTURAL RULES
EXPECTATIONS                  |         Age
    What I am guessing, hoping |         Sex
    and/or predicting that I   |         Race
    can do.                    |         Experience
                              |
                              |
```

"T-formation" is *not* used as an outline for a counselor-directed interview that has been cleverly disguised, we will not go over each category in detail in order to define what is a "scorable response." The T-formation is merely one way to sort out and chunk together the complex welter of information that pours forth from a client who is simply describing some aspects of his daily life. Thus, what will probably be the most helpful are the following examples of two persons with very different situations, and how the T-formation categories can help sort out the person-situation data in each case.

## Two Cases Using T-Formation Categories

### The Case of Jim Linton

Jim Linton, a twenty-year-old junior, requested an appointment at the University Counseling Center late in the spring. He explained to the counselor that he didn't know whether to stay at school during the summer and take a physiology course he needed, or whether to return home and work in the City Recreation Department as he had done last summer. So he thought maybe he could get some advice at the Counseling Center.

*Directions the Counselor Might Take:*

1. make a speech about the Counseling Center not being a place to get advice and that Jim will have to make the decision himself.
2. ask whether or not he can support himself if he stays on campus and if he really needs the physiology course now.
3. ask him to say a little more about his situation.

Alternative #1 could be done in a very friendly, helpful way and seemingly be an attempt to place responsibility in Jim's hands by gently refusing to take an advice-giving role. However, this early in the interaction, there has not been time to assess whether or not Jim will try to force the counselor to take over. A speech at this point would be an overreaction to the words "get some advice" and would be a put-down, no matter how helpful it sounded. It would represent the counselor's insistence that the client understand the counselor's role, rather than the emphasis being on the counselor understanding the client. Alternative #2 has the focus on Jim and his concerns, but is a premature, problem-solving effort that simply retards or interferes with the understanding process. The counselor who begins to ask specific questions at this stage is assuming that he knows better than the client what are the relevant bits of information. Unless the client is insistent on telling it his way, they will now enter a question and answer period in which the counselor takes the role of a detective sleuthing out clues. Alternative #3 is clearly preferred and produced the following information.

Jim is a premed major but he is unsure if he wants to go on in it. He has had quite a bit of trouble with chemistry and was on academic probation one term last year. He always thought he wanted to be a doctor. His father died when he was nine; his mother had been counting on his becoming a doctor. He has one older sister who is married and didn't finish college. His mother has been looking forward to his being home again this summer. She works in an office and is pretty independent, but she really relies on him. His dad left her enough money so things are really not tough financially, but she gets pretty lonesome. Last winter he moved out of the dorm into an apartment with his girl friend who is an English major. They don't know whether they will get married or not — they really like each other, but she wants to get a master's degree and then teach in a junior college, and he still has medical school. Jim thinks that she would really like him to stay at school this summer, although they haven't talked about it a lot.

*Directions the Counselor might take:*

1. Comment on how you have noticed that several of your clients who are cohabiting with someone, or who have similar living arrangements seem to be experiencing quite a bit of conflict.
2. Point out that the problem seems to be that Jim is caught between his mother's demands and his girl friend's demands on him.

3. Indicate that there seem to be at least two clusters of conflict and confusion: one concerning whether to stay at school or go home for the summer and the other concerning whether to continue in premed or to consider another major. Ask if it would be helpful to discuss one or both of these.

Alternative #1 is a thinly veiled rejection of Jim because of his choice to live with his girl friend. Although it sounds somewhat like an attempt to understand Jim's dilemma, it draws attention to the fact that he is one client among a professional counselor's caseload of troubled people. Such distancing from Jim would probably be a result of the counselor's inability to accept values different from his own coupled with the counselor's unwillingness to ignore the difference or state his biases openly. Alternative #1 does not further understanding, and it would probably be perceived as phoney. Alternative #2 does not reject Jim nor does it carry the phoney double message, "I'm concerned about you and think you're valuable, but I disapprove of you." However, Alternative #2 contains an interpretation (mother vs. girl friend) that is also a premature problem-solving attempt. Even though this is a good hypothesis and may turn out to be the case, it is too early to assume that the counselor has sufficient understanding of Jim and his situation to warrant formulating "the problem." Alternative #3 is preferred because it summarizes and organizes much of what Jim has said into two clusters. Jim can now reject or modify the counselor's formulations of his situation, or if they are accurate, Jim can indicate which one is the more important one to talk about first. Although they overlap in some ways, these two clusters represent two of the three life task areas, namely, Relationship and Work.

Alternative #3 resulted in Jim's talking about how much he wants to be able to help people and that he had always thought that becoming a doctor would be the best way. Jim said that he had been a camp counselor for the past two summers at a Recreation Department camp for predelinquent boys, and that he just seemed to be able to understand the boys and gain their confidence quickly. The camp director last year even suggested that he should consider that kind of work as a career. But somehow not going on in premed seems like running away. His science and math courses have been very difficult and he really disliked most of them, except general biology and embryology. One of his friends was a recreation major, and that seemed like it would be great, except it also seemed sort of Mickey Mouse. Although he doesn't think it's just the money and prestige attached to being a doctor, he recognizes that it's really important to him to make something of himself. He hasn't talked this over with anyone, except briefly with the camp director. He just figured he knew that he was going to be a doctor, and so there was no reason to think about anything else. But, as Jim says, "It's hard to be nearly twenty-one years old and still wondering what you're going to be when you grow up!"

The meaning or significance of an event or a thing is fully understandable only if the episode or thing is seen in context or against the backdrop of its situation. In Jim's case, the decision to go home or stay for summer session can be understood fully only when that decision is seen in relation to the many other transactions in his life. It would have been easy to jump to the conclusion that Jim had a "relationship problem" (mother vs. girl friend); however, when the uncertainty about whether or not to go home is seen in a wider context, it then is more accurately understood as Jim's uncertainty about the direction of his life work (medicine vs. recreation/juvenile counseling).

Referring to the T-formation, it is possible to sift out some of the personal/situational variables in Jim's life. We know about some of Jim's values or what he thinks he *ought* to do: help people, not run away from difficult situations or take the easy way out, make something of his life, be able to be proud of what he has achieved. We also have some leads about what Jim *likes* to do: listen to people, talk with people, be outdoors, participate in and lead camp activities. Using the Dictionary of Occupational Titles (1965) classification of types of work activities, namely, "people, data or things," we would probably describe Jim as most liking to do things that center around people and as least liking to do things that center around data. As far as what Jim is *able* to do, we know that he is struggling and barely managing a premedical course and that in contrast he rather easily is able to deal effectively with the recreation leader/juvenile counselor role. The final category on the Person side of the "T," *expectations* is perhaps the most unclear at this point. Until now, Jim has been telling himself and others that he was expecting to become a doctor because (1) he thought he was *able* to, (2) he thought he would *like* to, and (3) he thought he *ought* to. However, Jim has become less and less certain about the likelihood of this expectation. The probability of this possibility seems to be decreasing. Turning to the Situation side of the T-formation, we are unable to spot any major obstacles that hinder Jim from moving ahead in whatever direction he chooses. If Jim were black or poor or female, then we *would* find obstacles to his going ahead in a number of directions, including medicine. We do know a considerable amount about various aspects of Jim's situation. For example, we know something about Mother and the strong investment Jim perceives her to have in his future. It is less clear what role Jim's girlfriend plays in planning his future. We know that Jim's economic picture looks bright enough to not be a hindrance, but his undergraduate academic record casts a dark shadow over being selected for admission to a first-rate medical school. Finally, we know that Jim experiences the somewhat vague, but very real, social pressure on most young men his age to know what they are doing; to be undecided is viewed as immature, weak and stupid.

Given the information you have about Jim as a person in transaction with the world around him, there are probably other important aspects of Jim and his situation that you feel you understand or that you would like to understand more clearly. The T-formation is simply one way to sort out and keep track of these various dimensions of a person and his situation.

*The Case of Jennie Stevens*

Another way to think about the T-formation is to let the "T" stand for "trying," and use the categories to help sort through and understand what it is that a person is *trying* to do. When we use the T-formation in this way, our emphasis is on understanding the motivational aspects of a person and his situation. Trying, motivation, purposes, and goals are all terms we use to refer to two aspects of a person's behavior: (1) his *intentions*, which concern the direction of his actions, and (2) his *exertions*, which concern the effort or investment he makes. Intention discloses what a person is trying to do and exertion discloses how hard the person is trying to do it (Heider, 1958). In order to illustrate this use of the T-formation in helping sort through information and understand an individual, we will use the case of Jennie Stevens, a 14-year-old eighth grader who was referred to the junior high school counselor.

Jennie was asked to come to the girls' counselor's office following a conversation between the counselor and the home economics teacher, Miss Bailey, in which the teacher expressed concern over Jennie's recent lack of involvement in class and her apparent avoidance of the home ec. teacher. It seems that Jennie has been relatively close to Miss Bailey for over a year, ever since Jennie accompanied her to a local nursing home to deliver Christmas cookies which the home ec. class had baked. However, in the last two months, Miss Bailey has hardly been able to get Jennie to carry on even a very brief conversation. Miss Bailey also has noticed that Jennie has been eating lunch regularly with a group of ninth graders who have come to be known as the school hippies. This group of boys and girls dress differently from most other students, and they are reputed to be drug users. Jennie is not unknown to the counselor; she is the younger sister of last year's student body president. Jennie's parents requested a conference with the counselor at the beginning of the year. Their concern was how they could entice Jennie into studying harder and getting better grades now. They were worried that having already repeated one grade (fourth grade), and with intelligence test scores below normal, Jennie might not learn the proper study habits to insure her going to college.

Having agreed to respond to Miss Bailey's request for advice and/or assistance about relating to Jennie, the school counselor called Jennie to the counseling office. The counselor very openly stated how it came about that Jennie was called in — the home ec. teacher's concerns were summarized briefly and Jennie was asked if she would be willing to discuss the situation. Initially Jennie's response was hostile and defensive. She said she didn't know what business it was of Miss Bailey's, and that she hadn't done anything wrong.

*Directions the Counselor might take:*

1.  Explain to Jennie that she *is* the home ec. teacher's business and that nobody is accusing her of doing anything wrong, and that she should appreciate their efforts to help her.

2. State that unless Jennie is willing to talk about it, you have no choice but to alert her parents that trouble may be brewing.
3. State that it is understandable that Jennie would be angry about being hauled into the counselor's office because some teacher is up tight, but apparently she hasn't always felt that Miss Bailey is a nosey creep — does she understand how it all changed so much?

Alternatives #1 and #2 are both very rejecting, and place considerable distance between Jennie and the counselor. Whereas #1 is merely a defensive demand for Jennie to stop acting angry and be nice, #2 is an open threat designed to coerce Jennie into being cooperative — a contradiction both in terms and in basic values — coercion and cooperation simply do not go together. In Alternative #3, the counselor does not disown the fact that the situation is somewhat coercive (being hauled in), and the language legitimizes Jennie's anger (e.g., angry, hauled in, some teacher, up-tight, nosey creep). However, it also goes on then to a noncoercive inquiry about how Jennie views the situation.

In response to Alternative #3, Jennie burst into tears and said that Miss Bailey didn't like her anymore — ever since she quit going to Sunset Manor on Saturdays.

*Directions the Counselor might take:*
1. Reassure Jennie that of course Miss Bailey likes her or else she wouldn't be so worried.
2. Tell Jennie it probably isn't *that* serious, and that if she will just talk to Miss Bailey it will be all right.
3. Acknowledge that Jennie feels pretty badly about the situation and that you don't fully understand what it is like for her, and that you would like to understand it.

Alternatives #1 and #2 are tempting denials of Jennie's feelings. But they are cheap reassurances, since they are based largely on ignorance of the situation, and a benign belief that life really isn't so bad. With Alternative #3, the counselor does not deny or avoid Jennie's pain, but by wanting to understand it, the counselor communicates a sense of hope that is not easily overwhelmed. Alternative #3 functioned as an invitation to Jennie to talk more about her situation.

After the Christmas visit to the Sunset Manor Nursing Home, Jennie began visiting there every Saturday. The old people were very pleased with her, and many of them said it was the best part of the week. Each week on the following Monday, Jennie went in to talk with Miss Bailey about her Saturday visit. After about six weeks, however, Jennie's parents began to insist that she should either be studying at home or in the public library on Saturday, rather than going to Sunset Manor. Since she was barely passing in two subjects and failing a third,

Jennie felt that she couldn't argue. Jennie said that it has always been this way, ever since she had rheumatic fever in the second grade. She nearly died and her mother has worried and fussed over her ever since.

*Directions the Counselor might take:*
1. State that you are sure Jennie realizes that her mother probably is afraid something bad will happen and she worries because she cares about Jennie so much.
2. Ask Jennie if she knows why her parents want her to study hard and why her mother worries so much.
3. State that it must have been really hard to think about not going back to the nursing home on Saturdays.

Alternative #3 is focused on Jennie and her experience; the statement indicates that the counselor has a picture of and a feeling for what it must have been like, in short, that the counselor understands. Alternative #3 says, "I am with you; I understand; please go on." Alternatives #1 and #2 are both focused on Jennie's parents rather than on Jennie and thus they are distracting. Alternative #1 reduces to an attempt by the counselor to explain Jennie to herself, rather than an effort to encourage Jennie to describe herself to the counselor. The question in Alternative #2 is probably designed to find out if Jennie knows the right answer rather than to request clarification or correction of a counselor output. There is nothing intrinsically objectionable about asking a question; however, clumsy attempts to play Socrates and thereby lead the client to discover a startling insight which the counselor just had are inefficient at best, and most frequently quite offensive.

In response to Alternative #3, Jennie said she stopped going to the nursing home on Saturdays, but she didn't tell Miss Bailey how it happened because she *"knew"* that Miss Bailey was really disappointed in her and it was better not to talk about it. The Monday after the first Saturday that Jennie missed was just awful because Jennie was sure Miss Bailey knew she hadn't gone, but Miss Bailey didn't mention it to her so she knew it was better not to talk about it. After school Jennie was in the girls' room crying when Debbie Frazer came in. Jennie didn't know Debbie very well then, but Debbie asked what was wrong, and said she would like to help Jennie. Debbie is one of the "hippies." She and another friend who is also a hippie said they would walk home with Jennie. Jennie said that Debbie and some of the other hippie kids are nicer to her than anybody ever was. They don't seem to care that she gets bad grades or that she doesn't have very many friends. Jennie said she hasn't ever gone to any of their parties or anything, but they let her eat lunch with them every day.

The issue at hand is to illustrate how the T-formation facilitates our understanding of a person, especially in terms of what the person is trying to do. We know there are at least three clusters of things Jennie is trying to do: (1) *Work.* The question is, how can Jennie invest her time and energies so that she experiences herself as competently coping with life? (2) *Relationship*. The question is, how can Jennie manage her involvements with other people, e.g., her parents, Miss Bailey, Debbie and the other hippies, the old people in the nursing home, the counselor, so that they are satisfying to both herself and the others? (3) *Aloneness*. The question is, how can Jennie best come to terms with her own individuality — the person she is, apart from her relationships with others? In all three life task areas, answers to these questions depend on the interaction between what is inside Jennie and what is in the world around her. In order to understand Jennie and her situation there are many pieces of information that the counselor needs to know and many of these must come from Jennie herself. Before any plan to solve Jennie's "problems" is even considered, there are aspects of Jennie and her world that still need to be more clearly understood. For example, turning to the categories on the Person side of of the T-formation, what *are* Jennie's academic abilities? Was her potential limited by minimal brain damage incurred during a temperature accompanying rheumatic fever? Is there a sizeable discrepancy between what Jennie thinks she is *able* to do and what her parents believe she can do? What was it about the visits to the nursing home that Jennie *liked* so much? What is it about being with the hippies at lunch that Jennie *likes*? What kinds of things would Jennie *like* to do or have happen in the future? Does Jennie share her parents' opinion that she ought to study, get good grades, and go to college? When things don't work out as Jennie wanted them to, does she usually conclude that it's better not to talk about them? What does Jennie expect of herself? What does she believe her parents expect of her — that she will fail again, or that she will be okay this time? Does she, or do they, expect that she will pull through or just make a mess of things? What Jennie is trying to do (intention) and how hard she is trying to do it (exertion) depend on a combination of what she thinks she *ought* to do, what she *likes* to do, what she is *able* to do, and what she *expects* she will do. These dimensions of Jennie as a person (values, interests, abilities, expectations) interact with various dimensions of Jennie's world — her family, financial means to secure remedial tutoring for Jennie, the availability of skilled professional assistance to consult on special learning problems, social pressures on Jennie's parents to send all their children to college, cultural taboo against mental retardation, a school setting in which kids who are somewhat different are alienated by both students and staff, a group of alienated kids (hippies) who treat Jennie very kindly, a nursing home where Jennie was genuinely needed and wanted, a concerned but puzzled teacher.

As the counselor and Jennie work together to fill in the missing pieces, the picture becomes more complete and more understandable to both of them. With a more complete understanding, they are in a position to ask questions about the choices which Jennie faces and/or the changes she might want to see take place.

Thus far, we have been examining at close range the understanding process in counseling in terms of *what* the counselor and client are attempting to understand. In summary, we can say that *what* is to be understood is the client in transaction with his world; stated another way, what is to be understood is what the client is trying to do and the context in which he is trying to do it. A system for processing information called the "T-formation" was described as facilitating an understanding of client transactions, or what a client is trying to do, particularly in the three life task areas. A cautionary note was sounded, however, that the T-formation is not intended to function as a structured interview outline to which the counselor rigidly adheres. Therefore, it is important to separate consideration of *what* the counselor is attempting to understand, from *how* he goes about it. We turn now to ways of describing how the counselor receives information, sorts it out, checks its fidelity and stores it for later use.

## How to Become More Understanding

The day may come when we are able to describe and explain how a counselor understands a client as clearly and efficiently as we can describe and explain how a counselor changes a tire or finds an emergency towing service in the "Yellow Pages." However, until we can clearly and precisely specify each step or component of the understanding process, we will have to settle for somewhat vague approximations of the exact process, and we will have to endure the risk of destroying the very understanding we seek through misusing the word tools we possess. We are like children trying to capture a butterfly in flight. In our efforts to net, preserve, and display understanding, we are in danger of ripping the wings of the specimen we seek. But having acknowledged the present limitations of our ability to describe and explain the understanding process, we will proceed to some of our least crude efforts to capture the essence of understanding. We will explore several models or analogies, one or more of which will probably prove helpful to you in your pursuit of understanding.

### The "Movie-Making" Analogy

The process of understanding a client is like making a movie in your head. You are the "producer/director/cameraman," and your client is the "author/set designer/leading actor." The "producer" dimension of your combination of roles is intended to suggest that you underwrite or sponsor the endeavor through your active interest and concern; you invest yourself in the process at the beginning, long before it is clear what the returns will be. The "director" dimension of your multiple roles is intended to underscore your responsibility for deciding how to use the limits of time, place, and topic. Although you may extend considerable freedom to your "leading actor" client to determine where you will discuss what and for how long, there are boundaries and limits, outside of which the activity ceases to be counseling. To take an extreme example, suppose you are just beginning to work with a fifty-year-old woman who has been recently widowed, and is considering returning to school. In order to understand her ambivalence and indecisiveness, it is highly unlikely that it will be necessary for you to accompany her home to assist with decisions for redecorating her house. If she were to make such a request for help, it would be important to *direct* her efforts toward joining you in trying to understand what life is like for her now. How does it feel to be fifty and widowed and uncertain about the future? What are the alternatives open to her; what are the likely consequences of those alternatives? In the same way that an excellent stage director calls forth a fine performance from his cast, an excellent counselor calls forth from his client an active investment in portraying himself to the counselor. Whether the counselor facilitates or hinders the client's portrayal depends in large part on his skill as a "cameraman." Thus, the third dimension of the counselor's role emphasizes the necessity for an even, steady attention that is smoothly paced with the client, and keeps him in sharp focus.

The client in this movie-making analogy was cast as author, set designer, and leading actor. As such, the dramatic action that unfolds, the setting in which it occurs, and the portrayal of the central figure are largely the client's responsibility. The counselor will have his hands full supporting, guiding, and accurately picturing the client without also becoming involved in rewriting the story, redesigning the setting, or reinterpreting the leading figure's and supporting cast's roles. A reminder might be helpful at this point. We are talking about the process of understanding the client. It may well be that after a thorough understanding is accomplished, the counselor and client will contract to bring about some change in the client's life. At that point, redesigning some aspect of the setting or reconstructing the client's role may be precisely what is called for. However, before any treatment program designed to change a client's behavior is instituted, a thorough understanding of the client and his situation is necessary. Behavior modifiers or "operant conditioners" would likely refer to such an understanding in terms of specifying present base rates of the behaviors to be changed, identifying the contingencies presently controlling those behaviors, precisely describing the end-state to be achieved, and assessing what reinforcers are available to the client and counselor/therapist to utilize in a behavior modification procedure. Role construct theorists would refer to understanding in terms of being able to describe the manner in which the client construes various standard roles, e.g., mother, father, wife, husband, child, boss, friend, enemy, and designing and implementing new roles that will provide the client additional means for achieving his purposes.

The main thrust of this reminder is that regardless of your theoretical framework, or the contract that eventually may be negotiated, premature attempts to "solve a problem" or "alter the reinforcement contingencies" or "expand the role repertoire" interfere with achieving the degree of under-standing that is a necessary first step in any successful counseling or therapeutic effort. There are several advantages to viewing the understanding process as analogous to making a movie in your head. It casts the counselor in an active, facilitating role at the same time that the focus is on the client. It prevents the counselor from snatching responsibility out of the client's hands because the client is the primary source of important information and action. It discourages premature treatment efforts by insisting that before "the problems" can be formulated or "the choices" can be pinpointed, the person in transaction with his world must be seen clearly and comprehensively. It facilitiates remembering the content of a client's life by gathering and storing the information in meaningful episodes rather than as a collection of discreet facts. It facilitates the counselor's being able to step into the client's world and sense how the client experiences himself and his world. Sections of "the movie" can be replayed between meetings with the client for purposes of further clarifying the counselor's understanding or for purposes of identifying a fuzzy section that may need a retake.

Before presenting an example of understanding via movie-making, a cautionary note needs to be sounded. It certainly is possible to overdo the movie-making bit, and it would probably take the form of demanding that the client supply volumes of fine descriptive detail to satisfy a perfectionistic counselor's obsessive need to capture every nuance of feeling and action. Movie-making is intended to be a tool or means for reaching understanding. If it becomes an end it itself, it loses all therapeutic usefulness and becomes instead an implement of idle curiosity, or a clever excuse to maintain absolute control of the interaction, or it can even become a destructive device to satisfy a counselor's voyeuristic impulses. Employed properly, movie-making can help restore to seemingly mundane happenings much of the richness and vividness that characterizes any human experience which is viewed in its depth and complexity and uniqueness.

To illustrate the process of understanding via making a movie in your head, we will consider the experience of a Chicago physician who had just completed a routine physical examination for Steve Anderson, a high school senior.

> Steve is a very skilled black athlete who has already received three inquiries from professional football scouts and twelve scholarship offers from colleges and universities. Dr. Williams, who has been Steve's physician for the past three years, noticed that he seemed quiet and unresponsive, perhaps even despondent, which was in sharp contrast to his usual friendly and easy style of relating. Dr. Williams asked Steve if something was troubling him and was told that, yah, there was something driving on him all right, but Steve didn't know what it was — just a bad feeling. Steve said he couldn't get anywhere trying to decide which football offer to take or whether to take any of them . . . in fact, he said he couldn't even bring himself to accept invitations to visit the campuses. Dr. Williams asked Steve how he understood what was going on, and Steve said he just didn't know but somehow it was like how he felt when he was

a kid. "I guess I was about eleven years old, but everyone thought I was about fifteen. My old man had been gone almost a year and James, he's the oldest, had just shipped out for Korea. One of my older sisters was married so she didn't come around much. Marie, she's my other sister, she was working, but she had her own place — cross town. Well, anyway, Momma was trying to support the rest of us and there was five younger than me. Well, so every Saturday I used to go with her to this big old house where she cleaned and ironed and stuff. I would mow the lawn or wash the cars or burn the trash — stuff like that. The reason I got to work there was because once I had to go tell Momma that Daniel, he's one of the twins, fell and busted his leg. So the man saw me; he owned a couple of used car lots or something. Anyway, he saw me and told Momma that I looked strong enough to do a good day's work, and he'd be willing to try me out. He told her it would be good for me, and I'd probably be glad. So I started going every Saturday. Then his neighbor noticed me and asked him if I could come to his place on Sundays. Momma didn't want me to do that, so I traded off on Saturdays 'til summer. Then I worked for four of them up there all that summer."

If you have not read about, discussed, and experienced contemporary black-white conflicts and problems, then your chances of understanding Steve are indeed remote. However, if you have attempted to investigate racial issues and racism by reading and thinking, by suffering the pain of facing your own hidden prejudices, and by exposing yourself to Afro-American history and culture, then with no more information than has already been given, you are likely to reach considerable depths in understanding Steve. If you have even a minimal amount of racial sophistication and made a movie in your head of Steve and Dr. Williams, it might reveal something like this:

You see a powerfully built but beautifully graceful athletic young man — very black against the stark white of the physician's office. He is contained and controlled, showing no outward signs of the turmoil within, except for the intense eyes that seem to penetrate surfaces and fix themselves upon what lies beneath. You see Dr. Williams, cautious but direct, asking Steve what is bothering him, not merely to make conversation but because he really wants to know. You see Steve trust the authenticity of the question and risk revealing his own uncertainty and ambivalence about the football offers. You hear him say he has felt this way before. And now you begin to see a boy imprisoned in the too-soon body of a man. You see the proud and struggling mother trying to care for her too-many family. Dark, drab, dirty tenement blocks; spacious, green, clean suburb. A broken leg — pain and fear and hurry — but not even a possibility to telephone; Danny knows how out of place that would be. Neighbors bartering over the strong-as-an-oxen and not-lazy-either boy.

Colleges and universities hungrily waiting to tame and train and show their sleek, powerful, fast black cat.

As you allow your "mind's eye" to view these scenes of Steve when he was eleven and now when he is eighteen, it is not very difficult to grasp the meaning or understand his present ambivalence. When will he be something more than a magnificent body to be sold to the highest bidder? Will anyone ever value him just as a man – or will his worth always depend upon his ability to perform physically? What happens when his "gladiator" days are over . . . does he then find his meaning in peddling sports equipment or breakfast cereal? Does he have the right to care about what he thinks and what he feels or should he restrict his concerns exclusively to what he can do to guarantee a successful athletic career? What may have appeared to be a simple selection from among several good offers, takes on the magnitude of a critical life-choice that will be a major determiner of the kind of man Steve continues to become. You are hardly in a position to assist him in weighing alternatives until you can appreciate the fact that the man's identity as a human being is at stake. If you are white, or if you have never been poor, it is especially important to allow yourself sufficient time to vividly picture what the world of Steven Anderson is really like. You may find that thinking of understanding as analogous to making a movie in your head is a helpful way to grasp the full meaning of a person and a world that is even quite discrepant from your own.

### The Ballet Analogy

A second analogy that has proven helpful in communicating to beginning counselors the "how to" of understanding clients, is to compare understanding to attending a ballet. There are some obvious commonalities between the ballet analogy and the movie-making analogy; therefore, we will only highlight some of the special and unique dimensions of ballet and what they point up about the understanding process. In the ballet, we find expressed some of the most poignant and often tragic aspects of human experience. Music and dance are especially able to capture the vast range of emotions accompanying the vicissitudes of living. The story line and setting are less significant than are the intense human feelings being expressed through the soaring symphony orchestra and supple human forms which are beautifully blended, and yet strongly separate. Through sound and movement, the wordless drama unfolds. Ecstasy and joy flit about like hummingbirds or prance like spirited stallions; desolation and despair wander helplessly and hopelessly across an empty stage. All the while flawless precision and complete control yield an experience of ease and spontaneity and freedom. To say that understanding a client is like attending a ballet is to say: watch the movement of another person's life; listen to the sounds of another's joys and sorrows; be open to experiencing the ebb and flow of his feelings – sometimes bright and light, sometimes dark and heavy; capture the range of his experiences which extends from being torn apart in turmoil to being whole and serene and at peace within. Understanding via attending a ballet will be illustrated through a hypothetical case referred to Mr. Fred Collins, a DVR counselor (Division of Vocational Rehabilitation), whose assignment includes a Veterans' Administration Hospital in the Northwestern part of the United States.

Dale Weston, a twenty-five-year-old Caucasian male was returned from action in Vietnam that had left him with a spinal cord injury and a hideous new identity — paraplegic. Dale Weston, 100 percent service-connected and fully compensated, was almost totally disconnected from anything meaningful, and had decompensated to the point where he spent most of his day sitting in his wheelchair silently staring into space. The emptiness surrounding him was equalled only by the void within. Because of his depressed state, Dale had been sent to a neuropsychiatric ward following surgery that had failed to restore control or feeling to his legs. Through carefully regulated medication and participation in the ward treatment program, Dale finally decided that he was willing to at least talk with a DVR counselor, even though he was very pessimistic and skeptical about ever holding down a meaningful job.

During his first interview with Dale, Mr. Collins was struck with the overwhelming sense of resignation to a life of useless inactivity that pervaded Dale's references to the future. It was as if Dale had received an incommutable life sentence of futility. Even though his depression had lifted considerably since he had come to the hospital, he still seemed to adopt the posture of a condemned and penitent man whenever the possibility of future happiness was even suggested. In their discussion of previous work experiences and vocational aspirations prior to military service, it emerged that at one time Dale had considered going into the ministry. He and his family belonged to and were very active in a small fundamental church that placed heavy emphasis upon seeking and doing the Lord's will. Their faith was manifest in a close and constant walk with the Lord. A born-again believer could rest assured that when he sought and followed God's leading, the gifts of the Spirit were abundant, but when he knowingly strayed from what the Lord wanted for him, then he could expect to reap the wages of his sin. Because of his love of the outdoors and his desire to be active and doing, Dale had decided that seminary training was more time than he wanted to spend in school. Nevertheless, he was quite active in the church youth program all through his high school years. After graduation he went to work full-time on his father's dairy farm, and even then he continued to teach a junior high Sunday school class and to lead the singing for the Sunday evening service. Dale was Mr. Weston's only son, and so he was particularly pleased with Dale's plans to one day take over the dairy farm. It was very difficult for the whole family when

Dale was called up for active military duty. However, he was an expansive young man who welcomed life, and was eager for new experiences; generally optimistic and cheerful, he was confident that his faith would see him through. But Dale had never encountered anything like life in Vietnam: steamy hot jungle; the only references to God or Christ were oaths hurled at the enemy, the military, or no one in particular; writhing bodies wracked with pain; death and dying all around; atrocities on both sides that were beyond belief; totally unfamiliar forms of relief — drugs, alcohol, sex; absurdity and horror everywhere. In the midst of all this, the greatest absurdity Dale could imagine was whatever they meant back home when they talked about "seeking God's will for your life." Nobody could seriously consider God's will and Vietnam in the same sentence, or even the same world. The day he got hit, Dale was badly hung over from a night spent in a nearby village. During the long journey home, it was impossible for Dale to deny the thought that maybe he had committed the "unpardonable sin" and was beyond redemption. Although he believed God did not want people to suffer, and that God would welcome home even the most prodigal son, Dale still could not help thinking that he had brought his misery on himself and deserved all that was happening because he had given in to the desires of the flesh when he knew better, and because if he had been more alert, he might have spotted the mine and avoided it. Overcome with guilt and shame, Dale had relinquished any expectation of ever being happy or content again. Instead, he vowed he would simply accept his condition, and attempt to live out the remainder of his days without complaint.

Regardless of how you personally feel about Vietnam, fundamental religious beliefs, the use of alcohol, or physical disability, what is critical is that you are able to understand Dale and his world — as Dale himself experiences it. Drawing on the ballet analogy, Fred Collins was able to see Dale moving freely, energetically and with a self-assured style that carried him wherever he wanted to go. Collins could hear the throbbing beat and glorious harmonies of joyous gospel music. But the scene changes and the lively, responsive body slows to the faltering, trudging of an exhausted foot soldier and the heavenly choruses are drowned out by the hellish shelling of pounding mortars. And the curtain falls on a broken, limp body alone and silent. What Collins is up against is convincing Dale that his soul can dance again although his legs will never move; and that his spirit can sing again although he strayed away like a prodigal son. Finding a vocation with which Dale will identify, and a training program he will successfully complete, involves more than skillful interpretations of the GATB and the Kuder (General Aptitude Test Battery; Kuder Vocational Preference Record). The journey back to productive and meaningful existence is painful and arduous for the disabled client, but that journey has a better chance of getting underway when the counselor understands from whence his client must begin to move. Such an understanding may be facilitated by drawing on the ballet analogy.

### The Impressionistic Painting Analogy

The third analogy, suggesting yet another way to understand, is viewing understanding as similar to appreciating an impressionistic painting. Although viewing a painting may seem to lack the dynamic qualities of the movie-making and ballet analogies, appreciating an impressionistic painting is far from a static experience. As the name suggests, impressionism, whether in painting or writing or any other art form, concentrates on communicating the general impression of a scene or subject without the benefit (or distraction) of fine detail and elaborate finish. The power of such an artistic style comes in the interaction between the creation and the perceiver; exactly what gets communicated is heavily dependent upon what the perceiver brings to the interaction, and thus it is a highly personal experience. You have probably had the experience yourself or observed someone else demanding to know what a poem or painting or sculpture means precisely. It is often frustrating to encounter the ambiguity and lack of definitiveness in something that is supposedly there to communicate a message. If at that point, the perceiver tries to objectively scrutinize and analyze the artistic creation at close range, he most likely will only become more frustrated because careful analysis of each detail does not add up to an understanding of the creation as a whole. On the other hand, if he draws away a great distance and turns to a secondary source, such as a critical review of the work, he radically changes the experience by diluting or destroying the immediate, personal quality of the interaction between himself and the creation. In no way is it being suggested that careful analysis of details and consulting a secondary source should be avoided. Rather it is being suggested that the perceiver needs to know why he is doing that, and that he not merely be driven to it because he cannot tolerate the ambiguity of a direct encounter with the creation. Applying this to a counselor (perceiver) encountering a client (artistic creation), the parallels are striking. Some clients are very much like an impressionistic painting; there is a message to be communicated and understood, but the details are fuzzy and the experience of trying to understand the person is shot through with ambiguity and uncertainty. If a counselor moves too close, too quickly, and demands an explanation of each detail, or a precise statement of the person's meaning, he will most likely be met with a series of "I don't knows" and puzzled, confused expressions on the client's face which only add to the counselor's frustration. If, on the other hand, the counselor quickly draws away from his own firsthand, direct experience of the client and reduces the client to a personality test profile or a diagnostic category, he will significantly dilute or even destroy his relationship with the client. What is needed, at least initially, is for the counselor to remain sufficiently close to the client that psychological contact is maintained and the client does not feel abandoned, but to also remain sufficiently distant from the client that an overall impression of the whole client is possible without becoming entangled in fuzzy details. When both the client and the counselor are certain that they can meaningfully relate to one another, that they can gain some understanding of one another, and especially that the counselor is able to understand the client, then it is quite safe to zero in on some small unclear detail or to distance from the client by focusing on a test profile, without radically altering or threatening the quality of the counseling relationship.

The hypothetical case of Mary Chamberlain illustrates the use of understanding via appreciating an impressionistic painting analogy.

Mrs. Chamberlain is the forty-two-year-old mother of two college students. Her husband and children are all healthy and actively involved in satisfying lives. Of course, the other family members have their ups and downs, but none is in the depressed state that Mary finds herself. After consulting with their family physician and finding no physical basis for her condition, Mary accepts a referral to the local mental health clinic. She is interviewed there by a social worker, Helen Sullivan, who in contrast to herself, Mary perceives as young, vivacious, and a very competent woman. In the beginning of the interview, Helen's lively and attractive manner only made Mary more depressed, but the fact that Helen seemed genuinely interested in listening to her meant it was possible for Mary to try to talk about herself. The worst thing is that there is nothing to tell. After you describe two happy, healthy children who have become nearly independent and able to provide for themselves, and a husband whose needs are minimal and not unlike a million other husbands, what is there to say. Yes, she has been active in community volunteer work and that has been satisfying, but most of the activities have been coordinated with the children's interests and Mr. Chamberlain's activities, e.g., Boy Scouts, Camp Fire Girls, Demolay, Masons, Antique Automobile Owners Club, and some church work. "What was it about these activities that appealed to me the most? Oh, I don't know, just being with the family doing something we all enjoyed, I guess. No, I've never *really* thought about going to work, because I can't do anything. I finished a bachelor's degree in education in 1950, just before we were married, but I never did get my teaching certificate. I wish now that I had, except I'm not sure I could stand a whole classroom of children all day now. And the idea of going back to school is absolutely overwhelming; I wouldn't even be able to get through registration."

You probably know that unfortunately there are thousands of mature women, like Mary Chamberlain, who are experiencing a similar kind of emptiness and depression, and who cling tenaciously to a self-perception of uselessness and inability to cope with the drastic changes that occur when children have grown, and flown from the nest. If you, as counselor, insist that Mary tell you precisely what she likes to do, what she is able to do, what she thinks she ought to do, she will probably tell you she doesn't know what she likes or ought to do, and that she is really not able to do anything. Or if you too quickly administer a battery of interest, ability, and personality tests, Mary will probably politely listen to your test interpretation with mild interest but find it somehow not applicable to her and her situation. For a mature woman in the midst of a developmental crisis, it is very important that someone, perhaps a counselor, or someones, perhaps a counseling group, stand with her long enough and at an appropriate distance in order for her to risk exploring new ways of being herself.

Fortunately, Helen Sullivan was comfortable staying with Mary as she floundered and tentatively tried out new roles, both in their individual sessions and in the group. Because Helen and the other group members were willing to understand what had been true for Mary and the vague outlines of what might become true for her, Mary was able to explore and attempt to implement some new possibilities that seemed open to her. If Helen had not been able to tolerate the ambiguity and confusion that characterized Mary when she first came to the clinic, Mary probably would not have been able to begin the exploration that precedes carving out a new identity. Faced with similar vagueness and diffuseness in a client, it may help to think of understanding such a person as being analogous to appreciating an impressionistic painting.

### The Model-Building Analogy

The fourth and final analogy we will examine is that of understanding via building a model. Although we often associate model building with pre-adolescent boys, this activity is engaged in by a wide variety of people for quite different purposes. A molecular biologist trying to unravel the mysteries of DNA and RNA, an architect presenting his ideas to a city council, a Broadway set designer preparing for a new production, a retired Navy captain recapturing moments on the high seas, a social psychologist studying the decision-making process of different types of groups, and a father assisting with the construction of an Apollo space ship are just a few of the many ways humans use models to help them both work and play.

Even though there are many aspects of model building that apply to the understanding process in counseling, one especially interesting observation is that model building tends to be a masculine activity. This is not to say that a woman in the role of architect or set designer or molecular biologist or mother would not be capable of or interested in model building. Nor does it imply that little girls are odd if they like to build models. But it is difficult to think of many examples of model building in what would be labeled as traditional feminine activities. Because of this, understanding via building a model may be more useful to male counselors and/or it may be more applicable to male clients.

In addition to the sheer pleasure and sense of mastery derived from constructing a replica of a prized object, models are built when the real object is too large or unwieldy to work on directly. The model allows the builder to manage and master something even though it may be of tremendous dimensions and very complicated. Models are also built when something is quite rare or if the object or process is only partially known. In these cases the model makes it possible to deal with, or even discover what would otherwise be inaccessible. Some model builders begin their work with an exact goal in mind; they already have the end product clearly depicted as well as a set of instructions on how to assemble the separate parts. Other model builders have the designs and plans for only part of the model they are trying to construct, and after that portion is completed, they must begin improvising and trying out new possibilities in order to finish the job.

For many individuals, model building is a significant source of pleasure. For the counselor, understanding via building a model is also often a pleasure because of the sense of competence or mastery that he derives from being able to fit together the pieces of a client's life in a way that makes sense to both of them. All of us tend to think of ourselves and our lives as having some sort of structure by means of which we function. If another person, in this case a counselor, is able to put together the bits and pieces we communicate in a manner that truly seems to capture our unique structure and the special ways we function, we feel understood and that other person usually feels a sense of competence in being able to understand. However, model building in counseling is not done simply because it is fun or pleasing to do, but because it allows both the counselor and the client to get a handle on what is otherwise quite vast and complex, namely, a person's life. By building a model of the client, the counselor does not have to postpone working with the client until he knows every single detail of the client's past experiences, present situation, and expectations for the future. Building a model makes their interaction more manageable for both of them. In addition, when the counselor begins building a model of what his client presently knows and understands about himself, it assists both of them in discovering aspects of the client which may be currently inaccessible or only dimly understood. It is rare in counseling that a client has both a crystal clear picture of himself as he presently is and as he would like to become, together with a set of instructions on how to reassemble the parts to achieve the new model. On the other hand, it is equally rare that a client has no notion of what he presently is like, or no idea of what he would like to have be different, or not a clue as to how that might be achieved.

Whether Choice or Change or Confusion Reduction is the primary focus or goal, the most common situation in counseling is that the client can provide the counselor with many of the separate parts and some helpful hints on how to put them together, and he can serve as a "building inspector" who checks to see if the model is an accurate replica. However, the quality of the model is heavily dependent upon the model builder's skills, that is, the counselor's skills. If the counselor/model builder hurriedly identifies a couple of parts and then assumes he knows how the whole model goes together, and that he has no need for further directions from the client, his models will probably look very much alike, but bear little resemblance to the particular clients they are intended to represent. If a counselor is so perfectionistic that he becomes preoccupied with the model building and ceases to see it as merely a means to an end, namely, that of understanding the client, then he runs the risk of wearing out or even destroying a part because he cannot leave it alone unless it is perfectly in place. When the counselor/model builder encounters a situation where either a piece is missing, or it is unclear how to fit it in with the others, then he must be willing to experiment and improvise. With a blend of firmness and gentleness, the skillful model builder will carefully fit in a reluctant part, or he may even fashion a new part. And so it is for a counselor, who must gently try out different ways of construing the client, repeatedly checking to see if the pieces fit without forcing something into a place it really does not belong. At the same time, the counselor must actively and firmly attempt to fit pieces together that may not appear to belong together, and in fact, may turn out not to belong together. However, if there is not sufficient energy and certainty behind his efforts, both the counselor and the client will soon lose confidence in the counselor's skills and he will be seen as a pathetic, bumbling fool, or perhaps worse, a disgusting dilettante dabbling with someone's life. In the same way that craftsmen acquire and continue to improve their skills over a considerable period of time, skilled counselors are not trained overnight. Experience is particularly important in learning to balance gentleness and pressure in a counseling relationship. The pieces of a model will not magically fit themselves into place while the counselor merely smiles and nods, but neither will they stay in place if they have been hurriedly jammed and crammed together by an anxious counselor eager to demonstrate his problem-solving prowess.

There are several questions that a counselor can ask himself and his client which will assist in the process of building a model of the client. First, there is the question of size: What is the biggest thing in the client's life? How does he spend most of his time? Into what does he invest most of his energy and his caring? The biggest part of a client's life might be his work, another person, a group, a hobby, a set of beliefs, or any of a great number of things. Other questions deal with the functional relationships among parts of the client's life: Does one part support another and provide the energy for it? For example, does the client's home life serve as a foundation upon which other parts of his life are built, or is he most solidly grounded in his work which supplies the energy to participate as a family member? Some questions concern the spatial relations among individual parts: Does Part A fit inside of Part B, or does Part A encompass Parts B, C, and D? For example, do the client's religious beliefs encompass his attitudes toward other people, money, politics, child rearing, work, and his own self-worth? Or do his religious beliefs fit within a framework of economic and political conservatism? Still other questions focus on the compatibility of the present structure and its intended purposes or functions: Does the client attempt to accomplish multiple purposes, but have only one or two coping mechanisms at his disposal? For example, does the client express an intention to be well-rounded and have a diversity of interests in order to talk comfortably with a wide range of people, but spend his time and energy in such a way that he almost never meets a new person nor enters an unfamiliar setting? You can probably think of other questions that would help guide a model building effort. For example, how complicated or intricate are the various parts? How fast or slow, how stable or erratic is the model's usual pace of operation? How familiar is the client with his own equipment? How rapidly are various parts wearing out or becoming obsolete, and is there an effort to keep things in good running order?

For some counselors, understanding via building a model has the potential to provide still another means of accomplishing what has been acknowledged as a very important but difficult counseling activity, namely, grasping the meaning intended by another person. The hypothetical case of Gordon McKinley, a self-employed businessman who has just recently celebrated his sixtieth birthday, will be used to demonstrate understanding via building a model.

> Three days after Christmas, Father Landoni was about to leave his study for the day, when one of his parishioners knocked and opened the door. Recognizing Gordon McKinley as one of the men who had very faithfully served on the building committee for the newly constructed retirement home, Father Landoni invited him in. Other than his contacts with Gordon on that committee and two relatively brief visits when Gordon was in the hospital for cataract surgery, Father Landoni had not spent very much time with Gordon. Although he did not appear to be particularly depressed or anxious, Gordon seemed to want to talk with Father Landoni as soon as possible. As Gordon described it, he had been cleaning up his automotive repair shop earlier in the day — business at this time of year usually ground down nearly to a halt — and he had begun thinking about his age and retiring, his family, their finances, his failing eyes, how much better he felt when the shop was busy, and how empty it was when the boys were not around. The "boys," McKinley's Men, were a group of hoodlum-like high school dropouts who hung around Gordon's Repair Shop. The first couple of guys sort of wandered in and stuck around, mostly watching Gordon working on cars and listening to him talking with Frank, the other mechanic. At the end of this past summer, one of the original McKinley Men graduated from a two-year automotive mechanic's training program at the local vocational-technical school and now had his own repair shop in a new center across town.

As Gordon talked about the McKinley Men, and about how thankful he was that he and his wife were in relatively good health for their ages, and about how well both of his sons had done getting established financially, Father Landoni began to build a model in his head. He could see and feel the steady, solid, moderate pace at which Gordon operated. In contrast to a high speed computer or a finely tuned racing motor, Gordon seemed to function more like a four-wheel drive pickup, best equipped for strong and lasting effort even when the going is neither smooth nor easy. Most of his energy and effort seemed to be distributed evenly to his family, to his work, and to being an honest, responsible, and humble human being. It was clear to Father Landoni that Gordon McKinley valued primarily what a person did rather than what he said or how he looked. Gordon's success in relating to young men who were out of step with much of society was understandable in light of the importance he attributed to actions rather than appearances or words.

Father Landoni listened as Gordon talked about the future and how he was beginning to think about selling or leasing the shop. He mentioned plans to work on a mountain cabin, to do some fishing, to take his wife back to Minnesota to visit her older sister, and some thoughts about investing in a new company that was going to manufacture electronic equipment. But as Father Landoni listened, there seemed to be a piece missing. Where was the time and energy going to be directed that had been invested in McKinley's Men? Gordon made no mention of them in his comments about future plans. When asked about this, he attempted to dismiss it as something he would simply give up when he left the shop. Feeling that that did not really make sense or fit together too well, Father Landoni began to probe some in an effort to understand why Gordon would be thinking in terms of severing all ties with the young fellows he had helped so much. Gordon responded with how much he thought that the generations today were very far apart and had so little in common. Kids seem to look at life so differently nowadays that a man like himself could not seem to get through to them. But that still did not gibe with the model of Gordon that Father Landoni had been developing. The priest confronted Gordon with this by simply stating that the way he was talking about his relationships with younger people did not seem to fit the picture; Father Landoni said he was puzzled and wondered how they could understand it. Then Gordon began talking about his grandson, Tom.

Tom had done very well in high school; he lettered in two sports and was on the honor roll his senior year. He went to college and declared a predentistry major. But just before this Christmas vacation, he, along with five other students, was arrested for possession and use of marijuana and LSD. At this point, Gordon broke down and was unable to talk for a few moments. In those brief moments, Father Landoni could see the part that was missing. Gordon had always been confident that if a man worked hard, did his best, and did not lose perspective about what was really important in life, then he could expect that life would work out pretty well. Gordon had lived this way and, by example, had taught his sons to live that way. Until the shattering experience of having his own grandson charged with a felony which would probably ruin the boy's future, Gordon could point to his own life and the lives of his sons as silent testimonies that confirmed the value of his approach to life. But now, now what could he think! It was as if this tragic event had exploded in the center of his life and left a gaping hole which had once been filled with the confident and optimistic belief that if you give people a break and a chance to do something respectable, they will turn out okay. But Tom had had all kinds of chances and his schoolwork was something that everyone was proud of. Although he was never interested in working on cars, they had fished together many times. Gordon just shook his head, but his expression communicated the excruciating pain that a man feels when he neither understands nor can talk about his own people. Father Landoni seemed able to understand how shaken he was, how much he felt as if the bits and pieces of his life had just been randomly strewn about. The fact that Father Landoni was able to understand and to help make sense out of his helpless, hopeless feelings was the most encouraging thing that had happened to Gordon in the past week. For the first time since his son had called about Tom, Gordon could imagine that he might one day regain some of his old optimism and confidence about life and other people. Maybe if he could understand Tom and understand his own feelings, he could begin to rebuild instead of just sign off and retire from what was truly an important part of his life — the growth and development of young men.

You might have reached an understanding of Gordon McKinley by making a movie in your head of him and his world, or by watching a ballet of his life, or by appreciating him as you would an impressionistic painting, or by building a model, as Father Landoni did, or by a manner of understanding that is not described here. Whatever method allows you to grasp the meaning of another person, clearly and completely, is the preferred method. The four analogies suggested here will appeal to those counselors who find them easy to incorporate and a helpful way to think about how they could try to understand a particular person. To other counselors they may seem awkward or forced. That is to be expected, and in no way is it being suggested that all counselors will find them useful, or that one counselor will find them applicable in every situation. You may think of other analogies which are more suitable to you and to your particular style of understanding. There certainly is no one way to understand another human being that is superior to all other ways. Perhaps the position of greatest strength is to have several ways readily available to you.

## III ACCEPTANCE

Acceptance in counseling is mostly closely related to affective or emotional processes within the counselor, whereas understanding in counseling is most closely related to a counselor's cognitive processes. Understanding has most to do with what and how a counselor *thinks*; acceptance has most to do with what and how a counselor *feels*. According to Tyler (1969), "acceptance involves primarily two things – first, a willingness to allow individuals to differ from one another in all sorts of ways, and second, a realization that the ongoing experience of each person is a complex pattern of striving, thinking and feeling" (p. 34). When Tyler discusses acceptance, and Rogers describes unconditional positive regard, and Truax and Carkhuff speak of nonpossessive warmth, they are all talking about a set of attitudes and feelings that extends beyond a benign tolerance for others. *Acceptance in counseling is the celebration of diversity and complexity in others.* Using the television coverage analogy once again, we will first take an aerial view of acceptance in the context of human relationships in general. Next, we will move to a middle range view of acceptance in the counseling relationship and then move to a close-up view of *what* to accept about the client and *how* to accept it. As was the case with understanding, in the close-up views of what and how to accept, we will juxtapose descriptions of acceptance and hypothetical client-counselor interactions designed to illustrate a high degree of acceptance.

## Acceptance in the General Sphere of Human Relations

In the same way that taking an aerial view revealed that increasing degrees of understanding characterizes every human being's development, it is also the case that increasing degrees of acceptance characterize each person's development. While it is true that the degree of acceptance necessary for effective counseling is a relatively uncommon experience in most human interactions, the process of accepting another person is rooted in some very common human traits. Of all known creatures, the human being possesses the most curiosity, enjoys the greatest diversity, and seeks the widest range of novelty. In fact, "sameness" is highly noxious to a human. It is easy to document this statement either by examining the research on the debilitating effects of extreme states of sameness, usually called sensory deprivation and social isolation, or by simply reflecting upon your own distress whenever you have had to endure lengthy periods of repetitious inactivity. To be sure, extreme conditions of change are also debilitating and the human has an optimal range of change/constancy within which he functions best. Also, there are individual differences in what constitutes an optimal range of change/constancy for each person. What is important for our purposes is to note that a sense of stability and well-being comes from functioning within a range of activity somewhere between chaos and constancy (see Figure 7).

FIGURE 7.    Continuum of Human Activity

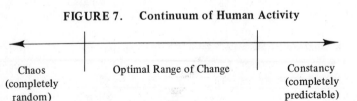

Whether we draw upon carefully controlled research studies or our own introspections, the conclusion is the same: We function best and feel most competent when our world is neither completely random nor completely predictable; a certain amount of ongoing change is necessary for optimal human functioning.

From the time of our birth each of us begins to interact with the world – touching, tasting, smelling, hearing, and looking, in an effort to discover, explore, and be able to cope with what is here, and perhaps to help create what is yet to come.

In recent years it has been pointed out that we cannot account for the tremendous amount of sustained effort directed toward mastering the environment which is expended by the developing infant, child, and adult by merely pointing to such basic biological needs as food, warmth, air, water, and sex. If becoming competent with the environment, including objects and people and ideas, were dependent upon physical deprivation and/or discomfort, e.g., an empty stomach or a full bladder, then it would take us a lifetime to learn the magnificent array of things each of us learns in the first few years of living. Studies of human development, including research on the human nervous system and on the growth of cognitive and perceptual abilities, point to the fact that living human beings are always interacting with their worlds to one degree or another. A great portion of the time, humans are in active pursuit of some part of their world and whereas we used to explain such activity solely on the basis of the need to fill some gastrointestinal or sexual deficit, it is now quite clear that humans, when they are neither hungry nor sexually aroused, are often very active simply because they possess human nervous systems.

The infant in his crib delighted with a new toy, the three-year-old busily removing the eyes from her stuffed giraffe, the seven-year-old gleefully mixing green and red to produce a lovely shade of mung, the ten-year-old determined to ride clear home without hands, the adolescent fascinated with teaching a rat in a

Skinner Box, the housewife struggling to become more skillful at throwing clay pots, the college sophomore venturing his first attempt at poetry-writing, the young, aspiring accountant learning Swedish because he wants to, the retired couple carefully planning how to see as much of Europe as they can on what they have saved, the arthritic widow gently grooming her prize-winning roses long after she has stopped competing in rose shows, constitute one small set of examples of how curiosity, novelty-seeking, and competence are expressed at all developmental stages.

In summary, human beings are by nature active organisms; imposed inactivity or sustained sameness are highly noxious conditions. Humans engage in a vast array of transactions with their worlds, i.e., with objects, ideas, and other humans. In fact, one of the hallmarks of humanness is the diversity and complexity of their activities, as individuals and as a species. Clearly, these activities are not merely for the purpose of filling gastrointestinal and sexual deficits, but rather these diverse and complex activities are associated with feelings of competence and mastery because they make something happen or have an effect on the environment, or because they result in learning something new or in creating something new. We are about to readjust the video camera to a middle range and focus on acceptance in the counseling relationship. Acceptance was defined earlier as the celebration of diversity and complexity in human behavior. From the aerial view we are about to leave, it is important to carry with us into the counseling relationship a profound appreciation of the fact that human diversity and complexity are deeply rooted in basic neurological, psychological, and social processes.

## Acceptance in the Counseling Relationship

If diversity and complexity are basic defining properties of humans, and acceptance is merely the prizing or celebration of human diversity and complexity, then why is acceptance a relatively rare experience for most people? Or, asked another way, why is it that all counselors, and especially inexperienced counselors, continually need to extend their capacities to accept others? At least a partial answer to these questions is found in what was described in Figure 7 as an optimal range of change along a continuum of human activity. There is, on the one hand, great effort to avoid a completely predictable, constant world devoid of novelty and change; on the other hand, there is an equally great effort to avoid a chaotic, random world in which nothing could be anticipated and prepared for. This, of course, is true whether we are talking about driving a car, accepting a check, listening to the weather forecast, getting an education, dropping a letter in a mailbox, or deciding to take another job. Only by anticipating or predicting what is likely to happen next, and preparing for it, are we able to maintain a stable existence.

We accomplish such stability or predictability in a multitude of ways, such as agreeing to a set of rules for traffic, football, business meetings, language, etc. Some of us achieve a degree of stability by identifying with the natural physical world, for example, protecting the trees and lakes, spending time at the ocean, or climbing a mountain. Some of us place our faith in an unchanging God, and thereby experience a sense of stability. What brings stability to one person does not necessarily stabilize the life of another, and we are once again faced with a great diversity among us. However, a fact of life that we all have in common is that other persons are our greatest source of unpredictability. Although the physical world, the world of ideas, and the spiritual world are not completely predictable, they are considerably more predictable and stable than is the world of other persons.

One of the major means we employ to cope with the lack of predictability in our experience with other persons is to surround ourselves with people who are very much like us, and to keep those who are different at a distance. We accept and welcome those persons we can count on to act as we do, and reject and retreat from those whose actions we are unsure of. In this way, we can achieve a high degree of predictability and stability, but at a very high price. The costliness of coping with unpredictability by closing off all persons who are or appear to be different, comes from the fact that because humans do differ so widely, we must reject large numbers of them in order to exclude those who are different. It is unquestionably the case that counselors cannot afford to pay such a price. Clearly, if counselors are to be of service to other than carbon copies of themselves, they must be willing to endure the unpredictability associated with human diversity and complexity.

Before we delve into the meaning of "celebration of diversity and complexity," we need to identify, in order to exclude, two extreme and antithetical interpretations of acceptance in counseling. Since the time that acceptance was first introduced as one of the essential characteristics of the competent counselor, it has suffered some very unfortunate mutations. Some counselors took the prescription that one ought to be highly accepting as an injunction against possessing and/or expressing any strong feelings — positive or negative — about a client. They fantasize an ideal counselor who is value-free, shockproof, rough-resistant, available in a no deposit/no return bottle, and whose body temperature remains normal under all conditions. Accepting a client was translated and twisted to mean passively receiving and blandly agreeing with anything and everything the client says or does. The image that comes to mind is that of a giant, warm sponge (Porifera Demospongiae Counseloriae). There are two major flaws in such a characterization of the competent counselor: passivity and blandness. Extending acceptance to a client is a very active and emotion-laden experience for both the client and the counselor.

However, this is not to say that counselors should be aggressive all of the time, or that each moment of the counseling interaction should be a pinnacle of emotional intensity. We are presently in the midst of a "feeling revolution" in some sectors of the counseling profession. The professional journals, as well as popular magazines, e.g., *Life, Playboy, Psychology Today*, and *Newsweek*, have been and are devoting considerable space to contemporary demands for intense emotional encounters via group and individual therapeutic experiences. Partially in reaction against the unpalatable blandness of earlier interpretations of counselor acceptance and partially as another instance of a larger cultural shift away from rationality and inhibition, some counselors have translated acceptance to mean extremely intensive emotional involvement between counselor and client. There are, of course, counselors who are sadly out of tune with their own feelings and quite fearful of strong emotion in either themselves or others. This shift within the profession to a greater emphasis upon affect is a very troubling and frightening turn of events for them. But there are also those within the profession who have capitalized on the current cultural trend to the point of exploitation. For those counselors, regardless of the client's purposes in seeking counseling, unless there are obvious displays of intense feelings, unless there are direct confrontive interchanges between themselves and their clients, and unless there are demonstrations of psychological and physical intimacy between themselves and their clients, they are unwilling to claim that they have accepted, or are accepted by their clients.

It is important to be very clear at this point; the purpose of these remarks is to define the boundaries of accepting behavior on the part of counselors. While it is helpful to note the contemporary cultural context within which counselor acceptance is being manifested, it is clearly beyond the scope of this book to present a critical analysis of the economic, political, psychological and social factors which are responsible for current cultural changes. We have simply declared a bland, passive posture to be a distortion of acceptance and to be outside the boundaries of what characterizes the competent counselor. At the other extreme, those definitions of acceptance which exclusively rely on an aggressive, confrontive, intensive, and intimate posture are also considered to be a distortion of acceptance and to be outside the boundaries of what characterizes the competent counselor.

Acceptance in counseling is certainly not a unidimensional trait, but rather a many-faceted set of attitudes and behaviors. However, if we are for the moment willing to think of counselor/client interactions on a continuum that extends from passive blandness to aggressive intimacy, we have in the previous discussion attempted to exclude the two ends of this continuum as being outside what is contained in the statement "the counselor accepts the client." We are, of course, left with a sizeable range of possible interactions between the two excluded extremes (see Figure 8).

**FIGURE 8.    Continuum of Counselor Acceptance**

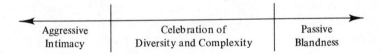

| Aggressive Intimacy | Celebration of Diversity and Complexity | Passive Blandness |

## Acceptance – The Celebration of Diversity and Complexity

The action word "celebrate" carries two connotations both of which are important meanings for a counselor. The earliest usage of "celebrate" refers to a solemn, public ceremony conducted to proclaim or extol the importance of something or someone. In many cases, the ceremony is a religious observance, such as celebrating Mass or Communion. A more recent usage of "celebrate" emphasizes the festive quality of a ceremony that is less solemn and formal, such as celebrating someone's promotion, or the coming of a new year. In both cases, however, the significance of something or someone is being recognized and proclaimed; the whole event is underscored by strong feelings which may range from solemn reverence to light-hearted exuberance. Although as few as two people may celebrate together, celebrating is a social event; that is, it must include a least one other person and usually includes many others. Whether it is a very serious event, or a more festive occasion, or a combination of the two, such as the marriage ceremony, celebrating means setting aside the ordinary business of the day to acknowledge the value of someone or ones.

The following list of words and phrases is offered in an attempt to capture the meaning of "celebrate" in the counseling situation:

> respecting
> valuing
> liking
> prizing
> being delighted with
> being concerned about
> caring for
> being genuinely interested in
> appreciating
> wanting to share the experience of
> receiving a person as he presently is
> having a deep regard for the basic worth of this human being

Upon reading such a list, some counselors may conclude that if this is what is involved in celebrating another's diversity and complexity, then only a saint would be capable of acceptance. From the outset of our efforts to define and describe acceptance, it is important to realize that celebrating another's diversity and complexity includes both positive and negative feelings. We are *not* talking about a syrupy, gushy, unreal devotion to mankind. Acceptance does not rule out all negative feelings. In fact, because you value and prize a client very highly, because you are concerned about him or care for him, you may be very irritated or angry with him on occasion. To take an extreme but nevertheless real example, whenever you are faced with a client who is seriously contemplating giving up, you may be furious if he attempts to commit suicide. You would probably feel a lot of other things too, e.g., inadequate, incompetent, frightened, confused, hurt, and helpless. But it would be quite understandable, and, in fact, expected that you would be angry because the person whose being you have chosen to feel strongly about, is choosing not to *be* anymore. The continued use of hard core drugs for an addict, or the repeated use of alcohol for an alcoholic would be other instances wherein it would be expected that a caring, concerned, accepting counselor would be angry or disappointed with his client. Because you are angry or hurt does not mean that you automatically rant and rave or chew out your client, or reject him for his choice. Possessing negative feelings about the client's choices does not automatically lead to rejecting him. You can accept someone fully at the same time that you have strong negative feelings about how he is treating himself. For any of us who have had the experience of being prized, valued, cared for, appreciated, deeply regarded, etc., we know that the other person who has accepted us to that degree does not always agree with us, and there are times when he or she is irritated or angry with us. Acceptance in counseling is not unlike such personal experiences. The depth of valuing and prizing a client comes from the fact that although the client may be very different from yourself, and although at times he may be very complicated and puzzling, and even though you may disagree with and be angry about some of his choices, you consistently maintain a deep regard for him as a person who is free to be different, puzzling, and even from your viewpoint, self-defeating.

We took extreme examples — attempted suicide, continued drug and alcohol use — to illustrate the upper limits of acceptance; such self-defeating choices are not frequent occurrences in the daily work of most counselors, unless they are in a setting specifically designed to work with such situations, e.g., a suicide prevention center, an alcohol and drug rehabilitation center, etc. Rather than an experience of being tested or pushed to the limits, accepting a client usually is a very natural and effortless activity. It is a high privilege to be able to share the experiences of so many different people; counselors are in an enviable role because they are able to interact with a very wide range of unique individuals at much more than a superficial, small-talk level.

"Every person is unique" is such a frequently recurring refrain in counseling circles that like a two-month-old hit tune, it does not turn anybody on any more. If we as counselors were expected to be excited about or feel reverent toward the factual statement that "every client is unique and different" or if we were expected to carry about a storehouse of enthusiasm for individual differences in general, then the outlook would be rather pessimistic. But fortunately that is not what is required for active acceptance of a client; the responsiveness that is demanded is to an individual — a particular person in transaction with his unique world. Or one might say, each client is another "hit tune" with his own particular melody and his own special lyrics. Although some songs may sound quite familiar, each is significantly different if you listen carefully. Accepting a person means hearing that difference, receiving it, and savoring it. Some songs may initially sound discordant and strange, but if you are open to new modes of expression, you may find that you even enjoy the once-strange song. Accepting a person means receiving and savoring even discordant differences, whether or not they ever become your preferences. Some songs may sound silly; they seem to be just pointless little ditties that simply fill up the air waves. Accepting a person means receiving and savoring the very simplest of melodies, even though your taste may run to intricately arranged, fully orchestrated symphonies. Some songs may sound unnecessarily complicated and convoluted, but if you are willing to continue listening, the important themes will likely emerge. Accepting a person means listening carefully to and appreciating his arrangement, even though it is at times awkward and belabored. And, finally, some songs may seem to carry contradictory messages or have other tunes hidden or embedded in the main theme. That may well be true, and the listener-counselor needs to be attuned to conflicting messages at different levels of communication. However, you can become so preoccupied with, or fearful of, missing some oblique message that the theme becomes lost in pursuit of possible variations. Accepting a person means listening carefully and taking seriously what he says, even though you detect another message which he presently denies is true.

A counselor works with and shares the experiences of people during periods when they are making profound choices and changes that will shape the entire course of their lives. Counseling is delightful, exciting, expansive, and rewarding work, depending upon how accepting you are. It is personally growth-producing if you can accept and allow yourself to be affected by the people with whom you work.

## Examples of Accepting and Rejecting Counselor Responses

In summary, we have said that accepting a client depends on your capacity to celebrate diversity and complexity in other people. By "celebrate," we referred to both a solemn, at times reverent, regard for another person, as well as a delighted, at times exuberant, liking of the person. Even in the face of great differences or clear disagreements about how things ought to be, the feeling of prizing, valuing, and caring for the person is sustained. We are now going to adjust our video-camera range again and zoom in on some examples of what acceptance is in the counseling relationship. We will "split the screen" and juxtapose descriptions of what to accept and hypothetical interactions between a client and an accepting and a rejecting counselor. This section on acceptance will close with a discussion of how to become a more accepting counselor.

The hypothetical cases presented below have been designed to demonstrate highly accepting counselor responses, and to illustrate the major barriers to communicating acceptance, namely:

1. *Overgeneralization* — "I've heard all this before; you're just like everyone else your . . . age, sex, race, class, etc."
2. *Conflict* — Discord between the counselor and client regarding values, interests, abilities, expectations, styles, etc.
3. *Disdain* — A haughty, arrogant, or aloof posture adopted by the counselor which places the client or his situation or his actions beneath the counselor.
4. *Impatience* — A restless, irritated, and hurried counselor style that tells the client that he is taking too long, not getting to the point, or that he is needlessly concerned and over-reacting.
5. *Cynicism* — A filter through which the counselor strains all his client's responses because he assumes that they are probably either malevolent or sick.

### The Case of Barbara

Barbara Stoddard is completing her sophomore year in a southern California metropolitan high school. During sixth period on a Friday, she approached Mrs. Carlson, the girls' counselor, to request an appointment. Mrs. Carlson, who had been busy helping the Senior Prom Committee with final arrangements for Saturday night's dinner-dance, was late for her sixth period open-office hour. When she arrived carrying a punch bowl, she recognized that it was Barbara who was waiting for her because Barbara had just been elected junior class treasurer. Also, Mrs. Carlson had met Barbara's father at a parents' night last fall; she was impressed then with how interested he seemed to be in Barbara's progress, even though he was obviously not well-educated. After she had put her things away, Mrs. Carlson invited Barbara in and indicated where she should sit.

Barbara began by saying that she had been doing a lot of thinking and some reading, and she had decided that she would like to become an architect. "I thought it would be a good idea to come in and talk with you about it because I'm not sure what courses I should be taking now or what college I should go to." Mrs. Carlson looked a little surprised and asked Barbara how she happened to decide on architecture. "Well, I've always like to draw things and to design stuff, and this year I helped Dean, my boyfriend, with his mechanical drawing and drafting homework, and I really liked it. And besides that, I went down and visited an architect in his office. Mr. Edwards helped me make the appointment."

### Directions the Counselor might take:

1. Ask Barbara if the architect told her how hard it is to be certified as an architect and that very few women ever make it — usually they go into drafting or interior decorating.

2. Let Barbara know that you think that is an interesting choice, but that it is a little premature to be worrying about next year's courses already, and that she probably should not be deciding on a career until she gets to college and knows if she really wants to be a career woman.

3. Tell Barbara that you are glad she has already begun thinking about her educational and career plans, especially if she is considering a profession, and that you will be happy to help her find out more about schools of architecture and the profession itself, as well as to help her think through what deciding to become an architect may mean to her.

If Mrs. Carlson were to take the direction indicated in #1, it would probably be based on a conflict between Barbara and Mrs. Carlson in values and expectations about appropriate jobs for women. Even though #1 is factually true, stated at this time, it would probably communicate that Mrs. Carlson thinks Barbara or any other woman should avoid architecture and find something similar that is "more feminine" and easier. In short, #1 says, "Barbara, your choice is unacceptable." The direction suggested by #2 is not as rejecting of Barbara's interests and ideas, but it also carries a discouraging message. Even if Mrs. Carlson were to be very sweet about it and display a concern for Barbara, the message is still clear — "Don't bother me with this now!" It is important to encourage youngsters not to decide on a career prematurely, and thereby close off any further explorations, but there is no evidence from Barbara's remarks that she is closed to all other possibilities and is unwilling to explore. In fact, Barbara indicated that was why she had come to see Mrs. Carlson, and if she were met with alternative #2, that probably would discourage further exploration.

Alternative #3 is, of course, the preferred direction to take because with it, Mrs. Carlson would be saying, "I have heard you; I take you seriously; I am pleased with you as you are; I want to help you in whatever way I can; I realize that there are still many things to think about in making a career decision."

### The Case of Vickie

Vickie Richmond never got to her junior year in high school because there was a rule in her district forbidding unmarried pregnant girls to attend school. Vickie's parents could not afford to send her to a private school, and besides, she decided to keep the baby, much to their disapproval. Since then she has worked for an industrial cleaning company that contracted to clean service station restrooms and telephone booths. But Vickie had to quit that job when she was six months pregnant with her second illegitimate child. When the second baby was a year old, Vickie enrolled her oldest child in a summer Headstart program. Living on ADC funds, commodity foods, plus some help from her mother once in a while, Vickie searched for a part-time job. As long as she was not working, she volunteered as a teacher's aide in the Headstart program two days a week. Midsummer, her caseworker quit to get married, and Vickie Richmond was reassigned to a new caseworker-counselor, Marvin Henderson. This was the fourth caseworker in two years that Vickie had been assigned to, and according to her they were all the same: "Rat finks for Welfare — some of them try to be human, but they are just part of a shitty system."

During his first week on the job, Marvin was making the rounds trying to become acquainted with his new caseload. He met Vickie at her place late one afternoon after she had spent the day at Headstart. He introduced himself, asked if they could talk, and accepted her invitation to enter the small, dingy, barren house. In response to his rather cheerful, "Well, how is life treating you these days, Mrs ... ahh ... Vickie?" Marvin was told rather flatly, without much feeling, "Mister, my life is so fucked-up, I don't know where it's goin'. But today I decided I wanna' be a school teacher, so maybe you can tell me how to get back in school."

*Directions the Counselor might take:*
1. State that you hardly think most mothers would be willing to entrust their children's minds to someone who has had as much "difficulty" and who feels as bitterly as Vickie does, and therefore, teaching seems a bit unrealistic.
2. Ask Vickie how her job hunting is going. Suggest that maybe the reason teaching looks so good is because she is having such a hard time finding a part-time job.
3. Tell Vickie that you know she has been volunteering as a teacher's aide at Headstart, and ask if that has contributed to her interest in, and excitement about teaching.
4. Tell Vickie that you are fairly new to the area and are not familiar with all the possible ways she might get help to return to school, but that you are very willing to explore it with her.

Although alternative #1 seems so obviously rejecting, it is not inconceivable that a counselor might be offended by some of Vickie's language, or be horrified that someone who had dropped out of school and borne two illegitimate children would dare to think of becoming a "molder of children's minds." If Marvin Henderson were going to take the direction stated in #1, it would probably be done in the name of representing reality to his client, and not reinforcing false hopes or unattainable aspirations. But it is a disdainful put-down and any client would certainly experience it as rejecting on the part of the counselor.

Alternative #2 is a less obvious rejection, but it is equally unaccepting. A counselor who made such a response would, with the question about job hunting, be denying that Vickie had just declared an interest in teaching and asked for help in making that possibility a reality. The second part of alternative #2 is a somewhat cynical or suspicious hypothesis that Vickie is not *really* serious about teaching, but is merely grasping at any way out of her present situation. Whatever Marvin's reasons might be for being suspicious of, or unwilling to deal seriously with Vickie's request, if he were to adopt alternative #2, it would communicate that Vickie's ideas about becoming a teacher are unacceptable.

Alternatives #3 and #4 are the most accepting responses, and one is not particularly better than the other. It is important that we not slip into a belief that there is one "right" response that is more accepting than any other. There are many different, equally accepting responses a counselor might make; we, of course, cannot review all of them. Instead we are trying to contrast some ways of rejecting a client with some ways of accepting a client, in hopes that the general principles of acceptance can be quickly applied in a variety of specific situations. With either alternatives #3 or #4, Marvin would be communicating, "I heard what you said, I'm interested in what you're interested in; I take your request seriously; I want to help in whatever way I can." In short, Marvin would be communicating, "I accept you."

In the last example, alternative #1 was labeled an unaccepting response that probably stemmed from the counselor's overreaction to a stylistic difference between himself and the client; namely, the use of obscene language. In order to be accepting of Vickie, it is not necessary to approve of prospective teachers using obscenity freely. What is required is to see that for the present such usage is quite irrelevant, and if Vickie were to undertake a teacher training course, she would have ample time to learn the "rules of the game" on how teachers should and should not talk. This kind of stylistic clash between counselor and client, whether it pertains to language, clothes, patterns of spending money, or preferences for spending leisure time, is fairly easy to spot because you can usually point to something and say, "That's where they differ, and that's what the counselor finds unacceptable!" The example we are about to consider involves a much more subtle, and thus difficult to detect, conflict between a counselor and client. The conflict in this case is not something you can easily point to, even though it centers on a particular decision, it nevertheless involves a person's whole approach to living.

### The Case of Owen

Reverend T. Owen Fremont is the assistant pastor for a large Southern Baptist church in West Virginia. Although he is only thirty-four, he has distinguished himself nationally as one of the most promising young Baptist clergymen, especially in the area of Christian Education and Youth Fellowship work. However, about eight months ago, at the close of a statewide campaign to strengthen the churches' outreach among high school students, Reverend Fremont approached another clergyman for counseling. When Reverend

Fremont first met with Dr. Alexander, a minister who had taken special work in pastoral counseling, he was experiencing a number of symptoms that his physician had labeled "psychosomatic." The two men had been working together for about seven-and-a-half months, meeting at least once a week. During that time Dr. Alexander was able to help Owen sort through a number of things that were troubling him. Also, Dr. Alexander had made arrangements for Owen to receive training in relaxation procedures, and had assisted him in establishing a routine that included some daily recreation. Although Owen had had to limit his state and local activities during the beginning of his sessions with Dr. Alexander, he was now able to function as fully as he ever had and was more efficient than he ever had been. Therefore, it came as somewhat of a surprise to Dr. Alexander when Owen announced at the beginning of their regular weekly session that he had decided to leave the ministry and return to school to study psychology. They had discussed this possibility thoroughly and on numerous occasions. Owen had left last week's session faced with having to submit a letter of resignation within two weeks if he expected to be in school for the fall quarter. But somehow Dr. Alexander found it almost impossible to believe he had actually decided to leave the ministry.

*Directions the Counselor might take:*
1. Remind Owen that almost all ministers go through a crisis like this at about his age and that making a major life change at this time may be a most regrettable decision.
2. Point out that few dilemmas are ever really resolved by running away, and that if Owen gives up now he may always wonder if he missed his calling or turned his back on God's will just to satisfy his own personal desires.
3. Tell Owen that you respect his right to decide whatever he wants to about leaving the ministry, that you are glad he has reached a decision, and that he will now no longer need to see you regularly.
4. Frankly acknowledge that you find Owen's decision difficult to accept; that try as you may to be unbiased, you really felt he should stay in the ministry and continue his excellent work — but you respect his ability to weigh things and you have confidence in his decision even though it is not what you hoped would happen.

Alternative #1 contains a two-stage put down: (1) "Owen, this is nothing but an average, run-of-the-mill, early-middle-age career crisis, so don't worry!" (2) "During these little episodes it's easier than it usually is to make a mistake, so it's better to be on the safe side and not make any decisions until the crisis has passed." Alternative #1 is a classic example of "overgeneralization" resulting in rejecting responses from the counselor — "Oh, you're just like everyone else; you're just going through a 'stage,' you'll soon grow out of it."

Such messages are painfully belittling to their targets because their implied meaning is, "Don't get carried away; this is really nothing more than something you will look back on, and laugh, and wonder what all the fuss was about." Dr. Alexander could deliver these messages in a most benevolent and fatherly fashion, believing all the while that he was only trying to protect the young man from something he would be sure to regret later. If Dr. Alexander did that, however, it would be clear that he believed that he had some special knowledge of what Owen would regret in the future. It follows from such an assumption that if Owen wants to be happy in the future, then he should choose what Dr. Alexander knows will make him happy, that is, remain in the ministry. In short, alternative #1 communicates that the counselor knows best how things ought to be, and therefore, the only sensible and acceptable thing for the client to do is go along with whatever the counselor subtly or obviously indicates is best.

Alternative #2 is very similar to #1 in some ways, and the exact opposite in others. Instead of belittling the seriousness of Owen's situation, alternative #2 overplays the gravity of the decision Owen has made. Through some special knowledge, Dr. Alexander apparently thinks he knows that the continued salvation of Owen's soul depends upon how Owen makes this decision. We do not need to debate whether or not it is *possible* for Dr. Alexander to have special knowledge (e.g., through prayer or leading of the Holy Spirit), because it is rare that "doing God's will" is understood to mean "going along with another human being." Among evangelical religious people and liturgical religious people alike, God's will is sought directly or through sacred rites and writings; but it is usually not thought to be contained in the opinion of another person, even a clergyman. If Dr. Alexander were to take the direction indicated in alternative #2, he would again be saying, "I know what is best for you and the only acceptable decision, Owen, is to remain in the ministry."

Alternative #3 is perhaps the most abruptly rejecting response that Dr. Alexander could make because even though he says he respects Owen's decision, he immediately threatens him with termination of their meetings. Terminating a counseling relationship that has existed for over seven months on a regular basis takes a little preparation. Owen would probably experience such a sudden ending of the sessions as being abandoned because he made the wrong decision. It may be that Dr. Alexander construed his contract with Owen to be a matter of assisting him get rid of some psychosomatic symptoms – but the possibility of Owen's leaving the ministry was more than he bargained for. If this were true and the contract had not been reviewed and clarified, then it is understandable, but indefensible, that Dr. Alexander might unknowingly adopt the attitude that "as long as you are working on improving your general psychological well-being as a minister, that's fine, but if you decide to stop being a minister, then our relationship must end."

The fourth alternative is clearly the most accepting response Dr. Alexander could make in the face of the conflict between Owen and himself. It is honest but at the same time definitely extends permission for Owen to disagree without losing Dr. Alexander's respect or concern. One of the clearest ways Dr. Alexander indicated that he accepted Owen's decision was by referring to it in the past tense (i.e., "I felt you should remain in the ministry ... I have confidence in you, though I hoped it would have gone the other way.") Alternative #4 also does not close off the counseling relationship just because a difficult decision has been made; there is every reason for Owen to expect that Dr. Alexander would welcome further discussion about his new plans.

There are counselors who would say that if Dr. Alexander felt quite strongly about Reverend Fremont remaining in the ministry, then he could not be objective about it and should have refused to see Reverend Fremont professionally. That may have been the ideal way to handle the situation, but often we are not able to achieve the ideal. If Dr. Alexander had refused to see Owen, it may have been impossible to accomplish a satisfactory referral, and Owen simply would have had to do without counseling. If after thorough discussion of the decision to remain in the ministry, Owen decides to leave, then Dr . Alexander needs to be able to respond in the manner suggested by alternative #4. But if Dr. Alexander were to find himself moving in the direction of alternative #1, #2, or #3, then he probably needs to re-examine some of his biases and expectations about Owen. The danger of a counselor having strong feelings about the outcome of a client's decision does not lie in the fact that the counselor cannot be "objective." Counselor objectivity is not the greatest good or zenith of fine counseling. The danger of a counselor's having strong feelings about a decision is, that his accepting the client may become conditional upon the client's choosing the counselor's preference. To neutralize such a danger, it is imperative that a counselor be able to guarantee to himself and to his client that his accepting a client does not depend upon the client always agreeing with him. In the example just presented, it is not Dr. Alexander's strong feelings that must be neutralized so that he will be indifferent to Owen's decision. Rather, it is imperative that Dr. Alexander be able to relinquish attempts to coerce Owen into remaining in the ministry, as illustrated by alternatives #1, #2, and #3, and to extend the genuine acceptance communicated by alternative #4.

We have concentrated heavily on this particular example for two reasons: (1) There are many ways in which it is like the conflicts between counselors and clients in many different settings, and thus we can generalize from this example to others. (2) We know from national surveys that a large percentage of people who are distressed or confused, or facing important decisions seek the assistance of clergymen first. If counseling as a profession is truly committed to providing assistance to individuals who are confused and who must make changes and choices in their lives, then we should make every attempt to provide relevant applications and illustrations of counseling principles for those persons who are doing most of the counseling, namely, clergymen.

*The Case of Bob*

The final hypothetical situation we will consider started out to be a "routine" educational-vocational planning session with Bob Hammond, a quiet, serious-minded senior high school student, but soon developed into a very emotion-laden encounter with Stan Weatherford, the boys' counselor. Mr. Weatherford is also the basketball and wrestling coach, but he did not know Bob very well because Bob had not turned out for sports. His time had been taken up primarily with a precollege math-science curriculum, participation on the award winning debate team, and a part-time job in a local supermarket. Bob was not an outstanding student and he had worked very hard to earn the B+ average that he carried. He had not particularly distinguished himself on the National Merit tests or on the College Boards, although his scores were high average. Bob and his best friend, Dick Endicott, were both planning to enter a small, but highly regarded liberal arts college in the Midwest and to declare premed majors. In contrast to Bob, Dick received mostly A's in his high school courses and did not study nearly as much. Dick also scored very high on the National Merit tests and there was a good possibility that he might win a scholarship award because of his test scores. In addition to the minimal time Dick spent on studies, he was a very skillful golfer and played at least twice a week, except in the winter. On the weekends and after school, Dick caddied and cleaned golf clubs at the local country club. A newly acquired interest in Far Eastern religions also took up some of Dick's time because he had read a great deal about them. Since they sat next to each other in a sophomore geometry class, Bob and Dick had been very good friends. Neither one of them dated much and when they were not working or with their families, they usually studied or just messed around together. They had decided about becoming physicians in their junior year, and had planned since then to go to the same college.

Knowing that the competition to be accepted, as well as to remain in the college which Bob had named was very stiff, Mr. Weatherford asked if Bob had applied to any other schools. Bob looked quite troubled and said that he hadn't applied anywhere else and that he really didn't know what he would do if he weren't accepted where Dick was going. When he heard himself say this, Bob seemed suddenly embarrassed and then blurted out, "Gee, that sounded kinda' queer, I guess."

*Directions the counselor might take:*
1. Reassure Bob that you're sure that's not true and redirect his attention to the importance of applying to more than one college.
2. Indicate that you were wondering if Bob's relationship with Dick maybe wasn't a little too "close" and that maybe going to different schools would be a good idea.
3. Summarize the feelings that you have heard Bob express by saying something like, "It's sort of frightening to think about the possibility

of being separated from Dick, but sort of troubling that he is that important to you."

Alternative #1 is a flat denial of the importance of Bob's feelings. Even though Mr. Weatherford might be trying to reassure Bob by not becoming alarmed, if Mr. Weatherford adopted the direction in #1, he would in essence be saying, "Such a possibility is unthinkable and such topics are unacceptable for us to discuss." Instead of being reassuring, alternative #1 would probably leave Bob thinking that having worries about homosexuality or having had any homosexual experience is so bad or so far-out that Mr. Weatherford could not even consider the possibility. Whether or not Bob has had any sexual experience that he would label "homosexual" is not at all clear from the information that Mr. Weatherford has. Indeed, if Bob has had any such experience, which should be no surprise according to our best estimates of homosexual contacts among males up to eighteen years in age, it is not something to become particularly concerned about. But adopting an unalarmed attitude while you respond to Bob's obvious distress over "sounding kinda' queer" can *not* be accomplished by doling out cheap reassurance that "you're sure that's not true." You are *not* sure that it is not true and your being certain about what is true or untrue at this point is totally irrelevant. The only thing that matters is that Bob's feelings – in this case, embarrassment and fear – are acknowledged and accepted.

Alternative #2 suggests a solution to a problem that the counselor just created on the spot. If Mr. Weatherford took this route he would completely bypass Bob's feelings. Instead of accepting and trying to understand Bob's distress, Mr. Weatherford would be using Bob's feelings to promote his own personal philosophy of friendship, namely, that high school boys should avoid getting "too close." Alternative #2 assumes that there is a problem of Bob and Dick being "too close" and rushes in with a solution. It may well be the case that Bob is overly dependent upon Dick, or vice versa, but Mr. Weatherford certainly could not know that from the information he has thus far received. In addition, it would be Bob and Dick who would need to decide if they are overly dependent upon one another. Mr. Weatherford might be of assistance in helping one or both of them explore their relationship, but it is not up to him to decide anything about it. Both alternative #1 and #2 cast the counselor in the role of evaluator or judge; in the first case, the judgment is that there is no need for Bob to be concerned about his relationship with Dick, and in the second case, the judgment is that there is definite need for Bob to be concerned about and to limit his relationship with Dick. Whenever a counselor sets himself up as a judge or allows himself to be set up as a judge, he is in no position to simply accept a client's diverse and complex feelings regardless of whether they are positive or negative.

Alternative #3 is a summary and reflection of Bob's feelings; it is probably the most accepting response Mr. Weatherford could make. Although there are many ways that Mr. Weatherford could say he hears and accepts Bob's distress, there are also many ways to summarize and reflect what Bob has said that would sound like the mindless productions of a parrot. For example, if Mr. Weatherford had said, "You don't know what you'll do if you are not accepted where Dick is and it sounds somewhat odd to say that," he would be summarizing and reflecting the content of Bob's statement, but not the feelings that accompanied the content. Such a content summary would probably communicate greater acceptance than would any of the judgmental comments in alternatives #1 and #2. But a counselor response that captures both the content and the feelings will communicate the highest degree of acceptance. The summary and reflection of feelings, together with content says, "I heard you; I understand how you feel; I am willing to just stand with you where you are; you are free to take us wherever it seems important to you to go next, whenever you want to go." When a counselor adopts this posture with a client, it also carries the message, "I trust and respect your judgment; I care enough to be in touch with your feelings, whatever they may be; I am not afraid of your thoughts and feelings; you are a valued person to me and if I can be of help, I would like to be." It is especially difficult for beginning counselors to believe that so much acceptance can be communicated with what appears to be such a simple statement. But it takes considerable skill to be able to quickly identify and reflect the significant content and feelings in a client's verbal and nonverbal communications. Often times an understanding nod of the head that says, "I am with you," is far more accepting than an elaborate summary that fails to capture the client's feelings.

Thus far we have been examining the "what" of Acceptance, what it means, what it is related to in human development, what it means in the counseling relationship; what the barriers are to being an accepting counselor, and what the differences are between accepting and rejecting counselor responses. We are now going to focus on the "how to" of Acceptance. Section Four of this book contains several training assignments designed to increase your capacity to accept others more fully and more easily. At this point, however, we will look at some general suggestions for becoming a more accepting counselor.

## How to Become More Accepting

All of the suggestions for becoming a more accepting counselor involve three processes: Exploring, Experiencing, and Expanding. As you explore the world about you, including ideas and feelings, objects and animals, but especially people, you will encounter new and unfamiliar thoughts, sensations, styles of expression, value systems, ways in which life is organized, and purposes for existence. By allowing yourself, or perhaps even pushing yourself, to experience fully these new and different discoveries, you will, of course, be changed by them. The changes will be in the direction of increasing your capacity to celebrate diversity and complexity.

### New Situations

One of the easiest ways to begin exploring and experiencing and expanding your capacity to accept others is to take yourself into new situations or settings. Regardless of the size and location of your particular community, there are undoubtedly dozens of settings in which people invest a great deal of time and energy, that you have never seen. For example, if you have never attended a Pentecostal Church service, then you probably are walking around with a vague stereotype of Pentecostals that falls somewhere between "mildly curious cult" and "wildly fanatical kooks." If you find yourself in this position, then it would behoove you to do some exploring and experiencing. There are several ways to begin, such as reading about Pentecostalism, making an appointment with a Pentecostal pastor and talking with him or her, and attending some services. It probably goes without saying, but just to be certain, it should be clear that the suggestion is that you enter and experience a new setting so that you will be changed, that is, freed of erroneous stereotypes, and enabled to be more accepting of what may have been very unfamiliar religious practices. It would be possible to adopt a "let's go look at the monkeys in the zoo" attitude and nothing would be further from the purpose of this suggestion. If you happen to be Pentecostal, then a more relevant setting for you to explore might be a Roman Catholic church.

Another setting that you may or may not have experienced is district court on Monday morning. The purpose of attending a court session would not be to see some fascinating criminal case that would rival a Perry Mason program, but rather to experience first hand the steady stream of individuals, seemingly locked into a self-defeating pattern of choices that almost defies disruption. Watch an eighteen-year-old grossly overweight girl, her face red and rumpled from crying, plead "guilty" to a shoplifting charge — involving a 39-cent bag of hair rollers and ask yourself about the role of the high school counselor. Observe an unshaven young man in white overalls and slippers provided by the city jail, plead "guilty" to a charge of nonsupport and wonder with him how an unskilled high school dropout is supposed to support a wife and four kids. You may feel overwhelmed; you may feel disgusted; you may feel angry, or pity or frustration, or all of these things, but you will probably feel stronger than ever about the importance of helping people make satisfying choices. If you are a high school counselor or an employment counselor, for example, you might invest a little more energy in and take a little more time with the next overweight student or potential dropout you encounter.

As we said in the beginning, there are dozens of settings or new situations that you could profitably explore. We will discuss one more example and then merely list some additional possibilities. Most counselors-in-training do not have first hand experience with people who are poverty-stricken, or people who are quite wealthy. Both groups pose a threat to most counselors because in either case the counselor is uncertain if *he* will be accepted. In addition, a counselor may harbor considerable hostility for wealthy people, simply because they have so much and so many have so little. If you find this to be true for you, that is, that you feel either self-conscious or resentful around wealthy people, then it is suggested that you take yourself into a setting that is frequented by well-to-do individuals. For example, most private country clubs have pro-shops where golf equipment and sports clothes are on sale to the public. Also many private clubs host golf tournaments that are open to the public to watch, usually for a fee. Whether or not you are interested in watching a golf tournament or browsing around a pro-shop, they provide opportunities to observe and interact with, on a limited basis, people that you may presently have encased in a velvet-lined, solid gold stereotype. The purpose of such an experience is not that you would become enchanted with rich people and immediately set up a private counseling practice to serve them. Rather, the value of experiencing such a setting would be that you could begin to regard a person's financial status as one of many important factors which account for the kind of person he is, but that it is not necessarily the most important factor, and certainly not the only factor. There are wealthy people who are frightened, some who are confident, other who are very responsible, some who could care less, still others who are quite confused. But they all perspire, put their trousers on one-leg-at-a-time, pass gas on occasion, suffer common colds, give birth to naked babies, and wonder about death.

You are in the best position to identify the settings that would be most helpful for you to explore and experience. But here are some suggestions that could result in encounters that would expand your capacity to accept others.

1.  The lobby of an old residential hotel that is heavily populated with older men.
2.  A Salvation Army Thrift Store or a Goodwill Industries Store
3.  A hospital emergency ward waiting room
4.  A bus depot, train station, and airport terminal
5.  A tavern, if that is an unfamiliar setting
6.  A coffee house or a teenage night club
7.  A dog show
8.  An auction
9.  A Tupperware party
10. An astrologer or palm-reader
11. A drag race; a stock car race
12. A dump

### New Roles

A second approach to increasing your capacity to accept others involves increasing your role repertoire. Each of us possesses several roles that we are relatively comfortable playing, e.g., friend, spouse, fellow worker, parent, officer of an organization, brother or sister, adviser or sponsor for a group, etc. Having an extensive role repertoire allows you to understand or empathize with people fully and quickly, as well as to be able to interact with them in ways that are comfortable and familiar to them. Some counselors-in-training resist this approach to becoming more accepting because they view it as a threat to their integration or their integrity. However, such resistance is usually found in persons who are pursuing integration by always trying to be the same. Usually such a pursuit is conducted under the guise of "being consistent and honest." Integration and sameness are quite different things. A well-integrated person behaves differently, depending in part on the situations and persons he encounters. A well-integrated male does not relate to his mother, his wife, his daughter, his secretary, a waitress in his favorite restaurant, his boss's wife, and his sister in the same way. Indeed, there will be some common elements in all of these relationships that have to do with the man's particular style of interacting, his beliefs and values about women, and his perceptions of himself. But there will also be some very important differences among the relationships that have to do with the way he and the other person define their roles. Personal integration is achieved through a core of common elements *plus* an absence of sharp conflict among your different role relationships. Trying to relate in the same way with each of the women would actually produce conflict and thereby prevent personal integration.

Possessing an extensive role repertoire does not mean you are a wishy-washy chameleon with a ditty-bag full of roles for every occasion. Instead we are talking about an individual who is sufficiently certain of his or her identity that he or she can risk relating in many different ways without getting lost in the process. For example, the well-integrated man we spoke of earlier could be patient and respectful in the face of his aging mother's lectures on how he should discipline his children, at the same time that with his wife he is unwilling to settle for anything less than thoroughly discussed and mutually agreeable discipline procedures for the children. Or he could be capable of romping and playing with his four-year-old daughter after work, although only hours before he was polite but rather formal and distant in response to his boss's wife's seductive overtures. This same man could well be his wife's greatest source of strength and emotional support, even though she held him until he wept himself to sleep the day his father was buried. He would likely be capable of laughing heartily at a crude and dirty joke, but be equally able to talk openly with his teenage son about the depth and range of meaning sexual intercourse can have. He might place a high premium on being good-natured and even-tempered, although he struggles against and sometimes loses to moodiness and periods of depression.

This quality and degree of integration need not be as idealistic or out-of-reach as it may first appear. What is required is a relatively clear sense of self or identity that is stable from one situation to another, and from one relationship to another, such as, seeing yourself as a person who tries to be as honest and open as possible; seeing yourself as a person who tries to help out or make things easier, it possible; seeing yourself as able to acknowledge disappointment but rarely able to admit to being angry at the time you feel angry, and so forth. The second requirement for being well-integrated is flexibility and skill in recognizing and accommodating to the role demands of different situations, different persons, and the same person on different occasions.

Most counselors-in-training have spent more time with and invested more energy in developing a stable self-concept than in acquiring flexibility and versatility in their repertoire of roles. However, the ability to celebrate diversity and complexity in others is very closely related to the condition of your role repertoire. There are several different ways to increase the number and range of roles which are readily available to you; some of these are presented as training assignments in Section Four. Here we will take up the things that are possible to do on your own, whether or not you are in a formal training program.

*Extending Your Role Repertoire through Reading*    One age-old method that for most of us has played some part in our developmental histories is reading about and identifying with real or fictional persons in novels, biographies, and plays. If your reading is an active, participative involvement with the characters and their situations and you are sufficiently identified with them that you have real feelings about what they do and what is done to them, then there is a very good chance that your role repertoire may be extended through reading. For example, if Mr. Weatherford had read and truly participated in a book by Chaim Potok called *The Chosen*, which includes an exquisite account of the birth and development of an intense, profound, and extremely constructive friendship between two teenage Jewish boys, then Mr. Weatherford might have been more accepting of Bob Hammond's fears. He would not have understood the fears any better, because the book does not in any way deal with that. The boys truly loved one another and there is no hint of their being embarrassed or worried about that fact. But if Mr. Weatherford could learn to allow two teenage boys to love one another as friends, without his becoming nervous or suspicious, then he likely would be able to accept Bob and Dick's friendship without alarm. Given that Mr. Weatherford really invested himself in *The Chosen*, he very likely could learn to allow, maybe even to celebrate, deep friendship between teenage boys. In the appendix there is a list of novels and plays that may be of assistance in your reading to expand your role repertoire. Your best resources, however, are probably a librarian, an English teacher, or a drama instructor.

*Extending Your Role Repertoire through Study of a Particular Role*    Another way to expand your role repertoire is to select a standard role, e.g., close friend, young father, respected teacher, skillful supervisor, etc., and begin to study intensively the myriad ways in which that one role is played. The ultimate purpose of such a study is to facilitate your being able to recognize and accept many different ways of filling a particular role.

When we attribute a role to someone, we then have expectations about how the person should act, think, and feel. For example, when we attribute the role of "leader" to someone in a group, we usually have expectations that the person will do something. We would probably expect him to take the initiative and either push the group toward realizing its purposes or facilitate attempts by group members to move the group toward realizing its purposes. If the "leader" just sits there and does nothing, then we would begin to question his right to be in the leadership role. In short, assigning a role to a person means we have expectations, and if the expectations are not met, then we find the person to be unacceptable in that role. Suppose you have a very narrow definition of a particular role, and thus very specific and narrowly defined expectations for how a person in that role should act, think, and feel, if you encounter someone who supposedly is in that role, for example a mother, and this particular woman does not act, think, or feel the way you expect a mother should, then you will most likely find her unacceptable as a mother. It is obvious how narrow role definitions can interfere with a counselor's ability to accept people. In order to avoid the difficulties in being accepting that are created by narrow role definitions, the counselor must be familiar with and appreciative of several different and equally acceptable ways a particular role can be filled. A counselor must give up the idea that there is one best way to be a mother, for instance, and recognize and appreciate several equally successful ways in which a woman could fill the role of mother.

In order to increase your willingness to relinquish narrow role definitions and thereby strengthen your capacity to accept several different ways of filling a role, you are encouraged to select a particular role that interests you and study it thoroughly. You will note that the need to change narrow role definitions is met by encouraging you to become actively involved in exploring the role and experiencing new ways of filling the role. Through your explorations and experiences, present role definitions that are too narrow will expand to accommodate greater diversity. Sometimes counselors will attempt to rid themselves of narrow role definitions by adopting a vague, ambiguous, unclear definition of a role. Instead of increasing the counselor's ability to accept diverse ways of filling a role, this usually results in hidden expectations that are not clear to either the counselor or the client. The counselor is just as narrow and rejecting as he was before, but now it is not clear why.

We will consider one example of selecting a standard role and studying it intensively in order to expand one's role definition and role expectancies. The role suggested for exploration is that of an "older sister." What follows are some suggestions for conducting an analysis of the standard role "older sister"; we will not present the analysis itself. Most persons either have a sister, or are someone else's sister or both, but few people have paid much attention to the great diversity of definitions the role "sister" takes on. This would be less true if you have been exposed to Adlerian family constellation theory, because the Adlerians have emphasized the importance of a person's position and role in the family for understanding that person. This, in fact, might be a good way to begin a standard role analysis; that is, to examine some of the descriptions of family constellations. For example, see Walter Toman, *Family Constellation*, 1961. In addition to reading the technical literature on a particular role, you can find other definitions and descriptions of the role in novels, plays, and biographies. Movies and television provide still other ways of intensively exploring and experiencing a particular role. (For example, *What Ever Happened to Baby Jane*, and *Georgie Girl, Days of Our Lives*, and *Peyton Place.*) It would be difficult if not impossible to exaggerate the influence these two media (movies and television) have on determining role definitions of all kinds.

A major part of your analysis of a standard role should involve observation of and interaction with representatives of the role. Spend some time watching and trying to understand; relate to and try to comprehend older sisters in their role as sister. You will be struck with how different they are, of course. Each older sister is a unique person, unlike any other older sister who has ever lived or ever will live. But you may be struck with some commonalities too; some characteristics that seem to be true of nearly all older sisters may become apparent. For example, many older sisters tend to be terribly responsible, and in later years, often assume responsibility quickly to the point of being officious at times. The purpose of conducting an analysis of a standard role is not so you can become a whiz at predicting how a person will behave simply by knowing a role relationship he or she occupies; but rather the purpose is to expand your awareness of and capacity to accept several ways of occupying the role. It is important for a counselor to be able to accept a client's references to "my older sister" even though the older sister may be depicted as a reliable, supportive, helpful person by one client and, in contrast, a diabolical, suppressive, vicious rival by another client. It is important that your role definition of "older sister" is not so narrow and rigid that upon hearing the role label "older sister" you immediately assume you know precisely what the client thinks and feels about his older sister, but rather your role definition is sufficiently broad that you can hear and appreciate a wide range of thoughts and feelings your client might express. Obviously this holds true for any other role reference the client makes.

*Extending Your Role Repertoire through Taking an Unfamiliar Role*    A third way to expand your role repertoire is to seek new situations and/or new relationships that will demand your taking on an unfamiliar role. There are some very simple ways to do this, as well as some very complicated and involved procedures. Something as simple as joining in the parlor game called Charades, in which you must act out a book title or movie title, a common saying, or a famous person's name without using any words, is a new situation that demands that you take on an unfamiliar role. Charades is usually played for fun and is hardly a serious activity; often you feel silly, for example, trying to look like a "watched pot that is not boiling," or like someone going "Up the Down Staircase." However, willingness to risk looking silly, and willingness to try something unfamiliar in the presence of other people is definitely related to willingness to allow and to prize diversity in others. If you are unwilling to risk being seen in any roles except the ones in which you feel safe and comfortable, then you are also likely to be unwilling to accept someone else in a role that makes you uncomfortable. For example, if you were unwilling to risk trying to play the role of the Biblical character, Jezebel, or to play the role of a madam in a house of prostitution for a game of Charades or for a skit, how could you claim to be able to accept a woman whose past or present life includes exploitative and illicit sexual practices. No one is suggesting that you should applaud the activities of a deceitful, destructive Jezebel, or a shady lady from a house of ill repute. But it you were called upon to counsel with either type of woman, you certainly need to be able to accept and appreciate her as a human being. Your being unwilling to allow yourself to even *appear* to be like such a person in a game or skit would be a dead giveaway of the degree of rejection you feel for this kind of woman.

Another and perhaps more obvious situation that demands a new role from you would be participating in the preparation and performance of a play. Almost all communities have drama groups that provide opportunities for even the most inexperienced to take part in a dramatic production. Such an activity usually requires considerable time and energy, depending on the size of the part you would be playing. A small part in the "crowd scene" or a minor character role are not as demanding of your time and talent, of course, but they are extremely important to the overall quality of any dramatic production. Small or large roles both afford an excellent chance for you to become involved in what could have considerable impact on your ability to experience and appreciate new and unfamiliar roles.

Besides seeking situations which would demand a new role of you, it was also suggested that you seek relationships that would demand a new role. For example, if you have never been in a teaching or supervisory role yith youngsters or older people or disabled persons, then you might consider chaperoning or sponsoring a group's activity on a special occasion, e.g., Valentine's Day, Halloween, Christmas, and so forth. Or if you are able to invest more time and attention, you could volunteer to assist with coaching a Little League team, tutoring the retarded, reading to and writing letters for a senior citizens' group, providing transportation for clients at a public clinic, becoming a Big Brother for a predelinquent adolescent, teaching a Sunday School class, etc. The emphasis here is less on the importance of volunteer work, which indeed is tremendously important, but more on pointing to another way in which you could seek new relationships that demand new roles of you. One of the issues that often arises in the training of counselors is their response to dependency on the part of a client. This is a very complicated issue and not one we can adequately cover in a brief discussion here. However, you can see that one of the dimensions you could begin to explore by putting yourself in some of the role relationships just suggested is how you respond to different kinds and degrees of dependency. How do you feel being the only link to the outside world for an aged, crippled shut-in? Is it unacceptable to you if an inarticulate, impoverished widow goes on and on telling you how much she appreciates your taking her young deaf son to the clinic each week? Or are you pushed out of shape if these needful people are not sufficiently grateful for your services? These are aspects of the "helper" role that you can begin to explore on your own; they are dimensions that will likely come up again in your training when you have the benefit of a supervisor with whom to consider them, but you can begin the process now.

The use of role-playing and psychodramatic procedures as a part of your training should be under the direction of a trained and skillful teacher. These procedures will be discussed in Section Three—Communication, and are only mentioned here as examples of other ways to expand your role repertoire.

*Extending Your Role Repertoire through Simulation*    We will discuss one final way to increase your general responsiveness to and your ability to accept diverse roles. Simulation and deception is involved in this procedure, and it therefore makes some people's ethical hair stand on end. One of the ways we have begun students' pre-doctoral internships in a mental hospital is by confining the students themselves to a mental hospital for one week. This was done without the knowledge of the hospital ward staff, other than the ward psychiatrist. There are some ethical problems involved here. But they have been dealt with as follows: The treatment staff agreed to participate in such a training program; they gave their permission to be kept uninformed as to the time when a student would be posing as a patient and as to which of the patients was in reality a student. At the end of the week, the staff and the student agreed to meet together and "debrief" the experience. The student is there to learn about himself and the role of a mental hospital patient; he has a responsibility to maintain his role and avoid being unnecessarily disruptive or demanding during the week. At the end of the week, the student has agreed to share, verbally and in written form, what he has learned; he is not there primarily as a spy or a critic, although some of the experiences he reports may reflect quite negatively on the staff. During the student's stay he, of course, becomes familiar with many of the patients; he has agreed to be bound by the same rules of confidentiality and professional limits after he leaves the ward that would be true if he were part of the ward professional staff. The chief psychologist at one of our internship agency settings initiated and implemented this simulation training procedure. All the students who have experienced it report that it is one of the most significant training experiences they have had. Usually, their reports include references to the simulation having expanded their awareness of and appreciation of persons in the patient role.

Whereas you probably are not in a position to arrange such an elaborate simulation, you can on your own simulate an unfamiliar role. For example, you could put on dark glasses, lined with black paper, and simulate the experiences of a blind person. It is easier and usually more helpful to ask someone to join in the experience. The person can both assist you during the simulation and help with the "debriefing" afterward. Going to a restaurant, ordering a meal, and eating it as a blind person, if done seriously and for the purpose of truly trying to feel what it is like to be blind, can be a profound experience.

You will have to deal with the ethical implications of appearing to be something that you are not, and settle the questions in ways that are satisfying to you. Some questions and considerations that might guide your thinking are: (1) There is never a time that we do not appear to be something that we are not; no one is in touch with some absolutely "real you" all of the time. (2) Because you do not "intend" to fool someone, such as when someone perceives you to be more interested in what they are saying than you really are, are you therefore less responsible for fooling them? In a simulation by which you are intending to fool someone, at least for a period of time, are you somehow more responsible than when you fool someone without intending to? (3) Are you sure your ethical objections are not merely a convenient way to avoid doing something that is frightening and that would make you uncomfortable? (4) There are ways to protect other people from the phoniness of your simulated role which will allow you to participate in a very authentic training experience. For example, if you are simulating a blind person, do not step off a curb in heavy traffic just to see what that would be like; or do not apply for aid to the blind wherein you would have to falsify records unless prior arrangements have been made with the agency to participate in the simulation. (5) Choose a role simulation that you are quite certain will not offend or endanger someone else; although you can best design your own simulation, some examples are:

1.  Rent a wheel chair and go shopping where you will not be recognized.
2.  Put on old clothes and accompany someone to the commodity food distribution center. A social worker or minister can often help you arrange this.
3.  Dress in shabby clothes and inquire about a bank loan for a car.
4.  Borrow or rent a hearing aid, simulate severe hearing loss as you inquire about opening a charge account at a department store.
5.  Design a questionnaire about attitudes toward open-housing; represent yourself as being from a pro-open-housing civil rights group and poll the houses in a wealthy, exclusive neighborhood and in a lower-middle-class neighborhood.
6.  With an opposite-sex member of a minority race, simulate a married couple going shopping or to a movie or to a restaurant, etc.

7.  Dress like a hippie and go to a coffee house or a bookstore frequented by hippies and then to a downtown store where hippies seldom go.

8.  Take an obviously retarded or crippled child to an ice cream parlor for a treat. You can probably make the necessary arrangements with a local special school or clinic. Go someplace where you are not known and the natural assumption is that you are the child's father or mother, brother or sister.

9.  Join in a sign-carrying, group-singing civil rights or antiwar demonstration.

10. Arrange to distribute religious tracts where you will not be recognized as not belonging to that religious group.

11. Design a role of someone quite unlike yourself; for example, if you are somewhat shy or reticent in initiating conversations, then design a role of a very friendly, outgoing, almost forward person. Take a short bus trip to a nearby community. Talk with someone on the bus, have a meal, and return, all the while remaining in the role.

12. Dress up in extremely sophisticated attire, which you could rent or borrow, and attend a concert, a play, or a ballet. Assume that you are highly cultured and very sophisticated and relate to the box office girl, the ushers, and anyone else you encounter, in that role.

13. Take a day and pretend that you are entirely alone; you have no family, are without friends, and work alone. Go to a park, to the library, to a cafeteria, and to a church during the day. In the evening go for a walk downtown by yourself.

14. Locate a very menial job that you could hold for one day such as picking fruit or vegetables, selling peanuts at a sports event, or working on a clean-up crew. If employment is not possible, dress appropriately and arrange to sweep the sidewalks and gutters in front of several stores, where you will not be recognized.

When you are planning a simulation, take care in creating the person you are going to be. Think about his past, his present situation, his values, abilities, interests, and expectations. Think about how others would likely respond to him and imagine how he would feel about that. Try to lose yourself in the role, but carefully attend to what is going on so that when you debrief or record the experience you can describe it fully and accurately. Some of the suggested simulations would not be simulations for you, because you may be blind or have a retarded child, or know what it is like to pick fruit. You will, of course, not need to simulate those experiences; you will learn much more from a role simulation that is very unfamiliar.

Let us close this discussion of how to increase your role repertoire, thereby expanding your capacity to celebrate diversity and complexity with a reminder that any of these suggestions must be entered into wholeheartedly.

Although you need not be somber, there must be a seriousness and a posture of good faith pervading your efforts or they can degenerate into the escapades of a con artist, or this week's entertainment for those who are bored with life. The suggestions here are given as ways of facilitating your becoming more deeply immersed in life and not as ways to exploit or toy with living.

## New Media

The third and final approach to increasing your capacity to accept others involves your exploring and experiencing new media. The suggestions in this discussion of exploring new and different media may appear to be a potpourri of things to do to fill your already busy life. It is unlikely that you could undertake all of the possibilities we will discuss. However, you can accomplish the purpose of these seemingly scattered activities by sampling from the total list because the unifying thread running throughout the collection is, simply, experiencing new and different ways of expressing yourself. Most of us are far more constrained in the ways we choose to give expression to our thoughts and feelings than we need to be. Most of us rely almost exclusively on spoken verbal messages delivered directly, face to face, to the intended receiver. A medium, as we are using it here, refers to the substance, channel, instrument, modality, or vehicle by means of which we express ourselves. The general recommendation is that you explore, experiment with, and experience new substances, channels, instruments, modalities, and vehicles of expression.

Individuals vary greatly in the media of expression that they prefer, with which they feel most comfortable and in which they are most able to express themselves clearly. For example, some adolescents could express more about what is most important to them, what things are uppermost in their thoughts and feelings, by showing you a series of photographs they had taken, than by trying to tell you the same things in words. If you saw a series of black and white photographs that included the grave marker of a child, the rat-infested rubble of a ghetto alley, the pleading eyes of a solitary face looking out through the wire fence surrounding a juvenile detention home, an old man patiently waiting in the park for nobody to come, a family of four romping on the beach, and a teenage boy and girl, outwardly appearing to be identical but inwardly searching the differences upon which they will build their separate identities; if you were privileged to share such a statement from an adolescent, you could probably learn more than you would in three hours of conversation.

Expanding the number and diversity of ways you are willing to try to send and receive messages about what you and others think and feel, extends the number and diversity of people with whom you can relate. In addition, the process of trying to express yourself through new media is usually somewhat frightening and frustrating, as well as exciting and fun. There is always the threat of not knowing exactly what to do and the fear that your efforts will come to nothing or, what is worse, that they will be hopelessly inadequate and an embarrassment to all concerned. If photography is a new or unfamiliar media to you, the thought of doing a photographic essay to communicate your ideas and feelings about family life, for instance, would probably be somewhat intimidating at the same time that it might sound enticing. Such a combination of fear and venturing forth, of intimidation and investment, is not uncharacteristic of the feelings many clients bring to counseling. Most persons seeking counseling do so with mixed emotions; they often want to invest themselves, but are also afraid that it will come to nothing or maybe even make things more confused than they already are. Few people are completely certain that counseling will help them decide what to do or change the way things are; most clients venture forth in the face of many uncertainties. There is a definite parallel between a client seeking counseling and your seeking new media for expression. Thus, in addition to expanding the ways you are able to express yourself and receive the expressions of others, exploring new media provides opportunities to capture and appreciate the mixed feelings that characterize most beginning clients.

The range of possibilities is almost limitless; the diversity of media almost defies classification. Rather than attempt to list all the possibilities within the fine arts, followed by the possibilities in the various crafts, in the graphic arts and photography, in music and dance, in literature and in science, we will settle for a miscellany of suggestions that span all of these fields. The examples were chosen primarily on the basis of their availability to persons in widely scattered parts of the country, living in communities of very different sizes and degrees of complexity. The examples are not presented as the best of all possible ways to explore new media, but rather as some highly probable ways you could begin your explorations.

Photography has already been mentioned and is a good beginning for many persons. Black and white snapshots, as well as movies can both be utilized. Some people have had a marvelous experience with coordinating a carousel of colored slides and a tape recording of appropriate music, sound, and noise. A growing interest of young persons is making "now" movies of people, scenes, action, and no-action which demands that the viewer become involved "now" and contribute to the meaning "now." Such a movie is experienced, not watched; its meaning is now, not rolled up on the reel and stored in a flat can. A small home-movie outfit or equipment borrowed from an audio-visual department will suffice for such a project.

The "now" movie has a collage-like quality that can also be experienced by cutting and pasting together pictures from magazines, newspapers, and "junk mail." Or larger pieces of junk, such as: the torn label from an expensive perfume; the box top from a highly formulated, thoroughly tested toothpaste; a discarded shoe polish applicator caked with chunks of white stuff; a used-up lipstick refill cartridge; rusty old razor blades; a broken eye lash curler and an assortment of hair curlers; cotton balls, cotton swabs, and cotton squares; a twisted, nearly empty tube of blemish cream that hides and heals in one operation; a strand of dental floss; a piece of broken mirror and a toothless, dirty comb; can be neatly arranged and glued to a board which has been covered with newspaper accounts of the war on poverty. This kind of personal statement can have at least as much impact as your saying in words that you are troubled by the inconsistencies, inequities, and absurdities of contemporary American life.

Two of the most obvious nonverbal vehicles for expression are painting and drawing. Some of you have undoubtedly tried your hand at oil, watercolor, charcoal, or pen and ink with varying degrees of success and satisfaction. If you have never attempted to communicate in these media, one way to begin is to purchase a set of bamboo-tipped colored pens which are now available in any dime store, or supermarket, and an inexpensive artist's sketch pad. Each day for a week choose something that you regard as worth keeping and try to represent it with the pens and pad. For example, you might want to capture the mood that pervaded a day, and the page could be covered with flowers of all shapes and sizes in all different colors, or the page could contain a long black box being lowered into the Past to rest alongside Yesterday and The Day Before. There might have been a pleasing phrase or a painful phrase that is personally worth keeping in some shape or form: "I'm really glad you called." "But you said . . ." "I love you. . . ." "It really doesn't matter . . . now." Or you might have seen a relationship in a new way, for example, between: You and Me, Love and Hate, Black and White, Young and Old, Was and Is, Alone and Together. Or there might be fragments of conversation that kaleidoscopically arranged in different styles of printing, capture that day: "Just fine, how are you? "Oh, that's too bad, how old was he?" "No, a scoop of vanilla and a scoop of chocolate almond on *one* cone." "Yes, but I've told you that a hundred times!" "Fill it up with regular." "Just fine, how are you?" "No, I hadn't heard . . . how long will it take?" "Yah, that's really funny." "No, black is fine." "Not if it isn't deductible, though." "Oh, not much, how about yourself?" "Thirty-eight, is that right?" "Well, hit him back." "Yah, see y'a around."

These are merely examples to provide some idea of what a colored pen journal might contain, in case you have never seen one. What is really important, however, is that *you* decide what *you* want to express and how *you* want to do that. It is possible that someday you might be asked to accept a client's feelings and thoughts expressed in this way; but whether or not that happens, the process of expanding the communication media with which you are familiar contributes to your overall ability to receive diverse communications.

There are many other substances or materials that are also potential vehicles for communication. Some of them require a considerable degree of skill or craftsmanship; some are expensive and require elaborate equipment. However, many of these materials are readily available, and often with no previous experience, you can devise ways to express yourself with them that are different and satisfying. You can probably add many more to the following list of materials: leather, copper, plastic, weeds for dry bouquets, wild flowers, brightly colored felt and yarn, stone for sculpting, wood for carving, clay for throwing pots, sea shells, driftwood and pebbles, and paper of all textures and colors. We are not assuming that highly accepting counselors are necessarily more creative or more skillful craftsmen. Rather, we are postulating that one approach to expanding your capacity to accept diversity and complexity in others is to expand the number and variety of communication media with which you are familiar and comfortable. And, secondly, we are postulating that the very process of exploring and experiencing new media is parallel to a client's experience of seeking and participating in counseling. Therefore, it is possible to generalize from an understanding and acceptance of your own experience with new media to an understanding and acceptance of the client's experience with counseling.

It should be pointed out that a more direct route to experiencing what it is like to seek counseling is simply to seek counseling yourself. However, there are many and differing schools of thought on that subject which range from "Yes, it is imperative and is therefore a part of any *adequate* training program;" to "Yes, it should be available to and encouraged among counselors-in-training, but it should not be a requirement;" to "No, it is an unnecessary and usually destructive practice which fosters inordinate dependency among trainees and thus should be avoided." We will not try to settle this long-standing controversy because what we are concerned with at this point is finding ways that you can, on your own and in the course of your daily life, become more accepting. Personal counseling might well facilitate this process but so will exploring and experiencing new situations, new roles, and new media.

## IV   SINCERITY

The third and final characteristic which is thought to be essential for the competent counselor is what Tyler calls Sincerity. Truax and Carkhuff have labeled this difficult-to-define attribute "genuineness" and "authenticity"; Rogers has used the term "congruence." All of these writers have acknowledged that not only is the quality difficult to define, but it is also very difficult to measure and to teach. A major problem is that it is impossible to specify precisely a set of behaviors that are sincere; "sincere" does not have a verb form. We can talk about Understanding as a process; you can understand somebody or something. We can talk about Acceptance as a process; you can accept somebody or something. But we cannot talk about Sincerity as a process; you cannot sincere somebody or something. No counselor can "do sincere"; he can only "be sincere." We cannot ask the questions: "What must I sincere?" and "How can I sincere it?" as we did with Understanding and Acceptance.

At the same time that it is impossible to point to specific actions called "sincerity"; sincerity is not some vague, ethereal vapor that encircles one's head, nor is it some mystical humor that courses through the veins of an elite group commonly known as competent counselors. Although sincere is defined as something a counselor is, not something he does, we are not saying that sincerity is unrelated to what a counselor does — quite the opposite. The diagram in Figure 9 will help us locate where in the counseling process the counselor's sincerity has its greatest impact.

**FIGURE 9.    Sincerity and the Counseling Process.**

Part of the counseling process involves the counselor receiving data from the world outside of himself; especially important in this aspect of the process is the information he receives from the client. The counselor's skill and capacity to understand and to accept the client govern the quality of this part of the counseling process. The other dimension of the counseling process involves the counselor giving data to the world outside of himself; particularly important in this aspect of the process is the information he gives to the client. Counselors give all kinds of information, including test results, new ways of looking at a situation, perceptions of the client, job entry requirements, procedures for alleviating anxiety, etc. But of particular concern to us at this point is the information the counselor gives about himself. Whether he is actually talking about himself or not, a counselor is communicating data about himself all the time. The quality of that communication is governed by the counselor's sincerity. You can think of the three counselor characteristics as filters: incoming data are filtered through the counselor's ability to understand and to accept; outgoing data about himself are filtered through the counselor's ability to be sincere. None of us does a perfect job of representing the outside world to himself; we all distort and deny some of what is out there as we try to understand and accept it. By the same token, none of us does a perfect job of representing himself to the outside world exactly as he is; we all distort and deny some of what we are as we give out information about ourselves to others. Knowing we fall considerably short of complete sincerity, the appropriate questions are: "How valid is the representation I give of myself?" and "How reliable is the representation I give of myself?" Sincerity in the counselor can be seen as the extent to which the counselor communicates a valid and reliable picture of what he is really like inside.

## Validity and Reliability in the Counselor

The terms "valid" and "reliable" are being used to describe the sincerity of a counselor's communications about himself in the same way that validity and reliability are used to describe the trustworthiness of a standardized test. Validity, when applied to psychological tests, refers to the degree to which a test actually measures what it purports to measure. For example, if a test is supposed to measure musical aptitude, then we want to be sure that other things are not interfering with measuring musical aptitude, such as reading ability or visual acuity. It is possible that a person with poor reading skills or poor vision might have very high musical aptitude. In order to have confidence in a test of musical aptitude, we would need to be certain that reading ability and visual acuity did not affect a person's score on the test. If it has high validity, then the test score will represent the person's actual musical aptitude rather than some other aptitude or ability.

Reliability, when applied to psychological tests, refers to the degree to which a test measures consistently and accurately. Again using the example of a test of musical aptitude, we would want to be sure that the test would yield the same score tomorrow that it does today. A person's musical aptitude does not change overnight and if the test were given under the same circumstances on two consecutive days then we would expect to get the same results. If the test is highly reliable, then we can assume that the person's true musical aptitude is accurately represented by his score. No test is perfectly valid or completely reliable and it is important to know how much confidence we should have in the scores it yields. For a discussion of test reliability and validity as they relate to counseling, see Tyler (1969, pp. 89–97).

In general, validity and reliability refer to the extent to which something actually is what it appears to be. When validity and reliability are low, we regard the appearance as a phoney and untrustworthy representation of the real thing. When validity and reliability are high, we regard the appearance as real, genuine, authentic, congruent, honest, and sincere.

To illustrate that a counselor communicates his sincerity by the degree of validity and reliability characterizing his messages about himself, we will compare the counselor to a radio station. You have no doubt had the experience of trying to listen to a particular radio program that was nearly obliterated with static. Even though you try very hard to tune in on the signal, something else keeps interfering with the program you are trying to get. Sometimes the interference is another program that is competing with the one you want to hear; sometimes the interference is just irrelevant, meaningless noise. Thinking of the counselor (Figure 9), it is important that he not send out competing and conflicting signals. It is important that the message he sends is a valid representation of what he truly is; otherwise it is very distracting and unpleasant to continue listening and most people will tune out. For example, suppose a counselor wants to transmit that he is very interested in what his client is saying because he knows counselors are supposed to be interested in their clients and most of the time he really is interested. On this particular occasion, the client is rambling through an episode concerning his mother that is apparently quite important to him. It just so happens that the counselor has recently had a sizeable argument with his own mother that is still unresolved. It is very possible that the counselor has devices for encapsulating his own personal parental difficulties so that they do not interfere with his ability to interact with his client about the client's mother. However, if the counselor is unable to suspend his concerns about his own mother and finds himself preoccupied with personal thoughts and feelings, then he faces a decision. He can either acknowledge that he too has had some recent difficulties with his own mother, and so he can readily identify with the client's concerns; or he can try to ignore or suppress his personal thoughts and hope they will not be obvious. The chances are good that if he tries to ignore or deny his preoccupation, it will only increase and he will begin to transmit conflicting signals; namely, "I am really interested in what you are saying," and "I don't really want to hear what you are saying." Or he will transmit one signal and some static: "I am genuinely interested in what you are relating, but there is also something else going on inside of me."

You can briefly acknowledge some personal experience without permanently snatching the spotlight from the client and his experience. In a situation like the one just described, if you allow your preoccupations to go unacknowledged, you run a high risk of sending out an invalid representation of yourself. Being sincere as a counselor means that you transmit a signal that communicates valid messages about yourself. Uncluttered by static or conflicting signals.

Continuing with the radio station analogy, you have probably also had the experience, late at night, driving in your car, of trying to listen to a distant station that keeps fading in and out. When the program comes through, it is loud and clear and free of static, but in a few minutes it fades to an inaudible level. This same thing can happen with a counselor transmitting information about himself. For example, suppose that a client is trying to decide whether or not to continue with a licensed practical nurses' training program and the decision is intertwined with another decision of whether or not to file for divorce at this time. The counselor with whom she is working believes strongly that she should finish the LPN program first and worry about the divorce later. It is possible that he can suspend his judgment on the basis of his belief that, above all, she should do what she thinks and feels is best. If the counselor is successful in achieving a position of neutrality on the matter, then he need not mention his beliefs one way or the other. However, he may find that he is actually committed to the position that she should finish training first. In that case, he faces a decision: He can either openly acknowledge his bias or he can try to ignore and deny it to himself. However, if he tries to suppress his opinion, it will probably find expression in the fact that he comes through loudly and clearly when discussing the advantages of finishing training, but fades out when discussing the advantages of settling the divorce first. We should not exclude the possibility of the client doing both simultaneously; however, the counselor may not even see that possibility if he is unknowingly, but rigidly, focused on allowing nothing to interfere with finishing the training.

You can acknowledge an opinion or bias without insisting that your client agree or else lose your approval. Oftentimes you will have an opinion about a decision facing your client, at the same time that you do not want to subtly manipulate your client into agreeing with you. By stating your opinion openly, the danger of subtle manipulation is less than it would be if you were to ignore everything the client said that did not support your position. For example, suppose that you are counseling an unwed, one-and-a-half-months pregnant junior high school girl, and that the law governing medical termination of pregnancy has been recently liberalized, but you are generally opposed to abortion under any circumstances. There are many decisions to be made in such a situation that involve the girl, her parents, the would-be father, school personnel, a physician, and perhaps a clergyman. However, you are in a very influential position as far as how seriously abortion will be considered as an alternative. By recommending a particular physician who you know shares your disapproval of abortion and by making vague references to "research which proves that young girls who have abortions suffer serious psychological damage," you can subtly reduce the probability that abortion will be considered. However, you could also simply state openly that you are very biased against abortion, and thus would find it difficult to discuss it as a real possibility, but that you believe it is important for her to discuss abortion with a competent counselor who is not opposed to it, if she would like to have that opportunity. You are in less danger of subtly manipulating her into not considering a legal abortion if you are frank about your bias. In addition, you are in less danger of transmitting messages about yourself that are inconsistent and unreliable. If one minute your seem to be attentive, interested, and helpful, but the next minute you seem to not hear what the client is saying and to have stopped trying to be helpful, then your message is not very clear. Being sincere as a counselor means that you transmit a signal that reliably represents your own position and that you not fade in and out according to how much your client agrees with you.

Of course, we know that how a radio signal is heard depends not only upon the transmitting station, but also upon the receiving equipment. However, as a counselor you only have immediate access to yourself as a transmitter. You cannot assume that each client has elaborate, high fidelity equipment that will pick up poorly transmitted signals. If you send out messages that compete with one another, if there is considerable static interfering with your messages, if your signal fades in and out, then you can expect that clients will tune out.

Being sincere as a counselor results in your reliably representing to your client a valid picture of what you are thinking and feeling. However, because the counseling process is focused primarily on the client and his situation, most of your messages about yourself are communicated indirectly and nonverbally. That, of course, makes the task of teaching and measuring sincerity quite difficult. It is impossible to say, for instance, "In order to communicate your sincerity you should behave in the following manner . . ." Nor can we say, "We can determine how sincere you are by counting the number of times you . . ." In actual counseling encounters, if you attempt to pursue sincerity directly, it is likely to have the opposite effect. Sincerity is similar to humility in that if you work very hard at being humble, you are sure to become "preoccupied with your own worth," which is the opposite of humility. If you work very hard at being sincere, you are sure to become "more concerned about the impression you are making, than about your client's needs," which is the opposite of sincerity. It is very unfortunate when a counselor tries to increase his sincerity directly by trying to be an exact replica of "genuine counselor," or by trying to always "act the same, no matter what." These pursuits are doomed to failure in that the counselor usually emerges behaving in a stilted, self-conscious, constricted, conforming, calculated, rehearsed, and mechanical manner. Sincerity becomes buried under layers of denial and distortion of who the counselor really is.

Even though it is difficult to describe counselor authenticity or sincerity, it is probably useful to review some of the ways that "representing yourself validly and reliably" have been conceptualized. In addition, we will discuss the internal processes that facilitate the growth of sincerity. This section will close with a discussion of how those processes can be developed in the interest of becoming a more sincere counselor.

## One Conceptualization of Sincerity

One of the ways sincerity has been conceptualized is in terms of opposite poles of several continua (see Figure 10).

FIGURE 10.  Sincerity Conceptualized as Opposite Poles of
Several Continua

| Closed | Open |
|---|---|
| Rehearsed | Spontaneous |
| Hidden | Visible |
| Disowned | Owned |

### *Open vs. Closed*

To be sincere means that you are open *to* your own thoughts and feelings, as well as the thoughts and feelings of others; and you are open *with* yourself and others about your own experience. The counselor who is closed to and with himself and others does not allow himself to be in close touch with the raw data of his own experience. For instance, most of us have had suicidal thoughts and feelings at one time or another. That experience need not be alarming, even though it probably was very unpleasant. What is alarming is the counselor who is so closed to allowing himself to explore irrational and destructive thoughts and feelings that he shrinks in horror from the very suggestion that maybe he has felt like committing suicide at some point. The reason that such closedness to the possibility of contemplating suicide is alarming is that if he is faced with a client who reveals suicidal thoughts and feelings, he probably will be very closed to his client also. In fact, he may not be able to take the client seriously and may attempt to deny that such a choice exists. Being open to and with the client at a time like this means that the counselor remains psychologically near and does not attempt to protect and shield himself from the harsh reality of the decision his client is considering. It may mean saying: "That is a frightening thought to me . . . I really do not want that to happen." It may mean saying: "I have never been exactly where you are, or felt exactly what you are feeling, but I can identify with you . . . I know what it is like to want to kill myself." It may mean saying: "I really haven't ever felt like killing myself, but I think I can sense the terrible emptiness you feel, and I can see how suicide could be an answer." What is important is that the counselor is honest, direct, and open about his thoughts and feelings. That, of course, does not mean you should deliver a lecture on the evils of committing suicide, nor does it mean you should recount the last time you narrowly escaped committing suicide. One of the most effective deterrents to a client's committing suicide is establishing some contract with you concerning steps he will take to prevent himself from attempting suicide. For instance, you might agree that before he followed through on the desire to commit suicide, he would contact you to discuss it. Or if he feels nearly overwhelmed with thoughts of suicide, you might work out a contract that he check in with you daily, until he feels he can manage without that contact.

There are many aspects of this example that are not possible to discuss here, e.g., importance of consulting, appropriateness of a referral, ways of assessing the likelihood of an attempt, etc. However, these may unfortunately be academic questions if you are unable to be open to and with a client who sees suicide as a likely possibility for himself. If you close off and fail to validly and reliably communicate your own thoughts and feelings, he will most likely tune out and make his decision without your help. Whether the issue involves suicide, divorce, religion, declaring an academic major, moving to a new town, coping with a difficult child, entering group therapy, quitting a job, etc., the minute you close off, the chances are good that your client will tune out and make his decision without your assistance.

One of the most common ways a counselor closes off is to surround himself with a stereotyped professional cloak of cold objectivity. An image that comes to mind includes a counselor behind a large desk, staring intently at the client's forehead, slowly bringing the tips of his outstretched fingers together and saying: "When did you first note the onset of self-destructive ideation?" Another image of a counselor, shielded by her professional mantle, includes an attractively dressed woman of forty, smiling pityingly at a dowdy A.D.C. mother holding an infant and saying: "I really think one ought to give careful consideration to the economic factors involved in such a move at this point, don't you, dear?" This last comment may, in fact, be what the counselor thinks, but stated this way, it also says that there are other thoughts and feelings which the counselor is closing off, e.g., "I think moving now is probably not wise," or "Before you do that, I really want you to look at it, 'cause moving now could be pretty bad." When clients talk about lack of sincerity in a counselor, they frequently mention things like: "He never says what he really thinks"; "I don't think she'd be really honest with me if she had an opinion"; "Sometimes I think he doesn't know what to do, but he always tries to act really cool."

### Rehearsed vs. Spontaneous

The second dimension, "rehearsed vs. spontaneous" is an important consideration in drama, as well as in counseling. When a counselor is said to be "spontaneous," we refer to a quality of naturalness that characterizes the way he or she behaves. In the theatre, it is critical that an actor achieve what is called "a sense of the first time"; nothing turns an audience off faster than an actor mechanically reciting lines and going through motions that seem worn out from practice. The irony of achieving a sense of the first time on stage, is that it comes from being absolutely certain of your own lines, completely clear about your own movement on stage, as well as that of other members of the cast, sure of your own ability to project the person you are portraying, and from a willingness to spend hours and hours going over the same lines and movements, again and again. Instead of the final outcome being a stilted, mechanical production, the actors feel free to live out the drama on stage, as if for the first time.

There is, of course, a significant difference between an actor on stage, and a counselor interacting with a client. The counselor is not playing a dramatic role, but rather is being himself in the professional role of counselor. However, the same over-practiced, rehearsed quality can render the counselor's performance ineffective. What is called for on the part of the counselor is a sense of freedom and spontaneity characteristic of an excellent actor. Being spontaneous as a counselor does not mean, however, doing and saying anything that randomly pops into your head.

For example, there are many times when a counselor needs to gain the client's permission and approval for having their session tape recorded, video taped or open to viewing by other counselors via one-way vision screens or closed circuit television. Most clients are not opposed or resistant to such an arrangement, given that they understand the purpose of it and are guaranteed that the same rules of confidentiality apply to anyone who observes the session. Nevertheless, introducing the topic often makes many counselors, especially relatively new ones, very uncomfortable, and they then become rather unspontaneous and contrived with their explanation and request. For instance, the counselor might say: "You may have noticed the tape recorder . . . I would like to record our session so that I can go over it later to check our progress . . . also, I don't like to take notes and this makes it easier . . . sometimes I may consult with another counselor, but no one other than a qualified professional person would ever hear any portion of it . . . You are also free to listen to it here, if you would like to. I assume that's okay with you . . . or maybe you have some questions." Some clients will have questions and some may have strong objections. You need to know clearly ahead of time, if you are willing to forgo the taping, if the client does object. What usually happens is that the client will say something like, "Yah, that's okay as long as it stays private." But at this point a nervous, new counselor who has rehearsed a lengthy argument for the advantages of recording, will not even hear the client give his permission, and will continue a monologue about how there is really nothing to fear, and if something gets too personal they can shut off the tape, and it really will be a help because his supervisor wants him to record everything, which is really a good idea because that's the best way to learn, and on and on. By this time, the client has probably stopped receiving the message that the counselor would like to do what seems reasonable enough and instead has begun to hear the message that the counselor is very unsure of himself. It would have been better if the counselor had said, after he heard the client agree to be recorded, "Good . . . I don't particularly enjoy being recorded myself, but I find I quickly forget it's even on."

These suggestions for what to say about recording are offered, of course, with the assumption that the counselor really does think and feel that way about it. If you are not at all intimidated by a tape recorder and have no qualms about asking a client for permission to record, then you need not worry about it because you will probably handle it quite naturally. However, if you are somewhat anxious about recording, the most authentic behavior would be for you to figure out how to say that you are somewhat uncomfortable about it in a natural manner. It is in this way that the paradox of the actor achieving a sense of the first time is quite applicable. By "rehearsing" in your mind or in a role play situation with another counselor, you can learn how to be natural and spontaneous about your own discomfort. If your reaction to a tape recorder has phobic proportions, it would be unwise to burden your client with that, and you would probably be well-advised to undergo a desensitization procedure to eliminate the phobia. But there is nothing wrong with acknowledging discomfort as long as it is not overwhelming. Sincerity within the counselor means a willingness to acknowledge discomfort and uncertainty, as well as ease and confidence.

### Visibility vs. Hiddenness

There is considerable overlap among the dimensions of sincerity; openness and spontaneity seem to go together in many ways. But each dimension tends to emphasize a slightly different aspect of sincerity; for instance, visibility vs. hiddenness tends to underscore the significance of shame within the counselor. We can think of shame as the feelings you have about yourself when you fall short or prove to be inadequate in some way. In contrast, guilt can be thought of as the feelings you have about yourself when you break a personal or social rule you have adopted. Shame involves not measuring up, whereas guilt involves overstepping a boundary. (For a thorough discussion of these constructs, see *On Shame and the Search for Identity*, Helen Merrell Lynd, 1961.) When a counselor feels as if he does not measure up, that he is inadequate, his shame will lead him to try to hide. When a counselor feels adequate and able to cope with the counseling situation, he is free to be uncovered and visible. Obviously, a counselor who is feeling ashamed and trying to hide his inadequacy cannot, at the same time, present a reliable and valid picture of himself.

A relatively common situation in which the counselor faces a choice to hide his inadequacy or to allow it to be visible occurs whenever a client brings up a topic and talks about it as if the counselor is familiar with it. If the counselor is not informed, but feels as if he ought to be, then he has something to hide. In an age when new jobs are being created at an unprecedented rate, it is not unlikely that an employment counselor would not be familiar with some technological specialty that a client is interested in exploring. A high school counselor might find himself in the position of having a young man hesitantly say that he feels just like Holden in *Catcher in the Rye*, but because he has not read *Catcher in the Rye*, he hasn't a clue as to what that means. A black student in a Job Corps Center makes reference to "the dozens" during a rare moment of trust in a white counselor, but the counselor does not have the foggiest idea as to what "playing the dozens" entails. In each of these situations, the counselor may be able to feign an understanding look in his eye, maintain an enigmatic half-smile and nod knowingly and thereby fool the client into thinking he really grasps what the client is trying to say. If he can hide his ignorance, the client may say enough that the counselor can fake it completely. There are two reasons why that is not a good idea: It seldom works and the client usually knows pretty quickly that you are faking and, more importantly, it deprives the client of an opportunity to give something of significance. Rather than the client feeling you are some obtuse oaf, he probably would respect your willingness to honestly admit you do not know everything. You could say: "I probably ought to know that, but I'm not clear on what you mean . . . could you help me out?" or "I have meant to read that and I'm almost ashamed to say I haven't, but you'll have to tell me how that is for you." or "That's a new one to me, I've never even heard of that job, but I sure am willing to find out about it with you." Being sincere as a counselor means that you are willing to be visible even when you feel inadequate; it means that you will struggle not to hide things or pretend you are something you are not.

### Owned vs. Disowned

The final dimension of sincerity which we will consider has more to do with denying what you are, than pretending to be something you are not. Rogers' term "congruence" emphasizes the extent to which a counselor "owns" his experience and the extent to which he denies and distorts his thoughts, feelings, and actions. To own your experience means that you freely and fully acknowledge, identify as your own, and assume responsibility for your thoughts, feelings, and actions. Some things are more easily owned than others. In general, we are more likely to disown strong, as opposed to moderate feelings; experiences close at hand are more difficult to own than are distant experiences; thoughts and feelings that are present now are more difficult to own than are those that were present then; and, finally, intimate experiences are more likely to be disowned than are impersonal experiences.

A situation that strains the sincerity of any counselor, but is especially up-ending to a new counselor, comes in the form of a serious challenge by the client to the counselor's competence. An outright request for credentials is usually not threatening, but an indirect undermining of the counselor's abilities often produces a very strong, here and now, highly personal reaction. For example, suppose you have been seriously struggling to understand and accept a high school junior's confused pacifist position. And after assisting him sort through some of his contradictory and vague thoughts and feelings about the military, national responsibility, personal responsibility, disapproval of his parents, legal implications, peer pressures, and so on, he says: "Well, I shouldn't expect someone your age from the Establishment to really understand it, anyway." Suppose that you are even quite sympathetic to a pacifist position, which should have been obvious from your unflinching willingness to accept draft resistance as a reasonable possibility for him. To be met with false accusations, a denial of your ability to understand and thorough rejection by your client, is likely to produce a strong, immediate, personal reaction. You have several choices at this point: (1) you can pretend that you did not hear the comment; (2) you can laugh it off as a bad joke, but assume he does not really believe what he is saying; (3) you can become openly hostile and make some snide remark to the effect that, of course, anyone as doddering and senile as yourself could hardly be expected to grasp the profoundly personal questions with which he was so manfully grappling; (4) you could label your own disappointment and puzzlement and irritation at being so grossly misinterpreted and request that you both work at trying to understand how that happened. Alternative #4 is the most sincere response, because with #4, you make no attempt to distort or disown your thoughts and feelings. You have freely identified, acknowledged and accepted the responsibility for your desire to understand what has happened.

Some people will balk at revealing irritation, resentment and anger to a client; but owning your experience means that if you feel hurt and angry, then you must be willing to share that too. Alternative #3 is a more hostile and destructive response; but owning your feelings does not mean that you irresponsibly let fly with a barrage of sarcasm. You can communicate strong negative feelings without unleashing a flood of venom. For instance, you might say: "Hey, wait a minute, I thought I'd done a pretty good job of getting with you and seeing how it looks from where you are . . . it's extremely important to me that I do understand you, and it makes me mad to think you would just brush it aside as if it were nothing." The most likely response from the client would probably include a realization that you care enough to get worked up over him, and that you are willing to "tell it like it is." We are not ruling out the possibility that you could choose to reflect the client's hostile feelings, rather than to share your own. For instance, you might say: "It really seems hopeless to communicate all the things you feel, and it makes you mad that you even try." The most likely response from the client would probably include a realization that the counselor really does understand. There is no sense debating the merits of confrontation vs. reflection in this case. Both counselor responses would be more or less effective with different types of clients. What is most important is that the counselor not disown his experience, positive or negative, at any time throughout his interaction with the client. For most of us that will mean acknowledging some rather delicate and tender positive feelings on occasion and some rather abrasive and stormy feelings on other occasions. Being sincere as a counselor means admitting to awareness and being willing to claim as yours a tremendous range of positive and negative thoughts and feelings.

Having reviewed some of the continua which have been used to describe the nature of sincerity within the counselor, we are ready to ask the question: "What will facilitate greater openness, spontaneity, visibility and owning of experience?" There are two internal processes upon which sincerity depends: self-understanding and self-acceptance.

## Self-Understanding

You have no doubt devoted considerable time and energy trying to understand yourself more fully; you certainly are not totally without self-understanding. However, each of us is such a complex and unique individual that we never really arrive at a point of complete self-understanding. By self-understanding we will be referring to three processes: description, explanation, and prediction. A person is said to understand himself when he can describe himself as he sees himself and as others see him, when he can talk about what and who he is. A person is said to understand himself when he can explain how he got that way and how different aspects of himself are interrelated A person is said to understand himself when he can predict what he will be like and how he will act in the future. For example, you may be able to describe yourself as a person who needs considerable reassurance and support whenever you face an unfamiliar task, but at the same time recognize that others would describe you as confident and willing to venture out onto unfamiliar ground. Your understanding of yourself on this point may go deeper, in that you can explain that you have very high expectations of yourself and find it exceedingly difficult to accept failure or even a mediocre performance, and that is why you need a great deal of support and reassurance. At the same time, however, you have learned over the years that you do not master new things unless you try, and that is why you are willing to venture out. You may also be able to explain the origins of these attitudes and behavior patterns in terms of the values and styles of coping which were characteristic of significant persons who influenced your development.

For instance, your parents may have placed greater value on trying new things and risking failure than on resisting new things and avoiding the possibility of failure; they may have rewarded and supported you for trying new things and punished you for running away from risk of failure. Of course, just the reverse may have been true for you, and you would explain your present unwillingness to try new things in terms of your parents' systematic withdrawal of support and their punishment of your trying something that failed. In essence, they rewarded you for holding back and avoiding failure. It should be noted that just because you can explain the origins of some personal trait does not mean you are no longer responsible for it.

Whether you are unwilling to venture out or quite willing to try new things, you would have an understanding of yourself on this point if you could describe what is true of you and explain how it developed. Finally, an even greater depth of understanding comes with being able to predict what is likely to happen in the future. For example, you may anticipate that when faced with an unfamiliar task from which you believe you could learn something, you will usually go ahead and try it, even though there is the horrible possibility that you might fail, and you will also seek more support and reassurance than you typically do. Or you may anticipate that when faced with an unfamiliar task, your energies will be devoted to avoiding the task if at all possible. In either case, if you understand yourself sufficiently to anticipate or predict what is likely to happen, you are in a position to choose what you want to have happen. None of us likes to think of himself as uncertain, fearful, needful of support and desperate for reassurance. None of us likes to think of himself as cowardly, unwilling to take a chance, and always avoiding risks. But if we are able to describe what is typically true of ourselves, if we have some explanation of how we developed as we did, and if we can anticipate when and where and how the situation is likely to arise, then we can cope with it directly and honestly.

The relationship between self-understanding and sincerity is that self-understanding puts us in a position to be open, spontaneous, visible, and responsible for our experience if we choose to be. A lack of self-understanding means that there are areas about ourselves that are unknown to us and we are more likely to keep them closed and hidden from others as well. Increasing self-understanding extends your capacity to be sincere, if you choose to be. You cannot be very confident that you are accurately and reliably representing a self that you do not understand. Later we will discuss some activities that are designed to increase your self-understanding so that you are in a better position to be sincere about yourself.

## Self-Acceptance

Earlier we defined acceptance as the celebration of diversity and complexity in others. Terms such as respecting, prizing, valuing, appreciating, wanting to share the experience of, etc., were used to suggest the tone and tempo of the action word "celebrate." Attention was drawn to the fact that "celebrate" can apply to a very serious event, or a more festive occasion; feelings may range from solemn reverence to lighthearted exuberance. But common to all forms of celebrating is the acknowledgment of the importance and value of someone or ones. As you contemplate directing acceptance toward yourself, it may appear that we are encouraging some form of personal idolatry. If indeed you were to seriously celebrate your own diversity and complexity, is there not a danger that you would wind up wallowing in a most obnoxious kind of self-worship? Can you respect and prize and be delighted with yourself; can you want to share your experiences with others and genuinely care for yourself without becoming a proud, arrogant, and conceited slob?

The position taken here is that the best way to avoid false pride, arrogance, and conceit is in fact to open yourself to all that you are and accept it. A phrase that is particularly useful in capturing what is meant by acceptance directed toward yourself is "to claim ownership of all that you are." What this involves, of course, is owning things about yourself of which you disapprove as well as things of which you approve; feelings that are hateful as well as those which are loving, thoughts that are destructive as well as those which are constructive, actions that are hurtful as well as those which are helpful. Self-acceptance means that in the face of all that you are, both good and evil, you affirm your own worth. This topic, as has been the case with many others we have discussed, has obvious religious implications. Our concern is with fostering sincerity in the counselor and the position has been taken that sincerity depends in part upon the counselor's ability to accept himself. We are not primarily concerned with the religious implications of self-acceptance. Nevertheless, many counselors-in-training may be blocked from further development of their capacity to accept themselves by religious training which they received as a youngster, or which is currently a significant part of their lives. For that reason, we will deal directly, although briefly, with some religious implications of self-acceptance.

If you take God as your standard of comparison, then clearly none of us measures up; we all fall short of perfection in our thoughts, feelings, and actions. Even if you set up a nontheistic standard of perfection and compare yourself to an ideal state of being, you also fall short of the ideal. In fact, there are very few, if any, persons who would claim that they measure up to what they would like to be, whether or not they compare themselves to an ideal or a standard of perfection. There is no way for any of us to base self-acceptance upon our own perfection; few, if any, would claim they are able to accept themselves because of the standard of excellence they have achieved. Therefore, to encourage counselors to become more self-accepting does not mean that they should claim to be perfect, or even to "think more highly of themselves than they ought to think." But it means that even though you are looking squarely in the face of your own wretchedness, you can affirm your own significance as did Job when he said: "Though he slay me, yet will I trust in him: but I will maintain mine own ways before him" (Job 13:15).

Throughout Hebrew and Christian teaching, a central commandment is to "love your neighbor as yourself." What would your relationship to your "neighbor" actually be, if it were modeled after the manner in which you love yourself. For many counselors, loving their neighbor as they love themselves would mean that they feel uncertain about, are disgusted with, ashamed of, hypercritical of, and punitive towards their neighbor, because those are the feelings they have about themselves. Strong negative feelings about yourself make it almost impossible to feel positively about others. Whether you turn to sacred writings or psychological research, the conclusion is the same on this point: self-acceptance and the acceptance of others go together and enhance one another.

Religious beliefs, rather than being a hindrance to self-acceptance, ought to facilitate self-acceptance. As far as our own imperfection in the presence of a Perfect Being is concerned, Judeo-Christian teaching encourages us to "maintain our own ways," and to "draw near boldly and with confidence." This does not mean that we lose sight of the fact that we fall short of perfection; in fact, we must not disown our own imperfection as we draw near. As far as our feelings about ourselves in relation to our neighbors are concerned, we are commanded to love both our neighbors and ourselves. This does not mean that we lose sight of the fact that at times we fail to love both ourselves and our neighbors, but again we must not attempt to disown any aspect of ourselves in an attempt to become more lovable.

For some of you, this discussion is totally irrelevant because Judeo-Christian teaching is irrelevant for you. However, we know that for a sizeable number of people, many of whom have chosen counseling as a career, Judeo-Christian teachings have significantly influenced their feelings about themselves. Unfortunately, that influence has for many people diminished their self-acceptance and their acceptance of others. Feeling negatively about oneself and others is definitely not the intended outcome of any religious system;

negative attitudes and feelings about oneself and others is an unnecessary and an unintended result of any religious system. All religions seek to foster a sense of meaning and worth in the follower, although the means for accomplishing that goal are widely divergent and sometimes in direct conflict with one another. What is important for our purposes, however, is to see that regardless of his religious beliefs and commitments, increasing his degree of self-acceptance is a desirable goal for any counselor.

The relationship between self-acceptance and sincerity is that self-acceptance gives us the courage to be open and spontaneous, and to claim ownership of what we are and what we experience in the counseling encounter. A lack of self-acceptance means that we are more likely to play a narrow rehearsed role that distorts and denies much of what we think and feel. If we cannot celebrate the diversity and complexity of ourselves, if we are ashamed of and uncertain about what we are, then we are more likely to hide and pretend in the counseling relationship. Increasing self-acceptance increases your courage and willingness to be sincere. You cannot be very confident that you are accurately and reliably representing a self that you cannot accept — that you do not prize and value. Later, we will discuss some ways in which you can increase your self-acceptance so that you become more willing and able to be sincere about yourself.

## Sincerity Within the Counselor — Three Hypothetical Case Studies

As Tyler (1969), and Truax and Carkhuff (1967) have noted, it is easier to pinpoint the absence of sincerity or the opposite of authenticity and genuineness than to point to the presence of this rather global counselor quality. In order to illustrate sincerity within the counselor, we will therefore examine the counseling styles of three people. The first counselor exemplifies a high degree of sincerity and is thus a somewhat idealized person. Nevertheless, his realness is what makes him such a model of sincerity. The next two counselors both manifest a low degree of sincerity which is related primarily to a lack of self-understanding in the first case and a lack of self-acceptance in the final case. By contrasting these three persons' counseling styles, the presence and absence of sincerity should become more clear-cut.

Bryan Bettencourt wanted to go to Alaska for the same reasons that take many men to that vast frontier; money and adventure. So with the ink barely dry on his diploma for a master's degree in rehabilitation counseling, Bryan left Seattle to accept a position with the VRS (Vocational Rehabilitation Service) in Alaska. He had received a number of offers all over the United States, but Alaska was his first choice and he was like a child on Christmas morning when the plane landed in Fairbanks. Bryan's delight was dampened somewhat when he attempted to talk with a group of teenage Indian boys who were in the terminal when he arrived. They just stood there with impassive eyes that did not meet his own warm gaze even though they were looking right at him. A uniformed man wearing a shoulder patch identifying him as an official from the Bureau of Indian Affairs intercepted Bryan and, after determining Bryan's federal employee status, explained that the boys were on their way to one of the boarding schools especially established for Alaska Indian children. The cardboard luggage tags tied to each boy's coat lapel bore his name and destination, and guaranteed he would not stray away or become lost.

The episode was unpleasant in a way that Bryan could not quite identify, but it quickly faded as he heard the announcement that meant his luggage was ready to be claimed. He found a place to stay and managed to see some of his new home before reporting for work on Monday morning. There were seven rehabilitation counselors in the office Bryan was assigned to and most of them seemed like fairly nice guys, at least at first meeting. But Bryan was particularly impressed with George Dunbar, a man of about fifty whom everyone called "Moose." The reason for the nickname was not apparent because George was not an especially large man; however, Bryan found out later that George had shot and killed one of the largest Kenai moose ever taken in that region. In a letter home, Bryan expressed how glad he was that Moose Dunbar had been designated as his supervisor during the time he was getting oriented to the job and the setting.

### The Case of Moose Dunbar

After a week of following Moose around, talking with him (although he was anything but talkative) and watching him work with his Eskimo clients, Bryan realized how little he himself really knew. As a boy, Bryan had seen lots of Indians, but they had always been in full ceremonial dress and doing tribal dances as part of the entertainment for fairs and rodeos in eastern Oregon. Now Bryan was confronted with a depressed people whose culture had been degraded and was dying, who lived in primitve housing, who received inadequate medical services and substandard educations, and whose work skills had been made obsolete by advanced technology; a people who had been exploited, abused, and beaten down to the point that survival depended upon passive, indifferent acquiescence to the white man's authority. Against this bleak and hopeless backdrop, Moose Dunbar's work glowed like a bright warm campfire. Everywhere he went people were obviously glad to see him coming. Cannery foremen trusted his judgment, and were willing to try someone out if Dunbar said the man could handle the job. The trade school admissions office knew that if Dunbar's signature was on the training recommendation, then the man was likely to complete the course. Other government agency workers knew that Moose would push as hard as he could to get assistance for a man, but that he would always tell them exactly where he stood and what he was trying to accomplish. But most significantly, the Indians with whom he worked obviously trusted him and dared to try things with his support that they would never have considered without it.

Bryan tried to analyze what it was about Moose Dunbar that made people respond to him as they did. Part of their confidence and trust came from the fact that "You always know where you stand with Moose," as some of them had expressed it. People in all walks of life, from kids to grandfathers, and in all kinds of positions, from chronically unemployed Eskimos to wealthy business-men, counted on things being the way Moose said they were, as if his statements were notarized affidavits. Although he did not brutally beat people with painful truths, Moose always would "tell it like it is," clearly and directly.

In addition to his uncommon honesty in describing the world as he saw it, and in representing himself as he saw himself, Moose also cared. It was not a matter of his whipping up mild enthusiasm to carry him through his job from eight to five; he cared deeply most all of the time. It was not just what Moose said to people, but it was more what he did with people that communicated his deep commitment and caring. For example, several years ago, there was an abrupt cutback in federal funds and a number of rehabilitation clients who were well along with plans for retraining had to be delayed or dropped. A young fellow for whom Moose had helped arrange training in radio broadcasting services was one of those whose plans were to be delayed indefinitely. Before his leg was crushed in a fishing boat accident, he was the sole supporter of his widowed mother, two sisters, and his own family of five. Moose scouted around until he located a businessmen's service club and a missionary group who were willing to sponsor the man and assist his family so that he could begin the training program. There were small things too, such as the number of times he had accompanied a client to the place where the client was to be interviewed rather than just sending the client, knowing he was frightened and unsure of himself. Moose was a quiet, easy-going man, but he had an unrelenting commitment to helping people locate what they wanted and thus experience more satisfaction in life. He was like a powerful iron hand encased in a soft, but tough chamois glove reaching out to help whomever he could. Bryan had sense enough to recognize that he could find no better person to teach him the many things he did not yet know.

### The Case of Dorothy Lee

In sharp contrast to George "Moose" Dunbar, who epitomizes the genuine and sincere counselor, we will consider two other counselors, Dorothy Lee and Karl Steiner, who are pitifully lacking in authenticity.

When school started in the fall, Chuck Jennings, the assistant principal, met with the eighth graders in the school cafeteria to discuss the testing program and the educational-vocational counseling that was to be conducted during the year. He talked about the importance of the decisions which the students faced as they began preparing for high school, and he urged them to take advantage of the opportunity to talk over their plans with either the girls' or boys' counselor. After the achievement test results were available, the two school counselors set up appointment schedules to meet individually with all eighth graders. It was not too long afterward that Mr. Jennings began to pick up some rumblings among the students and to receive some complaints from parents about one of the counselors, Dorothy Lee. The complaints all had the same theme running through them, that Mrs. Lee seemed to be interested in discussing only two things: "sibling rivalry," and how important it is to take high school courses and participate in activities that will get you accepted at a prestigious college. Mr. Jennings dropped by Mrs. Lee's office after school and found her getting out the cumulative records of the students she would be seeing the next day. After some small talk, he simply described some of the complaints he had received and told Mrs. Lee that he thought she would want to have such feedback, even though it was negative. She thanked him for his interest but immediately launched into a discussion of how junior high students know so little about what is ahead of them, and how sorry most of them will be if they get on the "wrong track." As she talked, it became clear to Chuck Jennings that Mrs. Lee had a very definite idea of what the "right track" was, and it involved: (1) taking college-bound high school courses together with undemanding electives in order to keep the grade point average high; (2) participating in lots of activities, especially of a social nature; (3) preparing early for the College Board Exams; (4) staying out of any disciplinary trouble; (5) looking as neat and clean as possible; (6) developing a healthy body, a healthy mind, and a healthy personality which people would find attractive; and (7) if a student had brothers or sisters, not being overwhelmed by the competition that naturally exists among all siblings. Because junior high students do not really know what they want yet, according to Mrs. Lee, the burden for careful guidance weighs heavily on the counselor's shoulders. Even though some students and their parents may not see the importance of what she is doing, she was certain that there would come a day when they would look back with gratitude for the sound advice and clear direction she provided.

As he listened to Mrs. Lee burble on about the dear little children innocently wandering into the harsh, cruel world of high school, and her protective and directive role, Mr. Jennings could imagine the routine each student was subjected to in Mrs. Lee's office. It was not hard to understand why the students regarded her as a big phoney — a kooky lady they had to endure. In fact, one student had described her session with Mrs. Lee as "like too unreal for words." In addition to her song and dance routine about the joys of going to a good college, Mrs. Lee seemed to have a real hang-up about competition and conflict among brothers and sisters. The stories carried home after a session with Mrs. Lee about the nature and dynamics of sibling rivalry were what had prompted the parents to call Mr. Jennings.

Suppose you were in Chuck Jennings' position. What would you do with or for Dorothy Lee?

### The Case of Karl Steiner

The final counseling style we will examine belongs to a young man who is also attempting to work with students. Karl Steiner had just completed his counselor training the summer prior to his taking a position at Bridgewater High School, a large metropolitan school on the East coast. Karl is small in stature and looks young for his age. He had taught high school English for three years before he returned to graduate school for a master's degree in counseling. Karl was able to establish rapport with most of his students during his teaching experience, but it usually took a while for the students to accept him. What seemed to bring them around was the fact that he frankly discussed several novels that are regarded as controversial or obscene in some school districts. Karl treated his students as if they were responsible, thinking, young adults who could handle controversial material maturely and critically. He avoided sensationalism and did not make a big production of teaching from "dirty books." Karl had always been somewhat of a loner, not necessarily by choice, but because he found it difficult to make friends. He was most comfortable in a small group of people who shared his literary interests and respected his command of the modern novel. Although Karl was reserved, he was also quite perceptive and sensitive to other people's feelings.

As you might expect, Karl had a difficult time being accepted as a counselor by the Bridgewater High students, and he was not much more successful with the teachers. He attended all of the football games and the Christmas concerts, but he remained largely on the outside and he felt quite alienated. After discussing the situation with a friend during the Christmas holidays, Karl decided what he needed to do was loosen up and become less inhibited. So he let his hair grow a little longer, he bought some brightly colored flower decals for his car, and in the evening he began wearing beads instead of his usual neatly tied four-in-hand. Karl bought a rather expensive guitar and a self-teaching series on how to play it; the guitar was rarely out of its case and occupied the back seat of his Plymouth. In his small office at school he put up a large poster of Bob Dylan to whom he kept referring as "Thomas," he bought a hashish pipe which was conspicuously displayed on his desk, and on top of a built-in storage cabinet he began burning incense each morning before school for fifteen minutes. On his door he hung a sign he had made and which he found to be riotously funny. In the center of a piece of white poster board he had fastened a black arrow that could be moved to point to the word "In" on the bottom left or "Out" on the bottom right of the sign. Using all different colors, Karl had carefully lettered across the top of the sign "The Guru Is."

With the exception of the hashish pipe which would probably be questioned as a decoration in any counselor's office in the nation, Karl's attempts to loosen up and become a "swinger" were not bizarre or unethical. It certainly is possible to imagine a respectable, responsible, competent high school counselor with the kind of personal style that could include flower decals, shaggy hair, beads on the weekend, a guitar, a poster of Dylan, and a funny sign on his door. But for Karl it just did not come off smoothly and he was soon the laughing-stock of the school. Instead of being impressed with how cool he was, the students recognized how phoney the whole scene was and he became their ding-a-ling in residence. The Administration did more than laugh and Karl was called in and told to change or resign. Frank Mitchell, the principal, whose duty it was to inform Karl of the precarious position he was in, was surprised to find him embarrassed, regretful, confused, and anxious about the situation. Karl kept saying, "Well, I thought that would help, but I can see now how dumb it was . . . but I don't really know what I should do."

Suppose you are in Frank Mitchell's position, what would you do with or for Karl Steiner?

### Differences in Sincerity Among the Three Counselors

If we had an opportunity to ask each of these three counselors — Moose Dunbar, Dorothy Lee, and Karl Steiner — what it was they were trying to do as counselors, each of them would probably say in one way or another that they were trying to help their clients. Each of them is probably sincere as far as his or her intentions are concerned, but somehow only Moose Dunbar is able to communicate his intention to be helpful in an effective manner. In contrast to Moose's open and spontaneous way of representing himself, Dorothy seems to be very closed to much of her experience as a counselor and to be playing an overly rehearsed role of what she thinks a counselor ought to be. Dorothy probably has very little insight and understanding about herself, both as a person and as a counselor. It is not so much a matter that she is ashamed and unsure of herself and thus is hiding or disowning who and what she is, but rather it is a case of not being able to accurately and reliably see herself as others see and experience her. Because she does not understand herself very fully, she is in no position to send clear and uncluttered signals about who and what she is. What gets communicated are competing messages that say, "Yes, I want to help you; I want to understand and accept you, *but* I have a particular way I am comfortable thinking and feeling and acting, and do not ask me to depart from it." If Dorothy Lee understood herself better, she would be in a position to present a more valid and reliable picture of all that she is, if she chose to do so.

Karl Steiner does not seem as insensitive to his own feelings and behavior as Dorothy does, but he also has difficulty communicating clearly and consistently who he is and what he experiences. Karl seems to be nearly overwhelmed with feelings of inadequacy and alienation in his role as school counselor. His pathetic attempts to do something about his inadequacy have thus far had the reverse effect. Instead of being more relaxed, uninhibited and open, he has become more contrived, distorted, and phoney. Karl also is in no position to send clear and unambiguous signals about who and what he is. What he does communicate is, "Yes, I want to be helpful; I want to understand and accept you; *but* I am so worried about and unsure of myself that I am really not free to attend to you." If Karl Steiner were able to accept himself more fully, he probably would not need to engage in what has become a ridiculous charade. In place of his pretending to be something he is not, Karl would have the courage to present a more valid and reliable picture of who he really is.

Earlier we raised questions about what could be done with or for Karl Steiner and Dorothy Lee; what could Chuck Jennings do or say that would help Mrs. Lee become a more authentic person, and what could Frank Mitchell do or say that would help Karl Steiner become more genuine and sincere? Frank Mitchell has a much better chance of helping Karl than Chuck Jennings has of assisting Dorothy.

There is no one way to be a counselor that is superior to all others; in fact, there are not even four or five best ways that could be precisely specified. However, there is one worst way to try to be a counselor that can be precisely specified: rigid, dogmatic adherence to a narrow view of other persons and their situations together with an unquenchable zeal for solving other people's problems. Individuals who fit that description do not make good counselors. A major difficulty with such persons is that corrective feedback never gets through the heavy filtering system that covers their window on the world. Rarely do they ask the question, "Is there another way to look at things that would be more useful or constructive, than the way I presently see them?" They are closed to any information except what fits their narrowly preconceived notions. Dorothy Lee tends to be this kind of counselor and the probability that Chuck Jennings can get through to her is very low. This does not rule out the possibility that she could learn to perceive things more openly or that she could learn to behave less rigidly. But we are not very successful, at this point, in retraining someone as thoroughly as would be required for Dorothy Lee, especially in view of the fact that she does not see any real need for change. Although this is a rather pessimistic conclusion, if we are being honest and realistic, we must recognize the limits of our ability to bring about change. It would be nice to be able to say "anyone can learn to be a good counselor." Possibly that is true, but in Dorothy Lee's case it probably is not. The most helpful approach that Chuck Jennings could take with Dorothy is to make it an honorable alternative for her to deselect herself from counseling. It is not uncommon that someone, like Dorothy Lee, has responded to the encouragement and pressure of a principal to fill the school counselor job, even though it is against his or her own best judgment. Often times "promoting" someone who seems to be just naturally suited for counseling works out quite well, but sometimes it does not. Fortunately, people who tend to be rigid and dogmatic often deselect themselves, if given an opportunity to do so without having to be irresponsible in the process.

There are several things that Karl Steiner has going for him that mean Mr. Mitchell could reasonably be optimistic about Karl's changing with some help. In the first place, Karl recognizes that something is not right and he is not trying to deny or disown his responsibility for changing whatever It is. Secondly, under different circumstances; namely, with the assistance of good curricular material and teaching skills, Karl has experienced considerable rapport with students. And finally, Karl's values and perceptions of the world do not alienate him from students; his personal style is what separates and isolates him. It is easier to learn new ways of doing things when there are not major attitude and value changes that also need to occur. Later we will consider some suggestions for increasing self-acceptance and that is what in general needs to change for Karl Steiner. If he could have some experiences that would increase his comfort with and valuing of himself, especially in relation to high school students, then he could cease ruminating about himself, relinquish his rehearsed role of a "swinger" and just be himself.

In summary, being open, spontaneous, visible, and willing to own your experience in the counseling relationship depends upon how thoroughly you understand and accept yourself. If you want to become more sincere and genuine as a counselor, you will probably have to expand and extend your self-understanding and self-acceptance. Both your thoughts about yourself and your feelings about yourself are involved in becoming more sincere. Although it is impossible to pursue sincerity directly, it is very possible to pursue self-understanding and self-acceptance.

Before we turn to suggestions for maximizing these personal, internal processes, there is one overriding message that is particularly important for you to be able to communicate validly and reliably. The message was readily apparent in Moose Dunbar's counseling. One of the most important characteristics that Bryan identified as responsible for Moose's effectiveness as a counselor was his profound caring for his clients. We have already noted that Dorothy Lee and Karl Steiner also seemed to care deeply for their students, but they were not as skillful in communicating that fact. In addition to self-understanding and self-acceptance, sincerity is also rooted in your capacity to communicate readily and clearly that you care about your client.

The reason that skill in communicating caring and helpfulness is especially important, is that clients find that message the most difficult to believe. Your sincerity as a counselor is most likely to be questioned and tested on this point. Clients, in general, do not have difficulty believing that you are able to understand them; after all, you are trained to do so. Clients, in general, do not have difficulty believing that you are able to accept them, again you are supposed to be trained not to be shocked or upset with what might bother the average person. But believing that you are genuinely interested in and care about them as persons, that is a different matter. Is it not your job to show an interest in and care about whoever comes through the door? You are paid to look fascinated and to feel deeply, are you not? It is not uncommon for a client to raise these questions directly, and it is quite understandable. It is a relatively rare experience, nowadays, to encounter someone who is willing to spend time and effort listening carefully to what may seem to be mundane details of an average life and to become involved in a nonjudgmental, noncoercive manner for the purpose of helping you. Thus, the most likely explanation for a counselor's interest and concern is that he is paid to do that — it is merely his job.

This issue is not an easy one to deal with, but there are several things you can do. In the first place, you can acknowledge openly that you are paid to be as competent a counselor as you can be, and that means caring about your clients. You can then add, if it is true for you, "Fortunately what the job calls for and what I really feel match very well . . . I do not find it a strain to like and care about many different kinds of people; in fact, it is personally very rewarding." If your sincerity has been questioned or challenged on the grounds that you probably are not really interested or concerned, then you can suggest in a nondefensive manner, "Let me invite you to test it out as you interact with me; it's a legitimate question and one I want you to be sure of, but I think you can trust your own ability to judge it as you interact with me. It's possible that I really am faking and would fool you, but I think the chances are good that you would detect that." From the client who is quite disbelieving about the genuineness of your interest and desire to be helpful, you may be hit with "You don't really care about me, because anybody who was talking with you, you'd care about too, wouldn't you?" It may be helpful to point out to this person, "Yes, you are right, anyone with whom I'd be talking, I'd be committed to caring about that person . . . but the person I am talking with is *you*, and it is *you* whom I am committed to caring about, that is the reality of my world right now."

Although it is useful to know ways to handle direct questions about and challenges to the genuineness of your interest and concern as a counselor, it is more important that you know how to communicate your caring quickly and simply and clearly. Therefore, in our discussion of ways to become a more sincere counselor, we will consider procedures for increasing your capacity to invest in other persons more readily.

## HOW TO BECOME MORE SINCERE

### Increasing Self-Understanding

It may seem paradoxical to recommend that you invest time and energy in focusing upon yourself in order to achieve greater capacity to be unpreoccupied with self and able to focus on others. However, the logic of the recommendation is illustrated by the unpleasant and familiar experience of arriving at a social event inappropriately dressed. It is as embarrassing to appear all decked out in your fanciest duds and enter a roomful of casually dressed guests as it is to show up in your grubbies for what turns out to be a formal occasion. There are times when you may intend to violate the expectations or "standards of proper attire," and that is a different matter. But on an occasion when you really had no intention of being different — maybe you find you are wearing different colored socks or only one earring or you are the only person who brought your spouse — at a time like that, it may be very difficult to not be preoccupied with yourself and how you appear to others. It would have facilitated your interactions with others if you had paid enough attention to yourself earlier so that when you arrived you would be free to forget yourself.

A similar experience can take place in a counseling interaction. For example, if you have been inattentive to some aspect of yourself, such as your attitudes toward religion or toward money, and these topics are central to a client's concerns, you may find yourself so entangled in your own thoughts and feelings that you really are not free to listen to your client. If you would invest some time and energy in struggling to describe, explain, and predict your own thoughts and feelings on such topics, it would probably increase your ability to interact openly and honestly with your client. The more things that you do not understand about yourself, the more places there are for you to want to protect yourself and hide from others. When that happens, others perceive you to be phoney. Thus, we can increase our capacity to be sincere by increasing our self-understanding.

### *Developing Ability to Describe Yourself: Four Analogies.*

Several of the exercises described in Section Four are designed to extend your self-understanding, but there are also some things that you can begin on your own which may also contribute to greater self-understanding. For example, each of the four analogies presented in the discussion of How to Understand; namely, making a movie in your head, attending a ballet, appreciating an impressionistic painting, and building a model can be directed toward yourself. You can practice describing yourself by selecting a period of time, for instance, yesterday morning from the time you awoke until the evening meal, and recall the events as if you were filming them. How clear a picture of yourself do you have? Next, recall a day about one year ago. You probably will not remember the day very clearly, unless you have chosen a special occasion, but try to imagine the kinds of things you were doing then. In your mind's eye, film the places where you spent the most time, the people with whom you were interacting, the activities that commanded your attention, and how you looked moving about in those scenes. Finally, go back in time far enough so that the places and people change. As you watch the movie in your head, check to see how you have changed from then until now. Can you describe the differences, as well as the similarities? Would your descriptions resemble those of someone who knew you well throughout this period of time? You, of course, can check out your answer to the last question by asking someone close to you to listen as you describe the "movies" you have made and comment on how his "movies of you" are different and how they are similar.

To practice describing yourself by means of the ballet analogy, select a recent episode about which you have very strong feelings. What music would you choose to capture the episode? What kind of movements would the dancers be executing? Which parts of the episode are best captured by solo performers, and which parts require the entire company? To check how your descriptions differ from someone else's descriptions, you could invite a person who was familiar with the episode to join you in creating a ballet or musical to capture the experience. It probably will not rival *West Side Story* or *Swan Lake*, but the process of trying it could be rewarding, once you surmounted feeling silly and self-conscious about doing something out of the ordinary.

In contrast to the veridical recording of fine detail that is possible with a movie camera, an impressionistic painting captures only the general impression of its subject and either omits or merely suggests the details. One way to use the impressionistic painting analogy to practice describing yourself is to consider various contrasting words that might be used to describe a painting, such as simple vs. complicated, light and airy vs. dark and heavy, bright vs. subdued, sweeping lines vs. short, broad strokes, subtle shading vs. intense coloration, evenly distributed vs. heavily concentrated, etc. If you were trying to capture the general impression that most people have of you when they first meet you, what terms would you use? Are you able to describe the general first-impression which you make so that others would recognize your descriptions? As people get to know you, they fill in the details of the picture out of their experiences with you. However, each new client experiences you initially in terms of the general impression you make. Can you describe that general impression accurately enough so that you are not surprised by the way others first respond to you? For example, a female counselor might know that many clients are initially skeptical about her competence because she appears to be a rather frail, young, subdued, and somewhat simple soul who would hardly be a person you would counsel with about major choices or changes in your life. If the woman understands this, if she is able to describe the general impression she gives others, then she is in a position to better understand their responses to her. Again, we have an example of self-understanding that facilitates our attending to and understanding someone else.

To illustrate the use of model building as a means of self-description, we will use a quite literal example. Suppose you were to design a building that would capture the essence of you as a counselor; what would it look like? For some counselors it might be a gymnasium-like structure where people would come either to work out or to be entertained. If they are coming to work out then they are probably interested in getting in shape or staying in shape. If they have come to be entertained then they usually expect to see a contest or a game and to watch one side win and one side lose. There are counselors who function very much like a gymnasium whose primary activity is game-playing for entertainment. Some counselors are built more like a fire station in which very little activity takes place until someone sounds an alarm. At this point there is a great flurry of excitement and a dashing away to douse the fire in order to avert tragedy. Most of the alarms are false alarms; but as is legitimate in the case of real firemen, the counselor views his activity as a necessary service. Some counselors are built like a library in that they are great depositories for all sorts of information. If you know how to use the card catalogue and if the "library" operates with an efficient retrieval system, then you probably can locate what you need, depending on how large and comprehensive its holdings are. Some libraries have a basic trust in their patrons and allow them to browse through open stacks. This is usually a more satisfying experience for both the library and the information-seeker because more of the library is utilized and the information-seeker need not have his requests always precisely formulated ahead of time. There are, of course, both "open-stack" counselors and "closed-stack" counselors.

Then there are counselors who are put together like city hall in that they are a center for the provision of a great many services concerning all aspects of life. City halls vary tremendously in how readily and efficiently those services are rendered. For instance, there are some city halls in which the overwhelming impression is that the most important considerations are that you walk on this side rather than that side, that you go up these stairs and down those, that you fill out this form before passing that point, that you maintain quiet and clear the building by 5:30 p.m., having refrained from spitting in the drinking fountain. In pleasing contrast there are also city halls in which most of the important information is communicated by human beings, for instance, an information clerk, rather than by lettered signs and printed forms. You may be quietly invited to stay a while if you like by the presence of chairs and a display of elementary school children's drawings on what would otherwise be barren and faded walls. If it suits you to describe yourself as a city hall-like structure, then which of these examples fits you best?

Finally, there are counselors who are built like sewage treatment plants. With the help of special equipment, certain technologies and particular chemicals, their function is to collect crud and transform it into inert material that can be disposed of safely. No one would dispute the importance of sewage disposal, although there is considerable disagreement as to what constitutes proper procedures. Depositing it in any old river satisfies some people; others believe it is worth investing whatever money is required to dispose of it permanently. The question for us is, does a sewage treatment plant, even with the finest modern equipment, provide an accurate model for counseling? There are many other types of buildings that may provide more suitable models by means of which you can describe yourself as a counselor, such as schools, medical centers, gambling casinos, chapels, conference halls, theatres, homes, etc. There are also many models in addition to types of buildings which you could use to describe yourself, such as types of machines, types of organizations, various art forms, etc. By allowing your imagination to go unchecked for a while, you may discover some new ways to describe yourself that contribute significantly to your self-understanding.

### Developing Ability to Explain Yourself

Model building provides a good transition from the first step in self-understanding, namely, description of self, to the second step in self-understanding, namely, explanation of self; because as you build a model you not only describe what is, but you also can see how different parts fit together. This, in turn, may suggest how you developed in the way you did, or in other words, the reasons for and causes of the way you are now. To explain something means to specify the reasons for, or cause of the something. We are interested in being able to explain ourselves for purposes of greater self-understanding. Although individuals vary tremendously in the extent to which they can specify the reasons for their thoughts, feelings, and actions, two things are obvious: (1) none of us will ever be able to give a complete explanation for all of his thoughts, feelings, and actions, and (2) each of us is already able to provide considerable explanation for his own thoughts, feelings, and actions. What follows are several suggestions for ways you can increase your ability to explain how you have developed as you have.

If you have access to old family albums of photographs, gather together a series of snapshots or portraits of yourself that were taken at different developmental stages. Some people will have to scrounge around through boxes of family records and forgotten memorabilia to locate baby pictures, childhood snapshots, school pictures, and photographs of special events in order to assemble a series that captures the full sweep of their own development from the cradle until the present. Other people will simply be able to request to borrow the album which their mothers began when they were first born and have kept up-to-date ever since. Whether you have to scrounge to find a few snapshots or spend time sorting through stacks of family albums, you can probably locate a sufficient number of pictures which will help you recall your own development. The process of gathering the materials together will likely remind you of events in your past that have heavily influenced the kind of person you are today. For example, you might be reminded of the time when your family moved to a new town. The deep loneliness and stark isolation you experienced as you struggled to make new friends was what led to your becoming completely absorbed in reading. Through the years reading has sustained as a major coping device and refuge. You might be reminded of a severe weight problem or skin disorder that turned your own adolescence into a nightmare of ugly exposure. The fact that now you are especially interested in working with that age group is certainly not a random happening, and probably was influenced by the agony of your own adolescence which has been translated into a compassionate concern for those who are confused and hurting as you once were. You might recognize the roots of an intensive striving to master the environment in early pictures of you trying to remove the training wheels from your tricycle, giving the dog a bath when the dog was twice your size, building a split-level duplex in a tree, directing a neighborhood summer stock theater group before you could pronounce proscenium. You might see the ever present shadow of a successful older brother or sister who made it difficult to try new things because you could never quite measure up. You might be able to spot the period in your life when discouragement was at a peak and begin to recall the mechanisms you developed to cope with defeats. There are endless examples of things you might see in a series of photographs of yourself which might help you explain the "whys" and "hows" of your present thoughts, feelings, and actions.

### Applying the T-Formation to Yourself

A somewhat more systematic approach to explaining your present development is to apply the T-formation (Figure 6) to yourself and at several points in your history with special emphasis upon the three content areas in counseling: Work, Relationship, and Aloneness.

For example, if Moose Dunbar did this task it might look like Figure 11.

You can speculate as to what Moose Dunbar's T-formation might have looked like even earlier, before he was married, and back in time to when he was ten or twelve. This would not provide a complete description and explanation of the fifty-year-old man we know today, but it would help us capture some of the significant events, patterns of choosing, emotional themes, and directions of movement that have resulted in the present person.

When you undertake a task like applying the T-formation to yourself, it is possible to become overwhelmed with the amount of information you possess which could be utilized. The purpose of this assignment is not to provide a complete analysis of your developmental history, rather we are interested in your becoming familiar with and comfortable with the major themes and directions that characterize your development. With the ability to describe and explain what we are today comes a greater willingness to be open and honest about ourselves. Applying the T-formation to your own development is merely one vehicle for journeying toward greater self-understanding; producing an elaborate T-formation is not the destination in and of itself. You might begin using this vehicle by selecting one category, such as Interests, and trace the developmental history of "what you like to do" regarding Work and Relationship and Aloneness. In this way you can determine for yourself whether the T-formation is a cumbersome old car that keeps breaking down or a reliable automobile that can be counted on to get you where you want to go.

### Using Psychological Theories to Increase Self-Understanding

The final suggestion for increasing your ability to explain your present patterns of thinking, feeling, and acting is an even more systematic approach.

Select a psychological theory of human behavior and apply it to yourself; attempt to explain your present behavior in terms of a recognized psychological theory of human behavior. We will not quibble over what is a theory and what is not, but will include in the label "recognized psychological theory of human behavior" such frameworks or systems as are present in the writings of Freud and his followers, Adler and his followers, George Kelly and his followers, Rogers and his followers, Victor Frankl and his followers, Miller and Dollard and their followers, and Skinner and his followers. It is not possible to provide a complete list of references, but you could get started in identifying the theory you would like to apply to yourself from the following list:

*Systems of Psychotherapy*, Donald H. Ford and Hugh B. Urban, 1963

*Theories of Counseling and Psychotherapy*, C. H. Patterson, 1966

*Theories of Personality*, Calvin S. Hall and Gardner Lindzey, 1957

Some theories give a thorough account of how individuals develop throughout the life stages, others make almost no mention of development after age six, and still others do not concern themselves with human development before adolescence. Some theories place major emphasis upon how individuals learn to think, feel, and act; some theories place major emphasis upon the way an individual's perceptions of himself and others determine his thoughts, feelings, and actions. Some theories explain personal motivation in terms of a steam engine; others prefer an analogue computer model. Some theories look at the situation within which the individual is functioning in order to understand the person; most theories attempt to look within the person in order to understand him.

No psychological theory of human behavior is complete; no psychological theory can completely explain your thoughts, feelings, and actions. However, it is the height of ignorance to therefore conclude that examining and applying theoretical formulations is a waste of time. Whenever you attempt to explain something about yourself, you make use of your own personal theory of human behavior. We cannot choose to avoid using theories. The only choice is whether or not we wish to be aware of the theories we are using. You can avoid the unexamined use of theory by intentionally and systematically applying a given theory to your own behavior. As a result you may gain greater ability to explain yourself and thus greater self-understanding. Obviously, this is not something that can be accomplished in an evening of reading and thinking, but you can begin the process anytime. As you read definitions of terms, think of examples from your own life that illustrate those terms; as you plough through discussions of major constructs, translate them into a discussion of your own experience. If there are research procedures that can be applied to yourself, take time to study yourself in those ways: for instance, collect base rate data on some of your own behaviors; engage in a free-association technique using a tape recorder; complete Q-sorts on attitudes toward yourself and others. You probably would find it both easier and more enjoyable to tackle a project like this if someone else were

# FIGURE 11    Application of the T-Formation

## THE PRESENT ("NOW")

SELF ←——————————————→ SITUATION

*Values – What I "ought" to do:*

*Work* – Do the best I can within the limits of time, resources, and the system.

*Relationship* – Be intimate with very few and value all othes equally.

*Aloneness* – Be able to continue functioning without the support and approval of others, if it is temporarily withdrawn or unavailable.

*Interests – What I "like" to do:*

*Work* – Be active, autonomous, and contributing to others.

*Relationship* – Share activities such as hunting, fishing, poker with a small group of long-time friends.

*Aloneness* – Walk at night; read about great men; collect Indian artifacts.

*Abilities – What I am "able" to do:*

*Work* – Help others to help themselves; train young men who really want to learn.

*Relationship* – Put others at ease and help them feel comfortable in talking about themselves.

*Aloneness* – Critically examine my own behavior and figure out ways to improve myself.

*Expectations – What I am predicting I "can" do:*

*Work* – Continue to do a satisfying job within a sometimes restricting system.

*Relationship* – Find more ways to accept those with whom I disagree.

*Aloneness* – Accept the horror of getting old.

*Family & Other Personal Commitments:*

*Work* – Continue working beyond earliest retirement possibility to provide for wife and aging father-in-law.

*Relationship* – Invest greater effort in trying to re-establish relationship with son who has adopted hippie way of life.

*Aloneness* – Re-examine wife's pleadings to consider becoming a Roman Catholic.

*Opportunities:*

*Work* – Enroll in in-service training course for computer-based vocational counseling.

*Relationship* – Join sensitivity-training group for older married couples facing retirement.

*Aloneness* – Accept an assignment to travel to a distant field office once a week for six months.

*Social and Cultural Rules:*

*Work* – Relinquish plan to change jobs; too late in life.

*Relationship* – Pressure for fathers and sons to respect one another is nearly intolerable in light of our estrangement.

*Aloneness* – Realization that there is no way to transcend totally the barrier between white man and Indian.

208

If Moose Dunbar were to apply the T-formation to himself and his situation fifteen years earlier, it might have looked like this:

## THE PAST ("THEN")

SELF ⟵⟶ SITUATION

*Values – What I "ought" to do:*

*Work* – Change the system so that better services are provided.

*Relationship* – Do not become intimate with or dependent upon anyone; treat everyone the same.

*Aloneness* – Do not seek or expect the approval or support of anyone be sufficient unto yourself.

*Interests – What I "like" to do:*

*Work* – Talk with employers and open up new training and employment possibilities.

*Relationship* – Teach two sons how to fish, hunt, and trap.

*Aloneness* – Avoid being by myself if at all possible.

*Abilities – What I am "able" to do:*

*Work* – Maintain a work load that is larger than any others' in the state.

*Relationship* – Command the respect of co-workers.

*Aloneness* – Decide what is best for me without depending on others for advice.

*Expectations – What I am predicting I "can" do:*

*Work* – Leave DVR and become a personnel consultant for a large corporation.

*Relationship* – Find more techniques for being persuasive and getting people to agree with me.

*Aloneness* – Conquer my fears of not measuring up to my idea of a successful man.

*Family and Other Personal Commitments:*

*Work* – Try to find ways to not let work rob me of time with the boys.

*Relationship* – Wie's support and encouragement most important factor in keeping going.

*Aloneness* – Father's death means there is no one left in the family, but me.

*Opportunities:*

*Work* – If I return to school to complete a master's degree, I must go on leave without pay.

*Relationship* – An old friend, who was recently widowed, has offered to pay for schooling, but she has expectations of an intimate affair in return.

*Aloneness* – A series of lectures on religion and my father's library started me reading again.

*Social and Cultural Rules:*

*Work* – Wife wants to work, but I just cannot accept it.

*Relationship* – No way to talk with sons about how much I love them and want them to be happy.

*Aloneness* – People think you are unfriendly if you do not want to go to play cards and booze it up all the time.

doing it also. You could share the difficulties and the insights you were having and you could assist one another in mastering the theory you selected to work with.

As was true of the other suggestions for finding ways to explain yourself, applying a psychological theory is a means to greater self-understanding and not an end in itself. Few things are more offensive than someone who bombards you with psychological jargon to describe and explain himself or, perhaps worse, to describe and explain you. The purpose of this task is a rather private and personal one, in that it is expected that you will allow the self-understanding which you achieve to serve as a cutting edge which you can use to pare off layers of defenses that keep you from being open and honest. However, unless someone has specifically agreed to join you in applying a psychological theory, it is something you should do by yourself, and it should never become a weapon to carve up another person's defenses.

### Predicting Your Own Behavior

The tasks suggested for increasing your ability to explain your own behavior carry us into the third stage of self-understanding, which involves increasing your ability to predict your own behavior. It should be made clear from the outset of our discussion that learning to predict your own behavior is not intended to make you a preprogrammed robot that responds in a calculated and mechanical manner. Quite the opposite; if in general you are able to predict how you would feel, what you might think, or how you might act in a particular new situation, then you do not have to be heavily guarded as you approach that new situation. If your self-understanding includes the ability to predict, in general, your own responses, then you are less likely to be surprised by how you feel, what you think, or what you do. For example, suppose you are able to understand yourself to the extent that you can describe how angry you become when someone you care about calls you "stupid" or "dumb" if you do something he disapproves of. Furthermore, suppose you can explain to yourself that you learned to be angry when this happens because the most shameful and embarrassing experience in your family was to behave stupidly; it usually resulted in being made fun of or rejected by other members of the family. If you were able to describe and explain your angry reaction to ridicule from a prized person, we would say that you understand yourself on this point quite well. If you were also able to predict that an encounter with a cared for individual is likely to include a discussion of something about which you disagree, that the other person is likely to make mocking remarks about your beliefs and if that happens you are likely to become angry, then you are in a position to do several things. You might decide to avoid the topic altogether; you might decide to initiate a discussion of how angry you feel when someone is scornful; you might decide to proceed with a conflict-ridden conversation and let the chips fall where they may. But you are freer to cope with the situation than you would be if you could not predict your own response and found yourself surprised by your anger and only able to explain it after it occurred. The degree of self-understanding that comes with being able to predict your own thoughts, feelings, and actions provides more ways of responding. You become more flexible, open, and honest and you become less anxious, threatened, and guarded in new and difficult situations.

In order to achieve a more thorough understanding of yourself, you can use the T-formation to project into the future. The category called "Expectations" on the T-formation does this to a limited degree, but we can further self-understanding by attempting to predict in all areas. For example, given that you can describe your present system of values and you can explain the developmental origins of those values, how do you think they will change in the next five or ten years, particularly in the areas of Work, Relationship, and Aloneness? On the basis of your present understanding of your interests, what they are and how they developed, you can extend your self-understanding by speculating about the direction they will take in the future. For each category on the T-formation, jot down two or three predictions about how you will change in the future.

A less global kind of projecting to increase self-understanding can be accomplished by projecting yourself into a presently hypothetical situation but one that is likely to occur in the future. On the basis of what you know about yourself, try to describe and explain what you would feel, think, and do in that situation. For example, if you have not yet faced the death of a loved one, you will. Although it may be a morbid and depressing task, try to predict your own thoughts, feelings, and actions in response to that inevitable situation. If you find yourself unwilling to engage in such a task for purposes of better understanding yourself, it calls into question your willingness to respond openly and fully to a client who is facing the death of a loved one. On the other hand, if you are willing and able to project yourself into the grief and anguish of death enough to more deeply understand your own responses, you are significantly more capable of responding authentically to a bereaved client. You can think of innumerable examples, some of which may have profound feelings accompanying them, and some of which may be nearly neutral emotionally. For example, predict the thoughts, feelings, and actions that would be characteristic of you in the following situations:

A long-haired, barefoot, beaded youngster standing on a corner makes the Peace symbol hand sign toward you, as you turn the corner in your car.

A ten-year-old boy in levis and a sweatshirt standing on a corner makes an obscene hand gesture toward you, as you turn the corner in your car.

Two apparently deaf adults seated at a nearby table are carrying on a conversation with hand signs in a rather expensive restaurant.

Ahead of you, two Afro-Americans with natural hair styles meet and greet one another with the raised, clenched fist of Black Power and are now blocking your path.

A priest bends over a small blanket-covered body in the middle of a glistening rain-soaked intersection and makes the sign of the cross while the officer examines your driver's license.

You may never encounter any of these situations; you may face any one of them tomorrow. The process we are trying to facilitate is your being able to vividly imagine any scene and see yourself moving about in it, thinking, feeling, reacting in ways that are characteristic of you. The particular situations do not matter as much as your ability to quickly place yourself in them; we arbitrarily selected several instances involving the use of a nonverbal signal, but any situation could serve the same purpose. The question you can ask yourself is: "Do I understand myself well enough to predict how I would respond to a great diversity of situations?"

## Self-Understanding through Analysis of an Episode

The final suggestion for increasing self-understanding is something that many people engage in almost automatically, but it may be unfamiliar to some of you. Select two episodes from this day, one about which you feel very positively, and one about which you feel very negatively. Analyze each episode by describing what happened, offering some explanation of how it happened and predicting what you would do if you could live it over again. In the case of the positive episode it would be important to understand how you contributed to making it a satisfying experience. In the case of the negative episode, the issues would be: "What would I like to have happened differently; how could I have acted differently to change things; when am I likely to have another opportunity to act differently?" The exact episodes will never present themselves again, but there are some existentialist writers who recommend that we live each moment as if it were a second chance to choose how we will act in a situation that we failed in the first time.

Some people feel weighed down and oppressed by such a philosophy. If we translate it into a counselor's life, it would mean that you would approach each counseling interaction as if it were a second chance to work with a client with whom you had been very unsuccessful the first time. Although to some counselors this sounds quite pessimistic and would mean that we would always be burdened down with feelings of failure, to others it has a very optimistic and hopeful sound. For the latter group, the emphasis is on how grateful they would feel to have a second chance, how seriously they would regard the opportunity, and how committed to making responsible choices they would feel. If analyzing past episodes, either positive or negative, has an oppressive and a burdening effect on you, then it will probably decrease self-understanding, rather than facilitate it. However, for many people analyzing past experiences carries with it the very hopeful expectation that by understanding themselves more fully in a particular episode, they are more likely to be able to maximize satisfying and meaningful experiences and to minimize or eliminate the incidence of particular negative experiences.

For those who feel they are on the brink of egomania and are in danger of being plunged into permanent narcissism, the suggestions throughout this section on self-understanding are probably not too helpful. However, many people who are drawn to counseling as a profession have spent an amazingly small amount of time studying themselves intensively. It is almost as if taking time to understand yourself is an egocentric, selfish, maybe even sinful activity. The position taken here is diametrically opposed to such an attitude. The capacity to forget oneself and focus upon another presupposes an understanding of oneself. Self-understanding means you have the ability to describe, explain, and predict your own thoughts, feelings, and patterns of action. Self-understanding puts you in a position to be open, spontaneous, visible, and to claim ownership of your experience, if you choose to. Self-understanding makes it more likely that you will be able to send reliable and valid messages about yourself to those with whom you interact. In your role as counselor, greater self-understanding makes it possible for you to reach a greater depth of sincerity.

## Increasing Self-Acceptance

Choosing to be honest and open with others concerning what you understand about yourself, demands a great deal of courage. It is often much easier to hide what you understand, to pretend not to know, to distort and deny what is painfully evident to you, and to disown thoughts and feelings that you recognize within as belonging to you. The courage to be sincere is rooted in self-acceptance.

We have described self-acceptance as a process of prizing, valuing, affirming the significance of yourself as a complex and unique person. We have discussed the importance of owning both positive and negative feelings and experiences in order to be fully self-accepting. We have acknowledged the ironical fact that becoming more fully self-accepting usually means a person is freer to try to be what he thinks and feels he truly ought to be, instead of just getting by with whatever it is convenient or popular to be.

There are three clusters of things you may find helpful for increasing your own degree of self-acceptance: (1) acknowledging personal limitations; (2) acknowledging personal power; (3) sharing yourself with other people. Each of us experiences the existential reality of being bound and limited by time and space. There is no escape from the hard, cold fact that you are dying on your feet. Life indeed can be beautiful, but nobody is going to get out of it alive. Even if you have confidence in a life after death, what is now, will one day no longer be for you. Because human existence is absolutely bound by time which flows in one direction, every hour you choose to spend doing something with one person cannot be spent with someone else.

## Acknowledging Personal Limitations

In contrast to the absolute and limited amount of time each of us has, we experience something very different when it comes to the amount of interest in and caring for others that we have. Being interested in and loving one person does not diminish your capacity to be interested in and love someone else. In fact, the opposite is more true, that caring deeply for more than one person enhances your capacity to love another individual. Parents often struggle to communicate the fact that loving one child does not reduce the love they have for a second or third child. But commitments to love and care for someone are made in space and time and, thus, it is an ongoing personal dilemma that your capacity to care is not limited in the same way or to the same degree as the time and space in which you can actualize your caring. If you commit yourself to caring for others solely on the basis of the nature of time, then your commitments will be limited, constrained, carefully measured, and steadily diminishing. If you commit yourself to caring for others without regard for spatio-temporal realities, then your commitments are likely to be unrealistic, misleading, conflicting with one another, and meaningless.

Another dimension of human existence which limits each of us, is the fact that we do not have boundless energy to invest during the time that is available. There are biological realities that differ among individuals, but which characterize every human being. You cannot escape the ebb and flow of energy that fluctuates according to your need for food, rest, and exercise, and according to the presence of disease. You cannot escape the reduction in energy accompanying the biological changes due to aging.

Still another dimension of human existence that underscores our limitations is that fact that we can raise questions about and be puzzled by far more than we will ever completely understand. Whether you look at mankind in general, or yourself as an individual, the extent of our knowledge is fantastic and the rate at which it is increasing is astounding. However, when you set what you know alongside what there is to be known about yourself, other persons, the world about you, and how they are interrelated, it is like hearing the opening bars of an unfinished symphony. There is no question that the composition will not be completed in your lifetime and there is reason to believe that the score will never be finished or, even if it were, we may be unable to develop the instruments and train musicians who could play it.

Genuine and total self-acceptance cannot occur outside the realities of human existence and that means within a context of limitations. For example, you may be one of the many persons who constantly chastize and devalue themselves for not reading more good novels, textbooks, and journal articles. In fact, you may be one of the many students who are puzzled by the fact that they hate the library. This is not so difficult to understand when you look at how ashamed you probably feel whenever you are faced with the volumes and volumes of excellent material you have never even attempted to explore. However, if you calculate the number of good novels it would be reasonable to read in your lifetime, you may be surprised at just how small the number really is, compared to what is available to read. For instance, if you read one a month for the next forty years, that is less than five hundred books. You have probably been handed lists of great books that you really should not miss that total more than five hundred and that does not take into account novels that will be written during the next forty years.

Another example of disregarding the limitations of time, space, and energy that leads some people to devalue and reject themselves concerns the maintenance of distant relationships. Many people are ashamed that they only communicate their good wishes to some of their friends once a year, at Christmas time for instance. Often they will apologize for not writing sooner and will promise to write more frequently. How much time do you think is reasonable to devote to letter writing? What will you stop doing in order to increase your letter-writing time? These are cold and objective questions that appear to ignore the feelings of the other persons. But if you are unwilling to ask such questions of yourself, then you are in greater danger of having ridiculous expectations of yourself that only set you up to feel ashamed and you will likely encourage others to have phoney expectations of you that only cause them disappointment and pain.

Finally, there is a trap that most of us fall into all too frequently that has to do with denying the limitations of our ability to thoroughly understand something and act rationally. If you are unwilling to admit that there are times when you are blinded by ignorance and strong bias, when you are debilitated by fatigue and frustration, and when you are immobilized by fear and anxiety, then you cannot warn another person that he may need to protect himself, nor can you help him know the most helpful ways to relate to you. We are not saying that because you are tired or sick or scared, you are no longer responsible. But what you are responsible for is giving other people enough information so that they can make some choices about how they will interact with you. For example, if you become cranky, demanding, uncooperative, and uncommunicative whenever you are ill, you are probably not going to change that easily or quickly. However, you can do two things while you are learning to suffer with greater dignity; you can learn to say, "I feel sick," clearly and directly and you can teach other people who have to deal with you when you are sick what is the most constructive way to approach you. If you are busy denying that you ever get sick or that you ever become unreasonable when you are sick, then you are not likely to figure out what the best ways to handle you are, so that you could teach someone how to cope with you.

A major block to greater self-acceptance is the denial of personal limitations. It is impossible to prize and affirm your own worth if you disregard the limits of time, space, biological necessity, and rationality, because you will be constantly overwhelmed with all that you are not.

### Acknowledging Personal Power

Within a context of the personal limitations that constrain all of us, self-acceptance grows and develops as we acknowledge and exercise personal power. In the same way that you may find facing your own limitations to be an unpleasant and anxiety-provoking process, facing your own power may be unsettling and even frightening. The word "power" itself carries connotations of danger and destruction for many people, and it is with some misgivings that "personal power" has been chosen to describe the dimension of human experience which we will be exploring. We could have used "ability" or "skills" to describe your potential for action; however, neither of these words connotes the strength and energy we wish to convey. Personal power refers to your capacity to make something happen, to have an impact, to change the way things are. There need not be anything destructive in the exercise of power; in fact, it is the creative, constructive, contributory use of power which we want to encourage.

In order to function optimally, a counselor needs to feel relatively free and unconstricted. This does not mean that we are making the metaphysical assumption that human behavior is undetermined. When we assume that human behavior is determined, we mean that it is not random, haphazard activity and that antecedent events cause consequent events. Instead of human behavior being an aimless, chaotic jumble of uncaused events, rather we assume that there is some order to the way things are and, that as time flows on, the things that are happening now are the results of what has happened before, and the things that will happen in the future will be caused by what is happening now. Does that mean that everything is predictable and people do not have choices? No, it does not mean that at all! Making choices, selecting from alternatives, deciding to do this rather than something else, is a reality we experience daily. But it is a matter of our subjective personal experience, which makes it no less real. It is important, however, to see that we are now talking about two different, though related, realms. In one realm the question is: "Do prior events cause later events and is human behavior random?" In the other realm the question is: "Do humans experience the freedom to make choices or is their experience that of being completely constrained, victimized, and controlled?" The first question is a metaphysical question; the other is a phenomenological question. We get into all kinds of difficulty by asking the wrong question; it really makes no sense to ask: "Is human behavior determined or free?" "Free" is something humans feel in varying degrees; "determined" refers to things being caused or uncaused, random or orderly. It is not a matter of human behavior being determined *or* free; human behavior is determined (caused and orderly) and human experience can be free. In fact, it would not be possible for you to experience yourself as free to make choices in a random, uncaused world. Although your feelings of freedom are caused and are not random events, they are no less real and no less free.

There is yet another realm of questions, which we cannot pursue in depth or exhaust here, but which should be mentioned. This realm has to do with how predictable human behavior is now, and how predictable it ever will be. At present, the fact of the matter is that human behavior is of limited predictability. There are some things we can predict with absolute certainty, such as if you cut off the supply of oxygen to the brain, eventually a person will die. There are some things which we can predict will probably happen, but we are not certain; for example, of you are verbally abusive and attack another person with words, he will probably stay and fight back or take flight from you. Questions about the predictability and unpredictability of human behavior are epistemological questions; namely, how we know about the way things are and the way things will be.

One of the major difficulties in trying to sort out the question, "Will we ever be able to predict everything with absolute certainty?" is that no matter how complete our knowledge of past events, no matter how capable the instruments we develop to assist us, e.g., high speed computers, making a prediction is a human act that occurs in time and space. The act of making a prediction thus becomes entangled in the causal chain of events about which we are predicting. For example, suppose you had access to all the necessary information for making a prediction about the next national election. Gathering the information in the first place and then making a prediction will affect the outcome. There is no way out of this dilemma, because gathering information and making predictions occur in time and space and cannot be completely separated from the events being studied and predicted.

Scholars take contradictory positions on the questions we have been raising here. It would be erroneous and foolish to represent this discussion as a series of answers to some age-old dilemmas. However, we can make some headway by trying to ask answerable questions and by identifying what are the most important questions for counselors to discuss. Figure 12 is presented in an effort to ask discussable questions.

**FIGURE 12**    Questions Concerning Determinism, Predictability, and Personal Freedom

| Is human behavior determined or undetermined?<br><br>A metaphysical question. | Is human behavior predictable or unpredictable?<br><br>An epistemological question. | Does an individual experience himself as free or controlled?<br><br>A phenomenological question. |
| --- | --- | --- |

It is quite possible to logically maintain a position that human behavior is determined, is of limited predictability, and can be experienced as free. In order to have a productive discussion and/or to think about these questions, it is important to keep track of the kind of question you are asking and to recognize the importance of the fact that time flows in one direction for humans. For example, is your reading this book determined? Yes, it is the result of prior conditions, including your own choices, and it is not a random event. Could someone have predicted that you would read this book? Yes, but only with a limited degree of certainty. Could you have chosen to not read this book? No, not now; your previous choice is fixed in space and time. Can you choose to not continue to read this book? Of course, that choice is still open to you. Will you choose to continue reading? No one can say, absolutely; hopefully, you will.

It is the third box and these latter questions that concern counselors the most: "What choices are open to a person?" and "Does a person experience himself as free to choose?" For instance, could you have been raised by more loving and consistent parents? No, not now. Could you have reacted differently to being rejected by white people? No, not now. Can you choose to be a more loving and consistent parent yourself? Yes, of course. Can you choose to react differently to racist white people in the future? Yes, of course.

There have been many attempts to describe the healthy, happy, well-adjusted, fully functioning, self-actualizing person. One theme which consistently appears in such descriptions is that the person feels free, unconstricted, not victimized, not controlled from outside, and not buffeted about by circumstances alone. In order to achieve a sense of personal freedom, it is not necessary to posit a random, undetermined, unpredictable world. It is necessary, however, to experience your own power as we have defined it above. In order to feel free, you need to know you can make something happen, you can have an impact, you can change things. The opposite of feeling free is experiencing yourself as the passive victim of outside influences, a person at the mercy of other people and things and circumstances. The suggestions given in the Acceptance discussion under the headings New Situations, New Roles, and New Media, are designed to expand your capacity to celebrate the diversity and complexity of human experience. You are asked to review these suggestions with an eye toward expanding your capacity to celebrate your own diversity and complexity. As you explore and experience new situations, roles, and media, welcome and prize the sense of personal power that comes with trying new things. You will not master everything you attempt; there are some situations and roles with which you will not be able to cope well. But there can come a sense of personal power with the knowledge that you were willing to try, that you are able to risk and endure failure. With many of your attempts to try new things, there will come the very satisfying experience of having learned to cope with or master a previously unknown dimension.

The links in the logical chain that extends from power to sincerity can be identified as follows: (1) The awareness and exercising of personal power means

"I am willing to try"; "I can cope with what it is"; "I can have an effect"; "I can make things be different"; and "I can create something new." (2) With such an awareness and experience of personal power come feelings of mastery and fitness — a sense of competence as a person. (3) A sense of personal competence is the foundation of self-acceptance — the basis for celebrating your own uniqueness and complexity. (4) With self-acceptance comes the courage to be open, spontaneous, visible, and willing to share yourself as a valuable and worthwhile person. (5) Openly and spontaneously sharing yourself with others is a definition of sincerity. This may seem to be a tortuous route or it may feel as if we will become shackled by the chain we are constructing. But it is necessary to trace the process of becoming more sincere back to a point at which we can intervene and take action. We cannot simply say, "Be more sincere"; nor can we say, "Be more courageous about being open and spontaneous." We cannot say, "Be more self-accepting"; nor does it help to say, "Feel more competent and powerful." But we can say, "Have an effect"; "Do something different"; "Create something new"; through exploring and experiencing new situations, new roles, and new media.

### Sharing Yourself with Other People

There is an additional step which will greatly facilitate self-acceptance. Within a context of personal limitations that constrain all of us, you can acknowledge and exercise your own power, plus you can share with someone else the new experiences of yourself which you are having. It is not necessary that the other person or persons actually participate; but as you explore and experience new thoughts and feelings and activities, share with someone else the ways in which you are expanding and growing. As you acknowledge your own power to yourself, you can also choose to share that experience with others.

There are many social-cultural rules that keep us from sharing ourselves. We are often very self-conscious when it comes to telling others about ourselves; we feel vulnerable and are reticent to risk boring someone with things that may be very exciting to us but not to them. The suggestion here is that you endure that vulnerability and take the risks involved in greater sharing of yourself with others. Of course, we are not suggesting that you stop some stranger on the street and launch into a lengthy description of how exciting your experiences are these days. But every day you ignore or avoid opportunities to share yourself with someone who would really like to hear what you think or feel, or what you have been doing that is important to you. Every day you choose to remain closed to someone with whom you could openly share a part of yourself. The process of self-acceptance is enhanced by sharing the things that are of significance to you and about you. When you talk with someone else about things that matter to you, you are affirming your own significance and worth. Sometimes it will not work out as you would like it to; the other person may fail to understand, be indifferent or openly hostile. Indeed there are risks in sharing yourself; but you can begin by entrusting something of yourself that will not devastate you if the other person proves unworthy of your trust and you can begin with someone who is quite likely to be able to cope with what you are entrusting to them. No doubt you already do this to a certain extent, but you probably can benefit from pushing yourself a bit more to reach out more frequently to more people, in an attempt to share yourself.

Some people find it easier to share negative things about themselves; some people are more willing to share positive aspects of themselves and their experiences. As has been said before, it is important to the self-acceptance process that you increase your capacity to own all aspects of yourself, whether you see them as positive or negative characteristics and experiences. Thus, it will enhance the self-acceptance process if you commit yourself to sharing all kinds of experiences, thoughts, and feelings, regardless of how positively or negatively you view them, with some other person or persons. One of the major purposes of the Basic Encounter Group experience, which has recently become very popular, is to increase self-acceptance using the same method of sharing yourself with others that we have been discussing. However, you do not need to wait for someone to convene a Basic Encounter Group in order to participate in the sort of sharing that will increase your own degree of self-acceptance. You can begin almost anytime: Surely at some point today, you have felt strongly about something and the chances are good that you will encounter someone today or tomorrow with whom you could share those feelings. Instead of adopting an attitude of "Oh, what difference does it make, they probably aren't interested anyway," push yourself to take a few minutes and share whatever was responsible for your strong feelings. There are few gifts more precious than giving someone the opportunity to give to you. Whenever you openly and honestly entrust a part of yourself to someone else, you are in essence giving him the opportunity to give in return through his understanding and acceptance of you. Increasing your self-acceptance can come through affirming that "What I think and feel really does make a difference," and risking that "Another person probably is interested." You can practice such a posture every day in the normal course of living your life.

## Investing in Others

We have seen that your sincerity as a counselor can be increased by extending and expanding your self-understanding and self-acceptance. In addition to maximizing your understanding and acceptance of yourself, the third suggestion for becoming a more sincere counselor is that you develop ways to communicate quickly and readily that you care about another person and that you want to be helpful. We will discuss this in terms of investing in others.

There are two meanings to the verb "invest" that are particularly applicable to our discussion of the sincere counselor. Apart from any reference to a helping relationship, to invest can mean to surround or envelop so that it might be said of someone, "Thoughtfulness invests his every action." To invest can also mean to commit something of value with the expectation of realizing a profit or achieving a goal so that it might be said of someone, "He invests nearly all of his time and energy in his work." The latter usage of invest includes the notion of risk-taking; usually the person doing the investing must endure a certain degree of vulnerability and risk in order to have an opportunity to realize a profit.

### Caring about Your Clients

There is an oriental aphorism recorded by Rabindranath Tagore (1960) that pledges to "Let my love, like sunlight, surround you, and yet give you illumined freedom." It is in this way that the authentic counselor invests in his clients. His caring surrounds and envelops like sunlight giving illumination and warmth and vitality; but he must be on guard that his caring not stifle or smother or bring darkness like a heavy blanket held over his client's head. Caring about your clients — investing time, energy, and concern in them — can be very risky in the sense of not being guaranteed a return on your investment. But that is precisely what the sincere counselor does, he envelops a client with his caring and endures the vulnerability of committing time, energy, and concern for someone who might or might not pay off. For example, there are times that a counselor after having worked hard and competently with a new client, is surprised and disappointed when the client fails to show up for the next appointment. Take another disappointing situation that is not uncommon in the schools: A counselor might initiate a conversation with one or more students, simply in an effort to be friendly, and he is met with either silence and sullen stares or suppressed laughter and nervous sidewise glances. Anytime a counselor is faced with a client who in one form or another is saying: "I don't care"; "It doesn't matter"; or "I won't try"; the risk of caring about that person is high. It is relatively easy to invest yourself in a client who is eager to be assisted, willing to try new ideas and behaviors, and who will work hard at your mutually agreed upon objectives. But the passive, seemingly uninvolved client requires greater willingness by the counselor to sustain a caring attitude without benefit of encouragement from the client and without promise of pay-off for his efforts. The risk of investing in a client does not only occur when an elaborate plan has been developed which the client must carry out; the risk occurs even at the stage when a counselor is trying to understand his client. Many clients will communicate by what they say or what they fail to say, "I am not worth the effort it takes to understand me"; or "The decisions I have to make are not important enough to bother about"; or "There's no use my trying to get you to understand me, nobody ever has, nobody ever will, and it wouldn't matter if they did!" The sincere counselor perceives that message, whether it is implicit in the client's behavior or explicitly stated, but goes on caring and trying and investing in the person even though many people would sign off with, "Fine, if that's the way you want it!" Without question there will be times that you will lose on your investment and if you looked back it would be easy to say, "Any idiot should have been able to tell that that client wouldn't come through." On the one hand every counselor has a responsibility to select the clients in whom he will invest the greatest time and energy with an eye to maximizing the services he can provide; but on the other hand, the counselor must be willing to risk caring about clients who may not look like winners during the first few encounters.

### Caring about People Who Serve You

It is possible to build up habits of investing in others, even when the pay-off looks doubtful or, at best, will not be very great. For example, there is a large category into which many different people fall, called "Persons Who Are Paid to Serve You." Many of the people in this category you rarely deal with directly, e.g., mailman, garbage collector, elected public official, cleaner and presser, hemotology lab technician, fry cook, photographic printer, etc. Many of those who serve you are related to you in highly superficial and ritualized ways, e.g., "Fill'er up with regular!" "Eighth floor!" "No, that will be all!" "I'd like that charged!" "May I have the check!" etc. And some of those who serve you, you interact with and invest in as you would a person who means more to you than simply being someone who provides certain services. Even though it is good public relations and good business to be nice to your barber or hairdresser or your secretary or your paper boy, kindnesses to people who might therefore serve you better are not being disparaged. You are encouraged to extend yourself in a helpful and friendly manner to all who are in positions of serving you.

However, the sort of investing in others that may have the greatest generalizability to your counseling, occurs when you extend yourself to someone whose services probably will not change simply because you are kindly or helpful. For example, the next time you attempt to place a long distance telephone call that does not go through or the next time you request a telephone number from Information, close the conversation with the operator with something like "Thank you for your assistance." Or the next time you are in an elevator that is not automated, as you exit at your requested floor, turn and thank the operator. These may sound like corny suggestions that ought to be confined to a young ladies' finishing school, but there *is* a certain naive quality that characterizes the sincere counselor. An authentic counselor is not preoccupied with himself or his position, and thus is free to acknowledge another person's efforts, even when they have as mundane a job as running an elevator. Now, of course, you can become obsessed with showing gratitude and make a big display of saying "Thank you" which would obviously defeat the purpose of the suggestions. What is intended is that in the course of a busy day, amidst a bustling crowd rushing frantically to reach a place where they will probably have to wait, you are the kind of human being who thinks it is worth the effort to recognize and confirm the humanness of the people-components in the giant machine known as modern society.

A less transient interaction and thus potentially more meaningful encounter is possible everytime you purchase something in a store or eat in a restaurant. You do not have to coerce a clerk or waitress into an extended conversation, particularly if she is being pushed to serve others, in order to acknowledge her humanness. For example, a simple comment such as "Pretty busy day, huh?" while she is serving your order or writing up the sales slip, affords you the opportunity to communicate a genuine degree of concern. You may be met with a terse "Yah" and nothing more, or it may give her an opportunity to share with someone a bit of what she is feeling, such as "Yah, and I've got four hours to go." Remember, we are talking about ways to push yourself toward readily investing in other people because that is one of the skills in communicating sincerity as a counselor. This does not mean, however, that you should henceforth strike up a conversation with every sales person and waitress you encounter, regardless of how you are feeling. In general, what is being suggested is that people who are paid to serve you are also paid to endure being treated like objects or machines but you do not have to participate in and contribute to such a depersonalizing and dehumanizing process. You can affirm the importance and value of other persons by insisting to yourself and acting in accordance with your belief that there is a difference between riding to the eighth floor in an elevator in which you pushed the button marked "eight" and riding in an elevator in which another person is paid to push the button marked "eight" for you.

### Caring about People Who Are Unable to Serve You

In addition to the category of those who serve you, there is another category of people who provide opportunities to increase your capacity for readily investing in others, namely, "Persons Who Are Unable To Serve You." Some of the more obvious examples of persons in this category are young children, aged people, disabled persons, and temporarily encumbered individuals. What we need to focus on in this category is not an individual's lack of ability to serve us, because all of the examples mentioned are able to give of themselves in many ways, but rather the fact that it is sometimes difficult for each of us to extend ourselves in a genuinely caring manner to someone who is permanently or temporarily disabled. For example, suppose you are pushing a grocery cart in a supermarket and as you enter the aisle containing cereals, you encounter a strapping young man about twenty years old who has obviously just knocked down a stack of "Cheerios" and "Grapenuts Flakes." You have several options: (1) you can move on without comment, as if you did not see the boxes strewn about; (2) you can quickly gather up as many boxes as possible, working even faster than he is to clean up the mess; (3) you can tell him you think it's terrible that the store places such hazardous items where an innocent person can run into them and that you would complain to the management and if they were not properly apologetic then you would threaten to sue them; (4) you can calmly pick up several of the boxes either without comment or with a simple acknowledgement that it probably was a surprise when they fell. There are many people who would defend the first option as being the best because it avoids any chance of embarrassing the young man further and besides he may not want your help. If the only way you know how to help is by making a big production of the whole thing, such as is done in options #2 and #3, then probably it would be better to simply move on. But if you have the ability to calmly acknowledge a mess or a mistake and quietly assist the person do the best he can to rectify it, as is the case with option #4, then your help would probably be welcomed. These same options exist in many situations, such as a child struggling with a heavy door, a crippled individual trying to operate a vending machine, an older person facing a flight of stairs without a railing, etc. Your offering to help may be met with a refusal or a clipped "I'd rather do it myself!" That has to be all right; you must be willing to allow someone to reject your offer without it resulting in your feeling hurt or angry. But a characteristic of sincere counselors is that they are willing to risk and endure rejection of their attempts to help. The sincere counselor is able to extend himself to someone else, even though he has not received an engraved invitation guaranteeing a warm reception. Most of the time your efforts to assist someone will be met with appreciation, if you extend yourself in the spirit of option #4. But sometimes there will be no payoff for your investment. Whether you are in a supermarket or on a street corner or in a counseling session, you must be willing to continue caring about other persons, even though some of them do not seem to care in return. The authentic counselor's investing in other persons is calm and quiet, but not indifferent; it is warm and friendly, but not fawning; it is matter-of-fact, but not blunt or harsh; it is open and optimistic, but not frantic. The sincere counselor's caring for another person surrounds and envelops, but frees the person to function more fully and more independently.

It is not a good idea to experiment with and try to practice investing in others and caring more deeply in your interactions with clients, because it takes the focus off the client and keeps you preoccupied with yourself. However, in your day-to-day encounters in stores, supermarkets, restaurants, offices, etc., it is possible to practice and extend your capacity to invest in other human beings and to communicate your caring quickly and readily.

In summary, the kind of counselor who is sincere in his relationships with clients is a counselor who feels and readily demonstrates deep concern for others and who possesses a high degree of self-understanding and self-acceptance. Although it is impossible to pursue sincerity directly, it is very possible to learn to communicate your investment in others more skillfully and to increase your self-understanding and self-acceptance. By so doing, you become more willing and able to be open, spontaneous, visible, and honest about yourself and your experience. You are more likely to represent yourself validly and reliably. In short, you will become more sincere.

# V   COMMUNICATION

Throughout this book, counseling has been viewed as a transactional process whereby a person, identified as "counselor," by means of Understanding, Acceptance, and Sincerity, negotiates a contract with another person, identified as "client," in order to assist him with Choices he must make and/or Changes he desires and/or Confusion he wishes to reduce in one or more of three life task areas, namely Work, Relationship, and Aloneness. The *content* of counseling has been viewed in terms of these three life tasks; the *purpose* of counseling has been viewed in terms of the three contracts which are negotiable. The *process* of counseling has been viewed in terms of the essential qualities characterizing an effective counselor, namely, understanding, acceptance, and sincerity. The single basic counselor skill which is demanded by and threaded through all these aspects of counseling is expertise in communicating (Tyler, 1969). We cannot think about the *process* of counseling without thinking about communication. Achieving the *purpose* of counseling is inconceivable without communication and the *content* of counseling does not exist unless it is communicated. Communication skills are inextricably interwoven with a counselor's values, attitudes, interests, and knowledge to produce the fabric of a competent counselor. It is no accident that communication is the last topic we will discuss; the ability to communicate skillfully is not merely fourth on the list of characteristics of the competent counselor, rather it permeates and summarizes all that has gone before. Therefore, as was the case for discussing counseling in general, we will consider skillful communicating in terms of its content, purpose and process.

Volumes have been written on communication; we will not attempt to survey or summarize what has been said. Extensive research has been conducted on communication; we will not attempt to survey or summarize the findings. The objective for this discussion of communication is relatively modest in that we will simply examine some dimensions of communicating, which hopefully will prove to be useful to a counselor-in-training.

In keeping with our practice of looking first at the behavior as it occurs in everyday experience, an aerial view, we will consider communicating in general. Then we will move in for a closer look at communicating in counseling and, finally, we will zoom in for a close-up view of specific communication skills which are included in the competent counselor's repertoire.

## The Content of Effective Communication

When you think about it, you have spent a tremendous amount of time learning to communicate with other persons. Especially if you are interested in counseling, you have very likely invested a great deal of energy improving your ability to communicate skillfully. We live at a time when there is unprecedented preoccupation with and necessity for communicating, person to person, group to group, and nation to nation. With the development of new communication media — color television, computers, satellites, Moog synthesizers, high speed copiers, etc. — we are experiencing radical changes in the form and function of communicating which are as far-reaching as was the invention of the printing press. You have personal, professional, and cultural reasons for being deeply concerned about communicating skillfully.

All of us know persons we would identify as generally skillful communicators. One of the characteristics that is common to people who are able to communicate effectively is that they are attuned to both the cognitive and affective dimensions of what is being communicated. The content of communication is made up of both thoughts and feelings, and the individual who is skillful at communicating is able to send and receive both kinds of signals.

### Attending to the Client's Thoughts and Feelings

In counseling interactions, it is especially important that both what the client thinks and what the client feels are acknowledged and dealt with. The material covered in successful counseling interactions ranges very widely and we could not specify topics which must always be covered nor could we list topics which are always irrelevant. Whether a topic is important and relevant, and thus contributes to communication being effective, depends upon the individual client, the individual counselor, and their particular situation. For example, you might find yourself spending time discussing the manner in which garbage is packaged and removed from a client's home as one instance of the many ways a boy and his mother are unable to relate to one another satisfactorily. To deal effectively with such a topic it is, of course, not enough to understand the bare fact that they have a running battle over carrying out the garbage. The feelings about one another which make carrying out the garbage a hassle must be understood as well. Whether you would opt for a behavioristic approach to reshaping both the mother's and the boy's responses or you would prefer to use insight into the dynamics of their interaction as the means of resolving their conflict, communicating effectively with one or both of them means you are able to deal with what they both think and feel about the whole mess.

At another time you might find yourself busily sending and receiving messages about the ecstasies of a Harley-Davidson, wide open on a nearly empty highway at dawn, as you struggle to understand why an eight-to-five job is unthinkable to this recently discharged veteran who is not too excited about utilizing his veterans' benefits. Clearly, it is not enough to communicate that you perceive that he enjoys riding his motorcycle and that working at a desk all day does not particularly appeal to him. The desire and needs for feelings of power, freedom, autonomy, and adventure associated with the cycle, must be part of what is communicated back and forth, if you are to be of any assistance in his choices about training and/or working.

These two examples have emphasized the necessity for communicating about feelings as well as thoughts in counseling, which presumes that most counselors are likely to be responsive to and able to communicate thoughts more readily than feelings. This probably is true of most beginning counselors; however, the other extreme is equally unproductive and is not an uncommon style among both experienced and inexperienced counselors. For example, you might find yourself faced with a thirty-five-year-old man who is dissatisfied with his job, his family, the town he lives in, the way the country is heading, and any number of things. You could encounter him in an employment service, a mental hygiene clinic, a college counseling center, your pastoral study, or in a conference about his retarded daughter's school performance. It is not enough to communicate with him about nothing but his feelings. Whether you see your job as one of helping him sort through the confusion, facilitating his making some plans and decisions, and/or assisting him in devising ways in which he can change things, what he thinks about himself and his situation is as important as what he feels. The content of effective communication with such an individual must include both what he thinks — what he believes to be true, how he construes his life, what his opinions are, how he relates the segments of his life, etc., and what he feels — his preferences, aspirations, disappointments, frustrations, deep longings, general discontent, etc. A counselor who was communicating skillfully with him would not ignore either aspect of the man's experience.

### Attending to the Spatio-Temporal Aspects of Communication

In addition to paying close attention to both the thoughts and feelings contained in a client's messages, the skillful communicator also attends to the spatio-temporal aspects of whatever is being communicated. It makes a great deal of difference whether the material being communicated was "there and then," is "here and now," or will be "where and when." For example, suppose a client says, "I get so mad when I can't say what I mean." That statement could easily mean, "*I was* so frustrated and angry with myself because I just couldn't make her understand." Or it might mean, "*I am* really frustrated and angry with you because you don't understand me." Or it might mean, "I don't want to try to explain it to her because she won't understand and then *I will* just get mad." The context in which the statement occurs should clarify what the client is trying to communicate. The counselor who is skillful in communicating will make certain that he indeed does know whether his client is referring to the past, the present or the future. In some ways, the importance of the spatio-temporal dimension seems terribly obvious; nevertheless, many communication breakdowns result from the counselor's failure to ascertain the time and place the client has in mind when he makes a statement.

There are a variety of techniques which a counselor can use to gain a clearer picture of the time-space context from which his client is speaking; we will discuss and illustrate these later. What is important at this point is that you recognize the significance of knowing the spatio-temporal context of your client's statements, if communication is to be effective. A long list of communication techniques is of little use to a counselor who does not know when to employ them.

For example, suppose you are a high school girls' counselor and a junior girl has been referred to you by her English teacher because her previously high quality performance has been steadily declining. In the process of your trying to understand what is happening with the English class, she reveals that: (1) she is having trouble concentrating; (2) she really likes English and is especially fond of her teacher; (3) she is confused; (4) she knows she must try harder; (5) she has been sick several days during the past two weeks; (6) her older sister quit school to get married last year; (7) she just broke up with her boyfriend. At this point she blurts out, "Mother always said I would probably disgrace the family." There are ways a counselor could respond to this that would be clearly wrong: "Oh, I didn't know your mother was dead"; "Yes, all mothers talk like that sometime or another"; "Well, I'm sure with a little self-discipline and hard work your mother will be very proud of you"; "I can really understand how you feel about it all." These responses are sadly lacking in understanding, they are for the most part rejecting and they are quite insincere. However, even more striking than the responses we can rule out as inappropriate, is the multitude of responses which would be very appropriate: "Could you say more about that?" "Mother really doesn't trust you"; "You feel like you've done a really bad thing?" "I'm kinda lost, can you help me see the connection between that feeling and what we've been talking about?" etc.

Whatever you say certainly should be aimed at receiving both the girl's thoughts and feelings, and it should also be aimed at identifying the time and space framework from which she is sending messages. Has she already disgraced her family? Is she fearful that she will disgrace them? Is it her performance in the classroom that is disgraceful? Is there something outside of the English class that she regards as disgraceful? Is she worried that she may do something outside of school that will be disgraceful? Does her mother prophesy daily that she will be a disgrace or was this something that was mentioned once, three years ago? These are questions that you probably would not ask directly, simply because it is more efficient to allow her to clarify what she means in her own way. However, if you are unable to place the message in time and space, then the context of her message has not been thoroughly communicated. It is as important that you know the difference between when a message has been communicated and when it has not, as it is to know techniques for clarifying the message further.

In summary, the content of counseling communications must include both thoughts and feelings and the content must be understood in terms of the time and place to which it refers. Therefore, the counselor who is skillful at communicating with his clients is attentive to and in tune with his client's thoughts and feelings and he receives those thoughts and feelings in terms of his client's time-space framework.


## The Purpose of Effective Communication

In general, communication can be a means to something or an end in itself. Communicating is intrinsically rewarding to humans from very early in their development; even prior to the acquisition of language, toddlers are fascinated with nonverbal exchanges among themselves. Teenagers spend hours on the telephone in what appears to those younger and older to be endless, goalless activity. College students engage in marathon rap sessions without burdening themselves by demanding an outcome or end product. Women's coffee klatches typically result in the exchange of considerable information, but again, the activity itself is more significant than any end product. Men from all socioeconomic levels are notorious, according to their wives, for sustaining lengthy conversations about the way things ought to be, although they do not expect anything will be different as a result of their conversations. Finally, the difference between an empty, meaningless day on a park bench or in a rest home and a day in which it is good to be eighty, may simply be someone to talk with. For all of us, some of the time, communicating is inherently worthwhile.

In counseling encounters, however, communicating itself is rarely an end goal, but rather the purpose of communicating is to reach some other goal such as exploring, informing, clarifying, formulating, planning, reinforcing, and evaluating in order to make choices or changes or to reduce confusion. Because communicating is generally rewarding to humans and particularly prized by persons attracted to counseling as a profession, you have to guard against allowing communicating to become the goal of counseling, instead of the means for achieving counseling goals.

This book makes no claim to provide you with all you will need to conduct effective counseling. There is, for instance, no discussion of how a counselor could enter the client's situation in order to modify the contingencies governing reinforcements for his behavior. We have not considered the kinds of interventions that are possible for altering the ways in which a client interacts with significant others in his world. We have not discussed techniques for teaching a client new ways to perceive the world of vocational possibilities from which he could choose, nor have we discussed tactics for engaging a client in planful decision-making, in general. Our efforts have been limited to examining the content, purpose, and process of counseling from its beginning stages up to the point of pursuing the objectives and thereby completing the contract established between the client and the counselor. Using Tyler's (1969) classification system, we have dealt with each level of counseling interaction up to the tactical level, which requires knowledge and skills in testing, computer assisted presentation of information, planning trial experiences, analysis of case records, behavioral observations, desensitization procedures, group and individual therapy, referral for medical evaluation and treatment, planning educational and training experiences, milieu therapy, and other experimental social interventions. Most particularly, we have concentrated upon the knowledge, attitudes and skills necessary for successful interviewing, which is a part of all strategies for bringing about change, choice or confusion reduction.

Communicating effectively is the essence of being a good interviewer. Nevertheless, communicating effectively is rarely, if ever, the goal of counseling; rather, skillful communication is a major vehicle for carrying you and your client to your mutually agreed upon destination. Much of the aimless wandering about that passes for counseling results from a counselor's not knowing what else to do and/or being so enamored with joyriding in his shiny new conveyance that he really does not want to reach a final destination. Failure to discern the difference between communicating as a means to an end and communicating as an end in itself, can block the forward movement of counseling and lock the client and counselor into a race track course of endless circular laps.

We will briefly examine both the sending and the receiving sides of communicating, followed by a short description of nonverbal messages and an illustrated list of verbal communication techniques.

## The Process of Communicating Effectively

It is not possible to *not* communicate with your clients. It is indeed possible to communicate poorly or ineffectively with your clients, but not communicating at all is *not* an option. You sometimes hear a counselor say in frustration and disappointment, "We just weren't communicating." What he means, of course, is that the communication which did occur between himself and his client was very unsatisfactory. Either the counselor sent signals which did not arrive as he had intended, or the counselor failed to receive signals which his client was attempting to transmit. In either or both cases the process of communicating does not stop, until the counselor and client are physically separated. During an interview, conversation may stop, understanding may cease, acceptance may terminate and sincerity may be nonexistent, but the process of communicating continues.

Effective communication can be understood to mean exchanges between the counselor and the client which contain both thoughts and feelings, within a spatio-temporal context, which facilitate the client's making choices, making changes, and/or reducing confusion in his life. Communicating effectively with clients is an interdependent process, that is, it is a transactional process that depends on both the counselor and the client. However, unless you want to limit your work to highly communicative clients who can readily adapt to your preferred style, the responsibility for communicating effectively is primarily yours. Your client has the major responsibility for the content of the communication; you and your client together determine the purposes for communication; but you bear the major responsibility for the process of communicating with one another. We will, therefore, focus upon the counselor's role in this basic transactional process, which is at the very center of counseling.

The counselor is both a sender and a receiver of messages and the process occurs both verbally and nonverbally. To illustrate these two dimensions of the communication process, namely, sending-receiving and verbal-nonverbal, from the counselor's point of view, several examples are given in Figure 13. A complete list of verbal and nonverbal messages received and sent by a counselor would undoubtedly be endless and Figure 12 includes merely a few examples.

### Nonverbal Communication

We approach the topic of nonverbal communication with two causes for trepidation: (1) it is clearly a terribly important mode of sending and receiving signals, about which there is not a great deal of practically useful advice to be given, and (2) preoccupation with this mode of communicating can easily sidetrack and confuse the beginning counselor. Perhaps the most useful approach to nonverbal communication is to point out that you probably know considerably more than you could say about this aspect of communicating. That is, you can very likely send and receive nonverbal signals in a way that facilitates the process of communicating, even though you would be hard pressed to describe and explain how you do it. In fact, if you were asked to monitor your own nonverbal signals and the nonverbal signals of your client as the process of communicating was moving forward, it would probably interfere with or prevent your going on. The utilization of nonverbal signals in counseling is an art. Skill comes through study and practice; but as is the case with any art form, the artist cannot necessarily describe and explain all the components which combine to produce an excellent performance. It is for this reason that artists separate practicing and performing, namely, pianists practice études, dancers rehearse individual movements, painters copy the masters, and singers practice scales.

Finding some analogous way for counselors to practice their skills in sending and receiving nonverbal signals is not an easy task. If you have never concentrated on the process of communicating nonverbally, you might find it useful to simply turn down the sound on a television set and watch a program, such as a late evening talk show. The number and complexity of nonverbal messages will be immediately obvious. The parlor game, Charades, in which one

FIGURE 13.   Two Dimensions of Communication

|  | SENDING | RECEIVING |
|---|---|---|
| **VERBAL** | Asking a question<br><br>Restating what client has said<br><br>Describing your own feelings<br><br>Explaining the implications of a test score<br><br>Summarizing a session<br><br>Assigning a task to be completed by next session | Hearing exactly what client has said<br><br>Imagining what an experience was like for client<br><br>Sorting and organizing a jumbled story<br><br>Placing a choice or problem in context<br><br>Listening for the feelings accompanying an episode |
| **NONVERBAL** | Gesturing toward chair in which you expect client to sit<br><br>Nodding and smiling<br><br>Frowning and looking away<br><br>Tapping your fingers on the chair arm<br><br>Touching arm of weeping client<br><br>Wearing a white coat; a white shirt and tie; a colorful polo shirt; a dirty sweatshirt | Hearing client's voice quality change, i.e., become husky, shrill, choked, etc.<br><br>Seeing a client squirm, wring hands, flush, perspire, etc.<br><br>Smelling scent of heavy perfume worn by 13-year-old girl<br><br>Watching client choose to sit in chair further away<br><br>Noting that client never takes his eyes off you, until you speak |

person must communicate without benefit of words the meaning of syllables, words, and phrases in a saying or book title or movie title, etc., so that others can guess what is being depicted, might be useful to increase your awareness of nonverbal signals. In addition, there are a variety of nonverbal exercises which have been developed to sensitize people to various aspects of human relations. For example, to give people a first hand experience of dependency, a nonverbal exercise which has been used involves allowing someone to lead you around a building while you are blindfolded and have agreed in advance not to talk to one another. Imagine that you are in the middle of an intersection, blindfolded, and a horn honks and brakes squeal. At the same time, the person who is leading you hesitates and momentarily loosens his grip on your arm; contrast that with his moving slightly closer and gripping your arm a little more tightly. In the first case, his nonverbal signals may heighten your sense of dependency, fear of being abandoned and anxiety associated with being vulnerable. The second set of nonverbal signals could well communicate a trustworthiness, reaffirm the person's commitment to protecting you from harm, and generally reassure you that your being dependent at that moment is acceptable. When you returned to the building for a debriefing session, assuming that there would be an opportunity to discuss your experience, you may have learned a great deal about dependency and about nonverbal signals during this exercise. Dependency, trustworthiness, reassurance, vulnerability, abandonment, support, and protection are clearly important issues in a counseling relationship and anything you learn about them will probably be useful. Communicating nonverbally is also an important issue in counseling. However, most of the nonverbal exercises such as the one just described, which are increasingly popular in group counseling, human relations groups, basic encounter groups, sensitivity groups, etc., have very limited generalizability to most counseling encounters. When you are assisting someone with choices, changes, and/or confusion reduction, the way in which you both send and receive nonverbal messages is quite far removed from leading someone blindfolded through traffic. There are many complex cognitive steps involved in generalizing from this kind of nonverbal exercise to an actual counseling encounter.

You will likely find other nonverbal exercises, such as exploring someone's face with your hands and eyes, but without speaking, or mirroring someone's posture, body movements, gestures and expressions, as well as being the recipient of exploration and mirroring, to be interesting, novel, fun, and instructive, depending on the skills of the person directing the exercises and debriefing session following the exercises. As was true of other new experiences and situations suggested in this book, you are encouraged to participate in such nonverbal exercises, provided they are directed by a reputable, trained person. If not, they will probably just be a waste of time, although sometimes they can be quite disturbing and stressful. However, it should be remembered that such exercises will probably have no direct effect on your skillfulness in sending and receiving nonverbal messages in counseling. They may help you become a more responsive person, in general, and to become more acutely aware of the process of communicating, but improving communication skills in counseling is very closely related to the counseling situation itself. Therefore, skills need to be practiced in a situation which is highly similar to the counseling situation.

The experience most likely to be instructive concerning your skill in sending and receiving nonverbal signals in counseling, is watching a video-taped playback of yourself counseling and then discussing what you saw with other counselors. The first time you watch yourself, there is a tendency to overreact to the particularities of your own behavior. For example, we all have developed idiosyncratic ways of sitting, nodding, gesturing, etc. Unless you have the stabilizing effect of feedback from other persons, you are likely to deny that some particular behavior is in fact typical of you and/or to conclude that every other gesture you make must be very distracting and should be eliminated. It may be true that some particularity is not helpful and may be a hindrance, but it is important to have that confirmed by trusted colleagues before you try to extinguish it.

Whether you have the benefit of video playback equipment or must rely on the verbal and nonverbal feedback descriptions of your colleagues, the important thing to look for is dissonance and discrepancy between your nonverbal behavior and your verbal behavior. For instance, you may feel very interested and talk as if you are interested in what a client is saying, but at the same time look very bored and impatient because of a habit of glancing out the window or rapidly moving your foot, of which you may be totally unaware. You may feel very warmly toward a client and be pleased with your interaction, only to be be startled to see how disapproving and angry you look because of a frown which typically accompanies concentration on your part.

Discrepancies between verbal and nonverbal signals are also important features of the client's communications. If a client says that a particular event or decision or person in his life is not especially important, but each time the subject arises he moves about in his chair, his voice changes, and he becomes less fluent, then you would likely conclude that what he says and what he feels are at odds. If you look closely at this conclusion, you will see that it assumes that increased movement, change in voice quality, and decrease in fluency are associated with strong feelings. These are probably good thumb rules, but herein lies the danger alluded to at the beginning of this discussion on nonverbal signals. We do not have anything approaching a catalogue of nonverbal signals and their associated meanings. If a counselor becomes preoccupied with interpreting the meaning of every twitch, stammer, squeak, and blush his client manifests, he is likely to lose track of the client's messages altogether. Neither is it possible to specify a set of counselor gestures, postures, expressions, colognes, or clothes which you can count on to communicate the same message to any two clients.

In general, nonverbal messages rarely stand alone in the counseling encounter, that is, they usually accompany a verbal message which they either confirm or contradict. For the counselor, the nonverbal messages he sends ought to confirm the verbal messages he transmits, thereby facilitating the process of communicating. From the client, it is helpful to receive both his verbal and nonverbal messages, especially when they are contradictory, since such dissonance often signals a significant subject has arisen. However, receiving a signal that something important is happening and understanding fully what that something is are very different matters. In order to understand fully the meaning of any nonverbal signal, the counselor must receive the signal in terms of the context surrounding it. A client's shifting in his chair may mean anything from "My leg has gone to sleep. . . ." to "I am nearly overwhelmed with anxiety whenever I think of changing jobs." The context, which includes the immediate situation, thoughts, and feelings about the past, and expectations about the future, gives the particular nonverbal signal, shifting in his chair, its meaning. In order to understand the context, you must rely heavily upon the verbal messages which are being transmitted. Several of the techniques which are described below, are designed to elicit and clarify the context of the client's concerns. Before we turn to the process of sending and receiving verbal messages, however, we will summarize the discussion of nonverbal messages.

1. Sending and receiving nonverbal signals is an art and thus requires study and practice in order to increase skill in performing.
2. Becoming preoccupied with the process at the same time you are engaging in it is usually disruptive and hinders rather than facilitates communication.
3. Therefore, studying and practicing nonverbal means to communicate should take place apart from a counseling interaction which is in process, but it should take place in a situation which is highly similar to the counseling situation.
4. The use of nonverbal exercises and, even more, observing yourself on video tape can help sensitize and alert you to your own, as well as others, nonverbal signals.
5. Dissonance and discrepancy between verbal and nonverbal messages *usually* means that there are relatively strong feelings accompanying whatever is happening, whether or not they are being acknowledged.
6. There is no standard set of meanings attached to various gestures, postures, expressions, manners of dress, etc. In order to understand a nonverbal signal, it must be interpreted in terms of the context in which it is embedded.

Sending and receiving *verbal* signals is no less complex and it also requires the skill of an artist, but it is easier to describe and explain how it is accomplished.

*Verbal Communication*

We can identify two simultaneous processes which, taken together, capture the essence of communicating verbally in counseling: making common and moving toward. See Figure 14.

"Common," in the way we will be using the term, does not mean "ordinary, mundane, or run-of-the-mill," but rather that which is shared, mutual, joint, namely, that which belongs to more than one. Both you and your clients have many thoughts, feelings, experiences, relationships, expectations, and aspirations which at the outset of counseling are unknown to one another. As you interact, many of these will be shared, especially those which originally

FIGURE 14.    The Process of Verbal Communication

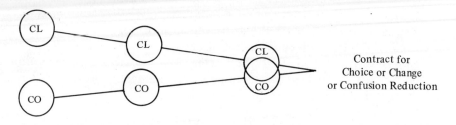

Contract for
Choice or Change
or Confusion Reduction

CL = Client and CO = Counselor

belonged to your client and were unknown to you. The process of communicating verbally is literally a process of using words to make thoughts, feelings,
experiences, etc., common to the two of you.

Earlier, the purpose of communicating was said to be a means for
achieving counseling goals; the purpose of communicating is to get from one
place to another. Therefore, the process of communicating involves movement
and direction. Initially, you and your client engage in a process of moving
towards a mutually agreed upon contract which describes what your expectations are in meeting together and how you are going to realize those
expectations. After the counseling contract is at least tentatively negotiated, you
and your client move towards fulfilling the contract which you have agreed
upon. Communicating verbally is the most important process which you and
your client will use to move towards a counseling contract. Depending upon the
nature of the contract you draw up, communicating verbally may also be the
primary process which you and your client use to move towards fulfilling the
contract.

Before we turn to a discussion of specific communication techniques for
making common and moving toward, it would probably be helpful to get our
bearings, that is, to look at the larger picture for a moment. We are about to
discuss face-to-face verbal exchanges between you and one or more clients. That
process has been described as the most important thing you do in formulating a
counseling contract, as well as one of the ways in which you can fulfill some
contracts. However, all of counseling cannot be reduced to face-to-face verbal
exchanges. In fact, there are many counselors and probably would-be clients
who feel that it is useless to sit around talking about how you would like things to
be, because wishing is not going to make it be that way. Instead of just talking
about it, they believe counselors ought to be out changing the situation so things
would be better for students, welfare recipients, wards of the court, hospitalized
patients, the aged, the unemployed, the disabled, minority groups, and other
disfranchised persons. In no way is the urgent need for constructive change of
present systems, which have people locked into a frustrating, debilitating and

dehumanizing existence, being minimized or denied. As private citizens, we all have grave responsibilities for bringing about changes that should have been accomplished hundreds of years ago. As professionals, we all have equally serious responsibilities for bringing about immediate improvements in the systems within which we function.

Some counselors have decided to concentrate all their efforts on such system change, and find it hard to understand how anyone could waste time doing anything else. Some counselors have also committed themselves exclusively to system change, at the same time recognizing the necessity for others to be working with individuals and groups who are trapped in the systems, but who must nevertheless make choices and decisions about themselves and what they are going to do in spite of the system. (Those choices include, of course, efforts to destroy present systems, as well as efforts to modify or tolerate them.) Some counselors recognize how bad things are for many people; they see the desperate need for change, but they are overwhelmed and immobilized by the enormity of the task. Some counselors do not care enough to look or are too stupid to see. Finally, some counselors recognize the necessity for some persons to be exclusively committed to system change and are highly supportive of their efforts, but have committed their own energies to working with individuals and groups within the constraints of the present systems. It is probably obvious that the writer believes that we need counselors who are committed to system change and expend themselves bringing it about, and that we also need counselors who are committed to system change, but who are willing to work within the present systems as the process of change takes place. Counselors who are overwhelmed, immobilized, uncaring, or stupid are of no use to anybody and a detriment to everybody.

For us to discuss the process of communicating verbally for purposes of assisting clients make choices and changes and reduce the confusion in their lives does not mean, implicitly or explicitly, that all people have a sufficient quantity or an adequate quality of choices and possibilities open to them. Nor does it mean that a client really can change whatever he wants changed, if he just tries hard enough. But all clients must make choices and many of them desire to make changes that could be accomplished regardless of how unsatisfactory their present situations may be.

Verbal communication is the major vehicle for assisting clients with confusion reduction and with many choices and changes; as stated above, communicating verbally involves two processes. These two processes — making common, and moving toward — were described as occurring simultaneously. That is, when you and your client share (make common) some aspect of your client's thoughts and feelings, you approach (move toward) a more thorough understanding of your client's whole existence. And, as you and your client move toward formulating and fulfilling a contract, the experiences and understanding you will have in common continue to increase. It is very important that the counselor recognize the fact that sharing and moving must be simultaneous communication processes and that any attempt to do one without the other interferes with accomplishing the purposes of counseling. For example, if you attempt to move too rapidly, without an adequate amount and quality of sharing, you will find yourself taking off and landing at some distant destination, only to discover you just made a solo flight. Arriving at mutually agreed upon goals or directions to pursue, depends upon you and your client sharing — making common — communicating with one another. On the other hand, if you attempt to do nothing but share the client's experiences, your counseling begins to look like an archaeological expedition with you busily digging up relics from the client's past to be carefully examined, catalogued, and preserved. The lack of forward movement in such over-extended sharing would likely undermine the client's commitment and the whole relationship would probably cave in. Sustaining a commitment to the counseling process depends upon both the counselor and client being able to see that things are moving forward — that their efforts at communicating are leading somewhere.

The communication techniques presented below contribute to both aspects of the communication process; some of them are especially useful for moving toward negotiating and completing a contract, while others are primarily used to make common the client's and counselor's experiences. Although we are somewhat beyond a Stone Age level of development in that counselors possess more tools than a couple of sharp, smooth stones and sticks, we are a long way from having an elaborate set of instruments like those of a modern mechanic or dentist. It is impossible to sort our communication techniques into neat categories, such as wrenches, screwdrivers, hammers, etc., and it is impossible to specify a precise order in which a counselor uses the communication tools which are available to him. Therefore, the best way for us to proceed is simply to describe and illustrate each communication technique, pointing out how it can be used both to make common and to move forward in a counseling interview. When and where and in what order you would employ these tools depend on your own judgment in each particular situation.

### Asking Questions

Most interviews begin with a question of some sort designed to determine what expectations the client has in seeking counseling. For example, a college counselor might ask, "What brings you to the Counseling Center?" or a high school counselor might inquire, "Did your teacher send you to see me?" But there is a world of difference in these two seemingly similar questions. The first one is what is commonly called an *open-ended question*, which means that in contrast to the second question, typically called a *yes-no question*, the first question places very little constraint upon the expected answer. There are hundreds of responses a client might make to "What brings you here?" There are probably only two responses a client would consider making to the second question, namely, "yes" or "no." There certainly is nothing intrinsically wrong with asking a yes-no question; it is the most efficient way to make a bit of specific information common to you and the client. However, yes-no questions do very little to move an interview forward. What usually happens is that the client will supply the requested information, pause and wait for the next question. Very shortly you are into a question-answer interaction that sounds more like an interrogation than a counseling interview.

It is the exclusive use of yes-no questions which needs to be avoided; but it should be remembered that yes-no questions do provide the most efficient means of determining whether something is or is not the case. A third type of question which combines the open-ended and yes-no questions is one in which the counselor provides several alternative answers among which the client chooses. This might be thought of as a *multiple-choice question*. It is not as constraining as the yes-no question, but it is less likely to move the interview forward than is an open-ended question. However, if you want to determine whether something is the case and to also rule out others ways of viewing it, then the multiple-choice question is very useful.

Examples of open-ended questions:

"Could you say more about that?"

"Is there an example or an incident that would illustrate the kind of thing you mean?"

"What does your husband think about it?"

"You've no doubt given this a lot of thought, what sorts of things have you come up with in trying to understand it?"

Examples of yes-no questions:

"Do you think Randy really misses his father?"

"Do you think Randy sees your mother as more in charge of the household than you are?"

"If you had enough money now, do you think you would start school right away?"

"Is it really more your mother's idea that you should have counseling than your own preference?"

Examples of multiple-choice questions:

"Do you see Randy as more confused by having both you and your mother in charge, or is it more that he is playing one of you against the other, or is it that he really isn't aware of the conflict between you and your mother and is just going along with whoever is in charge at the moment?"

"Do you see it more a matter of your wife treating you differently now, after the accident, or do you think you are acting differently now, or is it both?"

"Is it that since you moved here you've had trouble finding kids who are interested in being friends, or that making friends has always been a kind of hard thing to do, or more that since your family moved here you really haven't wanted to go through the hassle of making new friends 'cause your father may just be transferred again in another three years?"

"From where you stand does it look like your father wouldn't trust you now no matter what you did, or that if you went along with him and did the things he wants, then he'd respect you, or that time will probably take care of it and you just have to wait it out?"

### Misuses of Questions

Before we move on to the next communication technique, paraphrasing, we will briefly identify and discuss two of the most common misuses of questions, namely, random probing and coercive questioning. There are two reasons why counselors indulge in unplanned poking around in their clients' lives: (1) they do not know what else to do, and maybe something important will emerge, and (2) they have nose trouble, that is, they are unduly curious about and fascinated with the intimate details of other people's business. To avoid misusing questions for the first reason, you need to have some notion of how it will help you and your client to know some particular bit of information; any question ought to contribute to a mutual understanding of the client and to bring you closer to realizing the purposes for which you have agreed to meet together. If a counselor is misusing questions for the second reason, he probably would not recognize it because it casts doubt upon the quality of his motivation for becoming a counselor. Persons with intense needs to probe around in the intimate details of others' lives would be less harmful in a library full of cheap novels than in a counseling room.

In sharp contrast to random probing out of idle curiosity or ignorance, questions can be misused to coerce the client into viewing things as the counselor views them. Although the counselor may pose something as a question, the message is quite clear that the client had better agree. For instance, a counselor who has difficulty coping with strong negative feelings will often rush in with a "question" that denies or dilutes the strength of the client's feelings. "Don't you agree that most girls your age aren't very fond of their younger sisters?" or "Aren't there things *you* could do to make this school a nicer place?" or "Don't you think that God in His greater wisdom tests us *all* — actually for our own good?"

These two misuses of questions, random probing and coercive questioning, are more a result of insincerity and a lack of authenticity within the counselor than merely a lack of skill in asking questions. If you are sincere in your interactions with a client, if you are actively and planfully trying to understand

and accept your client, and if you are skillful in asking open-ended, as well as yes-no and multiple-choice questions, then you can be very certain that you will not misuse the questions you ask of a client.

### Paraphrasing

Restating with other words what the client has said is a device primarily used to move the interview forward. In general, paraphrasing has the effect of saying, "I'm with you; I understand; please go on." It is important that a paraphrase capture both the facts and the feelings contained in the client's statements. It is not enough merely to echo or parrot back what the client has said. For example, a sullen junior high boy plunks himself down in your office and says "Mr. Steele said I was supposed to report to you." You might paraphrase his statement with "The reason you're here isn't exactly 'cause you're dying to see me today." He would be more likely to volunteer the information concerning Mr. Steele's directive to report to the counselor's office, because your paraphrase captures the hostility and resentment which he appears to be feeling. If you merely said, "Mr. Steele sent you here and you don't want to be here," he is more likely to say, "Yah," and think to himself, "That's right, stupid, you figured it out."

Paraphrasing is used in all kinds of circumstances, not just to capture and reflect the client's hostility. However, it is usually directed toward identifying and disclosing the feelings which accompany an event or experience which the client is relating. For that reason, it is helpful to practice using metaphors and analogies to capture a client's meaning because figures of speech usually communicate feelings more poignantly than do simple descriptive statements. For instance, a high school senior has begun discussing how difficult it is to decide whether to remain with his father and graduate with his class or to accompany his mother to a city across the state to which she is moving while the divorce is in progress. His girlfriend and the basketball coach want him to stay, but he feels considerable responsibility to provide support and assistance to his mother, who is very confused and anxious about the whole situation. His father is encouraging him to stay if he wants to, but is not trying to force the issue because he knows that the woman he will probably marry does not like his son very well. The counselor might say, "It's like having a heavy rope around your legs and arms — pulling in four different directions — getting tighter and tighter as time goes on"; or, "It's like hearing about six telephones ringing all at once and you're somehow supposed to answer all of them and take care of what everybody wants and needs." Either of these paraphrases will communicate to the young man that you understand his feelings, that you are with him, and he should continue. If, however, the counselor said, "You feel pulled in several directions by your mother, father, girlfriend, and coach," he would probably acknowledge that, indeed, that was true, but wonder if the counselor really understands how he feels. He would probably continue but the paraphrase would have accomplished very little toward disclosing his feelings, other than to label them. Needless to say, even a paraphrase that understates feelings but is accurate, is better than a paraphrase which is inaccurate. For instance, the counselor might have said, "Everybody is so interested in your business, if they'd just leave you alone to work it out, things would be a lot better." That may be something the client thinks and feels, but it is definitely not the predominant feeling he was expressing; it is not a matter of being hassled by everyone's meddlesomeness, but rather being ripped apart by everyone's conflicting demands that he is feeling.

Now it is impossible to always utter the perfect paraphrase, no matter how skillful you are with analogies and metaphors. Fortunately, it is not necessary to achieve such perfection, because even if a paraphrase misses the mark and stops the flow of the interview, you and the client can make whatever effort is necessary to clarify the part you missed or distorted and then move on. In this way, paraphrasing is a process of making common, as well as moving toward. Within limits, it is better to risk giving an inaccurate paraphrase and stopping for further clarification than to sit there with an all-knowing look, nodding your head as if you understand, just so the client will move on. To accomplish both processes, making common and moving toward, it is most helpful if a paraphrase is cast in terms of a metaphor or analogy which is very familiar to the client. For instance, in the example of the senior high school student, pulling ropes and ringing phones are familiar images. However, if the counselor had chosen an analogy which was outside the experience of the young man, then it would not matter how emotion-laden it was, he could not identify with it as truly as capturing his feelings. "It's like a politician trying to please taxpayers, welfare recipients, lobbyists, and state officials about the budget"; or, "You are a little sailboat being blown about by shifting winds" are two examples of paraphrases which probably would not increase the common ground between the counselor and the senior high student.

Your best bet for developing skill with paraphrasing is to practice making brief statements, using familiar images, which capture strong feelings. One of the exercises in the next section is designed to provide such practice.

### Describing Behaviors and Feelings

A sizeable percentage of verbal communication in counseling involves the counselor listening to clients describe their own and others' behaviors and feelings. Clients usually do not make clear distinctions between overt behaviors, which anyone who was paying attention could observe, and feelings, which must be inferred from what a person says and does. It is up to the counselor to know the difference between a description of feelings, to which only the person who is experiencing them has direct access, and descriptions of behaviors to which any attentive observer has access. It is also up to the counselor to know which kind of description the client is providing. For example, an employment counselor might be told "So when he told me there'd be a two-week lay-off, I let him know I was pretty mad about it." This is primarily a feeling description ("I let him know . . ."). The employment counselor does not actually know if his client frowned and stomped off, cussed out the supervisor on the spot, calmly said he thought the lay-off was unfair, or just what behaviors were involved in "letting him know."

Listening for or requesting a description of behaviors and feelings is primarily for the purpose of making common the client's experience. The important thing to recognize is that if you are going to communicate fully with a client, you will need to share both the behaviors and the feelings which comprise a particular episode and that it is up to you to see that both kinds of descriptions are provided. For example, suppose you are the resident counselor for a dormitory of two hundred freshmen women and one of the women has come to you to discuss moving to another unit. Her reason for requesting a transfer is that she would like to live on a floor where at least one other Negro woman lives. She then recounts the many and repeated questions which have been directed to her during the term. "Can I feel your hair?" "Is it hard to comb a natural?" "Does your family eat soul food?" "What do you think of the Black Panthers?" "Do you want to go to Africa?" "Have you studied Afro-American history?" "Does your mother run your home?" As you listen to her describe the behaviors of the girls on her floor, you can make inferences about the way she probably feels, being a private Black-studies project for her dorm mates. However, only she can give you an accurate description of her feelings. She may feel very angry about being expected to spend time educating everyone and allaying their guilt feelings about Black people. She may feel quite inadequate being set up as an authority and expert on all issues concerning Afro-Americans. She may feel lonely and alienated because of being related to always in terms of her uniqueness and differentness as a Black woman. She may feel a combination of these things and many others. In order to communicate with her, you will have to share the feelings she has experienced as well as share the behaviors which produced them.

In addition to skill in listening for behavior and feeling descriptions, a counselor needs to be able to provide both types of descriptions. Generally speaking, when a counselor is giving a behavior or feeling description about himself, it is for the purpose of making common or sharing something. When the counselor is giving a behavior or feeling description about someone else, it is for the purpose of moving toward a goal. For example, suppose you are a junior high school counselor and you have just received a call from the school nurse asking that you come down to her office to talk with a ninth grade boy who has just been informed that both his parents have been killed in an auto accident. He is to wait at school until his grandparents arrive from a town about two hours' drive south. When you enter the nurse's office you see him sitting on the edge of a cot staring out the chicken wire reinforced window, tears streaming down his face, but no sounds. Nothing really makes sense at a time like this, except to acknowledge that nothing really makes sense. Probably the most helpful thing you can do is describe your own feelings, not in a way that demands he do something about them, but merely in an attempt to stand with him. You might sit down beside him and say in whatever way would be natural for you. "I'm really sorry, Mike . . . I feel helpless and awkward . . . like I should know what to say or do . . . but there isn't anything that's going to make it be right . . . all I can do is just sit here and be with you — knowing that that really doesn't help either . . . but caring about you means staying with you, even when there's nothing I can do." If the only way you could say something like this comes out as a subtle bid to be reassured that Mike really wants you to stay, then both of you would be better off if you said nothing. If you are confident that a person facing tragedy generally finds support in the presence of another human being who makes no demands, understands the despair and acknowledges that for now there is nothing to do but endure it, then you will probably be able to communicate by sharing your own feelings.

Tragedy is not the only circumstance in which a counselor describes his own behavior or feelings in order to make common his experience. However, it is a communication technique which should be used quite sparingly, since it takes the focus off the client. But there are times when describing your own behavior is a very efficient way to gain a better understanding of your client, as well as a way for your client to understand you better. For example, a campus pastor might hear a freshman girl refer to feeling guilty over thinking and talking about things which would horrify her parents. If he were counseling with her it could facilitate communication between them for him to describe his own behavior in this realm. He might say, "I think I understand what you mean because I sometimes experience something very similar. There are times when I find myself wondering if Christ ever slept with Mary Magdalene; after all, she *was* a prostitute before she met him and he was a very virile, attractive man and they were obviously very fond of one another. But then there is a tremendous rush of guilt and shame that envelops me . . . like how come I have to think about things like that . . . like I'm looking for some scandalous tidbit that will make me more comfortable or something . . . but then I think, why is that such a dirty, evil thought anyway . . . Is that the sort of thing you mean?"

The danger in a counselor describing his own behavior and feelings is obvious, but bears underlining. It is very easy to fall into a trap of shifting the focus off the client; counselors are usually highly verbal and introspective. It would probably be entertaining to both client and counselor to discuss the counselor's experience; it just does not happen to be why they are meeting together.

Finally, it is important for a counselor to be skillful in offering behavior and feeling descriptions of someone else; usually this is done in an effort to move toward a goal, more than to share something. For example, suppose you are an elementary school counselor who enjoys good working relationships with the teachers in a particular school. A relatively new teacher has asked you to observe his classroom and give him feedback on the way he relates to three youngsters who are performing considerably below grade level. After observing the class for an hour, you meet with him to discuss what you saw. If your feedback to the teacher is to help him plan how he might change, then it is important that you describe the behaviors you think are constructive and the behaviors you think he ought to modify. For instance, you might say, "I think your asking Freddie to hand out the booklets and check them in as others finished was a good way to help him feel like a useful and responsible member of the class. If those kinds of tasks could be assigned to the three underachieving students, it might help them feel more involved and invested in school." If you had said, "I think it would help if you made the three underachievers feel more involved in the class," and you had omitted the behavior description given as part of the original feedback message, you can see that the teacher would have much less information about how you observed him interacting with the three students.

Or, suppose you are a rehab counselor, working with a 48-year-old heavy equipment operator who has suffered a heart attack. Although he has recovered sufficiently to work an eight-hour day, his physician has instructed him not to return to operating heavy equipment. Because he knows a great deal about equipment and about road building and he describes himself as enjoying working closely with others (he is an officer in the local VFW chapter) you have suggested that he consider trying to locate an office job with the County Commissioners. This makes good sense to him and he agrees to make several appointments for interviews. However in your recent interactions you realize that even though he has recovered very well physically, he carries himself like a broken and feeble old man. Before he sets out on his job seeking interviews, it would probably be helpful if you would describe the behaviors he is emitting which make you feel that he is an unlikely employment prospect. Clearly, it would not be useful to ridicule, mimic, or scorn him for expressing in his body posture, gestures, and expressions what is probably a real change in the way he views himself. At the same time, he probably is not aware that he is communicating, nonverbally, that he is uncertain of his capacity to work anymore. It is not enough to toss off a few "Buck up, fella" platitudes about looking alive or putting his best foot forward. What is required is a careful description of his behavior and perhaps some role-play exchanges in which he could experience the difference between the image he is physically capable of projecting and the feeble figure you see projected.

Being able to give clear descriptions of behaviors and of feelings, of both yourself and others, can be a valuable resource for a client who is trying to understand and change some aspect of himself.

## Perception Checking

In the last two examples of an elementary school counselor and a rehab counselor offering behavior descriptions, it may be that if other counselors were observing the teacher and the cardiac client their perceptions would have been quite different. Although, it is not highly likely that counselors, or people in general, will have different perceptions of the *overt* behaviors they have observed. For instance, probably most counselors would agree on a behavior description of a teacher paying relatively little attention to three particular students, and they would agree on a behavior description of the shuffling, fumbling style of a rehab client. Nevertheless, there would be differences among different counselors observing the two situations. To identify, clarify, and perhaps resolve the differences in the way two or more people perceive a situation, they can do what is called "perception checking." Whenever you ask another person to listen to you describe your perceptions of a person or situation and to share his perceptions of the same person or situation, so that you can both see how well your separate sets of perceptions match one another, you are asking to check your perceptions.

Perception checking is used in counseling primarily to make common or to gain consensual validation for your observations. Without going into a lengthy discussion of the subjective nature of all human perception and without slipping into a solipsistic cul-de-sac, we can agree that our perceptions of what another person is doing and feeling are often highly subjective. That is, our perceptions, especially of another person's feelings, are affected by our own biases and emotions, the immediate situation, as well as our personal history with that other person. We can, however, reduce the discrepancies between our perceptions and someone else's perceptions, including the person's own perceptions of himself, by describing our perceptions and checking that description against the other's description.

For example, suppose you are a junior high school counselor and have been asked by a seventh grade physical education teacher to attend her conference with the irate parents of a girl who became somewhat upset during a discussion of sexual reproduction in health class. The parents look somewhat disapprovingly at you when you are introduced as the school counselor whose job it is to deal with a problem like this. The mother immediately declares that her daughter did not *have* a problem until they began talking about "personal intimate topics" that belong in the home. You respond with a paraphrase, for example, "Things were just fine with your daughter 'til the school began taking over what is rightfully a parent's responsibility." She goes on to express her belief that the breakdown of morals and all the loose living that goes on in the world is because sex is such a common topic and the schools are largely responsible for it. The father adds a comment to the effect that you can't expect kids not to get in trouble when the whole thing is discussed so freely and treated so lightly. He then says, "We believe sex is a sacred thing that is between a man and his wife . . . of course Sally would be upset, hearing all about it for the first time as if it was just some physical thing." At this point you decide you need to check your perceptions and so you say, "I need to see if I'm understanding you completely . . . it's not that you think Sally or someone her age ought to be kept ignorant of how babies are conceived and born, but rather that sex and reproduction are such important, personal, and sacred experiences, that they should be dealt with very carefully, so that the proper values are taught along with the facts . . . is that what . . . am I following you?" They nod "yes" and you go on to say, "The feeling I'm getting is that it's pretty difficult to see how in a health class you could talk about sex with the care you feel must be given to it and that in a sense the school has sort of taken advantage of your trust or tried to put one over on you . . . does that come anywhere near fitting with how you see it?" Until you and the parents and the teacher share a clear perception of how the parents see the situation and how they feel about it, there is no point in raising the question, "What shall we do about Sally and the whole situation now?" It would be particularly useless to try to educate the parents about the philosophy and purpose of sex education until they are ready to ask the question, "Why does the school want to teach these things anyway?" They are not likely to ask that question honestly, with a desire to hear the answer, unless you spend a sufficient amount of time and energy understanding their perceptions and letting them know you truly understand how they feel. In a situation as explosive as this one is, careful perception checking is an important technique for communicating. The following brief examples illustrate other ways perception checking can be used.

> "I saw you looking very expectantly, Judy, when you came into the room and I thought you were surprised and hurt when no one said anything. When you pulled out a book and started reading, I perceived you to be really angry and thought you'd probably decided to ignore everyone, if that's how they were going to treat you . . ."

> "It seems that you feel uncomfortable talking about this with me — like how do you know you can really trust me — at the same time that you feel you really need to talk with someone if you're going to get it sorted out — so it's yes, you want to, and no, you don't at the same time."

The major difference between a perception check and a paraphrase is that the perception check goes beyond what the person has said or implied and thus is a matter of inference on your part. In the last example, you may have accurately perceived the conflicted feelings ("Yes, I want to talk, and no, I don't want to talk"), but it may not be a matter of trust. The person may be worried about being late to another appointment or he may need to go to the bathroom; there are any number of reasons why he may feel conflicted, other than distrust of you. An efficient way to determine (1) whether he feels conflict, and (2) what it is related to is to check your perceptions with him. Care must be exercised on your part to be willing to let go of an unshared perception, at least for the time being, and try to understand how the client's perceptions are different. Perception checking should not lead to efforts to convince the client that you are right and he should see things as you do.

### Verbatim Playback

Restating what the client has previously said, using his exact words and intonation, is called a "verbatim playback" and is primarily used to move the interview forward. It is not uncommon for a client to lose track of what he or she was relating to you. Sometimes such "forgetting" can be attributed to anxiety over the topic or the counseling situation itself, but it often results from the sheer complexity of the counseling interaction. When a client begins to tell you about any aspect of his experience whether it relates to Work, Relationships, or his Aloneness, there are dozens of details and sidelights he will either include or omit, depending upon his conversational style and the cues he receives from you. Whether a client loses track of what he started to say because he got on a side issue suggested by the original topic or perhaps because you stopped to ask for clarification and to check your perception, it is important that you are able to assist him get back on track. One of the best ways to accomplish this is to quote exactly what he was saying just before he got off track. Usually, a verbatim playback of what he said will take him back to that point immediately and get him started again.

> For example, you have been listening to a seventeen-year-old girl who has recently had to assume major responsibilities for the care of her nine-year-old twin brothers because their mother is slowly recovering from abdominal surgery. Nicki came in to talk with you about the junior college she has been planning to attend in a year. With the situation changed at home, Nicki wants to know about loans and scholarships which might be available. In the process of your getting a clearer picture of what financial assistance she might expect from her family, Nicki begins telling you about how her grandfather left a little money for her and her older brother, but that somehow it is no longer available. This leads into a discussion of the relationships between Nicki's grandfather, father, and brother, and particularly how much more concerned Nicki's father is about her brother's education than he is about hers. You decide that it is important for you to understand this part of Nicki's situation and thus you spend some time paraphrasing and describing how you think she feels about the missing money. When it is clear to both of you, that you understand how hurt and rejected, but undaunted, she feels about there being no money for her education, the conversation stops. Then Nicki says, "I'm not sure

what you asked me," to which you reply, "I asked you about financial help from family and you said 'I'm not counting on *anybody* for money anymore,' and then we began talking about your grandfather and the money." "Oh, yah," replies Nicki, "well, my family isn't going to help and I wouldn't take it if they tried now — that's why I came to see you about loans and stuff."

In this case, your verbatim playback says to Nicki that you are listening very carefully, that what she says and even how she says it has some impact on you, and it is worth remembering. As is clear from the example, the verbatim playback facilitates refocusing on the main purpose Nicki had in coming to see you, namely, to find out about financial aids.

Sometimes a verbatim playback can be used to refer to a statement the client made during a previous interview. This is a good way to direct the client's attention to some earlier thoughts and feelings without your offering a lengthy interpretation of them.

For example, you are a junior high school counselor and in consultation with his family, his neurologist and the boy himself, who has begun having epileptic seizures, you agree to meet with the boy twice a week for about twenty minutes. The purpose of your meeting with him is to establish a place and a person he can count on to be available, simply to talk about whatever is on his mind, particularly while the neurologist works to get his epileptic condition controlled with medication. Earlier in the week, he was quite agitated and upset when he came in; there had been a misunderstanding between him and his mother about whether it was all right for him to shoot some baskets after school. They had had a big argument at breakfast about coming straight home from school that night. When he talked with you in the afternoon, he was still angry about his mother's overprotectiveness.

Three days later when you meet with him again, you decide it would be helpful to know if there is still a great deal of friction between the boy and his mother, whether your discussion of it gave him an opportunity to calm down, and whether he has followed through on your suggestion that he discuss it with his physician, since he was scheduled to see him the next day. There are several equally effective ways to ask about the situation, such as, "How did the deal about shooting baskets work out?" or, "Did you and your mom get settled on the basketball thing?" or, "Did you have an opportunity to talk to your doctor about shooting baskets?" etc. Even if you find out that the situation is now resolved, you may want to give him an opportunity to talk about how terribly frustrated and angry he felt. Rather than say, "You were pretty mad, weren't you?" you are more likely to reawaken to his feelings with a verbatim playback, for instance, "I remember your saying, 'I'd rather just be *dead* if I can't ever do anything anymore' — could we talk about that some more?"

Care must be exercised to avoid any hint of mimicry or of mocking the client when you use a verbatim playback to direct his attention or remind him of something. The purpose of this communication technique is to direct the interview to particular thoughts and feelings the client has previously expressed. The verbatim playback is not used to question or challenge or make light of those thoughts and feelings; it is merely a way to recapture a previous point.

The final example of using a verbatim playback to direct or refocus the interview illustrates its effectiveness when you are interacting with more than one person.

For example, suppose you are a vocational counselor in a community college and the parents of a young man who recently graduated from a small high school in a nearby town have accompanied him to your office to discuss various training programs. In response to your question about what sorts of jobs he has thought about as possibilities, he named police detective, mechanic, and forest ranger. He goes on by saying, "I don't know about mechanic though 'cause I'd like to be outside more or move around or something." At this point his mother begins telling about an uncle who is a policeman and who the young man admires greatly. The uncle was recently wounded while assisting with a riot and she expresses concern about the dangers of police work. The mother and son then begin debating whether police work is any more dangerous than auto mechanics.

It is a fairly delicate maneuver to refocus the discussion on the young man's vocational interests and aspirations without telling the mother to "shut up and let the kid talk." Even a statement such as, "Shall we get back to the reasons why Harold has selected the jobs he mentioned?" has a rather condescending ring to it. Your best bet for redirecting the interview, without making the mother feel defensive, is to use a verbatim playback. For instance, "Harold, I was particularly interested in what you meant by, 'I'd like to be outside more or move around or something.' "

There is little to be gained in confronting Harold's mother directly or in subtly letting her know you do not want her to talk. If your purpose in meeting with the family were to work on relationships among them, then you might well confront her. However, you can simply and directly focus the interview on Harold by returning to something he said earlier via a verbatim playback.

The ultimate in verbatim playback would be hearing a tape recording of what had been said; however, the awkwardness, inconvenience, and mechanical nature of using a tape recorder for this purpose overshadows its usefulness in keeping an interview on track. It is a relatively simple matter for you to perform this function yourself; it is a skill which you can practice and improve upon.

*Summarizing*

Another communication technique which is used primarily to move an interview forward is the brief summary. Generally speaking, a summary should identify the main points which have been discussed so the client can review with you and confirm or correct the overall picture you are getting. By gathering the separate strands of dialogue and weaving them together, you and the client can more easily see a pattern emerging. Summarizing can be used at the end of an interview to draw things to a close. However, summarizing is most valuable when it is used throughout the interview for purposes of integrating what has been communicated thus far so the interview can move forward more smoothly and in the direction you both want to go.

Here are three examples of a counselor summarizing:

"So far the picture I'm getting is that you are struggling to be mother and father to Randy and you have some real concerns about his feelings about his Dad moving out . . . and there are also problems with your mother letting him do things while you're at work that you've said he can't do 'til he finishes his homework . . . plus the frustration and confusion you feel about trying to go back to school and work part-time, or wait until you've saved enough to go full-time . . . were there other things I missed?"

"Let me sort of review what we've looked at thus far to be sure I'm getting a clear picture of how you see things. Before the accident you were regarded as a good worker and easy to get along with, but since you've been in the chair, the company has moved you to a different section twice because of personal conflicts between you and your supervisors. . . . At home the medical expenses and time-off have made things rough financially, but your wife says you've really changed besides, and then there is the concern you have about your daughter living with this guy, Shorty. Are there other things that figure in?"

"If I can summarize what we've covered so far, you feel your parents really don't believe you can manage your own life and they want you to live in a dorm. . . . You can see that they just are up-tight about things and want the best for you, but there's no way to get through to them that you're not a kid anymore and you think it's pretty important that you begin to break away from their control before you get much older. Then there are the problems with how involved sexually you want to be with Al before you are engaged or married and when or if you want to get married before you graduate. . . . And you mentioned some concern about whether getting a degree in political science is what you really want or whether you should get a teaching certificate — does that pretty much capture the major clusters of concerns you face now?"

You can see that summarizing also supports the process of making common, because it provides an opportunity for both the client and counselor to organize and arrange the material with which they are dealing in a similar manner. Summarizing facilitates your moving forward together.

### Formulating a Choice-Point

Oftentimes a summary in which several clusters of concerns have been identified will result in the client's turning attention to one of these clusters or themes and proceeding from there. However, it is sometimes helpful to actually formulate a choice-point for the client so that he consciously selects what he wants to focus upon. He may select the topic or theme that is the most pressing and troubling or he may select the area that is easiest to talk about and with which he feels safest. The choice he makes may not be the one you would make, if you were in his shoes. The area he chooses may not be the one which you feel needs to be dealt with first in order to make the changes or choices he desires. However, it is important for you to know where your client thinks attention should be directed. Unless you are prepared to tell the client that he is either avoiding dealing with what obviously must be dealt with or that he has misjudged what is the most important topic to discuss and your judgment is superior, then you had better follow the direction the client indicates. There will probably be occasions when you will need to disagree with a client and suggest that something other than what he wishes to discuss ought to be discussed first. But most of the time when you formulate a choice-point in the interview, you will be able to pursue the choice your client makes.

The following three examples of formulating a choice-point are related to the three summary statements given above.

"So there are like three clusters of concerns: Randy and his feelings about your ex-husband, your mother's role in raising Randy, and your decisions about work and school; which of these seems most important for us to look at first (they are so interwoven that they're probably hard to separate) . . . but which do you think we should consider first?"

"It seems as if there are two major themes: the ways you have changed — at work and at home — since the accident, and the problems with your daughter. Does one seem more the place for us to direct our attention than the other, or is one more pressing than the other; how do you want us to proceed?"

"There seem to be several questions: one has to do with greater independence from your parents — to live in the dorm being one example of that; another has to do with your relationship with Al; and then the questions about your major and the kind of career you want. These are all interrelated, of course, but does one stand out as more important than the other two as the place we ought to focus? . . . your parents, Al, or your major?"

In addition to the obvious effect of moving the interview in a particular direction, according to the client's choice, formulating a choice-point also gives the client another way to share with you what he regards as most important. You may have to ask the additional question of whether the selected topic was the most pressing concern or the easiest subject to talk about; but in either case you will have a rough idea of how things are rank-ordered in importance for your client. Formulating a choice-point might be thought of as a technique for achieving "client-centered directedness."

### *Facilitating Transitions in the Counseling Session*

Thus far we have been discussing communication techniques which can be used throughout an interview to receive and send accurate and reliable verbal messages. In short, they are ways of making your experience common and moving forward together. Although the process of understanding what the client means is a very complicated, demanding and necessary task, it alone is not sufficient. In order to fulfill the purposes of counseling, you must be able to address the task of doing something about what you now thoroughly understand. The remaining communication techniques are designed to facilitate the transition from How can we understand this? to What can we do about it?

From the moment you first begin interacting with a client, the question of what it is that the person would like to have happen as a result of your interactions should be kept in mind. We have discussed three types of contracts which specify what ought to happen as a result of counseling, *i.e.,* Choice, Change, and Confusion Reduction. You have also been warned repeatedly about the dangers of becoming prematurely preoccupied with solving a client's "problem." Therefore, to say that the question of what should happen as a result of your meeting together ought to be kept in mind is not to say that you ought to be thinking, "Well, what am I supposed to do about *that*?" each time the client makes a statement. There is a subtle but significant difference between having your thinking guided by: "How can I get a handle on what he is saying, so we can figure out what to do?" and thinking: "So I wonder what I'm supposed to do with that?" With the first line of thought you are most likely to communicate, verbally and nonverbally, to your client: "You and I need to understand this as well as we possibly can, so we can decide what we can do about it." The second line of thought is more likely to result in your communicating: "You tell me what's wrong and I'll figure out what you should do about it."

In the initial stages of the first interview, questions about what type of contract you and the client will negotiate are very much in the background; your task at that time is to understand thoroughly and accurately what he is saying and to sincerely communicate your understanding and acceptance of him. As the

254

THE PROCESS OF COUNSELING

interview moves forward and you and the client have begun to hold in common a picture of the client himself, his situation, and why he is talking with you, you will begin moving toward a contract that describes your reasons for continuing to talk. As we have noted before, this transition from understanding a client to negotiating a contract and even fulfilling the contract may be accomplished in less than an hour.

For example, a teacher may want to discuss a parent conference she has scheduled that afternoon. In less than an hour's interview with the teacher you may go from an initial phase of understanding the situation as she sees it, including her feelings about the whole thing, to a middle phase of establishing that she would like you to help her sort out the different ways to approach the parents and indicate what you think would be the most productive approach, to a final phase of actually clarifying alternative approaches and offering your opinion. Your opinion may be that it is better for you not to say what you would do if you were in her position, because it is best if she decides what would be the most natural and comforable approach for her. Or your opinion may be that it would be helpful for her to hear how you would approach the conference, if you were in her position. We are not interested, at this time, in what kind of opinion you offer, but rather we are concerned about your moving from the initial stage of understanding to the middle stage of negotiating a contract. Whether you have ten minutes or ten sessions to move from understanding to negotiating a contract, you need some specific communication skills to do it. The following three techniques can be used to bring about the transition from initial understanding to negotiating a counseling contract. In the example just presented, it is unlikely that you would use all three techniques, in large part because you have very little time to accomplish your purposes; however, each technique will be illustrated using the teacher, as well as other clients as examples.

*Gaining a Figure-Ground Perspective*   If you think about the hidden figure puzzles that often appear in the comics section of a newspaper's Sunday supplement, you may achieve a general feeling for this particular communication technique. You have probably struggled, at one time or another, to get an embedded figure to "stand out" from the rest of the drawing. Clients often present a somewhat muddled picture in which nothing stands out as the major focal point and yet they feel that there are problems or decisions embedded in the picture somewhere. When you assist a client place a choice to be made or a problem to be solved within a context and separate the figure (central set of concerns) from the ground (content surrounding the concerns) you are assisting the client gain a figure-ground perspective. By bringing the figure into focus against a background of the relevant situational factors, you are then in a position to shift from understanding the figure to raising the question of what shall we do about it? In other words, gaining a figure-ground perspective facilitates the transition from initial understanding to negotiating a contract.

Assume you are an elementary school counselor talking with a teacher.

"Ruth, if I understand the situation, there are several parties to be considered: there's the little girl's parents who are very angry and upset, but generally cooperative; there's the bus driver who seems to be in the best position to know what really happened; there's the boy's mother, who claims he has never lied to her and she knows he didn't do it; and then our beloved superintendent with his attitudes towards this kind of thing getting in the newspapers, and so on . . . but what you'd like us to do right now is find a way to sort it out so you're in shape to meet with the girl's parents this afternoon?"

Ruth confirms that your perceptions are accurate; her central concern is talking over the situation with you so she is better prepared to meet the parents. (Thus far assisting Ruth gain a figure-ground perspective is not greatly different from a perception check, with the exception that you are not checking your inferences about the way Ruth is feeling, which is generally a major reason for using a perception check.)

"Okay, well, let's try to identify what is at the heart of this rather complex matter. From listening to your description, what seems to stand out for me is that Mary's parents are most concerned about whether their daughter and other little white girls are going to be safe riding integrated buses and whether the school is going to guarantee their safety. As I get it, little Mary is not seriously injured, nor is she very upset about the broken arm, so her health is not an immediate problem. The insurance forms have been filed and the bus driver seems to think it was more mischievous teasing that got out of hand, than a malicious attack on Mary. So, again, it's a matter of reassuring the parents that we are *very* concerned about safety in general and racial incidents in particular on the buses or in any other part of the school. But it sounds like the relationship between school officials and Mary's parents is more central than the relationship between Mary and the Negro boy who pushed her. Does that make sense to you?"

If in fact Ruth has the same figure-ground perspective as you do and she agrees that the relationship between Mary's parents and the school is the focal point, then you are in a position to begin discussing the most effective ways to reassure Mary's parents that the school is greatly and genuinely concerned about the welfare of the children, especially in the painfully sensitive area of interracial relations. In this example, having gained a common figure-ground perspective, you and Ruth have also established a common goal, that is, you have formulated a contract, which you can now set to work fulfilling. How you fulfill the contract, that is, whether you use role-playing, discuss ways of making the parents less defensive, offer to join the conference, suggest that the principal join the conference, gather all the affected persons together for a conference, etc., depends upon the particularities of the situation. However, reaching a point in your interaction with Ruth where these possibilities can be discussed, depends upon your skill in getting the central issue well in focus. Thinking of this transition as gaining a figure-ground perspective will probably be useful to both of you.

Two other more brief examples of a counselor's assisting a client gain a figure-ground perspective follow.

"Although this whole situation is very complicated and it is hard to get a handle on it, what is beginning to stand out to me, as your primary concern, is your daughter's unwillingness to assume responsibility for what would typically be expected of a twelve-year-old. The way in which she keeps her room, coming home late from school, not helping her sister with the dishes, the sudden onset of baby-talk, her fear of her step-father, these kinds of things seem to be at the center. The problems with child support from your former husband, your son's long hair, your frustration with trying to lose weight, your recent conversion to Catholicism seem to be important aspects of your life space in which the difficulty with your daughter is happening. But the picture I'm getting has your twelve-year-old in the center and these other things as part of the background. Is that the way it looks to you or is there a more helpful way to sort it out?"

"One of the ways that we could try to understand what is going on and get a clearer picture of the decisions you face, is to try pulling out what seems to be the most central issue and what things seem to be more in the background. For instance, you mentioned that deciding to study for the ministry would mean that you would go to your church's college, rather than to State; we talked about your father's expectation that you would go into business with him after college and the fact that your folks fight a lot about religion . . . that your mother doesn't like Kathy, 'cause she thinks she's trying to trap you into marrying her . . . about your flunking the driving exam twice . . . and about how the happiest time of your life was counseling at the church camp last summer. It sounds as if the central question running through this is how you should make decisions — who should be considered, how much you should try to please others versus how much you should decide things for yourself. Does that seem to fit, or does something else seem to be the central question?"

In both of these examples you can see the movement from initial understanding of the client and his or her situation to identifying a central issue concerning Changes the client desires, Choices the client faces or Confusion the client wants to reduce. With this central issue in focus, that is, in perspective, you and the client are able to move on toward formulating a contract which will describe what you intend to do about the central issue. It should be added that often clients have more than one major concern they would like to deal with in counseling; there are often several figures which stand out from the background.

Gaining a figure-ground perspective is not used to force the client to arbitrarily choose one among several things which may have motivated him to seek counseling. The utility of this communication technique is in bringing each concern into sharper focus and separating it from the context in which it is presently embedded.

*Requesting a Contrast*   A second communication technique, which is particularly useful in moving from an initial understanding of the client's purposes in seeking counseling to a level of understanding that makes it possible to plan a way you can assist him with Choices, Changes or Confusion Reduction, is requesting a contrast. By suggesting that your client compare whatever you are attempting to understand with something which is significantly different or opposite, you can bring a developing picture into sharper focus.

Again, assume you are an elementary school counselor talking with a teacher.

> "Ruth, you said that Mary's parents have been cooperative in the past . . . that is, in contrast to the hostility you feel from them now, you have enjoyed a pleasant relationship in the past. Could you describe what you think the major difference is?" Ruth may simply say, "Well, they're mad now . . . that's what's different." You may need to clarify further that you are asking about the difference between the way they have felt towards her, the principal, the school, etc., compared to how she thinks they feel now. With this clarification Ruth goes on to say, "Well, I think they have had confidence in me, as a teacher, and as a person . . . they have supported the school and me . . . they have not been overly critical. They are probably frightened and distrustful now . . . that's probably the main difference."

Requesting a contrast between the way Mary's parents felt before the school bus incident and the way they probably feel now has brought your interaction with Ruth to a point where you can begin discussing ways to reduce the parents' fears and restore their confidence in Ruth and the school. Requesting contrasts is similar to gaining a figure-ground perspective in that they both facilitate the formulation of a contract concerning how Ruth can interact most effectively with Mary's parents.

Three other, more brief examples of a counselor's requesting contrasts for purposes of formulating a contract are given below.

> "Could you describe a time when you felt like you really knew where you were headed and how you were going to get there, in contrast to the lostness and purposelessness that characterizes now?"
>
> "Are there some times now when you are able to concentrate and work up to a capacity the full day, in contrast to days when you just can't get with it . . . and what seems to be the difference?"

"If you imagine an ideal relationship with your daughter, how would it be different from the way things are now?"

"Some of the decisions that have to be made seem to depend upon what's *out there* (circumstances and other people) and some seem to depend on what you think and feel *inside,* can we separate things that way for a minute . . . into "inside" and "outside"?

In each of these examples you can see how the counselor is attempting to reach a level of understanding whereby he and the client can know exactly what it is that should be different at the end of counseling. It is reasonable to assume that in the first instance the client hopes to achieve a keener sense of direction. But is that something he has never known, something he has recently lost, or something he has depended upon others or his work to provide? Is it part of a never ending religious quest or did it hit him on the morning of his fortieth birthday? You cannot possibly think of all the factors that might be involved, but you can help the client identify some of the factors upon which a sense of direction depends by requesting a contrast. You might also ask him to think of a person he knows well who seems to have the sense of direction he lacks and then ask him to compare himself to that person.

In the third brief example, we can assume that the client is having difficulties making decisions and that he sought counseling to get some assistance in making up his mind. By requesting a contrast between factors inside the client vs. factors outside the client, the counselor is moving the interview toward determining whether or not the way the client makes decisions is one of the issues they ought to deal with first. For instance, the client may say, "Oh, I don't have any trouble knowing what I want compared to what they think, but I just don't know enough about the law and conscientious objector status to decide yet." Or the client might have said, "Gee, I'd never thought about how I was actually going to decide . . . I mean we've never disagreed on something so much before." As was true in the other examples, requesting contrasts enables the counselor and client to formulate the client's reasons for seeking counseling in such a manner that a specific contract can be negotiated. The contract in this last example may simply be to provide the client with reliable information about the laws governing conscientious objector status or it might be to provide him with reliable information and to examine the process he has used in the past to make decisions, as well as the process whereby he would like to make this one. Which of these two contracts you negotiate will depend in part upon the client's response to your having requested a contrast between factors inside and outside of him.

*Introducing Concrete Examples*    In general it is more efficient for a client to generate his own examples of what he means; this usually follows an open-ended question by the counselor, for instance, "Can you think of a time when you felt this way recently?" However, there are occasions when it is helpful for the counselor to introduce a concrete example. By describing a hypothetical situation and suggesting how you think the client might respond, you can determine whether or not you have a grasp of the troublesome behaviors or choices with which the client is struggling. As was true of gaining a figure-ground perspective and requesting contrasts, introducing a concrete example has the effect of moving you closer to formulating a contract. All three of these communication techniques also facilitate the process of making common, because they extend the depth of your understanding. But their primary value is found in their usefulness in facilitating the transition from initial understanding of the client to contract negotiation with the client. If you can generate a hypothetical example which illustrates the behavior or dilemma the client is concerned about, then you undoubtedly understand his concerns thoroughly enough to begin discussing what might be done about them.

Once again, assume you are an elementary school counselor talking with a teacher.

> "What I hear you expressing, Ruth, is a fear that somehow you're just going to really blow it with Mary's parents. From what you've said, I gather that people who are really hostile are extremely difficult for you to deal with . . . for example, if the Taylors were really abusive and raised their voices and swore and demanded that you do something immediately, you would probably burst into tears and say something like, "I'm just one person and I'm only trying to do my job and I can't be responsible for everything!"
>
> Ruth grins and nods and says, "Yes, well that's probably what I would do all right . . . so that's why I thought I'd better talk to you before they arrive."

By introducing a concrete example of what might happen between Ruth and Mary Taylor's parents, you have nailed down precisely what it is that Ruth wants assistance with. You can now formulate a contract with Ruth, namely, to help her find ways to reassure the Taylors and guard against becoming overwhelmed with their hostility, if it is obvious and intense. It is not imperative that your example be accurate in every detail. For instance you might have said:

> "Sounds like you're really worried that you might just botch it completely with the Taylors this afternoon. From what I have heard you express, Ruth, I gather that you don't have much confidence in your capacity to remain calm and unruffled, if somebody is really mad. For example, if the Taylors are really nasty and sarcastic and demand that you see that the boy gets suspended or something . . . you might agree to recommend he be suspended, just to get them to shut up and leave you alone."
>
> Ruth quickly says, "No, I wouldn't agree to do that . . . I'd get

rattled allright, but I'd probably just tell them their little Mary is no angel and she probably asked for it in the first place ... but see, that wouldn't do any good and I'd be sorry and embarrassed, so that's why I decided I'd better talk to somebody before I see them."

Even when a concrete example is not completely accurate, it allows the client to specify more clearly what it is that concerns him. This, in turn, allows both of you to begin thinking about what can be done about his concerns, that is, it facilitates the formulation of a counseling contract.

Three, more brief, examples of a counselor introducing a concrete example follow.

"Suppose the relief man were late and you were delayed in getting to the lunchroom. If, when you walked in, you couldn't see your buddy anywhere, rather than join some guys you didn't know, then you would probably just go outside, smoke a cigarette and not eat lunch. Would that be an example of the kind of frightened of people you mean?"

"Suppose you discovered that there was a flaw in the nightgown you'd just purchased. You would probably just keep it and figure it was your fault for not seeing the flaw when you were in the store, rather than try to return it. Is that the sort of not being very forceful or standing up for your rights you mean?"

"Let's make up and example of a way you would know you'd made the right choice ... If your husband said, 'Look, I know you feel guilty about sending Larry to the State Training School, but I think Doctor Stone and Reverend Blake are right; both you and he would be better off in the long run,' then you'd feel okay about deciding to do it."

In each of these examples, the counselor and client are beginning to think in terms which will lead to the question, "What can we do about this?" How can we reduce your fear of people, so that you would feel comfortable sitting down at a table of strangers in the lunchroom? How can we increase your self-assertiveness, so that you would feel comfortable returning a defective garment? How can we approach this decision so that you will feel certain you are making the best possible choice?

This book does not deal with treatment strategies for actually accomplishing specific goals, such as those just mentioned. In an introductory practicum, you will have accomplished a great deal if you can master the communication skills necessary for (1) quickly establishing a constructive, helping relationship, (2) understanding the client and his situation, (3) letting him know you accept and are sincerely concerned about him, and (4) moving your interaction toward the formulation of a contract that would describe what could be done in order to achieve his purposes for seeking counseling. However, in order to function as a competent professional counselor, you would need to know much more about the particular setting in which you are counseling, the particular population of clients you are serving and particular counseling tactics for achieving specific outcomes. The writer assumes that this is not the only practicum you will complete in your training and that more advanced work on counseling settings, clients, and procedures will be included in your preparation for professional counseling.

# Section Four

**DESIGN
FOR A
PRACTICUM**

# I  OVERVIEW OF THE PRACTICUM

Each of the eleven practicum sessions has been designed to take three hours with a 15-minute break about midway through the session. The group should be no larger than six group members, plus one leader or two co-leaders; there should be no fewer than four group members. The sessions should be held in a relatively small room containing movable chairs. Although a private home would be preferred to a large classroom with bolted down desks, the room should resemble a typical counseling interview room as much as possible. It is assumed that each member will have acquired his own book prior to Session 1 and will thus have completed the pre-Session 1 assignment.

More than a dozen groups of six students have completed these sessions. Although the sessions are highly structured, the practicum is reported again and again to be a free, deeply personal, intense, and fast-moving learning experience. It rests with the leader, particularly in the beginning, to maintain the forward movement of the sessions. He or she must avoid rigidly adhering to a stop-watch precise pace, but at the same time keep the group from wandering aimlessly about, or going off on a tangent, or becoming bogged down in minutia. The leader needs to have a clear picture of what is to be accomplished during the session and sufficient sensitivity to individuals' feelings which allow him to discern when it is appropriate to move on to the next task from when it is appropriate to stay with a task until conflicts or misunderstandings which may have arisen are resolved. The leader must be willing to deal with the immediate feelings generated by the group members' interactions, but he must be willing not to identify and discuss every nuance of group process he perceives. For example, it may be fairly obvious in the beginning that a group member is skeptical or resistant to accepting the leader as a leader. If a power struggle emerges which interferes with the progress of the group, then clearly that must be dealt with and resolved. But the leader should avoid pouncing on a fleeting cue as an excuse to confront someone about his hang-up with authority figures.

If the group leader accepts the stated purpose which the group will have read is intended for that session, and if he follows the procedures closely, discussing any proposed departures with the group before he attempts to modify the session, then the group members will very quickly begin sharing the responsibility for moving the session forward at a comfortable pace.

## II   OUTLINE OF THE CLASS SESSIONS

### Session

1   Brief interviews concerning Work, Relationship and Aloneness.
2   Brief interviews continued from Session 1.
3   Practice using a variety of communication techniques.
4   Brief interviews concerning experiences with new situations, new roles, and new media.
5   Practice in giving and receiving positive and negative feedback.
6   Brief interviews concerning new experiences continued from Session 4.
7   Role-playing an insincere counselor.
8   Brief interviews concerning feelings associated with one of Erikson's developmental stages.
9   Brief interviews concerning Erikson's stages continued from Session 8.
10  Practice in giving and receiving positive and negative feedback.
11  Terminating the practicum group; debriefing and personal plans for further training.

## III   SUMMARY OF THE ASSIGNMENTS

### To prepare
### for Session

1   Read Sections One and Three.
    Prepare three episodes from life task areas: Work, Relationship, and Aloneness.
2   Set up your feedback log, which is to begin after Session 2.
3   Plan an experience involving a new situation, a new role, or a new medium.
    Prepare a list of analogies, metaphors, and similes which describe you.
    Review communication techniques in Section Three and read Section Two.
4   Carry through on your plan for a new experience.
5   Complete the second set of entries in your feedback log.

6    Review *Acceptance* in Section Three.
7    Review *Sincerity* in Section Three.
     Prepare a brief role play of an insincere counselor.
8    Review Section One and *Understanding* in Section Three.
     Recall and describe 16 personal experiences illustrating Erikson's developmental stages.
     Select one of these experiences to be shared with the practicum group.
9    Design an assignment for yourself and complete it.
10   Complete final entries in your feedback log.
     Review the written feedback you received previously.
11   Summarize the positive and negative aspects of this practicum experience.
     Describe your personal plans for further training.

## IV   NOTES TO THE PRACTICUM LEADER AND GROUP MEMBERS

### Session 1.

*Purpose:*   A small group of individuals who share the common goal of improving their counseling skills begin learning to work together in a cooperative, constructive, and honest manner.
Each group member begins attending to his skill in sending and receiving messages about himself and others in order to increase his capacity to understand and accept himself and others.

*Procedures:*   Prior to the first practicum session and in preparation for it, you are asked to read Sections One and Three of this book. Next, recall three brief but important episodes in your life which you are willing to share with the other practicum members.
Section One discusses three life task areas according to which the content of counseling can be classified. As was noted there, every human being must come to grips with:
     Work — the expenditure of time and energy in purposive activity; Relationship — the inherent social nature of contemporary human life; and Aloneness — the inescapable separateness and uniqueness that characterizes each person's existence. By our very nature we are able to function best when we: (1) are actively involved in something we regard as important and meaningful, whether or not we are paid to do it; (2) have developed mutually satisfying relationships with other people and learned ways of initiating and sustaining

such relationships; and (3) can understand and accept and become responsible for ourselves as individuals — separate and different from all other individuals.

Any given episode in your life probably contains elements of all three life-task areas. For instance, taking this practicum has implications for your work, your relationships with others, and your relationship with yourself. Even though these three categories of human experience are inextricably bound together, it is possible to identify episodes that emphasize one of the categories more than the other two. The three brief episodes, one of which you are asked to be ready to share with your practicum group should illustrate something about you and your work, about you in relationship with other people, and about you and your own separateness and uniqueness.

## Notes on Episodes in the Three Life Task Areas:

*WORK:*

*RELATIONSHIP:*

*ALONENESS:*

During the first class session, the leader should assume responsibility for seeing that each person knows everyone's name. Name tags are somewhat artificial and it is probably better to spend a few minutes going around the circle with each person saying his own first name and then the first name of the person on his left and of the person on his right. Any procedure for learning one another's names is in order, as long as it is not very time consuming or confusing. People will get to know one another in greater depth as they engage in the exercises and assignments, therefore this initial exchange of names is not intended to produce intense encounters.

*Optional Procedure:* Some groups have found it useful to stop at this point and have each member jot down a sentence or two about every other member, which describes the first impressions individuals have of one another. These six first impression statements (one for each of the five other group members and the leader) are retained by the individual who wrote them, until the feedback session — Session 5. At that time the statements are exchanged; each person will receive six first impression statements. If the statements are to be genuine first impressions, they must be written at this point in Session 1. The only drawback is that it can set a rather cold, evaluative tone early in the group's experience together. If the group is uncomfortable with this procedure, it should not be imposed. The advantages of completing the first impression statements are twofold: (1) Each person receives feedback on how he initially affects others. The same theme, appearing in several statements, is fairly good evidence that most clients will form a similar first impression. (2) Each person can later review what he has written and identify the biases and/or stereotypes which shape his first impressions. For example, what characteristics do you choose to focus on; which are seen as negative and which positive characteristics?

After names have been exchanged and the first impressions written, if desired, then the leader will ask for a volunteer to tell about one of the episodes he or she prepared for this first session and a volunteer to act as facilitator. The two volunteers should arrange their chairs so that they can easily address one another and at the same time be somewhat removed from the rest of the circle. They should not sit with a large table between them and/or the other members in their immediate visual field.

The interchange (brief interview) between the person recounting his experience (the "client") and the facilitator should be expected to take from 10 to 15 minutes. It does not matter if the "client" says ahead of time whether his experience involves primarily Work, Relationship, or Aloneness. It *does* matter that the experience be an important one to him; that is, an experience about which he has some feelings. The facilitator's task is simply to understand and communicate to the "client" that he grasps the meaning of what the "client" is trying to convey. The other group members are to attend carefully to the interchange so they are able to: (1) summarize what has been communicated, (2) paraphrase any part of the interview, and (3) offer feedback to the facilitator, in particular, and to the "client" regarding the interview.

Following the interview, the leader will ask that each group member give feedback to the facilitator and the "client." The most helpful kind of feedback is a combination of behavior description and feeling description. For example, "When you leaned forward and smiled and said, 'Let me see if I'm really understanding you, Dan ... ,' I felt like, if I were Dan, I would really be convinced that you wanted to get what I was saying." Or, another example, "Although I felt in general that you understood the facts and the details Mary was giving you, because you sat there motionless and expressionless, I felt that either you didn't really understand how she felt, or else you were afraid to express what you were feeling, or you didn't really care. . . . I think if I were Mary, I'd have been uncomfortable." Or, "It seemed like you weren't content to just receive and understand what Loni was telling you; you wanted to turn it into a problem you could help solve or something, like when you said, 'Does that still bother you now, Loni?' and I wasn't sure you really understood it yet."

Very likely the leader will be the most skillful at giving feedback. For this reason, the leader should offer feedback last; not so the others can hear "the right answer," but because it can be somewhat discouraging to the group to hear an eloquent and complete description before they offer their own feedback. Giving feedback is not something that comes easily to most people, especially when some of their observations are critical or negative. It is too easy for group members to avoid committing themselves with, "I really don't have anything to add to that."

After the leader has given feedback, the "client" then gives his or her feedback to the facilitator. Prior to this, the "client" should neither confirm nor disconfirm nor respond to the others' feedback, as it is being given. Finally, the facilitator makes whatever comments he has and concludes with a summary of the feedback, both positive and negative, which he has received. It will soon become obvious how difficult it is for some people to receive and acknowledge positive feedback. We seem to have a tendency to ignore positive statements about ourselves and to remember only negative statements. It is important that the group encourages the facilitator to hear and remember all of the feedback, both positive and negative statements.

You will be about midway through the session at this point and should probably take a 15-minute break.

When the group reconvenes, two more volunteers arrange themselves so that they can engage in a brief interview. The procedure is the same as it was for the first interview; one member is the "client" and another acts as facilitator. After the feedback is given and the facilitator summarizes what he has heard, the two remaining people get set up for the final interview. The procedure for the third interview and feedback is, again, the same as for the first interview.

Each group member will have been in the role of either "client" or facilitator. Every group member will have given feedback at least twice. During Session 2, those persons who were "clients" in Session 1 will become facilitators and those persons who facilitated will become "clients." The pairs of people need not stay together; and, in fact, it is better if they do not.

After the facilitator has summarized his feedback, following the third interview, the leader should distribute mimeographed Feedback Forms to each group member. If the leader does not have the resources to prepare Feedback Forms, each group member should prepare his own, following the examples given at the end of this description of Session 1. These forms are not to be completed until after Session 2, but it is helpful for each person to get the group members' names and to set up his Feedback Log this week. For a group of six members and two leaders, it will take:

   8 Notes on Self Forms
12 Group Leader and Practicum Feedback Forms
42 Group Member Feedback Forms.

Finally, draw the group's attention to the sample Feedback Forms at the end of this description of Session 1.

*Special Instructions to the Leader:*     There is, of course, no way to anticipate all possible problems which might arise and to offer suggestions about how to deal with them. However, some general comments may be helpful.

1.  If a group is relatively unskilled in communication techniques and/or naive about monitoring group process, then they are likely to need more direction and encouragement about understanding the *affective* components of the "clients" messages. They will tend to focus on the factual, cognitive components of the interaction. They are also likely to be very reluctant to offer negative feedback, because they fear all negative statements are hurtful and destructive. The leader is an important role-model in both of these cases. It is more effective *to demonstrate* sensitivity to the feelings accompanying a "client's" story and *to demonstrate* how critical feedback can be given constructively, than to tell people they ought to do it that way.

2.  If a group is relatively sophisticated and experienced with communication techniques and monitoring group process, then they are likely to need more direction and encouragement to *take time* to get a complete picture of what the "client" is saying, instead of focusing on contentless, raw feelings. They are also more likely to gravitate toward hostile, negative feedback as somehow being more real or genuine than is positive feedback. Again, the leader is an important role-model of someone who takes time to really understand the central message, the context in which it is embedded as well as the feelings accompanying the message. Also the leader is as sincere and real when he is giving positive feedback as when he is giving negative feedback.

3.  Because each person is asked to relate an experience which is important to him and one about which he has strong personal feelings, it is not uncommon that the "client" may cry or be unable to continue talking for a few moments. If that happens, it should be treated sensitively, of course, but it need not be alarming. The interviews are not exercises in gut-spilling; but neither are they exercises in self-control. It is probably better if the leader does not intervene, but allows the facilitator to handle the situation. We ought to be able to assume that the leader, as well as everyone else in the room, is committed to sincerely understanding and accepting each person there. Whatever arises in the group can be handled by the group. It does not require years of formal training to offer support to someone who is experiencing intense feelings. Simply, quietly standing by until the person is ready to continue is all that is necessary in most cases. An experience of a group member sharing intense feelings usually has a very constructive effect on the whole group.

4    In contrast to the person who takes the practicum very seriously and
     invests a great deal of himself, sometimes a person may have difficulty
     entering the situation in good faith or he may be very threatened by
     having to share anything of importance. The leader's task is not to
     diagnose paranoia. However, if a member is treating the interview and
     feedback in a cavalier, superficial manner, then the leader and the
     group need to inform the member of the negative feelings which
     result from being toyed with. If the individual persists in his unwilling-
     ness to be open and honest, then the leader and the group must decide
     how much time they want to spend on the matter. A person who is
     committed to remaining uncommitted can occupy the group for weeks
     if they allow that to happen.

As a final word, there are several beautiful and exciting discoveries that
occur in most groups even in this first session. A group of people, who in many
situations will be total strangers, can come together and, simply by revealing a
small portion of the fabric of their separate existences, can begin to discern the
pattern and texture of one another's lives. By giving themselves time to truly
understand one another, they are often amazed at the resources within
themselves and others which allow them to reach across age, sex, ethnic, and
value differences and experience another's world with him. By monitoring their
own responses and giving feedback to one another, they are also able to practice
and develop more effective ways of communicating understanding, acceptance,
and sincerity within a very real, immediate, and personal situation.

## NOTE ON SELF

Date_____          Following Session_____

Your Name_____

UNDERSTANDING:

ACCEPTING:

SINCERE:

GENERAL COMMENTS:

## FEEDBACK FORM — GROUP MEMBERS

Date_____          Following Session _____

Group Member's Name _____

Your Name_____

UNDERSTANDING:

ACCEPTING:

SINCERE:

GENERAL COMMENTS:

## FEEDBACK FORM — GROUP LEADER AND PRACTICUM

Date_____     Following Session _____

Leader's Name_____

Your Name_____

UNDERSTANDING:

ACCEPTING:

SINCERE:

GENERAL COMMENTS:

COMMENTS ON THE PRACTICUM:

$$\boxed{\text{SAMPLE}}$$

## NOTE ON SELF

Date___10-17-72_____                    Following Session ___2_____

Your Name___Don Nagel_____

UNDERSTANDING:   I seem to be able to get what someone else is trying to communicate pretty fast — sometimes I get impatient then and want them to move on before they're ready. I haven't spent enough time getting the whole picture or the context in which something happened.

ACCEPTING:   Same old problem — have to be right or look good; makes people feel rejected — like I'm trying to prove them wrong. Need to find ways to disagree with someone without making them feel rejected. Felt good to finally listen to and accept some negative feedback without giving a rebuttal.

SINCERE:   Most of the time I'm pretty honest and I think others see me that way — but I have trouble owning up to how much I want them to respect me — keep wanting to say it doesn't matter what they think — but it really does.

GENERAL COMMENTS:   Know this isn't supposed to be a sensitivity group, but I feel more open to this group than I usually do.

$$\boxed{\text{SAMPLE}}$$

## FEEDBACK FORM — GROUP MEMBERS

Date   <u>10-17-72</u>            Following Session <u>  2  </u>

Group Member's Name   <u>Sharon Smith</u>

Your Name   <u>Don Nagel</u>

UNDERSTANDING:   I feel like you think you have everybody all figured out and you don't need to listen to them to understand. When you were facilitating for me it seemed like you would nod and smile no matter what I said or whether you really understood it. I found it fairly easy to talk, but I wasn't sure you were getting what I meant.

ACCEPTING:   I did not feel judged or evaluated, you seemed to really accept me and the others. Because you did not fire questions at me, I felt that you really wanted me to tell the episode in my own way. I wonder if you could accept how angry I get at times though, because you never expressed any negative feelings to anyone during the meetings.

SINCERE:   I feel like you are genuinely interested in other people — including me; but I think some of your sweety-sweetness is phoney — like you couldn't admit a bad feeling if you had one.

GENERAL COMMENTS:   You are very easy to talk with; I feel at ease most of the time — but I am unsure how I'd feel if I had a really ugly thing to discuss, because I think you would try to say it was really beautiful or something.

SAMPLE

FEEDBACK FORM — GROUP MEMBERS

Date   10-17-72                              Following Session   2

Group Member's Name   Don Nagel

Your Name   Frank Patito

UNDERSTANDING:   When you were the facilitator and when you were giving feedback, you seemed to really understand how the other person felt; you seem very perceptive. Sometimes you jumped to conclusions too fast though, and then I felt as if you were arguing with the person you were trying to understand — almost like you were going to explain to her how she really felt.

ACCEPTING:   I don't know — I think you really like people, but it seems like you have to be right all the time or have the right answer — I feel like most of the time you probably are right, but if I didn't agree sometime, you would be impatient or irritated or want to argue.

SINCERE:   I felt you were really interested in me and the others and genuinely wanted to get to know us better — but you seem very closed to any suggestions on other ways to do things — because you try to argue with the other guy who's making the suggestion.

GENERAL COMMENTS:   As long as I was able to stand firm and not be overpowered, I think your ideas and perceptions were very helpful and accurate.

$\boxed{\text{SAMPLE}}$

### FEEDBACK FORM — GROUP LEADER AND PRACTICUM

Date    <u>10-17-72</u>                Following Session    <u>2</u>

Leader's Name    <u>Margaret Dean</u>

Your Name    <u>Don Nagel</u>

    UNDERSTANDING:    You seemed to listen very carefully and could see where I and the others were uncertain or unclear. It would have helped me to know that we were supposed to give feedback at the end of the first interaction before it began. You could have been more specific about what we were to do after each interaction. I felt you understood my questions and what I was trying to say, however.

    ACCEPTING:    Even though I know you can interview much better than anyone in the group, I thought you tried to accept the different ways that each of us went about it. I did feel put-down or "corrected" when you suggested another way of doing the facilitating. I think the enthusiastic way you introduced the tasks communicated that you really care about this practicum.

    SINCERE:    At first you seemed sort of nervous and I thought the introductions were a little strained, but I quickly felt at ease and comfortable with the group because you seemed to be very honest and open yourself.

    GENERAL COMMENTS:    I think I can learn a lot from you, especially about saying what I mean and without hurting someone. Also I need to learn to listen better.

    COMMENTS ON THE PRACTICUM:    So far so good. It's really interesting; I have some questions about whether it will make me a better counselor. Sometimes things seem to get bogged down in nit-picky points.

## Session 2.

*Purpose:*     Since Session 2 is a continuation of Session 1, the primary purpose is the same as that stated for Session 1. Secondarily, some attention should be given to the following communication techniques: asking questions, paraphrasing, behavior descriptions, and feeling descriptions.

*Procedures:*     To begin the session, the leader should determine how familiar the group members are with paraphrasing as an interview technique. After a brief description and explanation of its function in an interview (See Section Three—Communication) the leader should relate a brief personal experience and ask each practicum member to paraphrase the feelings involved. For example, the leader might say, "Yesterday when I arrived home I found my son sobbing in his bedroom because a sick kitten he had been caring for had died that morning while he was at school. I felt helpless and awkward and a million miles away 'cause there wasn't anything I could do to really make it right." The first group member who offers a paraphrase has the easiest task, of course. Nevertheless, there are literally dozens of words and phrases which will capture the central message and feelings the leader has expressed. Depending on how difficult the group finds the task to be, the leader or another person should offer other brief experiences to be paraphrased by each group member.

This communication exercise, paraphrasing round the circle, can be thought of as a warm-up device to start the group interacting immediately, as well as an opportunity to practice a very important interview skill. However, the primary purpose of this session is to have those members who were "clients" last session act as facilitators and receive feedback from the group. Therefore, after spending 20 minutes practicing paraphrasing, the leader should call for two volunteers to begin the interviews. The sequence to be followed is the same as in Session 1: a 15-minute interview concerning an experience involving Work, Relationship, or Aloneness, feedback from each group member to the facilitator, additional comments from the leader, feedback from the "client" and a summary of positive and negative feedback by the facilitator.

Following the first interview the leader should direct the group's attention to the success they are having in giving clear behavior descriptions and feeling descriptions in the feedback after the interviews. The leader and others may also want to point out the various uses of asking questions they have observed. After this discussion, it will probably be time for a 15-minute break.

When the group reconvenes, there will be two interviews plus feedback from the group to complete. The session should close with a discussion and clarification of the assignment for next session.

*Assignment for Session 3.*     The third session will be entirely devoted to communication exercises. In preparation for one of the exercises, each group member and the leader is to make a list of at least 10 metaphors and/or similes which are descriptive of feelings with which he can readily identify. For example, one person's list might include:

a child's discarded Teddy bear
an overly eager Cocker Spaniel puppy
an 8-day clock on day 7
a fine china ashtray which no one is comfortable using
an actor who has forgotten his lines
inside a glass bottle, crying, but no one hears
a door mat with WELCOME misspelled
sunshine on fresh powder snow
a Boy Scout without a compass
alone on an empty beach

These lists will be shared at the beginning of Session 3.

A part of Session 3 will also be used to practice the verbatim playback. In preparation for this, each practicum member and the leader is to work out plans for a new experience involving a new situation, a new role, or a new medium (See Section Three—Acceptance). During Session 3 each person will be asked to describe what plans he has made for a new experience and why he selected that particular new experience. These descriptions should take no more than five minutes. Another person will then "play back" the description, verbatim. Between Session 3 and Session 4, each person will actually carry out his plan and during Session 4 half of the group will tell about their new experiences with the assistance of facilitators. The other half will tell about their new experiences, with the assistance of facilitators during Session 6. The assignment to be completed between Sessions 2 and 3, again, is to plan a new experience based on the discussion in Section Three—Acceptance, and to be able to describe those plans in five minutes or less.

Finally, having now interacted with one another for two sessions, having seen everyone in both the role of "client" and of facilitator, as well as having participated in the give and take of feedback in the group, each person is in a position to complete the written Feedback Forms. It is very important that each person complete a form for every other person in the group before Session 3.

Many people find it quite difficult to commit themselves to giving written feedback. They postpone the task of completing the Feedback Forms until the last possible moment and then find they have not allowed themselves enough time. They either avoid Session 5 altogether because they do not have written Feedback Forms for everyone or they arrive feeling very guilty and apologetic. The people who do not receive written feedback feel very badly, as if others do not really care. Therefore, we have found that the most reliable and painless way to reach Session 5 with everyone the recipient of two sets of Feedback Forms, is for the leader to collect this first set at the beginning of Session 3. The leader should collect from each person 1 Note on Self, 5 Group Member Feedback

Forms, and 2 Group Leader and Practicum Feedback Forms for a 6 member/2 leader practicum. Since the Feedback Forms are of the greatest significance to the person receiving them, the leader should not read them. It probably makes some difference to the person giving the feedback to know that his statements are solely for the benefit of the person receiving the feedback and that it is up to the recipient to decide whether or not he wants to share his feedback with anyone else. Therefore, the leader should collect and later collate the Feedback Forms, but he should not read them.

For the first two written feedback assignments following Session 2 and Session 4, use forms like the samples given with Session 1 Notes. For the final written feedback, following Session 9, each person should design his own form.

## Session 3.

*Purpose:*    The primary purpose of Session 3 is to practice the communication techniques which are used to move an interview forward: verbatim playback, requesting contrasts, introducing concrete examples, gaining a figure-ground perspective and formalizing a choice-point (See Section Three—Communication). A secondary purpose of Session 3 is to begin to focus on becoming more Accepting. The first two sessions were focused on becoming more Understanding. With the sharing of plans to explore, experience, and expand in new situations, with new roles, and through new media, the group has an opportunity to hear one another's efforts to more fully celebrate diversity and complexity in themselves and others.

*Procedures:*    At the beginning of the session, the leader should collect the Feedback Forms from each member; the Forms can be collated later. The group should assume that the leader will not read the Feedback Forms unless he has raised the issue for discussion and, by consensus, another contract has been established.

To begin the interaction among the practicum members, the leader should ask each person to read several of the 10 figures of speech he chose to describe feelings with which he readily identifies. People may prefer to share their entire lists. This process will take about 30 minutes. In addition to the fun involved in hearing the kinds of phrases one another thinks of as personally descriptive, this particular exercise illustrates how words communicate both thoughts and feelings and how figures of speech are especially useful in communicating feelings. By whatever means the group can comfortably share with one another the thoughts and feelings contained in their individual lists is the way to proceed with this exercise.

On more than one occasion, it has been difficult to redirect the groups' attention after the "figures of speech exercise" because the activity is so enjoyable and people just keep thinking of more and more phrases. The leader may have to arbitrarily cut off the interaction after about 30 minutes in order to proceed with the verbatim playbacks.

Initially people are quite frightened of trying the verbatim playback exercise because they are certain they will block and not be able to remember anything. Usually, the whole group is pleasantly surprised to find that they are able to listen and remember things much better than they feared would be the case and that they also improve with practice. The leader should ask for a volunteer to describe, briefly, his or her plans for a new experience and the reasons for choosing that particular new experience. Next, another group member should volunteer to try a verbatim playback of the first person's description. The description should be brief – less than 5 minutes – immediately following which the second volunteer repeats *exactly* what he heard using the same words and same intonations. It is not advisable for the person doing the verbatim playback to attempt to mimic the first volunteer's gestures, posture, or voice quality. In no way is the verbatim playback intended to be a caricature or even an impersonation of someone. The intention, rather, is to hear and communicate that you heard precisely what the person said. After the verbatim playback of the description, the first volunteer and the other group members can fill in any details which were omitted. After the initial anxiety subsides, people find this exercise to be a lot of fun also. Two words of caution: (1) Do not get involved in a discussion of the person's plans for a new experience, simply receive that information; there will be ample time during Sessions 4 and 6 to discuss the new experiences after they have been carried out, and (2) it is probably best to identify the person who is to give the verbatim playback *before* the description occurs; it tends to increase anxiety to ask for a volunteer after the description has been given. Every group member and the leader should have a turn at describing their plans and at giving a verbatim playback of someone else's description.

You will now be about midway through the session and should take a 15-minute break. When the group reconvenes, the leader should introduce the last communication exercise by directing the group's attention to the vignettes given below. The leader or someone he designates should read one of the four vignettes aloud and then ask three of the group members to give three different responses which make use of "requesting a contrast." Next, someone should read another of the vignettes and ask the other three group members to give three different responses which make use of "introducing a concrete example." The third vignette should be read aloud and half the group asked to respond with different statements which make use of "gaining a figure-ground perspective" and, finally, the fourth vignette should be read aloud and the other half of the group asked to respond with different statements which make use of "formalizing a choice-point."

To minimize anxiety and confusion, a person should know, before a vignette is read, whether or not he is one of those expected to respond and which communication technique he is expected to employ. The goal of the second half of this session is to have each person practice as many of the different techniques for moving an interview forward as time will allow. The four vignettes can, of course, be reread and responded to with any one of the techniques. The group members will automatically give one another feedback on their various responses.

### Vignette #1:

Glen Stiller is a hard-working furnace repairman in a small town in Montana. He has never been much of a churchgoer, although his wife has always tried to get him interested. You met him when you baptized their twins two years ago. His wife, who is bright, attractive, and vivacious has begun taking some classes at the local State College. She has been studying music and literature, which Glenn finds hard to talk about or understand. He enjoys western music, but that doesn't seem to help. Not knowing where to turn, he thought maybe you could help, 'cause he just doesn't think things are right between them anymore.

### Vignette #2:

Reuben Schwartz has always been an active, capable youngster who last year was elected captain of the ninth grade debate team. You met him briefly during a sophomore orientation discussion you led at the beginning of school. It is the end of April and late one afternoon, you notice that Reuben is standing around outside your office appearing to read the bulletin board, but also appearing to decide whether to enter your office. You invite him in and notice that while he has grown an inch or so, he has also gained about 30 pounds. After responding to some initial questions about what he has been doing and how he likes high school, he begins telling you about how he never goes anywhere, he has no friends, he feels crummy all the time, he wants to work this summer but he hasn't learned to drive, even though he has had driver training, his parents have separated, his older brother was killed in Vietnam and he just doesn't see the point of anything anymore.

### Vignette #3:

Mrs. Carla Porter is the mother of a fourth grade boy who has been in and out of difficulties since his father remarried and moved to an adjacent state last summer. Mrs. Porter has asked for an appointment with you to see what "Michael's counselor thinks would be best for him," because Michael's father has invited the boy to come spend the summer with him and his new wife and to stay on and attend fifth grade there, if he wants to. Mrs. Porter was under psychiatric care for three months after the divorce but has not received any treatment nor taken any medication for over a year now. Mr. Porter lived in the same city for a year after the divorce, before he remarried and he saw Michael every week during that time. During your interview, Mrs. Porter talks about how her sister and brother-in-law think she shouldn't keep Michael from his father, that the men friends she has are not good for Michael, that she should find other work than being a cocktail waitress because of the hours. She says she doesn't have confidence in her own judgments of what's best for Michael, that he is the most important thing she has but that sometimes she gets weary of trying to raise him alone. On the one hand she wants what's best for Michael, but she can't stand the thought of him becoming more like his father than he already is — in addition she can't stand her ex-husband's new wife.

### Vignette #4:

You are a community college counselor and one of your colleagues, Frank Drummond, has asked to talk with you about his unhappiness with life. He has had several run-ins with the department administrator for failing to follow through on tasks he accepts and for missing meetings. He thinks this is related to how messed up his home life is because his wife wants to move back to a larger city near her parents. He has always planned to go on for a doctoral degree in counseling, but he has been out of school for six years now, since his master's degree, and the competition for admission is getting much stiffer. Lately he has developed a lot of interest in the stock market and spends quite a bit of time reading about and following different stocks. He explains how he thinks he has developed a way to invest without risking serious losses. He has always admired how content and satisfied with your life you seem to be,— like you've really figured out what's important or something. If he could just get a few things settled maybe he'd feel better.

If the group has difficulties generating responses using the various techniques for moving the interview forward, the following example may serve as a model from which to build responses to the four vignettes given above. (Also see Section Three—Communication.)

Joyce Thornton, an attractive young woman who just had her 23rd birthday, leans forward in her wheel chair and tells you that being an airline stewardess was all she ever really wanted to do. Joyce was in a car accident that left her paralyzed from the waist down; her fiancé, Tom, who was driving, was uninjured. He claims he still wants to marry her, but she thinks he is motivated by pity and guilt because their relationship was based largely on doing things together, such as dancing, water skiing, tennis, hiking, etc. A friend talked her into coming to the Counseling

Center on campus, because she has been talking more and more about how useless it is to go on living and that her fiancé would be better off if she had been killed completely. She is Roman Catholic and does not believe suicide is ever justified, but neither is being a lifelong burden to someone.

### Requesting a Contrast:

"Joyce, I think I understand your feelings of just being a weight around Tom's neck and that if he didn't feel so guilty and so sorry for you, he would probably not want to marry you now — but for us to get a better handle on this, suppose Tom really did want to marry you — not out of guilt or pity, but because of you — how would things be different from the way they are now? Can you compare how Tom is now with how Tom would be if he *really* wanted to marry you?"

### Introducing a Concrete Example:

"Joyce, from what you've said, I would guess that the kinds of things which have been most important to you are a combination of helping other people — making them confortable, giving them support — and actively going out to meet life — doing new and exciting things. So, for example, if you were to choose between paying to have a car specially built so that you could drive it, just using your hands, and paying a chauffeur to to drive you around — you'd choose the specially built car, even if it cost a little more and took more effort. Is that the case?"

### Gaining a Figure-Ground Perspective:

"Joyce, when someone suffers the losses which you've had to suffer, there isn't anything that isn't affected — your work, your relationship with other people, and your feelings about yourself. All kinds of decisions have to be made because of the tremendous change — can I ever work again? Do I want to? What shall I do with myself? Shall I marry Tom? How can I go on living? Maybe I should kill myself? Maybe I should just disappear? — Joyce, I think it would be helpful if we could try to see what's at the center of the questions and the decisions and maybe things will begin to fall in place a little more — it seems to me that the central issue is how Joyce feels about Joyce — are you *worth* the effort to try to find another equally meaningful career? Are you *worth* anyone's ever investing in, in the way marriage demands — Tom or any man? Are you really *worth* the effort it would take to make meaning out of the pieces of a shattered life? Joyce, I don't think you can answer such a question in the abstract or that this is the last time you'll have to answer it, but that seems to be the central question we are facing."

*Formalizing a Choice-Point:*

"Joyce, there's no question in my mind that you are worth the investment of trying to restore meaning and make new reason for being and there's no question in my mind that it would be worth it to you to risk hoping, searching, planning, and trying to find ways in which life can be useful and satisfying and whole again. You know and I know that we can't just wave a magic wand and everything will suddenly become gloriously meaningful — but of the things we've talked about — career and education, your relationship with Tom and with your friends and family, and the feelings inside you about you — which do you think would make the most difference, where would we begin to look at risking new possibilities?"

*Assignment for Session 4:*    Between Sessions 3 and 4 at least half of the group should volunteer to carry out their plans for a new experience and be prepared to tell about them with the assistance of facilitators. The format of Session 4 is very similar to that of Sessions 1 and 2 with half the group acting as facilitators for the other half who are in the role of interviewer or "client." During Session 6 these roles will be reversed and those who were facilitators during Session 4 will become interviewers, while the interviewees of Session 4 will become facilitators during Session 6. Session 5 is devoted to interacting with one another about the written Feedback Forms completed following Sessions 2 and 4. It should be clear in everybody's mind at the end of this session who will be the three interviewees for next session, 4, and who will be the three interviewees during Session 6. The three interviewees for next session obviously have just one week to carry out their new experience plans, whereas the three interviewees for Session 6 have three weeks to carry out their plans. It is probably a good idea to complete the new experiences as close as possible to the time you will be interviewed, rather than let the experience fade over a two- or three-week period.

## Session 4.

*Purpose:*    Three group members will have an opportunity to share the results of their efforts to increase their capacity to celebrate diversity and complexity through experiencing new situations, new roles, and new media. The other half of the group will have an opportunity to practice and receive feedback about their skill in communicating Acceptance, while in the role of facilitator.

*Procedures:*    The format for this session is very similar to that of Sessions 1 and 2, that is, one group member, the interviewee ("client") describes his or her new experience to another group member who is acting as a facilitator. Following a 10 to 15 minute interview, the other group members and the leader give feedback to the facilitator. Next the "client" gives feedback to the facilitator, especially concerning the extent to which the facilitator communicated Acceptance of the "client" and his new experience. Finally, the facilitator summarizes both the positive and negative feedback he received.

The range of possibilities for new experiences is very large. One facilitator may find himself being asked to respond to an episode wherein the "client" simulated a role which resulted in his feeling self-conscious, frightened, isolated, and powerless. Whereas the next facilitator may find himself being asked to respond to a collage which the "client" has brought to the group, along with a story of how exhilarating and personally rewarding it was to create something which was unlike anything he had ever attempted before.

The third facilitator may be asked to respond to a "client's" story about entering a situation into which he had never dared venture before. The facilitator may in fact be very familiar with the setting and thus find it particularly challenging to communicate acceptance of what to him, personally, would be an ordinary, unremarkable episode.

It is assumed that the group will have read Section Three—Acceptance and that they will have identified Acceptance in counseling as an active process of receiving and prizing another person as he presently is, as well as valuing and caring about what he is in the process of becoming. As is always the case, a combination of behavior descriptions and feeling descriptions is the most useful feedback the facilitator can receive. By identifying the particular verbal and nonverbal behaviors which the facilitator emitted that resulted in feelings of being accepted and feelings of being devalued and rejected, the facilitator is in a better position to alter or sustain those behaviors accordingly than if he is merely told, "I think you are a very accepting person most of the time and you make me feel accepted."

The experiences which are related by the interviewees and the feedback to the facilitator are both likely to be more complex and time-consuming than was the case in Sessions 1 and 2. The leader should watch the time so that all three group members who come prepared to share a new experience are in fact given an opportunity to do so. The 15-minute break will probably fit best after the second interview. There may be time, following the third interview for the group to engage in a discussion of the meaning and significance of sharing one another's new experiences.

Although the leader's participation in interviewing and being interviewed is not specifically programmed in the sessions, it is assumed that the leader will determine the extent to which he should take part in any of the exercises according to the group's needs. On the one hand, the leader should not be an aloof, nonparticipant observer who directs things from a safe distance, but on the other hand, the practicum is intended to give the *students* enrolled in it the greatest amount of practice which time will allow, learning to communicate understanding, acceptance, and sincerity, as well as learning skills for moving an interview forward. The leader should participate whenever his doing so facilitates the group's relating to him as a real person, rather than an impersonal authority figure and whenever his participation serves as a role model through which group members actually see techniques demonstrated which are described in this book. But he should guard against taking time unnecessarily, and thereby limiting the time students can focus their attention on one another's efforts.

*Assignment for Session 5*    At the beginning of Session 5 each group member and the leader will receive two sets of written Feedback Forms. After each person has had an opportunity to read through what every other person has written about him after Session 2 and after Session 4, the members will interact in dyads and triads about the written feedback. Therefore, the assignment for Session 5 is to complete the second set of written Feedback Forms: 1 Note on Self, 5 Group Member Feedback Forms, and 2 Group Leader and Practicum Feedback Forms, given to a 6 member/2 leader group.

## Session 5.

*Purpose:*    At the close of this session each person should be able to summarize the major strengths and weaknesses in his interviewing skills which others have observed. Each person should also develop greater confidence in his ability to give constructive feedback, positive and negative, to his colleagues.

*Procedures:*    To begin the session the leader should distribute the first set of written Feedback Forms and the group members should distribute their second set of Forms. With approximately 16 Forms before him, each person will need an opportunity to read through them looking for: (1) the similarities and the differences between the first and second sets of Forms; (2) the repeating themes in both sets of Forms; (3) the similarities and the differences between the Note on Self and the other Forms in the set; (4) statements which are unclear and those which are especially helpful.

If the group engaged in the optional procedure suggested in Session 1, involving writing down initial impressions of the other practicum members, these can also be exchanged during this session.

After everyone has finished reading through his Forms and developed some general impressions, the leader should assist the group members organize themselves into dyads and triads, depending upon the total number present, to interact with one another concerning the written feedback they received from each other.

In approximately 15 minutes, the group leader should indicate that it is time to reorganize and begin interacting with another member of the group. This procedure should continue until each person has had an opportunity to interact with every other person in the group. During each interaction the people involved should concentrate on clarifying and understanding the written feedback they have given and received from one another. While someone may disagree completely with what someone else has written, the task is to understand what has been written rather than to debate its validity. The leader will need to watch the time so that everyone does have a chance to interact with everyone else. Whereas the leader should avoid becoming a drill sergeant, it is necessary to maintain somewhat of a schedule, or else people will miss interacting with some of the other group members and/or the leader. If the group has access to more than one room, that would, of course, make it easier to conduct the four simultaneous interactions which are required during this session. The group members should confine their discussions to the feedback which they have received from, or given to, the person with whom they are interacting. That is, comments which you have made about another group member and comments which another has made about you are not to be discussed with a second group member. The interaction between you and another group member provides an opportunity to clarify the written feedback you gave and to respond to the written feedback you received. Undoubtedly this process will result in your sharing with one another information and insights about yourselves which are related to experiences outside this practicum, as well as sharing self-understanding which has developed within the practicum.

After everyone has interacted with everyone else in the group, the leader should reconvene the members in a large group. The leader will then ask each person to summarize and comment upon the feedback he has received. The leader, of course, should participate in this along with all the group members. During and after the summaries of feedback received, the group will probably engage in a general, but personal, discussion of their feelings about *giving* feedback and how they have changed since the first session. There will very likely be references to the kind of feedback which is most difficult to receive, that which has been the most helpful, and that which has been the most surprising.

This session may be one of the most personal and self-disclosing sessions the group has thus far experienced together. In addition to the importance of their immediate experience of sharing with one another in this particular group, some attention should be given to the nature and quality of professional peer relationships in general. That is, not only is it important and helpful and satisfying to share feedback within this practicum group, but professional people who work together in any setting ought to be able to benefit from such shared feedback among themselves. Each practicum member should therefore attempt to understand those things which facilitate and those which hinder his participating in a constructive sharing of positive and negative feedback.

*Assignment for Session 6.* Those persons who acted as facilitators during Session 4, will be the interviewees during Session 6. They will, therefore, be engaged in completing their plans for a new experience utilizing new situations, roles, or media, between Sessions 5 and 6. All group members are asked to review Section Three—Acceptance in preparation for a discussion of the "What" and "How to" of Acceptance in counseling.

## Session 6.

*Purpose:*   Since this session is largely a continuation of Session 4, the purpose stated for Session 4 applies to Session 6 as well.

*Procedures:*   The leader should ask for a volunteer from among the three people who have not yet shared their new experience with the group and a volunteer to act as facilitator from among those who did not facilitate during Session 4. These two group members are to arrange themselves, as has been done in past sessions so they can interact while the rest of the group observes their interaction. The facilitator should draw this brief interview to a close within about 15 minutes. The group members and the leader should then give feedback to the facilitator concerning the brief interview he just conducted. Following this, the "client" gives feedback to the facilitator who then clarifies and summarizes the feedback he has received. This same sequence is followed for the remaining two brief interviews about new experiences. The group will likely want to take a 15-minute break after the second interview.

At the close of the third interview, after the facilitator has summarized his feedback, the leader should invite the group to review some of the dimensions of Acceptance in counseling which they have identified and/or experienced, particularly during this session and Session 4. For example, the discussion may focus on the ways in which the group has experienced some of the words and phrases used to define Acceptance in counseling:

> Respecting, valuing, liking, prizing, delighted with, concerned about, caring for, genuinely interested in, appreciating, wanting to share the feelings of, receiving a person as he is, having a deep regard for the basic worth of another human being.

Or the discussion may focus on the tremendous diversity and complexity within the group and how valuable and important those differences are. The discussion may focus on the frightening, but exhilarating feelings of venturing out to explore and experience and thereby expand the kinds of people and situations with which each group member feels at home. Some members of the group may want to share their growing awareness of the barriers which block them personally from communicating greater Acceptance, such as overgeneralizing or stereotyping, having disdain for another's efforts, being impatient with, being cynical about, and needing to garner approval or agreement from.

This discussion is not intended to be an intellectual exercise, but is rather an opportunity for the group members to integrate and summarize the range of experiences they have had which bear on the nature and function of Acceptance in the counseling relationship.

*Assignment for Session 7:*   Each group member is to prepare a brief (5 to 10 minute) role-play in which he will depict an insincere counselor. A member is free to invite as many of the other practicum members to join him in the preparation as he desires. For instance, a person may want to play the role of a counselor working with a married couple and would thus need two other people; or he may want to be an elementary school counselor working with two siblings and their mother and would thus need to ask three other group members to assist him. Or, two people may want to work together on two role-plays, with one person the counselor in the first role-play and the other person the counselor in the second. However the members want to team up to prepare their role-plays is fine; what is important is that each person arrives at Session 7 having prepared an episode in which he plays an insincere counselor.

This exercise forces each member to think through what it is about a counselor's tone, manner, voice quality, choice of words, facial expressions and gestures that communicate phoniness, inauthenticity, and insincerity. It is very important that the members strive to capture the subtle, difficult-to-pinpoint ways in which a counselor closes off, hides, disowns his experience, and is contrived and rehearsed, rather than presenting a caricature of a counselor doing a crummy job. Portraying a blatantly dogmatic dolt, who is obviously a big phoney, is no challenge. It may seem as if we are going at this backwards or practicing the wrong things. However, as was discussed in Section Three— Sincerity, you really cannot practice sincerity directly. Studied attempts to appear sincere always backfire. In fact, that is one way to play the role of an insincere counselor, namely, try very hard to be *very* authentic and it is sure to come off as being phoney. By becoming sensitized to the ways in which counselors in general communicate a lack of sincerity, the group members are in a better position to monitor the ways in which they personally affect clients.

Some examples of insincere roles which might be portrayed and thus provide a way to look at sincerity are: the overly solicitous counselor; the aloof, inscrutable counselor; the smiling, benevolent authoritarian; the impatient problem-solver; the nervous, self-conscious counselor; and the dogmatic, rigid counselor who does not listen well.

Again, it should be underscored, that the role-plays are useful if they are sufficiently subtle so that the group can identify with the insincere counselor. If all the members feel, "Oh, I would never do that!" then they will miss the experience of seeing how easy it is to communicate insincerity.


## Session 7.

*Purpose:*   This session is devoted to identifying the subtle ways in which counselors in general communicate insincerity and the particular ways in which each group member is most likely to communicate a lack of genuineness.

*Procedures:*   The leader should ask for a volunteer to begin the session with his role-play of an insincere counselor. Following the role-play, the group should be asked to identify the ways in which they felt the counselor was insincere and how he communicated his lack of authenticity. Different group members will be affected differently, of course, and some much more intensely than others. Some forms of insincerity are minimally distressing to some clients and terribly offensive to others. Ample time should be taken to allow everyone who was observing the role play to respond to it; after which the person playing the insincere counselor should comment on the type and quality of insincerity he was attempting to portray.

In addition to the specific feeling descriptions and behavior descriptions of the observers, they will likely find themselves thinking and saying, "Boy, I've seen counselors just like that!" and "I can see myself falling into that kind of trap," etc. It will be very helpful if the leader and others can identify the particular places in the role-plays where the counselor faced a choice to hide his feelings or disclose them, open himself or close off, disown his feelings and thoughts or claim them as his own, go through the motions of listening or really hear the client, etc. Those points should be identified and more authentic responses, than the one given by the insincere counselor, should be described.

The leader will need to watch the time so that all eight role-plays, plus a discussion of each one, as well as a break midway through can be completed during this session. Also a few minutes should be reserved for clarification of the Session 8 assignment.

*Assignment for Session 8:*    The next two sessions, 8 and 9, are designed: (1) to give each group member, while in the role of a facilitator, an opportunity to work with an individual who is communicating very intense feelings and (2) to reveal to each member that his own history is a rich resource and foundation for understanding and accepting a tremendous range of human emotions. To accomplish the second goal of Sessions 8 and 9, increasing awareness of oneself as a resource for understanding another's feelings, each group member and the leader is to complete the following exercise:

Erik Erikson (1959) has formulated a psychosocial model of human development which specifies Eight Developmental Stages through which every person passes with differing degrees of success. There are basic developmental tasks required of the individual at each stage, and how well he masters the tasks at one stage influences how competently he will cope with the next stage. The personal feelings associated with competently coping with developmental tasks contrast sharply with the feelings associated with failing to cope adequately. Figure 15 is a chart which names Erikson's developmental stages, identifies the developmental tasks required at different stages and lists words and phrases which have been added to describe the feelings associated with successfully mastering the tasks and the feelings associated with failing to master the tasks.

# FIGURE 15. ERIKSON DEVELOPMENTAL STAGES (Adapted from Erikson, 1959, p. 166.)

| | STAGE | TASK | SUBJECTIVE EXPERIENCE |
|---|---|---|---|
| I. | INFANCY<br>Trust<br>vs.<br>Mistrust | To get<br>To give in return | Secure; sure of self; trusting in the world; expecting the best from others; certain that difficulties can be met and pain relieved; having faith and hope in life<br>vs.<br>mistrust; apprehension; uncertainty; fear; ambiguity; feeling that life is very risky, painful, chaotic |
| II. | EARLY CHILDHOOD<br>Autonomy<br>vs.<br>Shame, Doubt | To hold on<br>To let go | Independent; able to manage oneself; aware of own strengths; confident; sturdy; resourceful; self-reliant; curious; able to meet others' demands; able to make choices on basis of one's own preference<br>vs.<br>ashamed; doubting; exposed; surprised; inadequate; caught off guard; powerless; helpless; dependent |
| III. | ACTIVE PLAY AGE<br>Initiative<br>vs.<br>Guilt | To go after<br>To play like | Able to channel energy; showing self-control; can hold self in check; able to express enthusiasm and exuberance constructively; others pleased to see me coming; lively and expansive; able to question rules and to challenge authority freely, openly, directly without losing control of self<br>vs.<br>guilty; hostile; aggressive; out of control; hurting; breaking; getting carried away |
| IV. | SCHOOL AGE<br>Industry<br>vs.<br>Inferiority | To complete things<br>To make things together | Competent; productive; capable; can take things in stride; having energy that flows freely into planned activities; can see something through to completion; showing pride in what one is able to do; eager to invest self; eager to encounter new situations and new people<br>vs.<br>incompetent; inferior; inadequate, falling short of standards and expectations; unable to cope; afraid to venture forth; unwilling to try |

| | | | |
|---|---|---|---|
| V. | ADOLESCENCE<br>Identity<br>vs.<br>Role Diffusion | To be oneself<br>To share being oneself | Stable; reliable; unique; comfortable in sex role; comfortable with career plans; inner-directed; having a sense of agency; having a sense of vocation<br>vs.<br>fragmented; outer-directed; overly dependent; conforming; confused about and rejecting of sex role; being unpredictable for its own sake; unwilling to set limits or rule things out |
| VI. | YOUNG ADULTHOOD<br>Intimacy and Solidarity<br>vs.<br>Isolation | To lose and find oneself in another | Connected; being close without smothering; accountable to; able both to receive and give with enthusiasm; respectful; acceptant of diversity in others; open; spontaneous; able to be naked in body and spirit with another; willing to abandon self to another; willing to make resonable demands<br>vs.<br>isolated; alienated; insulated; fearful of ego loss; unable to give or get close; unwilling to receive; avoiding dependency and closeness at all costs; either making no demands or having to possess totally |
| VII. | ADULTHOOD<br>Generativity<br>vs.<br>Self-Absorption and Stagnation | To make be<br>To take care of | Nurturant; caring for; responsible; dependable; protective; encouraging, supportive; able to laugh at self; innovative; willing to try new things; able to negotiate, revise, renew<br>vs.<br>stagnating; rigid; static; immobilized; closed; authoritarian; narrow; limited; constricted; highly conventional; uncaring; humorless; resistant to change; not curious |
| VIII. | MATURITY<br>Integrity<br>vs.<br>Despair | To be through having been<br>To face not being | Having a healthy narcissism; feeling a sense of accomplishment; pride in one's efforts; useful; involved; adapting to rapid change; optimistic; at home with self and cosmos; sturdy in the face of diminishing strength; able to go on alone<br>vs.<br>disgust; despair; hopelessness; having nothing to strive for or enjoy; bitter over losses; pessimistic about most everything; unwilling to acknowledge and accept reality or limits; sensing meaninglessness; being unresolved |

As you examine the chart it will be clear that you have had experiences which produced feelings characteristic of both sides of *all* the Erikson stages. Even though you have not reached Maturity, chronologically, you have experienced many of the feelings associated with aging. Although you are no longer an infant, even now you frequently have feelings which are associated with both sides of Erikson's first stage, Infancy. Within the same day it is not uncommon to feel that the world is a trustworthy place in which pain and difficulties can be resolved but, at another point in the day, to feel that life is uncertain and ambiguous and, at best, painful and chaotic. Even though you may have mastered the developmental tasks at Stage I and developed an overall Basic Trust of Life, you still can know approximately how it feels to have a Basic Mistrust of Life because of those life experiences which have produced mistrustful, apprehensive, and fearful feelings in you — however fleeting or enduring they may have been.

After examining each stage and the tasks and subjective feelings which characterize success and failure at that stage, recall sixteen personal experiences, recent or distant, which were dominated by the feelings associated with both success and failure at each developmental stage. For example, for Stage V—Adolescence, ask yourself, "When have I felt most stable, reliable, unique, comfortable in my sex role, comfortable in my career plans, etc?" Then ask yourself, "When have I felt most fragmented, overly dependent, conforming, confused about my sex role and unwilling to define and limit myself?" There may be episodes in your life within this past week that produced both of those sets of feelings. Search through your own developmental history, drawing on different periods, and identify sixteen different episodes about which you felt very strongly. You do not need to find an episode that actually occurred during your own adolescence to identify the feelings associated with success and failure during the Adolescent Stage of Development. What is important is that you recall at least sixteen different episodes, which together cover the full range of feelings represented by Erikson's developmental model. Use the format on pp. 297-98 to make brief notes to yourself about these sixteen experiences.

During sessions 8 and 9, each group member will select one of these intensive, personal experiences to share with the group, with the help of a facilitator. In this way, the first goal will be accomplished, namely, to give each group member an opportunity to work with an individual who is communicating very intense feelings.

## Session 8.

*Purpose:* This session is designed to give three group members an opportunity to receive feedback on their ability to communicate understanding and acceptance and sincerity while assisting another person recount a life experience which was of great personal significance and thus carries intense feelings. In

## PERSONAL NOTES FOR SESSION EIGHT ASSIGNMENT

| DEVELOPMENTAL STAGES | DEVELOPMENTAL TASKS | PERSONAL LIFE EXPERIENCES |
|---|---|---|
| I. INFANCY<br><br>Trust<br>vs.<br>Mistrust | To get<br><br>To give in return | POSITIVE:<br><br><br><br>NEGATIVE: |
| II. EARLY CHILDHOOD<br><br>Autonomy<br>vs.<br>Shame, Doubt | To hold on<br><br>To let go | POSITIVE:<br><br><br><br>NEGATIVE: |
| III. ACTIVE PLAY AGE<br><br>Initiative<br>vs.<br>Guilt | To go after<br><br>To play like | POSITIVE:<br><br><br><br>NEGATIVE: |
| IV. SCHOOL AGE<br><br>Industry<br>vs.<br>Inferiority | To complete things<br><br>To make things together | POSITIVE:<br><br><br><br>NEGATIVE: |

addition to this primary purpose, each person will have an opportunity to experience the richness of his own developmental history as a basis for understanding and accepting a vast range of human feelings.

*Procedures:* Each group member will have prepared sixteen different personal experiences which carry a diversity of deep, personal feelings. At the beginning of the session the leader should ask for a volunteer who will share one of his sixteen experiences; another volunteer should be requested to act as facilitator.

| DEVELOPMENTAL STAGES | DEVELOPMENTAL TASKS | PERSONAL LIFE EXPERIENCES |
|---|---|---|
| V. ADOLESCENCE<br><br>Identity<br>vs.<br>Role Diffusion | To be oneself<br><br>To share being oneself | POSITIVE:<br><br><br>NEGATIVE: |
| VI. YOUNG ADULTHOOD<br><br>Intimacy and Solidarity<br>vs.<br>Isolation | To lose and find oneself<br>in another | POSITIVE:<br><br><br>NEGATIVE: |
| VII. ADULTHOOD<br><br>Generativity<br>vs.<br>Self-Absorption and<br>Stagnation | To make be<br><br>To take care of | POSITIVE:<br><br><br>NEGATIVE: |
| VIII. MATURITY<br><br>Integrity<br>vs.<br>Despair | To be through having<br>been<br><br>To face not being | POSITIVE:<br><br><br>NEGATIVE: |

The group, having become very familiar with this format, should arrange themselves so the two volunteers can interact easily and the others can observe the interview readily.

The facilitator should draw the interview to a close within about 20 minutes and invite feedback from the observers and the "client," in turn. After the feedback has been given and clarified, if necessary, the facilitator should summarize what he received. This same procedure should be followed for the other two interviews, as well.

Because the assignment for this session asks the three "clients" to select an intense personal experience to share with the group, it is not unlikely that the "client" may re-experience the emotional intensity of the episode he is sharing. It is up to the facilitator to respond to the emotional intensity of the immediate situation, as well as to respond to the historical meaning of this episode from the "client's" past. The sincerity and skill with which the facilitator responds to the "client" should be the focus of the feedback following the interview.

By now the group has experienced a great deal together and the members should be able to interact with one another very frankly and openly. They should be able to give both positive and negative feedback with the confidence that it will be received in good faith. The facilitators should expect an unusual degree of honesty and clarity.

*Assignment for Session 9*    The facilitators and "clients" of Session 8 will exchange roles for Session 9 and follow the same procedures. The group members prepared for Session 9, as well as for Session 8, when they completed the exercise using the Erikson develomental model to identify sixteen significant personal experiences. The assignment for the period between Sessions 8 and 9, therefore, is to design and complete a task which will contribute to your further growth and development as a counselor. The number of possible tasks is nearly limitless; included would be work on specific communication techniques, reading one of the books listed in the Appendix, completing another new experience, completing one of the suggestions given under increasing self-under- standing in Section Three — Sincerity, completing one of the suggestions for increasing self-acceptance also given in Section Three — Sincerity, or your self-designed assignment might be something quite different from anything suggested thus far. At the close of the practicum you will be asked to share with the group your plans for the next step in your training. The self-designed assignment which you develop after this session, 8, may also help you begin thinking about the kinds of further training experiences you need most.

## Session 9.

*Purpose:*    Since Session 9 is a continuation of Session 8, the purpose stated for Session 8 also applies to Session 9.

*Procedures:*    The format for this session is the same as that for Session 8, with the exception that those group members who were facilitators last session will be "clients" this session and those who were "clients" will now be facilitators. It is not necessary to describe the schedule in detail. The group is thoroughly familiar with the brief interview/feedback/summary sequence that has been used in previous sessions. However, it is probably impossible to overemphasize the importance of giving explicit feedback to the facilitator concerning his ability to understand and accept emotion-laden communications.

During this session, as was true of last session, each of three members will share an episode from his past, recent or distant, which he defines as having a great deal of personal significance. It will be the hope and reasonable expectation of those three members, that the individuals who are facilitating will be able to thoroughly understand and accept the feelings being disclosed. Each facilitator should be able to accompany the "client" for whom he is facilitating wherever the "client" wishes to go. By now the facilitator should be able to assist his "client" explore and experience intense feelings without the facilitator overreacting to or being consumed by the "client's" affect and without abandoning the "client" or trying to banish his feelings. It is exceedingly important that a counselor be able to respond to a client's strong feelings without becoming overwhelmed by them and without minimizing their significance. This is a difficult posture to maintain and all counselors get off-balance from time to time. It is imperative that a counselor be able to recognize when and how he begins floundering, so that he can acknowledge it and thereby restore the balance.

> For example, it might be necessary for a counselor to say "It is clear to me that this means a great deal to you and that you're feeling the impact of it very strongly, but I don't feel I'm really with you, yet — that I'm really seeing and feeling it as you do — can you help me get a better sense of what it's really like for you?"
>
> Or it might be necessary for a counselor to say "I think I really understand what you are saying and how it feels — it's almost like I'm feeling it with you and it's nearly overwhelming — in order to get some perspective on the feelings, I think it would be helpful if we could step back and look at the larger picture of which this episode and the feelings are a part."

In the first example the counselor needed to reduce the distance between himself and his client's feelings; in the second example the counselor needed to gain some distance and perspective on the client's feelings.

The feedback to facilitators should be very explicit and specific, particularly regarding skill in communicating genuine understanding and acceptance, as evidenced by the facilitator's ability to maintain his balance while responding to his "client's" intense emotional expressions.

*Assignment for Session 10*   During Session 10 the group members will once again have an opportunity to interact in dyads and triads about written feedback they have prepared for one another. Each person is asked to design whatever format best allows him to write constructive, evaluative comments on each of his fellow group members, himself, and the leaders. In preparing the written feedback to be exchanged at the beginning of Session 10, each member should consider the type of information and the areas he would like to have covered in the written feedback others will be preparing for him. This is probably the best guideline to follow in deciding what to write about the other group members. The leader may wish to instruct the group about a format he would like the group to use to evaluate the practicum training experience as a whole.

## Session 10.

*Purpose:* The purposes of this session are (1) to help each group member and the leader assess his own major strengths and weaknesses as an interviewer; (2) to allow individuals to clarify or explain the nature of the written feedback they have given to one another; (3) to provide an opportunity for each member to summarize the written feedback he has received, together with his own assessment of himself, in the presence of his peers.

*Procedures:* At the beginning of the session, the written Feedback Forms prepared for this session should be exchanged. Each person should then have before him seven written statements from other group members and the leaders, as well as a personal evaluation statement. The leader should give the group members at least 15 minutes to read their written Feedback Forms before he initiates organizing the members into dyads and triads to discuss the feedback. Some members may want to refer to their previous sets of written Feedback Forms, in an effort to see the progress and development which has occurred from the time they entered this practicum. Since the group has experienced this format during Session 5, elaborate description of the procedures is not necessary. However, as was true earlier, the leader will need to watch the time closely so that each person has an opportunity to interact with all the other group members and the leader(s). The leader or someone he designates should assume responsibility for limiting the brief interactions and assisting the members reorganize into new dyads and/or triads for each feedback interaction.

The same expectations apply to this session, as were true of Session 5, namely, people should discuss with one another only that which they have written about one another; the feedback should be discussed and clarified, rather than debated; and both positive and negative evaluative statements should be given, received, and, later, summarized.

After all members have interacted with one another, the leader should reconvene the group and ask for a volunteer to begin the final summary of written feedback. After each person has summarized his feedback and commented upon it, and the group seems ready to close this session, the leader should clarify any questions about the assignment for Session 11.

*Assignment for Session 11:* In preparation for the final session, review the previous ten sessions and answer the following questions:

1. What did you find to be most valuable in this practicum?
2. What did you find to be least valuable?

Also, for Session 11, each person should be able to describe the direction in which he would like to move in his training and what he sees as the next step he plans to take. Group members will likely have a considerable variety of plans for furthering their training. Some members may focus upon the characteristics of particular client groups which they would like to study, e.g., junior high school students, hospitalized patients, physically handicapped children or adults, persons with marital or family problems, college students, preretirement adults, etc. Some members may want to master specific techniques and strategies for bringing about behavior change; others may want to focus on mastering techniques for facilitating planning and choice-making; others may view learning techniques for reducing confusion through perceptual restructuring as their training priority.

Some members may want to turn their attention to areas of their own personal development. Whatever the direction of professional development selected, each member should identify a specific plan for moving in that direction, which he expects to implement. Such plans might involve additional courses, individual reading, personal counseling, practicum experience in a particular setting, working closely with an experienced and skilled practitioner, etc. During the final debriefing, Session 11, each member's plans will be presented and discussed.

## Session 11.

*Purpose:* This being the final session, each member should have an opportunity to comment on the ways in which the total practicum experience has met his expectations and the ways it has failed to meet his expectations. Also, each member should terminate with a clear idea of the direction in which he would like to move, an outline of a plan for moving in that direction and a specific plan for taking the next step in his professional development.

*Procedures:* The leader should open the session by asking for someone to identify the most and least valuable aspects of the practicum experience, i.e., how it met and failed to meet his expectations. Other members may find that they identified identical strengths and weaknesses in the practicum; some members may have reached just the opposite conclusions. What is most important during this discussion is that each person have an opportunity to comment and be understood.

It is not uncommon for people to be quite resistant to dissolving a group which has worked together well, experienced some very personal and intense times together, and developed an identity and cohesiveness which is not easily duplicated. A discussion of strengths and weaknesses of the practicum is one way of assisting the group terminate. Looking back at the positive and negative aspects of a past experience is one way of gaining closure on that experience.

A second way in which closure can be facilitated is through looking forward to anticipated experiences. When it seems that the group has reviewed the practicum sufficiently to let go of that discussion comfortably, the leader should direct the members' attention to hearing one another's plans for future professional development. Again, someone will need to volunteer to describe the general direction in which he wants to move and his specific plans for moving ahead. After several members have presented their plans, the group will likely begin to identify both commonalities and diversities in the directions and plans represented in the group. Group members should be encouraged to offer constructive concrete suggestions to one another, regarding additional ways plans might be implemented. As has been true in the past, it is expected that the leader will participate in this discussion by sharing his own intended direction and plans for continued professional development.

While it would be possible to whip through a superficial summary of each person's thoughts and feelings about the practicum and his future plans, if the purpose of this final session is to be realized, it will take the full time to bring the practicum to a close. Individual members of the group are more likely to continue in their professional growth and development, if they have worked out a plan and shared it with others.

*Final Note:*

I would value very highly receiving a summary description of your group's experience with this book. In order to facilitate your sending such a summary, I am including a Feedback Format, which you may or may not wish to use.

Susan K. Gilmore, Ph.D.
DEPARTMENT OF COUNSELING
UNIVERSITY OF OREGON
EUGENE, OREGON 97403

## Feedback Format—S. K. Gilmore

*General Descriptions of the Group* (size, setting, age, professional area, and level of training, etc.):

*Summary of Positive and Negative Aspects of the Practicum:*

*General Comments and Suggestions:*

# Appendix

## SUGGESTED READING

The following list of books is offered as suggested reading for increasing your Acceptance of others by expanding your role repertoire (see p. 105).

*Another Country*, James Baldwin, 1960.

*Forbush and the Penguins*, Graham Billing, 1966.

*I'll Get There: It Better Be Worth the Trip,*
John Donovan, 1969.

*Invisible Man*, Ralph Ellision, 1947.

*Midnight Cowboy*, James L. Herlihy, 1965.

*Beneath the Wheel*, Hermann Hesse, 1953.

*How We Live*, P. C. Hills and L. R. Hills (Eds.), 1968.

*One Flew Over the Cuckoo's Nest*, Ken Kesey, 1962.

*To Kill a Mockingbird*, Harper Lee, 1960.

*They Shoot Horses, Don't They*, Horace McCoy, 1935.

*The Ballad of the Sad Cafe*, Carson McCullers, 1951.

*The Heart is a Lonely Hunter*, Carson McCullers, 1940.

*The Member of the Wedding*, Carson McCullers, 1946.

*The Chosen*, Chaim Potok, 1967.

*Summer of '42*, Herman Raucher, 1971.

*The Little Prince*, Antoine de Saint-Éxupery, 1943.

*Catcher in the Rye*, J. D. Salinger, 1951.

*Franny and Zooey*, J. D. Salinger, 1961.

*Nine Stories*, J. D. Salinger, 1953.

*Of Mice and Men*, John Steinbeck, 1937.

*The Red Pony*, John Steinbeck, 1937.

*Travels with Charley*, John Steinbeck, 1962.

*The Graduate*, Charles Webb, 1964.

*The Glass Menagerie*, Tennessee Williams, 1945.

## REFERENCES

Bach, G. R. and Wyden, P., 1969. *The intimate enemy; how to fight fair in love and marriage.* New York: Morrow.

Bandura, A., 1969. *Principles of behavior modification.* New York: Holt, Rinehart and Winston.

Becker, G. M. and McClintock, C. G., 1967. Value: behavioral decision theory. *Annual Review of Psychology*, 18, 239–286.

Dreikurs, R., Corsini, R. J., Lowe, R. N., and Sonstegard, M. A. (Eds.), 1959. *Adlerian family counseling. A manual for counseling centers.* Eugene, Oregon: University.

Erikson, E. H., 1959. Identity and the life cycle. *Psychological Issues*, Monograph 1. New York: International University.

Ford, D. H. and Urban, H. B., 1963. *Systems of psychotherapy; a comparative study.* New York: Wiley.

Frankl, V. E., 1963. *Man's search for meaning; an introduction to logotherapy.* Boston: Beacon.

Franks, C. M. (Ed.), 1969. *Behavior therapy appraisal and status.* New York: McGraw-Hill.

Gardner, J. W., 1965. *Self-renewal: the individual and the innovative society.* New York: Harper & Row.

Gibran, K., 1951. *The Prophet.* New York: Knopf.

Ginott, H. G., 1965. *Between parent and child.* New York: Macmillan.

Goldman, L., 1961. *Using tests in counseling.* New York: Appleton-Century-Crofts.

Hall, C. S. and Lindzey, G., 1957. *Theories of personality.* New York: Wiley.

Hammond, K. R. (Ed.), 1966. *The psychology of Egon Brunswik.* New York: Holt, Rinehart and Winston.

Heider, F., 1958. *The psychology of interpersonal relations.* New York: Wiley.

Kanfer, F. H. and Phillips, J. S., 1970. *Learning foundations of behavior therapy.* New York: Wiley.

Kanfer, F. H. and Saslow, G., 1969. Behavioral diagnosis. In C. M. Franks (Ed.), *Behavior therapy: appraisal and status.* New York: McGraw-Hill.

Kelly, G. A., 1963. *A theory of personality.* New York: Norton.

Krumboltz, J. D. and Thoreson, C. E., (Eds.), 1969. *Behavioral counseling.* New York: Holt, Rinehart and Winston.

Lederer, W. J. and Jackson, D. D., 1968. *The mirages of marriage.* New York: Norton.

Lynd, H. M., 1958. *On shame and the search for identity.* New York: Harcourt, Brace.

Maher, B. (Ed.), 1969. *Clinical psychology and personality: the selected papers of George Kelly*. New York: Wiley.

Morris, C. W. (Ed.), 1934. *Mind, self and society from the standpoint of a social behaviorist. George H. Mead*. Chicago: University of Chicago.

Neff, W. S., 1968. *Work and human behavior*. New York: Atherton.

Niebuhr, R., 1932. *Moral man and immoral society*. New York: Scribner's.

Patterson, C. H., 1966. *Theories of counseling and psychotherapy*. New York: Harper & Row.

Potok, C., 1967. *The chosen*. New York: Fawcett World Library.

Rand, A., 1961. *The virtue of selfishness*. New York: New American Library of World Literature.

Rogers, C. R., 1951. *Client-centered therapy*. Boston: Houghton-Mifflin.

Rogers, C. R. 1957. The necessary and sufficient conditions of therapeutic personality change. *Journal of Consulting Psychology*, 21, 95–103.

Roth, R. M., Hershenson, D. B., and Hilliard, T. (Eds.), 1970. *The psychology of vocational development*. Boston: Allyn & Bacon.

Salinger, J. D., 1961. *Franny and Zooey*. Boston: Little, Brown.

Saslow, G., 1966. A case history of attempted behavior manipulation in a psychiatric ward. In L. Krasner and L. P. Ullman, *Research in behavior modification*. New York: Holt, Rinehart and Winston.

Simon, P., 1969. *Bridge over troubled water*. New York: Charing Cross Music.

Steinbeck, J., 1962. *Travels with Charley: in search of America*. New York: Viking.

Strauss, A. (Ed.), 1964. *George Herbert Mead on social psychology*. Chicago: University of Chicago.

Szasz, T. S., 1961. *The myth of mental illness: foundation of a theory of personal conduct*. New York: Hoeber-Harper.

Tagore, R., 1960. *Fireflies*. New York: Macmillan.

Toman, W., 1961. *Family constellation; theory and practice of a psychological game*. New York: Springer.

Truax, C. B. and Carkhuff, R. R., 1967. *Toward effective counseling and psychotherapy: training and practice*. Chicago: Aldine Pub. Co.

Tyler, L. E., 1963. *Tests and measurements*. Englewood Cliffs, N.J.: Prentice-Hall.

Tyler, L. E., 1961. *The work of the counselor*, 2d Ed. New York: Appleton-Century-Crofts.

Tyler, L. E., 1969. *The work of the counselor*. 3d Ed. New York: Appleton-Century-Crofts.

Ullmann, L. P., 1969. From therapy to reality. *The Counseling Psychologist*, 1, 4, 68–72.

U.S. Department of Labor, 1965. *Dictionary of occupational titles, Vols. I and II*. Washington: U.S. Government Printing Office.

Vonnegut, Jr., K., 1963. *Cat's cradle*. New York: Holt, Rinehart and Winston.

White, R. W., 1960. Competence and the psychosexual stages of development. In M. R. Jones (Ed.), *Nebraska symposium on motivation*. Lincoln: University of Nebraska.

White, R. W., 1959. Motivation reconsidered: the concept of competence. *Psychological Review*, 66, 297–333.

Whitely, J. M. (Ed.), 1969. Behavioral counseling. *The Counseling Psychologist*, 1, 4, 1–108.

# Index